DRAWING UPON THE
SPIRITUAL TREASURES
OF THE

STEPHEN L. FLUCKIGER

CFI
An imprint of Cedar Fort, Inc.
Springville, Utah

© 2024 Stephen L. Fluckiger
All rights reserved.

No part of this book may be reproduced in any form whatsoever, whether by graphic, visual, electronic, film, microfilm, tape recording, or any other means, without prior written permission of the publisher, except in the case of brief passages embodied in critical reviews and articles.

This material is neither made, provided, approved, nor endorsed by Intellectual Reserve, Inc. or The Church of Jesus Christ of Latter-day Saints. Any content or opinions expressed, implied or included in or with the material are solely those of the owner and not those of Intellectual Reserve, Inc. or The Church of Jesus Christ of Latter-day Saints. Permission for the use of sources, graphics, and photos is also solely the responsibility of the author.

Paperback ISBN 13: 978-1-4621-4701-4
eBook ISBN 13: 978-1-4621-4767-0

Published by CFI, an imprint of Cedar Fort, Inc.
2373 W. 700 S., Suite 100, Springville, UT 84663
Distributed by Cedar Fort, Inc., www.cedarfort.com

Library of Congress Catalog Number: 2024934014

Cover design by Shawnda Craig
Cover design © 2023 Cedar Fort, Inc.

Printed in the United States of America
10 9 8 7 6 5 4 3 2 1
Printed on acid-free paper

*For Michael, Yeni, Ben, Landon, Amelia,
Lincoln, Isaac, Addie,
Peter, Ruby, Claire, Charlie, Eliza, Ember,
Charlotte, Eleanor, Lucas*

Contents

Acknowledgments ix

Introduction xi

Chapter 1
The Spiritual Treasure of God's Divine Love — 1

Chapter 2
The Spiritual Treasures of Reverence, Worship, and Worthiness — 11

Chapter 3
The Spiritual Treasures of Making and Keeping Covenants — 27

Chapter 4
The Spiritual Treasure of Increased Faith to Follow Jesus Christ — 39

Chapter 5
The Spiritual Treasure of Increased Power to Gather Israel through the Keys Restored by Moses — 53

Chapter 6
The Spiritual Treasure of Power to Build a People Prepared for a Temple — 63

Chapter 7
The Spiritual Treasure of Sacrifice or Daily Repentance — 91

Chapter 8
The Spiritual Treasure of Proxy Baptisms and Confirmations — 103

Chapter 9
The Spiritual Treasures of Washings and Anointings — 119

Chapter 10
The Spiritual Treasure of "Beautiful Garments"   129

Chapter 11
The Spiritual Treasure of Being Given and
Called by Sacred Names   139

Chapter 12
The Spiritual Treasures in the Endowment Instruction   153

Chapter 13
The Spiritual Treasure of Living God's Higher Laws   177

Chapter 14
The Spiritual Treasure of Communing with Heaven   191

Chapter 15
The Spiritual Treasure of Passing through the Veil   209

Chapter 16
The Spiritual Treasures from the
Dispensation of the Gospel of Abraham   215

Chapter 17
The Spiritual Treasures from the Mission and Keys of Elijah   237

Chapter 18
The Spiritual Treasure of Eternal Families   253

Chapter 19
The Temple's Ultimate Promise and Spiritual Treasure   279

Epilogue   291

Appendix 1
Sacrifices and Offerings of the Mosaic Law   299

Appendix 2
Promises Made and Ordinances Given to Abraham
Were Renewed with Isaac and Jacob   305

Works Cited   321

About the Author   341-

"Christ the Fountainhead" or "Women at the Well," bas-relief mural originally created by Torleif Knaphus for the exterior of the Cardston Alberta Temple.

ACKNOWLEDGEMENTS

Thanks to Dru Huffaker, my publisher; Kimiko Hammari, my editor; and Shawnda Craig, designer extraordinaire, for their efforts in bringing this volume to fruition.

I thank Denis Barney, Hal Kendrick, Emily Wheelwright, and Emron Pratt for their helpful comments and encouragement on early drafts. Hal, Gordon Foote, and Stuart Alleman were among my most enthusiastic early supporters when our individual studies about temple doctrine and practices were the subject of frequent conversations in the temple.

Recognition would be incomplete without mentioning the sealers, staff, leaders, and workers in the Dallas Texas Temple, whose consecrated service gives real-life substance and form to the spiritual treasures the temple can bring to our lives.

Special thanks to my sweetheart, Dorothy, the love of my life, for believing in and encouraging my passion for writing about the most profound and interesting subject in the universe—God's perfect plan of happiness for His children.

Introduction

"The temple is where you will receive your highest spiritual treasures."[1]

—Russell M. Nelson

What Are the Spiritual Treasures of the Temple?

In his talk in the general women's session of the October 2019 general conference entitled "Spiritual Treasures," President Russell M. Nelson addressed a theme that he had echoed in previous conference addresses[2] and, more importantly, that he has repeated in virtually every general conference since becoming the senior apostle of the Church: "Every woman and every man who makes covenants with God and keeps those covenants, and who participates worthily in priesthood ordinances, has direct access to the power of God." Through the ordinances of the priesthood, "both covenant-keeping women and men have access to '*all* the spiritual blessings of the church' or, we might say, to all the spiritual treasures the Lord has for His children."[3] These gifts or treasures come from making and keeping covenants, especially our temple covenants.

When President Nelson addressed the sisters in 2019, my wife and I had just returned from a mission in São Paulo, Brazil. A few months before we completed our mission, a member of the First Presidency had visited with us via video conference, calling us to serve in the Dallas Texas Temple. Our service began a few weeks after this conference address. The shock of that call still with me, I realized as I listened to the prophet that I needed to understand better what these "spiritual treasures" were, including the endowment of power that I had received forty-eight years previously in the Salt Lake Temple before embarking on my first mission to Brazil.

Of course, over those intervening years I had studied extensively many of the things President Nelson urged the sisters in that powerful talk to "study prayerfully" "about the profound endowment of knowledge and power" we "receive in the temple," including "the scriptures and teachings by modern prophets, seers, and revelators."[4] However, I felt a particular need at that time to claim the specific blessings he promised: "As your understanding increases and as you exercise faith in the Lord and His priesthood power, your ability to *draw upon this spiritual treasure* that the Lord has made available [in the temple] will increase. As you do so, you will find yourselves better able to help create eternal families that are united, sealed in the temple of the Lord, and full of love for our Heavenly Father and for Jesus Christ."[5]

President Nelson's reference to "drawing" upon the Lord's power, which He makes available to us through temple ordinances and worship, brings to mind the Savior's conversation with the Samaritan woman at the well (see cover illustration). Drawing upon the spiritual treasures of the temple is, indeed, drinking the Living Water. "Whosoever drinketh of the water that I shall give him shall never thirst; but the water that I shall give him shall be in him a well of water springing up into everlasting life." To "draw upon" the spiritual treasures of the gospel requires that we act in faith. We must come "hither," that is, to the well, to the source of the Living Water, even the Savior (and to no other person or thing), to draw upon His power (John 4:13–15). "Therefore with joy shall ye draw water out of the wells of salvation" (Isaiah 12:3).

As I have continued my studies since President Nelson's seminal 2019 address, I have grown to appreciate more deeply what these spiritual treasures, gifts, and powers are, how we can "draw upon" or receive them in our own lives, and how we can use them to bless the lives of others, especially our families. In fact, the doctrines and features of temple ordinances that are highlighted in the chapters herein could be viewed in their broadest sense as "spiritual treasures" or blessings, including:

- Power to recognize and receive the extraordinary influence of God's divine love (chapter 1);
- The transforming power that comes from regularly and

consistently reverencing and worshiping God in the temple (chapter 2);
- The power of understanding the central role covenant-making and covenant-keeping have in God's law and perfect plan of happiness, which we receive as we study and better comprehend the covenants we make in the ordinances of the "preparatory gospel" (Doctrine and Covenants 84:26) and the endowment and sealing ordinances (chapters 3, 8, 10, 13);
- The power of increased faith in and obedience to the Lord Jesus Christ (chapter 4);
- Increased power to gather Israel on both sides of the veil, which we can gain from the examples of and our strengthened appreciation for and submission to the priesthood keys restored by Moses, Elias, and Elijah (chapters 5, 6, 16, 17);
- The power of daily repentance, which is at the heart of the law of sacrifice (chapter 7);
- The power to be cleansed, to be sanctified or made holy (chapters 8 and 9);
- The power of divine calls, appointments, or anointings (chapter 9);
- The power of being clothed in the garment of the holy priesthood (chapter 10);
- The power of names received in the temple, including the power of taking upon ourselves the name of Christ in baptism and the endowment (chapters 8 and 11);
- The power that comes from increasing our understanding of the "endowment of power" given in the ordinance of the endowment, including the symbolism and role of the temple's veil (chapters 12, 15);
- Greater power to part the veil and receive answers to our prayers (chapter 14);
- The power and blessings associated with temple sealings (chapters 16 and 18); and
- The power to become "one" with God and receive of His fulness (chapter 19).

In truth, the spiritual and temporal blessings (Mosiah 2:41; Doctrine and Covenants 14:11) God has prepared for those who "love [Him] and keep all [His] commandments," or "seek" so to do (Doctrine and Covenants 46:9), are as many and varied as the number, lives, and circumstances of His children, even a "multiplicity of blessings" (Doctrine and Covenants 97:5, 28; 104:2, 33, 38, 42, 46; 124:13).

How Do We Begin to Gain a Greater Understanding of Temple Ordinances and Doctrine?

While urging us all to "really study"[6] to better understand temple ordinances and doctrine, in particular to understand better how to "draw liberally" upon "God's power" that "flow[s] from [our] priesthood covenants," President Nelson observed that the effort would not necessarily be "quick or easy." But he did promise that it would be "spiritually invigorating."[7] I can testify that my own efforts to follow the prophet's counsel have been so. As you begin or continue your own study, you will discover insights for yourself and have your own awakenings.

Where should we begin? With the scriptures, the *best* source of information about the temple. As one student of the temple wrote, the scriptures "will reveal deeper and broader meanings about the temple. Within their pages are the keys to much of the temple symbolism." "Since the endowment is scripture, and since scripture is the best commentary on other scripture, in our reading of the Standard Works we should expect to find insight about the endowment."[8]

In this regard, President Nelson suggested that members going to the temple for the first time read explanations in the Bible Dictionary about scriptural references to such temple topics as "anoint," "covenant," "sacrifice," and so forth.[9] Searching the scriptures related to such topics in this fashion often leads to other related topics and raises further questions. For example, a search for scriptures answering the question, "What do the scriptures teach us about gospel covenants?" leads to further questions such as, "What is the Abrahamic covenant?" "How does the Abrahamic covenant relate to temple ordinances?" "What exactly are the 'promises' made to (or blessings of) Abraham, Isaac, and Jacob referred to so often in the scriptures?" And perhaps more fundamentally, "Who were Abraham, Isaac, and Jacob?" and "Why are their lives relevant to me today?" It is possible to view the scriptures through the lens of the temple, even with "temple eyes."[10] For me, viewing the lives of the patriarchs (and their wives) through the lens of the temple ordinances they jointly received[11] is one of the best ways to visualize the effect these ordinances can have in my life.

In Doctrine and Covenants 18 the Lord explains that the words communicated to prophets as they write or declare scripture "are not of men nor of man, but of me . . . for it is my voice which speaketh them unto you; for they are given by my Spirit . . . and save it were by my *power* you could not have them; *Wherefore, you can testify that you have heard my voice, and know my words*" (vv. 34–36).[12] In other words, we should look first to the scriptures in learning about the temple because through them we can "hear Him," that is, be taught by the power of the Holy Ghost.[13]

For me, there is another wonderful blessing that comes from regularly immersing myself in the scriptures to find answers to my gospel questions. Revelation from God comes to prophets "in their weakness, after the manner of their language" (Doctrine and Covenants 1:24). The context of the revelations is nothing but the ordinary and the extraordinary events in the lives of the prophets and their wives, children, extended families, and associates in the work of the Lord. In the details of their lives,[14] just as with the descriptions of the Savior's ministry in the Gospels and other standard works, we grow to know them and to love them. For this reason, and particularly because of their seminal role in the restoration of priesthood keys related to temple work, chapter 6 focuses on the ministry of Moses; chapter 16 on Elias and the lives of Abraham and Sarah; chapter 17 on the ministry of Elijah; and appendix 2 on the lives of Isaac and Rebekah and Jacob and Rachel. As you read about their lives, ask yourself, "What can I learn from their experiences about the purposes and potential impact temple ordinances can have in my life?"[15] As Jesus beckons us to follow Him, the scriptural and biographical accounts of the lives of the Lord's prophets, seers, and revelators (ancient and modern) show us what it looks like to do this—to be and become disciples of Jesus Christ.

In addition to searching the scriptures, the next best resource for learning more about the temple is the insights and testimonies of apostles and prophets. I have especially benefited from President Nelson's temple teachings since his ordination in 2018, which I reference throughout this study. Church leaders have also given us a helpful resource for improving our understanding of temple ordinances and doctrine in recently updated sections of the *General Handbook: Serving in The Church of Jesus Christ of Latter-day Saints*.[16]

Why Are the Spiritual Treasures of the Temple Important?

Why has the prophet emphasized so often "experiencing" or receiving for ourselves, "understanding" and better "comprehending," regularly attending,[17] and having "spiritual insights" and "awakenings"[18] about the temple and temple ordinances? According to President Nelson, the temple's "sacred ordinances and covenants are pivotal to preparing a people who are ready to welcome" the Savior at His Second Coming[19] and "to fulfill our divine mandate" to prepare "ourselves and the world for the Second Coming of the Lord."[20] The "world," of course, includes our families. Ultimately, however, our temple study and worship help us come to know God. As the Savior explained in Doctrine and Covenants 93, ordinances, covenants, and all associated gospel laws and principles are given so "that you may understand and know *how* to worship, and know *what* you worship, that you may come unto the Father in my name, and in due time receive of his fulness" (v. 19).

Doctrine and Covenants 84 explains the central role the priesthood and priesthood ordinances play in obtaining the spiritual treasures of knowledge and power our prophets have urged us to better understand and apply: "And this greater priesthood administereth the gospel and holdeth the key of the mysteries of the kingdom, even the key of the knowledge of God. Therefore, in the ordinances thereof, the power of godliness is manifest. And without the ordinances thereof, and the authority of the priesthood, the power of godliness is not manifest unto men in the flesh; For without this [power of godliness] no man can see the face of God, even the Father, and live" (vv. 19–22). In other words, the ordinances of the priesthood are the means God has ordained for us to receive the "power of godliness" in our lives.[21]

The Lord continues in the next two verses (as discussed in more detail in chapter 6), describing how Moses "plainly taught" this doctrine "to the children of Israel in the wilderness." Moreover, the Lord continued, Moses "sought diligently to sanctify his people that they might behold the face of God. . . . But they hardened their hearts and could not endure [God's] presence; therefore, the Lord . . . swore that they should not enter into his rest while in the wilderness, which rest is the fulness of his glory" (Doctrine and Covenants 84:23–24).

What lessons do the experiences of Moses and the children of Israel teach us? As Moses, Joshua, and other faithful Old Testament prophet leaders were sanctified by receiving and being true to the ordinances of their day and entered into the rest of the Lord, so too can we receive gospel covenants and ordinances of our day and likewise have greater power to do and be good. As Elder David A. Bednar taught, "As we invite into our lives the 'power of godliness' by receiving priesthood ordinances and making and keeping sacred covenants, we are blessed with strength beyond our own to overcome the temptations and challenges of mortality and to do and become good."[22]

What Resources Has the Church Developed to Help Us Understand the Temple?

The booklet *Preparing to Enter the Holy Temple*, which was adapted from *The Holy Temple* by President Boyd K. Packer and is the student manual for the Temple Preparation Seminar,[23] and *Endowed from on High*, the teacher's manual for such course (and any updates the Church may prepare),[24] are (and will be) must-reads both for individuals preparing to receive their own endowment, as well as for members "who have previously attended the temple" and want "to know more about the temple."[25]

The "Temples" pages of the Church's website contain information about all of the Church's temples under the "Find a Temple" tab, as well as helpful and extensive information under the "About Temples" tab, including such topics as "Why Latter-day Saints Build Temples," "History of Temples," and "Ordinances and Covenants." In addition, the "Attending Temples" tab includes such topics as "Prepare for the Temple," "About the Temple Endowment," "About the Temple

Sealing," among others.[26] Included at the end of the topic "About the Temple Endowment" is a link to "General Conference Addresses" about the temple, which includes more than 170 general conference addresses by the apostles, prophets, and other Church leaders about temple ordinances and doctrine.[27] The principal sources I relied on in my study are accessible through the Church's website.

Understanding Doctrine about the Spirit World Enhances our Temple Experience

Students of the temple invariably describe temples as places "where heaven meets earth"[28] or "portals to heaven."[29] Indeed, after his experience with God described in more detail in the supplemental reading in appendix 2, Jacob referred to the "house of God" as the "gate of heaven" (Genesis 28:17). Such descriptions beg questions such as: "How many of those whose temple work is performed will accept the work done for them?" "Do they get to witness or participate in the work being done for them?" "How close is the spirit world to ours, especially the temples where so many labor on behalf of those who have passed on?"

To this last question, President Dallin H. Oaks described the following as doctrine originally taught by the Prophet Joseph Smith: "The spirits of the just are exalted to a greater and more glorious work . . . [in] the world of spirits. . . . They are not far from us, and know and understand our thoughts, feelings, and motions, and are often pained therewith." He also suggested that our deceased ancestors might "be allowed to prompt" their descendants in finding information needed to perform "their proxy ordinances on earth so they can be baptized and enjoy the blessings of the Holy Ghost (see Doctrine and Covenants 138:30–37, 57–58)."[30] President Ezra Taft Benson taught similarly that "the spirit world is not far away. Sometimes the veil between this life and the life beyond becomes very thin. Our loved ones who have passed on are not far from us."[31]

Interestingly, in the very article which President Oaks cited in his general conference message, Brother Brent Top, a Brigham Young University professor who has focused his academic career in part on this subject, also cited Joseph Smith's statements about the spirit world, including his testimony that, after his passing, "I would not be far away from you, and if on the other side of the veil I would still be working with you, and with a power greatly increased, to roll on this kingdom." These doctrinal insights first declared by the Prophet Joseph Smith, Brother Top comments, underscore an "important doctrine of the restored gospel repeatedly taught by prophets and apostles, and that is that the spirit world is right here on earth and the spirits of our departed loved ones are in reality among us. To me, this is also a vital principle of consolation. This doctrine is as comforting to the Saints as it is unique among Christian beliefs of the afterlife. Our deceased family and friends are not gone, neither are they far, far away in some distant heaven." In summary, Brother Top concludes, "The teachings of the early Brethren emphasized the nearness of our family, the nearness of the spirit world, the relationship between the two realms, and the fact that spirits continue to be interested and intimately involved in the Lord's work on both sides of the veil."[32]

The prophets teach that many, if not most, will accept the temple work done for them and that they are aware of the work being completed. This emphasizes that the culture of reverence and holiness temple workers and patrons seek to establish while in the house of the Lord is not just for their benefit but for those whose involvement on the other side is all important. In the April 1894 general conference, President Wilford Woodruff announced that it was the will of the Lord for members "from this time to trace their genealogies as far as they can, and to be sealed to their fathers and mothers" and to have children sealed to their parents and "run this chain through as far as you can get it." He further explained that "there will be very few, if any, who will not accept the Gospel."[33]

President James E. Faust noted in general conference that "those for whom the work is done [in the temple] may accept it or not, as they choose,"[34] suggesting that those on the other side of the veil must be aware of our efforts in their behalf on this side of the veil. In short, in order to accept ordinances that have been performed in their behalf, the dead must know about them. The Lord has not seen fit to reveal to the world exactly when and how this happens. But many leaders and members of the Church have testified privately, as President Joseph F. Smith taught, "We move and have our being in the presence of heavenly messengers and of heavenly beings. We are not separate from them."[35] This is especially true in the temple.[36]

Knowing these things greatly increases our love, both for our ancestors and for the Lord, who made these vicarious ordinances available to us and to them. Indeed, love of God and our fellow man (particularly, in this context, our deceased family members) is not only the overarching principle of the gospel but also one of the most fundamental of the many spiritual treasures we receive through temple and family history work.

Endnotes

1. Russell M. Nelson, "Spiritual Treasures," *Ensign*, November 2019, 76. Unless otherwise noted, all emphases in scriptural and general conference quotations are mine.
2. See, for example, Russell M. Nelson, "A Plea to My Sisters," *Ensign*, November 2015, 95 ("We need women who . . . understand the power and peace of the temple endowment; women who know how to call upon the powers of heaven to protect and strengthen children and families"); Russell M. Nelson, "Ministering with the Power and Authority of God," *Ensign*, May 2018 ("The restoration of the priesthood of God, including the keys of the priesthood, opens to worthy Latter-day Saints the greatest of all spiritual blessings. We see those blessings flowing to women, men, and children throughout the world").
3. Nelson, "Spiritual Treasures," 77 (emphasis in original), quoting Doctrine and Covenants 107:18 ("The power and authority of the higher, or Melchizedek Priesthood, is to hold the keys of all the spiritual blessings of the church"). See also Russell M. Nelson, "The Power of Spiritual Momentum," *Liahona*, May 2022 ("Ordinances and covenants give us access to godly power"); Russell M. Nelson, "Peacemakers Needed," *Liahona*, May 2023 (in the temple "we are endowed with God's power, giving us the ability to overcome Satan").
4. Nelson, "Spiritual Treasures," 77–78. President Nelson suggested starting such study with two of the great revelations on priesthood power, Doctrine and Covenants 84 and 107 (and, I would add, section 121) (Nelson, "Spiritual Treasures," 79). It is noteworthy to me that the Lord introduces section 84 as "the word of the Lord . . . for the gathering of his saints to stand upon Mount Zion [a reference to the temple], which shall be the city of New Jerusalem," wherein a "house shall be built unto the Lord" (Doctrine and Covenants 84:1–5). In this unique house of the Lord, "the sons of Moses and Aaron," who include all worthy Melchizedek Priesthood holders, "shall offer an acceptable offering and sacrifice" (vv. 31–34). In short, this and other revelations on priesthood power explain, authorize, and direct the ultimate work of the priesthood that goes on only in temples of the Most High. For a discussion of what constitutes this "acceptable offering and sacrifice," see chapter 5, "When We Serve as Proxies in Temple Ordinances We Offer Unto the Lord an 'Offering in Righteousness.'" President Nelson renewed his "invitation for [members] to increase [their] understanding of priesthood power and of temple covenants and blessings" in the October 2020 general conference (Russell M. Nelson, "Embrace the Future with Faith," *Liahona*, November 2020).
5. Nelson, "Spiritual Treasures," 79. See also Russell M. Nelson, *Heart of the Matter: What 100 Years of Living Have Taught Me* (Salt Lake City, Utah: Deseret Book, 2023), 182 ("Seek now to understand what the temple can teach you about . . . learning how to *draw upon* the precious privileges of the endowment" [emphasis added]).
6. Russell M. Nelson, "Come, Follow Me," *Ensign*, May 2019, 88. See also Nelson, *Heart of the Matter*, 182 ("I plead with you to seek—prayerfully and consistently—to understand temple covenants and ordinances. Spiritual doors will open").
7. Nelson, "Spiritual Treasures," 77.

8. S. Michael Wilcox, *House of Glory: Finding Personal Meaning in the Temple* (Salt Lake City, Utah: Deseret Book, 1995), 20.
9. Russell M. Nelson, "Personal Preparation for Temple Blessings," *Ensign*, May 2001, 32. Read together, reviewing multiple scriptural passages on any given gospel topic reveal a more complete picture of the subject or principle and the contexts or circumstances in which such principle finds application, the conditions associated with such principle, and the blessings and consequences, or curses, associated with living or not living the principle. President Nelson gave us an incredible example of how such a study can bless our lives when describing how he "read and underlined every verse cited about Jesus Christ, as listed under the main heading [under Jesus Christ] and the 57 subtitles [thereunder] in the Topical Guide," consisting of "more than 2,200 listings . . . in those 18 pages of the Topical Guide." Asked about the impact of this study on him he replied, "I am a different man!" Of this description, Elder Neil A. Anderson exclaimed, "He [President Nelson] was a different man? At age 92, a different man?" "If a renewed study of the Savior [or other gospel topic] helped prepare President Nelson," surely it can help "us as well." (See "Prophets, Leadership, and Divine Law," Worldwide devotional for Young Adults, Jan. 8, 2017, https://www.churchofjesuschrist.org/church/events/january-2017-worldwide-devotional-for-young-adults?lang=eng, quoted by Neil L. Anderson, "We Talk of Christ," *Liahona*, November 2020, 88). President Nelson shares how, "in the midst of a busy surgical practice and raising a large family," he felt that he was "not making any spiritual progress." His solution? He "got up an hour earlier [at 4:30 a.m.] each day to study the scriptures and learn to play the organ" (Nelson, *Heart of the Matter*, 153; see also his account of his challenge to the young single adults to increase their testimony of the Savior [Ibid., 154–56]).
10. Personal conversation with Steve Anderson, Recorder, Dallas Texas Temple, attributed to remarks reportedly made at the Bountiful Utah Temple dedication. See also "Temple Clothing in the Scriptures," Relief Society Women: To Know the History, Purpose, and Destiny of the Relief Society, August 24, 2008, https://www.reliefsocietywomen.com/blog/2008/08/24/temple-clothing-in-the-scriptures/ ("As we read the scriptures with our 'temple eyes', we will 'see' what the Lord wants us to see, and the deeper meaning in the scriptures that exists for those who have received the temple ordinances").
11. "Adam and Eve, Noah and his wife, Abraham and Sarah, Lehi and Sariah, and all other devoted disciples of Jesus Christ—since the world was created—have made the *same* covenants with God. They have received the *same* ordinances that we as members of the Lord's restored Church today have made: those covenants that we receive at baptism and in the temple" (Russell M. Nelson, "Come, Follow Me," *Ensign*, May 2019 [emphasis in original]).
12. The Lord similarly told Hyrum Smith, "[Believe] in the power of Jesus Christ, or in my power which speaketh unto thee; For, behold, it is I that speak . . . and by my power I give these words unto thee" (Doctrine and Covenants 11:10–11). (See Nelson Baker, *The Process of Atonement*, 2016, 347.)
13. Russell M. Nelson, "Hear Him," *Ensign*, May 2020, 88. On another occasion, the Prophet promised that the Holy Ghost would be our "personal tutor"

as we "seek to understand what the Lord would have [us] know and do" as we seek to learn how to "draw the Savior's power" into our lives (Nelson, "Spiritual Treasures," 77).

14. Highlighting the importance of the "stories" related in the scriptures in an essay about "richness" or complexity, on the one hand, and simplicity or truth on the other, Daniel C. Peterson notes:

    The Gospel must not be misunderstood as an attempt at a philosophical system. It doesn't purport to answer every question that might be raised by a graduate seminar in analytic philosophy. That isn't its purpose. It need not define philosophically precise answers to questions about divine foreknowledge, the nature of preexistent personhood, or the ultimate origins of morality. Such definitions are no part of its intent.

    There are good reasons why Latter-day Saints have distinguished themselves in journal-keeping, the recording of history, and historical writing but have not produced systematic theologians. *Our scriptural texts are often couched as stories.* They are never presented as manuals of doctrine, let alone as theological treatises. The Gospel is about building a relationship with the Father, Son, and Holy Ghost and about entering into covenants with God. It is not simply a list of propositions to be affirmed, whether deep or shallow. (Daniel C. Peterson, "De Profundis," *Interpreter: A Journal of Latter-Day Saint Faith and Scholarship,* https://journal.interpreterfoundation.org/de-profundis/ [emphasis added]).

    Noting that he has known "personally ten of the sixteen men who preceded [him] as President of the Church," President Nelson adds, "prophets are extraordinary role models" and that "the finest leaders to walk the earth are prophets of God" (Nelson, *Heart of the Matter,* 140).

15. President Nelson has reminded us that "temple ordinances and covenants are ancient" (Russell M. Nelson, "The Temple and Your Spiritual Foundation," *Liahona,* November 2021, 93). Thus, he has taught, studying passages in the "Old Testament and the books of Moses and Abraham in the Pearl of Great Price" that shed light on temple ordinances and doctrine (and I would add reliable scholars who study ancient temple patterns and practices) "is even more enlightening *after* one is familiar with the temple endowment. Those books underscore the antiquity of temple work" (Nelson, "Personal Preparation for Temple Blessings" [emphasis in original]). Elder David B. Haight also highlighted the ancient origin of temple ordinances and their influence on the world: "The gospel in its fulness was revealed to Adam, and undoubtedly all religious practices are derived from the remnants of the truth given to Adam. Some religious practices given in those early days have, no doubt, been corrupted as they have been handed down through the ages. But faithful members who understand the eternal nature of the gospel—of God's holy purpose to bring to pass the eternal life of man—understand clearly why the history of man seems to revolve around the building and use of temples" (David B. Haight, "Personal Temple Worship," *Ensign,* May 1993, 23, quoting John A. Widtsoe, "Temple Worship," Utah Genealogical and Historical Quarterly, April 1921, 53–54).

16. See, for example, *General Handbook: Serving in The Church of Jesus Christ of Latter-day Saints 3*, "Priesthood Principles," and 27, "Temple Ordinances for the Living" (referred to hereafter as *General Handbook*).
17. Nelson, "The Temple and Your Spiritual Foundation" (The *Lord* "is the One who wants you to understand with great clarity exactly what you are making covenants to do. *He* is the One who wants you to experience fully *His* sacred ordinances. *He* wants you to comprehend your privileges, promises, and responsibilities. *He* wants you to have spiritual insights and awakenings you've never had before [emphasis in original]). President Nelson has urged us to "spend more time in" and "regularly" attend the temple in virtually every general conference since his ordination. For example, in October 2022 he urged members to "spend more time in the temple, and seek to understand how the temple teaches you to rise above this fallen world" (Nelson, "Overcome the World and Find Rest," *Liahona*, November 2022, 98). In addition, he testified, "I promise that increased time in the temple will bless your life in ways nothing else can" (Nelson, "Focus on the Temple," *Liahona*, November 2022, 121). In October 2021, he urged members: "Please make time for the Lord in His holy house. Nothing will strengthen your spiritual foundation like temple service and temple worship" (Nelson, "Make Time for the Lord," *Liahona*, November 2021). In April 2020, he said, "Please schedule regular time to worship and serve in the temple. Every minute of that time will bless you and your family in ways *nothing* else can" (Nelson, "Hear Him" [emphasis in original]). In October 2018 he said: "My dear brothers and sisters, the assaults of the adversary are increasing exponentially, in intensity and in variety. Our need to be in the temple on a regular basis has never been greater. I plead with you to take a prayerful look at how you spend your time. Invest time in your future and in that of your family. If you have reasonable access to a temple, I urge you to find a way to make an appointment regularly with the Lord—to be in His holy house—then keep that appointment with exactness and joy. I promise you that the Lord will bring the miracles He knows you need as you make sacrifices to serve and worship in His temples" (Nelson, "Becoming Exemplary Latter-day Saints," *Ensign*, November 2018).
18. Nelson, "The Temple and Your Spiritual Foundation."
19. Russell M. Nelson, "Closing Remarks," *Ensign*, November 2019.
20. Russell M. Nelson, "A New Normal," *Liahona*, November 2020. See also Nelson, "The Future of the Church: Preparing the World for the Savior's Second Coming," *Liahona*, April 2020, 9.
21. See, for example, Ed J. Pinegar, *The Temple: Gaining Knowledge and Power in the House of the Lord* (American Fork, Utah: Covenant Communications, Inc., 2014), 234–35.
22. David A. Bednar, "Let This House Be Built Unto My Name," *Liahona*, May 2020, 86.
23. "Preparing to Enter the Holy Temple," The Church of Jesus Christ of Latter-day Saints, 2002, https://www.churchofjesuschrist.org/study/manual/preparing-to-enter-the-holy-temple/preparing-to-enter-the-holy-temple?lang=eng.

24. *Endowed from on High: Temple Preparation Seminar*, Teacher's Manual, 2003, https://www.churchofjesuschrist.org/study/manual/endowed-from-on-high/title-page?lang=eng.
25. *Endowed from on High*, iv.
26. See https://www.churchofjesuschrist.org/temples?lang=eng.
27. https://www.churchofjesuschrist.org/general-conference/topics/archive?topic=temples&lang=eng&page=1.
28. See, e.g., Truman G. Madsen, *The Temple: Where Heaven Meets Earth* (Salt Lake City, Utah: Deseret Book, 2008).
29. Andrew C. Skinner, *Temple Worship: 20 Truths That Will Bless Your Life* (Salt Lake City, Utah: Deseret Book, 2007). (See especially chapter 17, "A Portal to Heaven.")
30. Dallin H. Oaks, "Trust in the Lord," *Ensign*, November 2019.
31. Ezra Taft Benson, "Life Is Eternal," *Ensign*, June 1971, 33. See also Neil L. Andersen, "My Mind Caught Hold upon This Thought of Jesus Christ," *Liahona*, May 2023 (relating how Matt Johnson and his four daughters "deeply felt their love and eternal bond with [their recently deceased wife and mother,] Sarah" as they performed proxy baptisms in the temple).
32. Brent L. Top, "What's on the Other Side? A Conversation with Brent L. Top on the Spirit World," *Religious Educator*, vol. 14, no. 2, 2013, 51–52 (citations omitted), https://scholarsarchive.byu.edu/cgi/viewcontent.cgi?article=1623&context=re. See also Madsen, *The Temple: Where Heaven and Earth Meet*, 31. ("There are laws that enable [our kindred dead] to have some influence upon us and we upon them. In the temple these laws are fulfilled. Parley P. Pratt taught that, for the pure in heart, when we receive communication from 'kindred spirits, . . . spirit communes with spirit, thought meets thought, soul blends with soul, in all the raptures of mutual, pure, and eternal love.'") See also Brent L. Top, *What's On the Other Side? What the Gospel Teaches Us about the Spirit World* (Salt Lake City, Utah: Deseret Book, 2012), 17–24. Similar testimonies can be found on the Church's website. For example, "President Brigham Young taught that the postmortal spirit world is on the earth, around us" (see *Teachings of Presidents of the Church: Brigham Young* [1997], 279 and Gospel Topics, "Spirit World," https://www.churchofjesuschrist.org/study/manual/gospel-topics/spirit-world?lang=eng). President Ezra Taft Benson, quoting President Brigham Young, added: "The spirit world is not far away. From the Lord's point of view, it is all one great program on both sides of the veil. Sometimes the veil between this life and the life beyond becomes very thin. This I know! Our loved ones who have passed on are not far from us. [President Brigham Young] asked, 'Where is the spirit world?' and then answered his own question: 'It is right here. . . . Do [spirits] go beyond the boundaries of this organized earth? No, they do not. They are brought forth upon this earth, for the express purpose of inhabiting it to all eternity.' He also said, '. . . If the Lord would permit it, and it was His will that it should be done, you could see the spirits that have departed from this world, as plainly as you now see bodies with your natural eyes'" ("Because I Live, Ye Shall Live Also," *Ensign*, April 1993, 4, quoting Brigham Young, *Journal of Discourses* 3:369, 368 from "The Spirit World and the Redemption of the Dead," Introduction

to *Family History Student Manual—Religion 261*, 9.2.2 [Salt Lake City, Utah: Seminaries and Institutes of Religion Curriculum The Church of Jesus Christ of Latter-day Saints, 2012, https://site.churchofjesuschrist.org/study/manual/introduction-to-family-history-student-manual/chapter-9?lang=eng]).
33. Wilford Woodruff, "The Law of Adoption," April 1894 general conference, *Deseret Weekly*, April 21, 1895, 541–43, http://contentdm.lib.byu.edu/cdm/compoundobject/collection/desnews7/id/7443/rec/16, cited in Jennifer Ann Mackley, *Wilford Woodruff's Witness: The Development of Temple Doctrine* (Seattle, Washington: High Desert Publishing, 2018), 286. This teaching was repeated by President Lorenzo Snow in general conference in 1893: "When the Gospel is preached to the spirits in prison, the success attending that preaching will be far greater than that attending the preaching of our Elders in this life. I believe there will be very few indeed of those spirits who will not gladly receive the Gospel when it is carried to them. The circumstances there will be a thousand times more favorable" (*Millennial Star* 56:50, quoted in Dale C. Mouritsen, "The Spirit World, Our Next Home," *Ensign*, January 1977). John W. Taylor "concluded that only one in ten would refuse the ordinance" (Madsen, *The Temple: Where Heaven and Earth Meet*, 31).
34. James E. Faust, "The Restoration of All Things," *Ensign*, May 2006.
35. Top, "What's on the Other Side? A Conversation with Brent L. Top on the Spirit World," 52.
36. Matthew B. Brown shares accounts of individuals from the spirit world appearing to those on this side of the veil to request help with and witness the performance of their proxy ordinances in *The Gate of Heaven: Insights on the Doctrine and Symbols of the Temple* (American Fork, Utah: Covenant Communications, Inc., 1999), 260–71. Summarizing these accounts, he concludes:
    It is clear from the scriptural record and eyewitness accounts that there are temples in the spiritual world. Even though we are not aware of precisely what goes on inside those heavenly buildings, we have been informed by latter-day prophets that some form of work is performed that ratifies the temple work that is performed upon the earth. President Ezra Taft Benson taught that the "work we are performing here has [a] direct relationship to the work over there. Someday you will know that there are ordinances performed over there, too, in order to make the vicarious work which you do effective. It will all be done under the authority and power of the priesthood of God" [*The Teachings of Ezra Taft Benson*, 252–53]. And from President John Taylor we learn that "God is looking upon us, and has called us to be saviors upon Mount Zion. . . . If we are saviors, what have we to do? Build temples. What then? Administer in them; and others in the heavens are engaged in the same work as we, but in another position and in other circumstances. They preach to spirits in prison; they officiate in ordinances with which we have nothing to do. We administer in ordinances which God has revealed to us to attend to; and when we attend to them correctly, God sanctions them" [*Journal of Discourses* 22:308–09] (Brown, 270–71).
    See generally, Joseph Heinerman, *Temple Manifestations* (Salt Lake City, Utah: Joseph Lyon and Associates, Inc., 1974).

CHAPTER 1

The Spiritual Treasure of God's Divine Love

"God 'loveth those who will have him to be their God' (1 Nephi 17:40). This is exactly why, as part of the covenant, a special mercy and love—or hesed—*is available to all who enter this binding and intimate relationship with God, even 'to a thousand generations' (Deuteronomy 7:9)."*[1]

—Russell M. Nelson

Covenants Provide Access to God's Love and Mercy

In his October 2022 *Liahona* message, "The Everlasting Covenant," President Russell M. Nelson describes the very "special kind of love and mercy" God extends to those who make covenants with Him and the intimate relationship that we can develop with Him as we strive to keep our covenants. "In the Hebrew language," he wrote, "that covenantal love is called *hesed* (חֶסֶד)." Noting the difficulty Bible translators had translating the term *hesed*, rendering it often as "lovingkindness," or as "mercy" and "goodness," *hesed*, he wrote, encompasses the idea of "a covenant relationship in which both parties are bound to be loyal and faithful to each other."[2] Learning by the power of the Holy Ghost the reality of this vital scriptural truth about God's love for us, which I have always felt especially strongly in sacrament meetings and in the temple, changes everything.

Even when we stray from the covenant path, in large or small degrees, God "will help [us] find [our] way back to Him," the prophet testified, "offer [us] opportunities to change," and "forgive [us] when [we] repent."[3] Service in the temple can renew in us feelings of God's faithfulness, patience, and long-suffering toward us in our "weakness" (Ether 12:27) *and* our weaknesses[4] like nothing else can. There we are assured, as President Nelson notes, that our Heavenly Father and our Redeemer "will never tire in [Their] efforts to help us, and we will never exhaust [Their] merciful patience with us."[5]

The Love of God Permeates the Spirit World and Fills His Holy House

In his address about the spirit world, President Dallin H. Oaks described how even those of our ancestors we least expect to respond to invitations to accept the gospel—"the unrepentant, and the rebellious"—"can be freed from their bondage and go forward to the blessings a loving Heavenly Father has in store for them."[6] Even so, as temple patrons we may wonder about those in the spirit world for whom we serve as proxies—"is he or she here today or know that I am here?" And so it came as a welcome reassurance when Elder Gerrit W. Gong of the Quorum of the Twelve shared the sacred experience of one such temple patron who came to know for herself that her temple service was welcomed by such a "converted soul":

> When they joined The Church of Jesus Christ of Latter-day Saints, my friend and her husband joyfully learned family relationships need not be "until death do you part." In the house of the Lord, families can be united eternally (sealed).
>
> But my friend did not want to be sealed to her father. "He was not a nice husband to my mother. He was not a nice dad to his children," she said. "My dad will have to wait. I do not have any desire to do his temple work and be sealed with him in eternity."
>
> For a year, she fasted, prayed, spoke a lot with the Lord about her father. Finally, she was ready. Her father's temple work was completed. Later, she said, "In my sleep my dad appeared to me in a dream, all dressed in white. He had changed. He said, 'Look at me. I am all clean. Thank you for doing the work for

me in the temple.'" Her father added, "Get up and go back to the temple; your brother is waiting to be baptized."[7]

With some notable exceptions like that related by Elder Gong, much of the time we may not know for sure whether the individual for whom we are serving as a proxy is aware of or has accepted the ordinance we are officiating in in their behalf. But we *can* always know through the power of the Holy Ghost that our Father in Heaven is aware of our temple service.

The scriptures contain abundant evidence that the Savior "doeth not anything save it be for the benefit of the world; for he loveth the world, even that he layeth down his own life that he may draw all men unto him" (2 Nephi 26:24). It should not surprise us, then, as Brother Top observed in his study of near-death experiences, that "love is the supreme element of . . . heaven." "Those who have had positive near-death experiences invariably testify to the ascendancy of love in the realm of righteous spirits."[8] He further noted, "In virtually all recorded near-death occurrences, the love transmitted by the light" that near-death witnesses see and feel as they transition from mortality to life in the spirit world "is the most extraordinary and unforgettable aspect of the experience."[9] Brother Top explained:

> The following [reported experience] is typical: "A dazzling brightness infiltrated the mist and, ultimately, cradled me in a way that I cannot describe. . . . My thoughts? I had none. But feelings my cup did, indeed, run over. Bliss . . . rapture . . . joy . . . ecstasy, all of the above, and in such measure that it cannot be compared or understood. As the light continued to surround me and engulf me, my consciousness expanded and admitted more and more of what the light embraces: peace and unconditional love."[10]

Similarly, prophets who have seen Christ often focus on the singular feeling of love they come away with through their experience. For example, in the first recorded account of the First Vision, Joseph Smith reported that after the vision "*my soul was filled with love*, and for many days I could rejoice with great joy."[11] When Nephi saw the tree of life his father, Lehi, had seen and asked the Spirit of the Lord the meaning thereof, he was shown Mary, "the mother of the son of God" and the newly born "Lamb of God, yea, even the Son of the Eternal Father" (1 Nephi 11:18, 21). Whereupon Nephi was taught and knew that the tree (and the fountain of living waters) was a representation of "the love of God, which sheddeth itself abroad in the hearts of the children of men; wherefore, it is the most desirable above all things" (1 Nephi 11:22, 25). Lehi later described to his sons his feelings at the time of his marvelous vision: "Behold, the Lord hath redeemed my soul . . . ; I have beheld his glory, and I am encircled about eternally in the arms of his love" (2 Nephi 1:15; see also Doctrine and Covenants 6:20). Nephi similarly testified that God "hath filled me with his love, even unto the consuming of my flesh" (2 Nephi 4:21). The Atonement of Christ is the greatest manifestation of love in the universe!

Notably, the impetus for President Joseph F. Smith's great vision of the redemption of the dead was his "pondering over the scriptures; [a]nd reflecting upon the great atoning sacrifice that was made by the Son of God, for the redemption of the world; [a]nd *the great and wonderful love made manifest by the Father and the Son* in the coming of the Redeemer into the world" (Doctrine and Covenants 138:1–3). Similarly, Orson F. Whitney, later called to be an apostle, while serving as a less than fully converted young missionary, expressed similar feelings about the Savior's love upon witnessing the tenderness and depth of His sorrow and compassion for all humankind, which were manifest during His suffering in Gethsemane:

> One night I dreamed—if dream it may be called—that I was in the Garden of Gethsemane, a witness of the Savior's agony. . . . After telling [Peter, James, and John] to kneel and pray, He passed over to the other side, where He also knelt and prayed. . . . 'O my Father, if it be possible, let this cup pass from me: nevertheless not as I will, but as thou wilt.' As He prayed the tears streamed down His face, which was toward me. I was so moved at the sight that I wept also, out of pure sympathy with His great sorrow. My whole heart went out to Him. I *loved Him* with all my soul and longed to be with Him as I longed for nothing else.[12]

The scriptures testify that many of the prophets saw God. All heard His voice by the power of the Holy Ghost. Their testimony of God's love for His children no doubt derives, in part, from what they felt during those experiences.

Love of God and Neighbor Is the Principal Fruit of Christ's Personal Ministry

> **Acts 2:44–47**—And all that believed were together, and had all things common; And sold their possessions and goods, and parted them to all men, as every man had need. And they, continuing daily with one accord in the temple, and breaking bread from house to house, did eat their meat with gladness and singleness of heart, Praising God, and having favour with all the people. And the Lord added to the church daily such as should be saved.

In their study of the negative impact sixteenth-century theological dogmas have had on the "plain and precious" truths about God's nature, Fiona and Terryl Givens describe the "radical love and community" the first Christians exhibited, as alluded to by Luke in the verses in Acts cited above. This love, which Christ constantly exhibited for His disciples, was simply the reflection in Christ of His Father's love for His children. "Infinite love and goodness," they write, "have a form, a face, a healing hand—that reaches out to touch, to embrace. This, we discover to our shock and surprise, this is God. For Christ, we learn, is not a mere earthly version of a distant, unapproachable, 'foggy' God. God the Son is the perfect reflection of exactly who God the Father always was and is: 'He that hath seen me hath seen the Father' (John 14:9)."[13]

This understanding of the true nature of God transformed the Church of Jesus Christ in the Old World. "The first Christians['] . . . understanding of the interrelatedness of the human family as a whole was utterly transformative of every connection, every gesture, every aspiration toward genuine community. . . . 'What marks us in the eye of our enemies [wrote Thomas] is our practice of lovingkindness: "Only look," they say, "how they love one another.'" These first Christians turned ad hoc communities into a society governed by love."[14] Likewise, the Nephites, after Christ's visit, exhibited a similar love for God and for one another because of the constancy and power with which they felt God's love for them: "And it came to pass that there was no contention in the land, *because of the love of God which did dwell in the hearts of the people*. . . . And surely there could not be a happier people among all the people who had been created by the hand of God" (4 Nephi 1:15–16).

The abundance of God's divine love that we feel as we attend the temple is surely one of the most important spiritual treasures we receive through our temple covenants. As we feel this soul-satisfying love, we are reminded of our relationship to our Father in Heaven—a beloved spirit son or daughter, inheritors of His divine nature. We feel His confidence and trust in us and leave energized, ennobled, and uplifted thereby. Surely the profound renewal of strength is one of the reasons President Nelson has urged us repeatedly "to make an appointment regularly with the Lord—to be in His holy house—then keep that appointment with exactness and joy."[15]

Endnotes

1. Russell M. Nelson, "The Everlasting Covenant," *Liahona*, October 2022. GotQuestions.org contains the following entry on the meaning of hesed:

    Many biblical words such as mercy, compassion, love, grace, and faithfulness relate to the Hebrew word *hesed* (חֶסֶד), but none of these completely summarize the concept. *Hesed* is not merely an emotion or feeling but involves action on behalf of someone who is in need. *Hesed* describes a sense of love and loyalty that inspires merciful and compassionate behavior toward another person. *Hesed*, found some 250 times in the Old Testament, expresses an essential part of God's character. When God appeared to Moses to give the Law a second time, He described Himself as "abounding in" or "filled with" *hesed*, which is translated "love and faithfulness," "unfailing love," "faithful love," "steadfast love," and "loyal love," depending on the Bible version (Exodus 34:6–7). The core idea of this term communicates loyalty or faithfulness within a relationship. Thus, *hesed* is closely related to God's covenant with His people, Israel. [The] trustworthy, ever-enduring, loyal aspect of God's covenantal love resonates throughout the Old Testament (Nehemiah 1:5; Daniel 9:4; Jeremiah 32:18). . . .

    God's covenant relationship with His people results in His loyal love and faithfulness [*hesed*], even when His people are unfaithful to Him. Always at the heart of *hesed* lies God's generous sense of compassion, grace, and mercy. *Hesed* surpasses ordinary kindness and friendship. It is the inclination of the heart to show "amazing grace" to the one who is loved. *Hesed* runs deeper than social expectations, responsibilities, fluctuating emotions, or what is deserved or earned by the recipient. *Hesed* finds its home in committed, familial love, and it comes to life in actions.

    The message of the gospel—God's act of forgiveness and salvation in Jesus—is rooted in *hesed*. *Hesed* describes the disposition of God's heart not only toward His people but to all humanity. The love of God extends far beyond duty or expectation. His forgiveness of sin fulfills a need that is basic to all other needs in the relationship between human beings and God—the restoration and continuation of fellowship with God in Jesus Christ. God's *hesed* manifested in forgiveness makes a relationship with Him possible. That forgiveness comes to us freely as a gift from God based on the sacrificial act of Christ. (https://www.gotquestions.org/meaning-of-hesed.html)

2. Nelson, "The Everlasting Covenant." See also Nelson, *Heart of the Matter*, 36–38.
3. Ibid.
4. In the previously oft-cited verse, Ether 12:27 ("If men come unto me I will show unto them their *weakness*. I give unto men *weakness* that they may be humble; and my grace is sufficient for all men that humble themselves before me; for if they humble themselves before me, and have faith in me, then will I make weak things become strong unto them"), Moroni uses the singular term "weakness" twice and once again in the next verse. The term *weakness*

suggests that while the Lord gave us a mortal, fallen body and world in which we are subject to Satan's influence through the flesh (unlike translated beings [see 3 Nephi 28:39] and little children [see Doctrine and Covenants 29:47]) so that we can "work out [our own] salvation" (Philippians 2:12; Alma 34:37) and "prove" ourselves (Abraham 3:25), learning from our own experience the difference between righteousness and wickedness, He does not necessarily give us our weaknesses. These, it seems to me at least, we bring to mortality with us as a result of our individual choices and progression from the "beginning" (Doctrine and Covenants 93:29–31) or "foundation of the world" (Alma 13:3–5). Otherwise, if God gave us our individual weaknesses, we could blame Him for the problems such weaknesses may cause. (See Dale G. Renlund, "Accessing God's Power through Covenants," *Liahona*, May 2023, note 7 ["we should not doubt the Savior's ability to help us with *our* weaknesses"]).

5. Nelson, "The Everlasting Covenant."
6. Oaks, "Trust in the Lord."
7. Gerrit W. Gong, "Happy and Forever," *Liahona*, November 2022. Interestingly, in footnote 3 to this "unusually direct" sacred experience, Elder Gong noted: "There are many sacred experiences of hope and promises for change as we and those we love come to Jesus Christ through temple ordinances and covenants on both sides of the veil." President Joseph F. Smith declared, "Our fathers and mothers, brothers, sisters and friends who have passed away from this earth, having been faithful, and worthy to enjoy these rights and privileges, may have a mission given them to visit their relatives and friends upon the earth again, bringing from the divine Presence messages of love, of warning, or reproof and instruction, to those whom they had learned to love in the flesh" (James E. Faust, "A Royal Priesthood," *Ensign*, May 2006, 51, quoting Joseph F. Smith, *Gospel Doctrine*, 5th ed., 1939, 436).
8. Brent L. and Wendy C. Top, *Glimpses Beyond Death's Door* (American Fork, Utah: Covenant Communications, 2012), 101, 103.
9. Top, *Glimpses*, 87.
10. Ibid., quoting from *The Return from Silence*, 122.
11. Gospel Topic Essays, "First Vision Accounts," https://www.churchofjesus-christ.org/study/manual/gospel-topics-essays/first-vision-accounts?lang=eng (as quoted in the 1832 account). See Karl Ricks Anderson, *The Savior in Kirtland* (Salt Lake City, Utah: Deseret Book, 2012), 109–11 (documenting how, through His many interactions with the Prophet Joseph Smith, the Savior showed and taught of His "loving, kind, [and] compassionate nature"); see also ibid., 159–65 (reviewing historical accounts of Joseph Smith's testimonies of his First Vision).
12. The rest of Elder Whitney's classic account tells us not only about the character of the Savior, but also how important it is to convert our (sometimes temporary) feelings of love for Him into a daily commitment to follow Him:

> Presently He arose and walked to where the Apostles were kneeling—fast asleep! He shook them gently, awoke them, and in a tone of tender reproach, untinctured by the least suggestion of anger or scolding, asked them if they could not watch with Him one hour. There He was,

with the weight of the world's sin upon His shoulders, with the pangs of every man, woman, and child shooting through His sensitive soul—and they could not watch with Him one poor hour! . . .

All at once the circumstance seemed to change, the scene remaining just the same. Instead of before, it was after the Crucifixion, and the Savior, with those three Apostles, now stood together in a group at my left. They were about to depart and ascend into heaven. I could endure it no longer. I ran out from behind the tree, fell at His feet, clasped Him around the knees, and begged Him to take me with Him.

I shall never forget the kind and gentle manner in which He stooped and raised me up and embraced me. It was so vivid, so real, that I felt the very warmth of His bosom against which I rested. Then He said: "No, my son; these have finished their work, and they may go with me, but you must stay and finish yours." Still I clung to Him. Gazing up into His face—for He was taller than I—I besought Him most earnestly: "Well, promise me that I will come to You at the last." He smiled sweetly and tenderly and replied: "That will depend entirely upon yourself." I awoke with a sob in my throat, and it was morning (Orson F. Whitney, "Gospel Classics: The Divinity of Jesus Christ," *Ensign*, December 2003 [citations omitted]).

13. Fiona and Terryl Givens, *All Things New: Rethinking Sin, Salvation, and Everything in Between* (Meridian, Idaho: Faith Matters Publishing, 2020), 11, 13.
14. Ibid., 14–15 (quoting Elaine Pagels, *Beyond Belief: The Secret Gospel of Thomas* [New York: Random House, 2003], 10).
15. Nelson, "Becoming Exemplary Latter-day Saints."

CHAPTER 2

The Spiritual Treasures of Reverence, Worship, and Worthiness

In explaining to friends not of our faith the meaning and purpose of temples, start by "call[ing] attention to the words etched on the temple's exterior: 'Holiness to the Lord: The House of the Lord.' . . . Each temple is a holy place; each temple patron strives to become more holy. All requirements to enter the temple relate to personal holiness."[1]

—Russell M. Nelson

A Divine Pattern—Ascending the Mountain of the Lord

The Lord set the pattern for how we should approach Him anciently. To Moses he said: "Draw not nigh hither: *put off thy shoes from off thy feet*, for the place whereon thou standest is holy ground" (Exodus 3:5). The temple is a place "for the Most High to dwell" (Doctrine and Covenants 124:27), a "place of [His] holiness" (109:13), a place that He "may reveal [His] ordinances . . . unto [His] people" (124:40). It is also referred to as the "mountain of the Lord," "mountain of the Lord's house," and the "holy mountain" (Isaiah 2:2–3; 30:29; 65:11; 66:20; Daniel 9:20; Joel 2:1; Zechariah 8:3). "And many people shall go and say, Come ye, and let us go up to the mountain of the Lord, to the house of the God of Jacob; and he will teach us of his ways" (2 Nephi 12:3). In fact, one of our most beloved latter-day prophecies of the establishment of the iconic Salt Lake Temple uses this appellation: "But in the last days it shall come to pass, that the *mountain of the house of the LORD* shall be established in the top of the mountains, and it shall be exalted above the hills; and people shall flow unto it" (Micah 4:1; see also verse 2).[2]

The imagery of the temple as a "mountain" is apt. In our journey home, we ascend from our telestial state to Heavenly Father's home in a celestial sphere, which is symbolic of our moral journey as we progress through the power of Christ's Atonement unlocked by ordinances and covenants from telestial, then terrestrial, and finally to celestial habits. Our ability to live a celestial law enlarges as we spiritually progress toward a celestial character.[3] As Bruce Porter put it (and as we will explore throughout this study), the "endowment of power" is all about change or growth—"without a change of character, there is no power in the ordinances of salvation or exaltation. . . . The power of the ordinances lay[s] in the individual choice to change one's character in a way that will foster the relationship with God, His Son and the Atonement which is needed to make the [promises of the] ordinance a reality."[4]

In likeness of our spiritual journey upward, ancient temple patrons and temple workers physically ascended the temple mount, including climbing steps as they entered the temple grounds and progressed through the outer and inner courts of the temple into the holy place and finally the holy of holies.[5] Scholars have noted that the location of the temple in Jerusalem on the top of Mount Moriah, "halfway between heaven and earth," "served as an ideal meeting place for God and man."[6] Prophets such as the brother of Jared[7] and Moses ascended to mountaintops to commune with God and receive sacred temple ordinances. Latter-day temples have been similarly designed to remind us that our journey to our heavenly home necessarily ascends ever upward.[8]

Temples provide the "holy ground" or sacred spaces previously reserved for divinely selected mountaintops. "We regard a temple," President Nelson taught, "as the most sacred structure in the Church."[9] Elder Lionel Kendrick of the Seventy shared his belief that "the temple is . . . the most sacred and holy place on earth and should be treated with the greatest degree of reverence and respect. Reverence in the temple is an expression to the Lord that we consider [the temple] to be sacred and that we recognize it to be, indeed, His holy house."[10] "Ye shall . . . *reverence my sanctuary*: I am the Lord" (Leviticus 19:30; see also Leviticus 26:2).

Reverence, a Deep respect for Sacred Things

The Guide to the Scriptures defines reverence as a "deep respect for sacred things; wonder." It is closely associated with the verb "honor," which, "as usually used in the scriptures, [means] to show respect and reverence to someone or something." Christ taught the ultimate meaning of reverence when He explained that the honor or respect, reverence, and obedience that all created things afford God the Father is the source of His power. "The devil," the Savior said, who "was before" and "tempted" Adam in the Garden of Eden, "rebelled against me [speaking by divine investiture for the Father], saying, Give me thine honor, which is my power" (Doctrine and Covenants 29:36). Like the bread cast on the water, as we honor God, He honors us. "If any man serve me, let him follow me; and where I am, there shall also my servant be: if any man serve me, him will my Father honour" (John 12:26).[11]

Another synonym of reverence is "fear." The Guide to the Scriptures notes: "*Fear* can have two meanings: (1) to fear God is to feel reverence and awe for Him and to obey His commandments; (2) to fear man, mortal dangers, pain, and evil is to be afraid of such things and to dread them." The Bible Dictionary makes the same point. On the one hand, "fear of the Lord" (Ps. 111:10; Eccl. 12:13; Isa. 11:2–3; Luke 1:50) and "godly fear" (Heb. 12:28) are "frequently spoken of as part of man's duty." This type of fear "is equivalent to reverence, awe, worship, and is therefore an essential part of the attitude of mind in which we ought to stand toward the All-holy God." Scriptural uses of godly "fear" include:

- "Gather me the people together, and I will make them hear my words, that they may learn to fear me all the days that they shall live upon the earth" (Deuteronomy 4:10);
- "Thou shalt fear the Lord thy God" (Deuteronomy 6:13; Joshua 24:14; 1 Samuel 12:24; Proverbs 24:21; Ecclesiastes 5:7; 1 Peter 2:17);
- "God require[s] of thee, but to fear the Lord" (Deuteronomy 10:12; Micah 6:8);
- "All Israel shall hear, and fear" (Deuteronomy 13:11; 21:21);

- "Serve the Lord with fear" (Psalm 2:11);
- "Secret of the Lord is with them that fear him" (Psalm 25:14);
- "Eye of the Lord is upon them that fear him" (Psalm 33:18);
- "Fear of the Lord is the beginning of wisdom" (Psalm 111:10);
- "Blessed is the man that feareth the Lord" (Psalm 112:1);
- "Ye that fear the Lord, trust in the Lord" (Psalm 115:11);
- "In the fear of the Lord is strong confidence" (Proverbs 14:26);
- "Fear of the Lord tendeth to life" (Proverbs 19:23);
- "Woman that feareth the Lord, she shall be praised" (Proverbs 31:30);
- "It shall be well with them that fear God" (Ecclesiastes 8:12);
- "Work out your own salvation with fear and trembling" (Philippians 2:12; Mormon 9:27);
- "Fear God, and give glory to him" (Revelation 14:7; Doctrine and Covenants 88:104);
- "Prophets stirred up the people continually to keep them in the fear of the Lord" (Enos 1:23);
- "They who do not fear me, I will disturb and cause to tremble" (Doctrine and Covenants 10:56);
- "He that feareth me shall be looking for the signs of the coming of the Son of Man" (Doctrine and Covenants 45:39; see also Topical Guide, "Fear of God," "Respect," "Worship").

The scriptures repeatedly teach that fear of man and life's challenges, on the other hand, is "something unworthy of a child of God, something that 'perfect love casteth out' (1 Jn. 4:18)." Moreover, the Bible Dictionary adds, one of the greatest causes of this type of fear, sin, "destroys that feeling of confidence God's child should feel in a loving Father and produces instead a feeling of shame and guilt. Ever since the Fall God has been teaching men not to fear, but with penitence to ask forgiveness in full confidence of receiving it."[12]

Elder M. Russell Ballard combined these concepts in his definition of reverence: "*Reverence* may be defined as a profound respect mingled with love and awe. Other words that add to our understanding of reverence include *gratitude, honor, veneration,* and *admiration*. The root word *revere* also implies an element of fear. Thus, reverence might be understood to mean an attitude of profound respect and love with a desire to honor and show gratitude, with a fear of breaking faith or offending."[13]

Why Are We Commanded to Reverence God?

As the foregoing and many other scriptures testify, as our first and most important priority in life, we are to love, revere, and worship God: "Thou shalt love the Lord thy God with all thy heart, and with all thy soul, and with all thy mind, and with all thy strength: this is the first commandment" (Mark 12:30). Why has God commanded us to love and reverence Him? Because to reverence or worship Him, which means to "show reverence and adoration" for God; to "honor with religious rites,"[14] helps us receive or develop the divine attribute of holiness, which the Father and Son possess in perfection.

The Guide to the Scriptures defines "worship" as "love, reverence, service, and devotion for God," citing Doctrine and Covenants 20:19, which states: "And [God] gave unto [man—male and female] commandments that they should love and serve him, the only living and true God, and that he should be the only being whom they should worship." "Worship includes prayer, fasting, church service, participating in gospel ordinances, and other practices that show devotion and love for God."[15] Some scriptural examples this entry gives of commandments to worship God include:

- Worship the Father in spirit and in truth (John 4:23);
- Worship him that made heaven and earth (Revelation 14:7; Doctrine and Covenants 133:38–39);
- Worship him with all your might, mind, and strength (2 Nephi 25:29);
- They believed in Christ and worshiped the Father in his name (Jacob 4:5);
- Zenos taught that men should pray and worship in all places (Alma 33:3–11);
- Worship God, in whatsoever place ye may be in, in spirit and in truth (Alma 34:38);
- The people fell down at the feet of Jesus and worshiped him (3 Nephi 11:17);

- All men must repent, believe on Jesus Christ, and worship the Father in His name (Doctrine and Covenants 20:29);
- This one God only will I worship (Moses 1:12–20).

Thus, reverence for and worship of Heavenly Father and Jesus Christ include family prayers and scripture study; participation in the sacrament, temple ordinances, and gospel discussions in classes and quorums; attendance at ward, stake, and general conferences; and even family and church activities that accomplish God's purposes and increase faith in Him.

Paul taught, "Be ye therefore *followers* of God, as dear children" (Ephesians 5:1). The footnote to the word "followers" in the King James Version says "imitators." The verb "to reverence" includes the idea to "venerate."[16] Actively and consistently fearing or reverencing the Lord, which includes our efforts to imitate or pattern our lives after the example He gave us, allows Him to sanctify us in His own way and time. "Neither shall ye profane my holy name; but I will be hallowed among the children of Israel: *I am the Lord which hallow you*" (Leviticus 22:32).

Worshipping and Worthiness—What Is Required to Participate Worthily in Priesthood Ordinances?

When He introduced the ordinance of the sacrament to the Nephites, Jesus directed His disciples (priesthood leaders of that day) to "not suffer any one knowingly to partake of my flesh and blood unworthily" (3 Nephi 18:28). Paul taught that we should "examine ourselves" before partaking of the sacrament lest we eat or drink "damnation to" our self, meaning that we would be damned or stopped from receiving the blessings sought and promised in the sacrament—the companionship of the Holy Ghost (1 Corinthians 11:27–29). What does it mean to be worthy to partake of the sacrament? The *Doctrines of the Gospel Student Manual* answers this question with a general conference statement by President George Albert Smith: "Before partaking of this sacrament, our hearts should be pure; our hands should be clean; we should be divested of all enmity toward our associates; we should be at peace with our fellow men; and we should have in our hearts *a desire to do the will of our Father and to keep all of His commandments*. If we do this, partaking of the sacrament will be a blessing to us and will renew our spiritual strength."[17]

The *General Handbook* also emphasizes that when we participate in or perform an ordinance we must "be worthy," which means generally to keep the standards "associated with holding a temple recommend" (18.3). It goes on, however, to teach a principle about worthiness that should be instructive to all of us as we participate in gospel ordinances, including the temple: "As guided by the Spirit and the instructions in this chapter, bishops and stake presidents may allow fathers and husbands who hold the necessary priesthood office to perform or participate in some ordinances and blessings *even if they are not fully temple worthy*. A priesthood holder who has unresolved serious sins should not participate." Of course, this is not to suggest that we can or should enter the temple unworthily, which the final question in the temple recommend interview questions outlined below clearly requires us to be. Rather, it is to encourage us, in answering the question, "Am I worthy?" as we approach the sacrament and the temple, to avoid inappropriately feeling that we need to be "perfect," or being so self-critical that we deny ourselves the sanctifying influence the Lord intended His ordinances to provide in our strivings for completeness or "perfection."[18] For example, Bradley R. Wilcox taught in general conference, "God's message is that worthiness is not flawlessness. Worthiness is being honest and trying. We must be honest with God, priesthood leaders, and others who love us, and we must strive to keep God's commandments and never give up just because we slip up."[19]

President Nelson elaborated on the theme of "holiness" and worthiness in his concluding remarks of the October 2019 general conference: "All requirements to enter the temple relate to personal holiness." In an earlier general conference message on temple preparation, President Nelson taught that just as each temple bears the inscription "Holiness to the Lord," "those who enter the temple are also to bear the attribute of holiness." Then he added this important qualifier: "We can acquire holiness only by enduring and persistent personal effort. . . . As temples are prepared for our members, our members need to prepare for the temple."[20] In other words, acquiring holiness is a process requiring "persistent personal effort" not achieved in a one-time interview or single visit to the temple.[21] Just as the ordinance of the sacrament and our worship in sacrament meetings are designed to help us "grow up into [Christ] in all things" (Ephesians 4:15), so the endowment and sealing ordinances and regular temple worship are intended by the Lord to assist us in our efforts to "grow up" in Christ, as He declared in His revealed prayer dedicating the Kirtland Temple (Doctrine and Covenants 109:15).

In the October 2019 general conference, President Nelson listed the following requirements to enter the Lord's holy house, some of which had "recently been edited for clarity":

1. Do you have faith in and a testimony of God, the Eternal Father; His Son, Jesus Christ; and the Holy Ghost?
2. Do you have a testimony of the Atonement of Jesus Christ and of His role as your Savior and Redeemer?
3. Do you have a testimony of the Restoration of the gospel of Jesus Christ?
4. Do you sustain the President of The Church of Jesus Christ of Latter-day Saints as the prophet, seer, and revelator and as the only person on the earth authorized to exercise all priesthood keys? Do you sustain the members of the First Presidency and the Quorum of the Twelve Apostles as prophets, seers, and revelators? Do you sustain the other General Authorities and local leaders of the Church?
5. The Lord has said that all things are to be "done in cleanliness" before Him (Doctrine and Covenants 42:41). Do you strive for moral cleanliness in your thoughts and behavior? Do you obey the law of chastity?
6. Do you follow the teachings of the Church of Jesus Christ in your private and public behavior with members of your family and others?
7. Do you support or promote any teachings, practices, or doctrine contrary to those of The Church of Jesus Christ of Latter-day Saints?
8. Do you strive to keep the Sabbath day holy, both at home and at church; attend your meetings; prepare for and worthily partake of the sacrament; and live your life in harmony with the laws and commandments of the gospel?

9. Do you strive to be honest in all that you do?
10. Are you a full-tithe payer?
11. Do you understand and obey the Word of Wisdom?
12. Do you have any financial or other obligations to a former spouse or to children? If yes, are you current in meeting those obligations?
13. Do you keep the covenants that you made in the temple, including wearing the temple garment as instructed in the endowment?
14. Are there serious sins in your life that need to be resolved with priesthood authorities as part of your repentance?
15. Do you consider yourself worthy to enter the Lord's house and participate in temple ordinances?[22]

"Why are these issues so crucial?" President Nelson asked in 2001. Because they help each of us "discern if we are willing to live in accord with the will of the true and living God or if our hearts are still set 'upon riches and . . . vain things of the world.'" In other words, these standards, which "are not difficult to understand,"[23] give us specific spiritual milestones to reach for in the ongoing journey of growth that we have been on possibly for millennia. We should not be discouraged if we do not reach them all within a day, week, month, or another length of time from our baptism, return to activity, or whatever point we are at in our lives. Nor should we be complacent or cease striving to meet these standards because they are difficult. He will help us if we let Him.

Reverencing That Which Is Holy Brings the Spiritual Treasure of Communion with God

Doctrine and Covenants 97:15–17—Inasmuch as my people build a house unto me in the name of the Lord, and do not suffer any unclean thing to come into it, that it be not defiled, my glory shall rest upon it; Yea, and my presence shall be there, for I will come into it, and all the pure in heart that shall come into it shall see God. But if it be defiled I will not come into it, and my glory shall not be there; for I will not come into unholy temples.

Elder Lionel Kendrick spoke in general conference about the importance of cultivating the attribute of reverence in connection with our temple worship, noting that it is "no minor nor mundane matter," as our demeanor and conversations in the temple are "an outward indication of an inner feeling that we have" for the Lord. "We should always remember that it is by His invitation that we come to His holy house, the temple of the Lord. We should respond to His invitation by being worthy, by being prepared, and by having the temple as a priority in our lives." Some of the things we can do to show the profound feelings of awe and gratitude we should feel toward the Lord in His house, he suggested, are (1) to be "aware" of "what is taking place"; (2) have a "desire to learn and to be receptive to the promptings of the Spirit"; (3) strive "to seek added light and knowledge" and (4) speak "in reverent tones."[24] As the Lord taught the early Saints of this dispensation, when we fail to reverence or treat "lightly" the things God gives us, our minds will be "darkened" (Doctrine and Covenants 84:54).

The Cautionary Tale of Korah Teaches the Importance of Meekness in Our Quest to Be Worthy

Korah, a Levite and one of the princes of Israel, led a rebellion against Moses and Aaron, showing the folly of aspiring to callings in the Church and the importance of meekness[25] and humility. "Now Korah," the account in Numbers relates, "took men: And they rose up before Moses, with certain of the children of Israel, two hundred and fifty princes of the assembly." These were leaders in the ancient church, "famous in the congregation, men of renown." Their presumption and pride is evident in their complaint against the Lord's anointed: "Ye take too much upon you, *seeing all the congregation are holy, every one of them, and the Lord is among them*: wherefore then lift ye up yourselves above the congregation of the Lord?" (Numbers 16:1–3). It seems that Korah and his companions mistakenly presumed that the visible manifestations of the Lord's presence in His tabernacle and among the congregation of the hosts of Israel, as well their status as "princes" and "fame" as "men of renown," including their appointment as members of the tribe of Levi to bear the holy Levitical Priesthood, qualified them as "holy." But as Jesus so often preached, it was not merely the Jews' citizenship in a nation of the "chosen people"[26] (or as we would analogize, our membership in the true Church), but their personal righteousness that would qualify them as a "holy nation" (Exodus 19:6).

Directing them each on the morrow to bring a censer and "put fire therein," Moses prophesied that the Lord would show "who are his, and who is holy" (Numbers 16:5). In essence, the Lord declared through Moses, in coveting that which they *had not* been called to do, they neglected to appreciate and magnify that which they *had* been called to do. "Seemeth it but a small thing unto you, that the God of Israel hath separated you from the congregation of Israel, to bring you near to himself to do the service of the tabernacle of the Lord, and to stand before the congregation to minister unto them? And he hath brought thee near to him, and all thy brethren the sons of Levi with thee: and seek ye the high priesthood also?" (JST, Numbers 16:10). Korah and his companions went on to falsely accuse Moses of the very thing they sought through aspiring to the higher priesthood, to be "altogether a prince [or despot] over us" (Numbers 16:13).

While the pettiness of their perceived wrongs is so apparent with millennial hindsight, is it as obvious to us when we second guess our leaders today? Rather than show respect to their offering, "the earth opened up and swallowed the leaders of the rebellion (Numbers 16:31–33), and fire came down and consumed the other two hundred and fifty who presumed to take priesthood power unto themselves (v. 35)."[27] Thus, the Lord taught His covenant people, and teaches us, the true nature of holiness: becoming humble and meek, even as a "little child" (Matthew 18:4).

Endnotes

1. Nelson, "Closing Remarks," *Ensign*, November 2019.
2. Chaim Richman of The Temple Institute in Jerusalem cites Isaiah's prophecy as evidence that "the Temple of God" would be rebuilt in Jerusalem at "the end of days," a belief that is shared by Latter-day Saints (see, for example, "Ezekiel 37:26–28. A Latter-day Temple in Jerusalem" in "Prophecies of the Restoration: Ezekiel 25–48," *Old Testament Student Manual 1 Kings–Malachi—Religion 302*, Church Educational System, The Church of Jesus Christ of Latter-day Saints [Salt Lake City, Utah, 2003], https://www.churchofjesuschrist.org/study/manual/old-testament-student-manual-kings-malachi/chapter-27?lang=eng). Describing the centrality of the temple to the Jewish faith, he writes, "It was Abraham who declared that the Temple of God would be established on Mount Moriah. . . . Over a period spanning nearly 1,000 years, the Holy Temple was the center of Jewish life." Recognizing the fulfillment of the many prophecies of the gathering of Israel in the latter days, he goes on to note, "In our own days, the prophecy of redemption is being fulfilled before our eyes, stage by stage . . . with the ingathering of the exiles and the liberations of the Land" (Chaim Richman, *A House of Prayer for All Nations: The Holy Temple of Jerusalem* [Carta, Jerusalem: The Temple Institute, 1997], 5–6). To what end? In its "Statement of Principles," the Temple Institute website declares that the Institute "is dedicated to all aspects of the Divine commandment for Israel to build a house for G-d's presence, the Holy Temple, on Mount Moriah in Jerusalem. . . . We hope that by doing our part, we can participate in the process that will lead to the Holy Temple becoming a reality once more. . . . Every prophet of Israel, without exception, prophesied that the Temple would be rebuilt, ushering in a new era of universal harmony and peace unparalleled in the history of man. Thus, the 'movement' to rebuild the Holy Temple is not new. It was born almost 2,000 years ago, at the moment of the Second Temple's destruction. For when the Holy Temple stood in Jerusalem, it was the soul of Jewish people . . . and the entire world . . . as we believe it will be once again" (The Temple Institute, "Statement of Principles," https://templeinstitute.org/statement-of-principles-2/).
3. See Nelson, *Heart of the Matter*, 45 ("During this mortal life you get to choose which laws you are willing to obey—those of the celestial kingdom, or the terrestrial, or the telestial—and, therefore, in which kingdom of glory you will live forever" [footnote omitted]); Ibid., 46 ("He who is not *able* to abide the law of a celestial kingdom cannot abide a celestial glory"; quoting Doctrine and Covenants 88:22 [emphasis added]). See also Russell M. Nelson, "Think Celestial!" *Liahona*, November 2023 ("If we unwisely choose to live telestial laws now, we are choosing to be resurrected with a telestial body"; in the temple we "are shown how to progress toward a celestial life" "and given greater access to His power"); Dallin H. Oaks, "Kingdoms of Glory," *Liahona*, November 2023 ("We know from modern revelation that 'all kingdoms have a law given' and that the kingdom of glory we receive in the Final Judgment is determined by the laws we choose to follow in our mortal journey").

4. Bruce Porter, "Endowed with Power: The Purpose of Creation Accounts," 7–8, https://www.bhporter.net/_files/ugd/c71091_56228d3862334530898f4df6a7de1e6c.pdf.

5. For a detailed review of the ascent theme in the rituals of the temple of Solomon, see David J. Larsen, "Ascending into the Hill of the Lord: What the Psalms Can Tell Us About the Rituals of the First Temple," *Interpreter: A Journal of Latter-Day Saint Faith and Scholarship*, https://journal.interpreterfoundation.org/ascending-into-the-hill-of-the-lord-what-the-psalms-can-tell-us-about-the-rituals-of-the-first-temple/. See also Daniel C. Peterson, "The Temple as a Place of Ascent to God," https://www.fairlatterdaysaints.org/conference/august-2009/the-temple-as-a-place-of-ascent-to-god. See "Uncovering the Pilgrimage Road to Jerusalem—Revealing the Sacred Ancient Journey" by the Israel Nature and Parks Authority for images of the ascent taken by pilgrims anciently to the Temple Mount, https://www.youtube.com/watch?v=XTkCrQHBF0o.

6. Brown, *Gate of Heaven*, 111–12. Brother Brown, summarizing the findings of some biblical scholars who argue that the Garden of Eden, "archetypically" or actually, was the first temple, notes, among other scriptural examples, that "in Ezekiel 28:11–16 it is implied that the Garden of Eden was located 'upon the holy mountain of God' (compare Isaiah 56:7)" (Ibid., 27–28). Likewise, God commanded Enoch (Moses 7:2–4) and Nephi (1 Nephi 17:7; 18:3) to climb mountains, where He communed with them.

7. See M. Catherine Thomas, "The Brother of Jared at the Veil," in *Temples of the Ancient World: Ritual and Symbolism*, ed. Donald W. Parry (Salt Lake City, Utah: Deseret Book and FARMS, 1994), 388, www.ldsscriptureteachings.org/staging/4108/wp-content/uploads/2019/10/Temples-of-the-Ancient-World-Ritual-and-Symbolism-Parry-full-text.pdf.

8. Bruce C. and Marie K. Hafen, *The Contrite Spirit: How the Temple Helps Us Apply Christ's Atonement* (Salt Lake City: Deseret Book, 2016), chapter 6 and text accompanying note 12. Brother and Sister Hafen observe, "When temple work for the dead was first fully instituted in 1877 in the St. George Temple, temple patrons would take each name through each step in the complete sequence of ordinances, rather than doing only baptisms and confirmations, or only initiatory ordinances, or endowments, or sealings on a given day." Thus, they note, "in [this and other] older temples, in order to complete all of the needed ordinances in their natural sequence, patrons began each set of ordinances in the temple's basement or lower level. Then they walked physically upward (in some cases only slightly, but still upward) from room to room—starting with the baptistry, then up to the creation room, up to the garden room, up to the world room, up to the terrestrial room, up to the celestial room, and finally up to the sealing room. This climb symbolizes the 'step-by-step ascent' that President McKay [described as an] "ascent into the eternal presence." See chapter 6, text accompanying note 8 (citing David O. McKay, Los Angeles Temple Dedication, quoted in Truman G. Madsen, "House of Glory," BYU Ten-Stake Fireside address, March 5, 1972, 7). Even in newer temples the symbolism of "ascension" has been retained. For example, in the

San Antonio Temple where my wife and I serve, the hallway to the celestial room (and, I assume, the transition from the first instruction room to the second, representing our journey from the telestial to the terrestrial worlds) noticeably slopes upward.

9. Russell M. Nelson, "Closing Remarks," *Ensign*, May 2019.
10. L. Lionel Kendrick, "Enhancing Our Temple Experience," *Ensign*, May 2001.
11. See also Doctrine and Covenants 76:5 ("For thus saith the Lord—I, the Lord, am merciful and gracious unto those who fear me, and delight to honor those who serve me in righteousness and in truth unto the end"); Doctrine and Covenants 75:5 ("And thus, if ye are faithful ye shall be laden with many sheaves, and crowned with honor, and glory, and immortality, and eternal life").
12. Bible Dictionary, "Fear."
13. M. Russell Ballard, "God's Love for His Children," *Ensign*, May 1988 (emphasis in original).
14. See Google Dictionary (definitions from Oxford Languages).
15. Guide to the Scriptures, "Worship," https://www.churchofjesuschrist.org/study/scriptures/gs/worship?lang=eng.
16. See https://www.dictionary.com/browse/reverence. The word "worship" "is derived from the Old English weorþscipe, meaning 'worship, honour shown to an object', which has been etymologised as 'worthiness' or 'worth-ship'—in the sense of giving, at its simplest, value to something" (*Wikipedia: The Free Encyclopedia*, "Worship," https://en.wikipedia.org/wiki/Worship#:~:text=The%20word%20is%20derived%20from,its%20simplest%2C%20worth%20to%20something (accessed July 17, 2023)(emphases added). Thus, "worship" and "worthiness," which is derived "from Middle English worthynesse, equivalent to worthy + -ness (Wiktionary, "worthiness," https://en.wiktionary.org/wiki/worthiness#:~:text=Etymology,to%20worthy%20%2B%E2%80%8E%20%2Dness), are related etymologically.
17. *Doctrines of the Gospel Student Manual*, chapter 20, "The Sacrament, A Memorial Ordinance," citing George Albert Smith, in Conference Report, April 1908, 35, https://www.churchofjesuschrist.org/study/manual/doctrines-of-the-gospel-student-manual/20-sacrament?lang=eng. In the *Doctrines of the Gospel Teacher Manual* discussion about standards and safeguards "regarding those who would partake of the sacrament," it notes first Paul's counsel in 1 Corinthians 11 and explains that "a person who partakes unworthily brings damnation to his soul because his spiritual progression is damned, or halted." Then, pointing out that as Paul taught, each person is responsible for "determining his own worthiness to partake of the sacrament," and, ultimately, once an individual qualifies for a temple recommend, for attending the temple as well, the teacher manual refers to President George Albert Smith's statement quoted above from the student manual (https://www.churchofjesuschrist.org/study/manual/doctrines-of-the-gospel/chapter-20?lang=eng).
18. The entry "Sacrament" under Gospel Topics counsels that members "do not need to be perfect in order to partake of the sacrament, but they should have a spirit of humility and repentance in their hearts."

19. Bradley R. Wilcox, "Worthiness Is Not Flawlessness," *Liahona*, November 2022. See also Vern P. Stanfill, "The Imperfect Harvest," *Liahona*, May 2023; Gerrit W. Gong, "Room in the Inn," *Liahona*, May 2021 ("Perfection is in Jesus Christ, not in the perfectionism of the world. Unreal and unrealistic, the world's 'insta-perfect' filtered perfectionism can make us feel inadequate, captive to swipes, likes, or double taps. In contrast, our Savior, Jesus Christ, knows everything about us we don't want anyone else to know, and He still loves us. His is a gospel of second and third chances, made possible by His atoning sacrifice. He invites each of us to be a good Samaritan, less judgmental and more forgiving of ourselves and of each other, even as we strive more fully to keep His commandments"); Matthew L. Carpenter, "Wilt Thou Be Made Whole?" *Ensign*, November 2018 ("If you have committed a sin that impacts your temple worthiness, I invite you to counsel with your bishop"); Joy D. Jones, "Value Beyond Measure," *Ensign*, 2017 ("Let me point out the need to differentiate between two critical words: worth and worthiness. They are not the same. Spiritual worth means to value ourselves the way Heavenly Father values us, not as the world values us. Our worth was determined before we ever came to this earth. 'God's love is infinite and it will endure forever.' On the other hand, worthiness is achieved through obedience. If we sin, we are less worthy, but we are never worth less! We continue to repent and strive to be like Jesus with our worth intact. As President Brigham Young taught: 'The least, the most inferior spirit now upon the earth . . . is worth worlds.' No matter what, we always have worth in the eyes of our Heavenly Father. Despite this marvelous truth, how many of us struggle, from time to time, with negative thoughts or feelings about ourselves?").
20. Nelson, "Personal Preparation for Temple Blessings."
21. Anthony Sweat observes that "unwrapping and utilizing this gift presented in the endowment ceremony takes time. Some things can be learned only through experience" (*The Holy Covenants: Living Our Sacred Temple Promises* [Salt Lake City, Utah: Deseret Book, 2022], 12–13). Commenting on the Lord's promise to bestow upon couples who are faithful to the covenants they make in the new and everlasting covenant of marriage "thrones, kingdoms, principalities, and powers, dominions," as we will read about in more detail in chapter 18 below, Brother Sweat adds, "Before we get too excited, these exalted blessings are currently beyond our capacity. Most all of us are still figuring out the basics. I don't know about you, but I'm not ready to sit on eternal thrones and have angels subject to me (see Doctrine and Covenants 132:20) when sometimes I struggle to sit in my car and subject my frustration with traffic."
22. Nelson, "Closing Remarks," *Ensign*, November 2019.
23. Nelson, "Personal Preparation for Temple Blessings."
24. Kendrick, "Enhancing Our Temple Experience."
25. See David A. Bednar, "Meek and Lowly of Heart," *Ensign*, May 2018, 30.
26. Deuteronomy 7:6 ("For thou art an holy people unto the Lord thy God: the Lord thy God hath chosen thee to be a special people unto himself, above all people that are upon the face of the earth"); Deuteronomy 14:2 ("For thou art an holy people unto the Lord thy God, and the Lord hath chosen thee to be a peculiar people unto himself, above all the nations that are upon the

earth"); Psalm 33:12 ("Blessed is the nation whose God is the Lord: and the people whom he hath chosen for his own inheritance"). See also Isaiah 43:20; Daniel 11:15; Helaman 15:3.

27. "Numbers 13–36 Wilderness Wanderings, Part 2," *Old Testament Student Manual Genesis–2 Samuel,* https://www.churchofjesuschrist.org/study/manual/old-testament-student-manual-genesis-2-samuel/numbers-13–36–wilderness-wanderings-part-2?lang=eng.

CHAPTER 3

The Spiritual Treasures of Making and Keeping Covenants

"We increase the Savior's power in our lives when we make sacred covenants and keep those covenants with precision. Our covenants bind us to Him and give us godly power."[1]

—President Russell M. Nelson

Blessings and Laws of the Gospel Are Received by Covenant through Ordinances

President Russell M. Nelson has taught repeatedly in his general conference messages about the importance of *covenants* and *ordinances*. He and others have referred to this as the "covenant path."[2] President Nelson describes covenants with God as "protective" not "restrictive," helping us to "filter out of our minds impurities that could harm us," just as "we filter the water to screen out harmful ingredients."[3] According to the Bible Dictionary, "The gospel is so arranged that *principles and ordinances are received by covenant*," meaning that the recipient solemnly promises upon receipt of the principle or law to abide by it. Another scriptural term for making a covenant or solemn promise is to "vow" or "vow a vow." In Numbers 30:2 the Lord said, "If a man vow a vow unto the Lord . . . to bind his soul, he shall not break his word, he shall do according to all that proceedeth out of his mouth." Simply stated, a covenant involves a "two-way commitment between God" and His children in which "God sets the terms, and we agree to those terms. In exchange, God makes promises to us."[4]

Because of their central importance to our eternal progression, we should prepare ourselves and "clearly understand" what we are agreeing to do before making these sacred commitments, Elder Dale G. Renlund adds. Then we must "absolutely honor" our commitment, for "we make a covenant only when we intend to commit ourselves quite exceptionally to fulfilling it."[5] The seriousness of our covenants is illustrated by the New Testament story of Ananias and Sapphira, who in calculatingly breaking their covenant of consecration and lying to Peter (meaning to God) about it forfeited their very lives (Acts 5:1–11).[6] When truth is sought from God, He holds the seeker accountable to live by that truth when it is revealed. In other words, the law of obedience, discussed in chapter 4, is the foundational principle that gives covenant-making and covenant-keeping their incredible power in our lives, now and in the eternities.[7]

Heavenly Father will always keep His covenantal promises. "All those who receive the priesthood," the Lord declared, "receive [the] oath and covenant of my Father" associated with the priesthood, "which [the Father] cannot break, neither can it be moved" (Doctrine and Covenants 84:40). In other words, the promises God makes to us through covenants are sure.

Covenants Are Governed by God's Law to Fulfill His Divine Purposes in Man

> **2 Nephi 2:10–13**—Wherefore, the ends of the law which the Holy One hath given . . . [are] to *answer the ends of the atonement*—For it must needs be, that there is an opposition in all things. If not so, my first-born in the wilderness, *righteousness* could not be brought to pass, neither wickedness, neither *holiness* nor misery, neither *good* nor bad. . . . Wherefore, . . . there would have been no purpose in the end of [the creation of "all things"]. Wherefore, this thing must needs destroy the wisdom of God and his eternal purposes. . . . And if ye shall say there is no law, ye shall also

say there is no sin. If ye shall say there is no sin, ye shall also say there is no *righteousness*. And if there be no righteousness there be no *happiness*. And if there be no righteousness nor happiness there be no punishment nor misery. And if these things are not there is no God. And if there is no God we are not, neither the earth; for there could have been no creation of things, neither to act nor to be acted upon; wherefore, all things must have vanished away.

And now, my sons, I speak unto you these things for your profit and learning; for *there is a God*, and he hath created all things, both the heavens and the earth, and all things that in them are, both things to act and things to be acted upon.

In his masterful theological explanation to his son Jacob before his death, Lehi explained the "ends" or purposes of divine law, God's "plan of happiness" (Alma 42:8, 16), and the Atonement—the eternal verities upon which all existence rests. In essence, Lehi taught that through God's law or plan, agency exists both to be obedient or righteous, or disobedient or sinful. Further, obedience to divine law results in blessings and happiness, whereas disobedience results in punishment and misery. Without divine law and its fruits, "there is no God" and if there is no God, "we are not" nor would there be an earth or the "creation of things" (2 Nephi 2:13).

Of course, there is a God, who is the source of divine law and creator of "all things." "All things," Lehi explains, are divided into two grand groups or classes, "things to act" and "things to be acted upon." Things to be acted upon include, of course, "element" or matter, including the elements that make up "the tabernacle of God" (Doctrine and Covenants 93:33, 35) and man, showing the importance of gaining mastery over our physical appetites. Things to act, on the other hand, include "intelligence." From the Doctrine and Covenants we learn that "intelligence, or the light of truth, was not created or made, neither indeed can be" (93:29). The Guide to the Scriptures defines intelligence as "the spirit element that existed before we were begotten as spirit children" (see also Abraham 3:21–22). Intelligence is "independent in that sphere in which God has placed it, to act for itself" (Doctrine and Covenants 93:30), meaning that even our elemental "self" had agency and will to make moral choices. "Behold, here is the agency of man, and here is the condemnation of man; because that which was from the beginning is plainly manifest unto them, and they receive not the light" (Doctrine and Covenants 93:31). Conversely, the crown of man comes through receiving and living by God's light, law, and truth.

What is the end or purpose of God's law or plan for His children? "To bring to pass the immortality and eternal life of man" (Moses 1:39). How does He do this? Through the plan of happiness or plan of salvation, which centers on the Atonement of Jesus Christ. In the scriptural record we see this pattern of "manifesting" or revealing truth repeated. From the beginning of man's journey on earth, Heavenly Father sent divine messengers to Adam and Eve to reveal the principles of eternal progression—His laws, commandments, and covenants. In short, God's purpose, the purpose of His laws and gospel, is to help each and every soul to progress as far and as much as they desire or choose to—potentially to become even as He is and to have all that He has. He has been doing this since the very "beginning" even before we became His spirit children, manifesting "plainly" truth, His eternal laws and principles, which we have been and continue in this life to be free to accept and apply in our lives and thereby grow and progress, or not.[8]

In the revelation known as the "Olive Leaf," the Lord further explained the role of divine law. He revealed that "there are many kingdoms; for there is no space in the which there is no kingdom," some of which are "greater" and others "lesser," but all of which "have a law given" and "unto every law there are certain bounds also and conditions. All beings who abide not in those conditions are not justified" (Doctrine and Covenants 88:36–39), meaning that they are ultimately unable to live in that kingdom. Father's purpose is to prepare us and to help us grow, line upon line, from "grace to grace" as the Savior did. If we keep our covenants, we also "shall receive grace for grace" (Doctrine and Covenants 93:20) and, ultimately, be able to live the law of a celestial kingdom. For, as the Lord explained, "they who are not sanctified through [or able to live] the law which I have given unto you, even the law of Christ, must inherit another kingdom, even that of a terrestrial kingdom, or that of a telestial kingdom. For he who is not able to abide [keep or live by] the law of a celestial kingdom cannot abide a celestial glory" (Doctrine and Covenants 88:21–22).[9]

In the end, God makes possible exaltation—it is a gift, indeed, the "greatest of all the gifts of God" (Doctrine and Covenants 14:7), as, in fact, are all the kingdoms of glory. Even those who reject all covenants, all law, receive a gift. "And they who remain [after all others receive a kingdom of glory] shall also be quickened; nevertheless, they shall return again to their own place, to enjoy that which they are willing to receive, because they were not willing to enjoy that which they might have received" (Doctrine and Covenants 88:31–32).

When we accept and enter into the covenants God has given us, in essence we exercise our moral agency to undertake the process He has ordained by which we *receive* the blessings or accept the gifts (or "treasures") He so intensely wants to bestow upon us. "For what doth it profit a man if a gift is bestowed upon him, and he receive not the gift? Behold, he rejoices not in that which is given unto him, neither rejoices in him who is the giver of the gift" (Doctrine and Covenants 88:33).

God's Covenants Enable Him to Bless Us with His Power and Eternal Family Relationships

Through His covenants, God invites us to establish a deep and abiding personal relationship with Him. As President Nelson taught, "When you and I enter [the covenant] path, we . . . create a relationship with God that allows Him to bless and change us. . . . If we let God prevail in our lives, that covenant will lead us closer and closer to Him."[10] The whole burden of the Church's *Come, Follow Me* curriculum can be summarized thus: God *wants* to have a deep and unbreakable relationship with each of His children. Jesus pled, "Learn of me" (Matthew 11:29), "Come after me" (Matthew 19:21), "Come and follow me" (Luke 9:23). President Nelson affirmed: "The covenant path is all about our relationship with God—our *hesed* relationship with Him." God "will always keep His word. He will do everything He can, without infringing on our agency, to help us keep ours."[11] What is more natural for a parent than this? As imperfect mortals, we would do anything to help our children be happy and successful in life. Could He want or do anything less?

The New and Everlasting Covenant Defined

Doctrine and Covenants 22:1–3—Behold, I say unto you that all *old covenants* have I caused to be done away in this thing; and this is a *new and an everlasting covenant, even that which was from the beginning.* Wherefore, although a man should be baptized an hundred times it availeth him nothing, for you cannot enter in at the strait gate by the law of Moses, neither by your dead works. For it is because of your dead works that I have caused this *last covenant* and this church to be built up unto me, *even as in days of old.*

As explained in the *Encyclopedia of Mormonism*, "the new and everlasting covenant is the gospel of Jesus Christ. The sum of all gospel covenants that God makes with mankind is called '*the* new and everlasting covenant' and consists of several individual covenants, each of which is called '*a* new and an everlasting covenant.' It is 'new' when given to a person or a people for the first time, and 'everlasting' because the gospel of Jesus Christ and plan of salvation existed before the world was formed and will exist forever."

"All covenants between God and mankind," the entry continues, "are part of the new and everlasting covenant (Doctrine and Covenants 22; 132:6–7). Thus, celestial marriage is a new and an everlasting covenant (Doctrine and Covenants 132:4) or the new and everlasting covenant of marriage. Some covenants, such as baptism, have force in all dispensations. Other covenants are made for special purposes in particular dispensations; circumcision as a sign of a covenant is of this type."[12]

That the Lord chose to define His gospel as a "covenant" suggests how central covenants are to the Father's plan for our eternal progression. The end or purpose of God's plan is eternal life—His life, which He knew would (and He designed to)[13] be unattainable without His divine power and help. He ordained that we would receive such help through a personal, even intimate relationship with Him, which is developed as we make and keep sacred covenants received and renewed through the ordinances of the gospel. In essence, He offers to reveal Himself to us, to walk with us, to show us who and what He is so that we might come to "know" Him or become like Him.[14] No wonder President Nelson urges all to seek to understand with greater "clarity" not only what we covenant "to do," but the essential purpose and role of covenants in our Heavenly Father's plan for our eternal progress, His plan for us to achieve our "divine destiny."[15]

Endnotes

1. Russell M. Nelson, "Drawing the Power of Jesus Christ into Our Lives," *Ensign*, May 2017, 41. See also Nelson, "Spiritual Treasures," 77 ("Every woman and every man who makes covenants with God and keeps those covenants, and who participates worthily in priesthood ordinances, has direct access to the power of God. Those who are endowed in the house of the Lord receive a gift of God's priesthood power by virtue of their covenant, along with a gift of knowledge to know how to draw upon that power."); Nelson, "The Temple and Your Spiritual Foundation," 94 ("[The Savior's] essential ordinances bind us to Him through sacred priesthood covenants. Then, as we keep our covenants, He endows us with His healing, strengthening power"). See also Nelson, *Heart of the Matter*, 203 ("The reward for keeping covenants with God is heavenly power—power that strengthens us to better withstand our trials, temptations, and heartaches").

2. See, for example, Nelson, "Drawing the Power of Jesus Christ into Our Lives" ("As faithful disciples, we repent and follow Him into the waters of baptism. We walk along the covenant path to receive other essential ordinances"); Russell M. Nelson, "We Can Do Better and Be Better," *Ensign*, May 2019 ("Whether you are diligently moving along the covenant path, have slipped or stepped from the covenant path, or can't even see the path from where you are now, I plead with you to repent. Experience the strengthening power of daily repentance—of doing and being a little better each day"); Nelson, "Come, Follow Me" ("Jesus Christ invites us to take the covenant path back home to our Heavenly Parents and be with those we love"); Russell M. Nelson, "Moving Forward," *Ensign*, November 2020 ("We are here on earth to be tested, to see if we will choose to follow Jesus Christ, to repent regularly, to learn, and to progress. Our spirits long to progress. And we do that best by staying firmly on the covenant path"); Russell M. Nelson, "Let God Prevail," *Ensign*, November 2020 ("If you have sincere questions about the gospel or the Church, as you choose to let God prevail, you will be led to find and understand the absolute, eternal truths that will guide your life and help you stay firmly on the covenant path"). The term "covenant path" appears first in a general conference message by Sister Elaine Dalton, "Stay on the Path" (*Ensign*, May 2007, 113). Elder D. Todd Christofferson used the term twice in his April 2009 general conference message, "The Power of Covenants" (*Ensign*, May 2009, 19). According to the website https://www.lds-general-conference.org/, between 2013 and 2019, the term "covenant path" appeared in general conference messages 106 times and in general conferences from 2020 through 2022, 111 times. See, for example, Renlund, "Accessing God's Power through Covenants."

3. Nelson, "Personal Preparation for Temple Blessings." In April 1995 President Nelson used another medical analogy, comparing our covenants to spiritual inoculation, which comes as we receive and understand the doctrine associated with and taught through gospel ordinances. He explained, as he often likes to do, the derivation of the word "inoculate," which "comes from two

Latin roots: *in*, meaning '*within*'; and *oculus*, meaning 'an eye.'" "*To inoculate*, therefore, literally means 'to put an eye within'—to monitor against harm." Unlike physical diseases, however, sin requires a different remedy. "Jesus chooses not to inoculate, but to indoctrinate. His method employs no vaccine; it utilizes the teaching of divine doctrine—a governing 'eye within'—to protect the eternal spirits of his children" (Nelson, "Children of the Covenant," *Ensign*, May 1995, 32 [emphasis in original]).

4. Nelson, "The Power of Spiritual Momentum," footnote 5. The Bible Dictionary pointedly notes that the parties to the two-way promises in covenants "do not stand in the relation of independent and equal contractors. God in His good pleasure fixes the terms, which man accepts. The [word covenant] is sometimes rendered 'testament.'"

5. Renlund, "Accessing God's Power through Covenants."

6. Bible Dictionary, "Covenant."

7. Another example of how the law of obedience is fundamental to covenants, and the potentially severe consequences of treating our covenants lightly, is when the Prophet Joseph Smith asked the Lord, as he was translating the Bible, why He "justified [His] servants Abraham, Isaac, and Jacob, as also Moses, David and Solomon [in] their having many wives and concubines." "Behold," the Savior responded, "I am the Lord thy God, and will answer thee as touching this matter. *Therefore, prepare thy heart to receive and obey the instructions which I am about to give unto you*; for all those who have this law [or any heavenly law] revealed unto them must obey the same" (Doctrine and Covenants 132:1–3). The "instructions" and "law" referred to in these verses (described as a "covenant" in verse 4) is the new and everlasting covenant of marriage. "The same revelation [section 132] that taught of plural marriage was embedded within a revelation about eternal marriage—the teaching that marriage could last beyond death." Thus, both "monogamous and plural marriages performed by priesthood power could seal loved ones to each other for eternity, on condition of righteousness." (Incidentally, the topic notes, "During the years that plural marriage was publicly taught, not all Latter-day Saints were expected to live the principle, though all were expected to accept it as a revelation from God. Indeed, this system of marriage could not have been universal due to the ratio of men to women. Women were free to choose their spouses, whether to enter into a polygamous or a monogamous union, or whether to marry at all" [Gospel Topics, "Plural Marriage in the Church of Jesus Christ of Latter-day Saints," https://www.churchofjesuschrist.org/study/manual/gospel-topics-essays/plural-marriage-in-the-church-of-jesus-christ-of-latter-day-saints?lang=eng]).

While revealing to Joseph Smith glorious new truths about celestial marriage (discussed more in chapter 18), the Lord reminds him, and us, about the all-important principle that we must receive, or obey, "all things" given "by revelation and commandment," by God's "word," which means through proper priesthood channels, as did Abraham (Doctrine and Covenants 132:29). To make the point crystal clear, the Lord noted that "Abraham was *commanded* to offer his son Isaac; nevertheless, it was written: Thou shalt not kill. Abraham, however, *did not refuse*." In other words, notwithstanding his personal aversion (as a victim of attempted human sacrifice) and all logic to the contrary, Abraham obeyed God, as did Nephi to a similar commandment years later. *"And it was accounted unto [Abraham] for righteousness"* (Doctrine and Covenants 132:36).

How difficult was it for Joseph Smith to accept and live the truths God revealed to him about plural marriage? "Joseph [Smith] told associates that an angel appeared to him three times between 1834 and 1842 and commanded him to proceed with plural marriage when he hesitated to move forward. During the third and final appearance, the angel came with a drawn sword, threatening Joseph with destruction unless he went forward and obeyed the commandment fully" (Gospel Topics, "Plural Marriage in Kirtland and Nauvoo," https://www.churchofjesuschrist.org/study/manual/gospel-topics-essays/ plural-marriage-in-kirtland-and-nauvoo?lang=eng). See Dale G. Renlund, "A Framework for Personal Revelation," *Liahona*, November 2022; particularly the discussion accompanying note 23.

8. Spencer W. Kimball, "Privileges and Responsibilities of Sisters," *Ensign*, November 1978 (God and your "mother in heaven" "gave your eternal intelligence spirit form, just as your earthly mother and father have given you a mortal body. You are . . . made of the eternal intelligence which gives you claim upon eternal life. . . . The whole intent of the gospel plan is to provide an opportunity for each of you to reach your fullest potential, which is eternal progression and the possibility of godhood").

9. Nelson, "Choices for Eternity," Worldwide Devotional for Young Adults with President Nelson—May 2022," https://www.churchofjesuschrist.org/study/broadcasts/worldwide-devotional-for-young-adults/2022/05/ 12nelson?lang=eng ("During this life we get to choose which laws we are willing to obey—those of the celestial kingdom, or the terrestrial, or the telestial—and, therefore, in which kingdom of glory we will live forever"). See also Nelson, "Think Celestial!" and Oaks, "Kingdoms of Glory." President Nelson further explains the role of "absolute truths" and the "power of divine law" in chapter 2 of his book *Heart of the Matter*.

10. Nelson, "The Everlasting Covenant."

11. Ibid.

12. D. Cecil Clark, "New and Everlasting Covenant," *Encyclopedia of Mormonism*, https://eom.byu.edu/index.php/New_and_Everlasting_Covenant. As Elder Marcus B. Nash of the Seventy explained, "The new and everlasting covenant 'is the sum total of all gospel covenants and obligations' given anciently and again restored to the earth in these latter days" (citing Doctrine and Covenants 66:2). "In the scriptures the Lord speaks of both 'the' new and everlasting covenant and 'a' new and everlasting covenant. For example, in Doctrine and Covenants 22:1, He refers to baptism as 'a new and an everlasting covenant, even that which was from the beginning.' In Doctrine and Covenants 132:4, He likewise refers to eternal marriage as 'a new and an everlasting covenant.' When He speaks of 'a' new and everlasting covenant, He is speaking of one of the many covenants encompassed by His gospel. When the Lord speaks generally of 'the' new and everlasting covenant, He is speaking of the fulness of the

gospel of Jesus Christ, which embraces all ordinances and covenants necessary for the salvation and exaltation of mankind. Neither baptism nor eternal marriage is 'the' new and everlasting covenant; rather, they are each parts of the whole" ("The New and Everlasting Covenant," *Ensign*, December 2015).

13. It is worth considering, what is there in the nature of a celestial life or world, in which all are organized in perfect order and unity of purpose in all things (in other words, in which the individual, of his or her own free will and choice, subjects or aligns his or her will with the will of God), such that the divine plan to achieve such celestial life requires us to depend wholly upon the "merits and mercy" or power of God to achieve such life? As to this question, as in all things, Christ's perfect example is instructive: "Nevertheless not as I will, but as thou wilt" (Matthew 14:9). Yielding His will to the Father's in all things enabled Him to achieve the "oneness" described in John 17:11, 22–23 (being "made perfect in one"). See John 10:30 ("I and my Father are one"); 3 Nephi 11:27 ("Behold, verily I say unto you, that the Father, and the Son, and the Holy Ghost are one; and I am in the Father, and the Father in me, and the Father and I are one"). See also verse 36; 3 Nephi 28:10; Doctrine and Covenants 38:27 ("Be one ["as I am"]; and if ye are not one ye are not mine"); Doctrine and Covenants 50:43 ("the Father and I are one. I am in the Father and the Father in me; and inasmuch as ye have received me, ye are in me and I in you"); Doctrine and Covenants 93:3 ("I am in the Father, and the Father in me, and the Father and I are one."). The alternative, of course, is to choose, rather than to align our will to God and His law, to "become a law unto [your] self" (Doctrine and Covenants 88:35), thus alienating yourself eternally from everything and everyone who is good, which, in my view, would be the ultimate form of loneliness.

14. In describing how through Christ's "divine power" we might be "partakers of [Christ's] divine nature," Peter essentially equates the "knowledge of our Lord Jesus Christ" with the process of becoming like Him, adding to our faith, by "giving all diligence," the Christlike attributes of "virtue," "knowledge," "temperance," "patience," "godliness," "brotherly kindness" and "charity." "For if these things be in you, and abound, they make you that ye shall neither be barren nor unfruitful in the knowledge of our Lord Jesus Christ" (2 Peter 1:2–8). President Ezra Taft Benson, citing verse 8, affirmed that "to know the Savior, then, is to be like Him" ("What Manner of Men Ought We to Be?" *Ensign*, November 1983).

15. "The Family: A Proclamation to the World," https://www.churchofjesuschrist.org/study/scriptures/the-family-a-proclamation-to-the-world/the-family-a-proclamation-to-the-world?lang=eng ("In the premortal realm, spirit sons and daughters knew and worshipped God as their Eternal Father and accepted His plan by which His children could obtain a physical body and gain earthly experience to progress toward perfection and ultimately realize their divine destiny as heirs of eternal life").

CHAPTER 4

The Spiritual Treasure of Increased Faith to Follow Jesus Christ

"Talk about the temple with your family and friends. Because Jesus Christ is at the center of everything we do in the temple, as you think more about the temple you will be thinking more about Him."[1]

—Russell M. Nelson

How Is Jesus Christ at the Center of My Temple Experience?

It took many years of temple attendance, indeed a call to temple service, for me to fully appreciate that faith to follow Jesus Christ, the first principle of the gospel, is also the first principle of the temple. The "Temples" page on the Church website declares, "Everything in the temple points us to Jesus Christ."[2] In fact, increasing our faith in and helping us "draw nearer to Heavenly Father and Jesus Christ" is not only the central purpose of the temple, but, as the *General Handbook* states, the central purpose of everything we do in the Church.[3] President Nelson taught, "Every activity, every lesson, all we do in the Church, point to the Lord and His holy house." Moreover, he added, "The basis for every temple ordinance and covenant . . . is the Atonement of Jesus Christ."[4] One of the objects of this study is to increase our understanding about how our own temple experiences can do this—increase *our* faith in, and draw *us* nearer to, our Father in Heaven and His Beloved Son Jesus Christ through the ministration of the Holy Ghost.

Scholars and other careful observers of the role temples and temple ceremonies have played throughout history confirm that "symbolically speaking, the endowment is entirely Christocentric. Every aspect of it—covenants, commands, clothing, signs, tokens, etc.—is about Christ."[5] In later chapters we will focus on how the Savior is represented, seen, and experienced through the tokens, sacred gestures, ceremonial clothing, altars, and veil of the temple.[6] We also explore in this study how the Savior is the central focus of the five laws or "sacred covenants" made in the endowment, which are listed in the *General Handbook* as the law of obedience, the law of sacrifice, the law of the gospel of Jesus Christ, the law of chastity, and the law of consecration.[7] In this chapter we explore how the temple increases our faith in Jesus Christ and His Atonement, the subject of the first question in the temple recommend interview and the first principle of the gospel. We also explore how faith in Jesus Christ, a principle of action and power, leads and empowers us to follow or obey Him—in essence to live the first covenant of the temple, the law of obedience.

Knowing the Nature and Purposes of God and Jesus Christ and Our Relationship to Them Are the First "Mysteries of the Kingdom of Heaven" Taught in the Temple

> **Doctrine and Covenants 84:19**—And this greater priesthood administereth the gospel and holdeth the key of the *mysteries of the kingdom*, even the key of the knowledge of God.
>
> **Doctrine and Covenants 107:18–19**—The power and authority of the higher, or Melchizedek Priesthood, is to hold the keys of all the spiritual blessings of the church—To have the privilege of receiving the *mysteries of the kingdom of heaven* . . . and to enjoy the communion and presence of God the Father, and Jesus the mediator of the new covenant.

As the Lord revealed in the two great revelations on the priesthood cited above, the greater or Melchizedek Priesthood "administers" the gospel, which includes the "mysteries of the kingdom." The mysteries of God and of His kingdom are defined as "spiritual truths known only by revelation,"[8] meaning that, in the first instance, God revealed the truth to His prophet, who recorded it in scripture and, secondly and most importantly, that He will reveal or declare the truth of any such mystery or revelation to us individually by the power of the Holy Ghost (Moroni 10:5). How important are these spiritual truths that constitute the "knowledge of God"? The Savior responded, "This is life eternal, that they might *know thee* the only true God, and Jesus Christ, whom thou hast sent" (John 17:3). In other words, without the special knowledge we receive in the endowment, we cannot have eternal life. The President of the Church holds the "keys of the mysteries" (Doctrine and Covenants 28:7), or the right to declare the doctrine of the Church. He also holds the keys to oversee the administration of all priesthood ordinances, through which we not only receive the "power of godliness" (Doctrine and Covenants 84:19) but also, especially in the rites and sacred instruction received in the temple, mysteries[9] or knowledge that is necessary for us to be able to "behold the face" or "enter into the rest" or fulness of the glory of God (Doctrine and Covenants 84:22–24).

What truth is among the most central and critical of these mysteries or spiritual truths? As declared in the Family Proclamation, it is that each human being, male or female, "is a beloved spirit son or daughter of heavenly parents." As God's spirit children "in the premortal realm," the Family Proclamation continues, we "knew and worshipped God as [our] Eternal Father and accepted *His* plan by which His children could obtain a physical body and gain earthly experience to progress toward perfection and ultimately realize [our] divine destiny as heirs of eternal life."[10] The key element of the Father's plan, we learned in the Grand Council in heaven[11] described by Abraham and Moses, is that He would "provide a Savior,"[12] without whom we would be unable to accomplish the purpose of the plan, "to progress toward perfection," enabling us to live with our Heavenly Parents again.

God asked, "Whom shall I send? And one answered like unto the Son of Man [Jehovah]: Here am I send me" (Abraham 3:27), adding, "Father, thy will be done, and the glory be thine forever" (Moses 4:1). But another, a "son of the morning" whose premortal name was Lucifer,[13] also answered but in words dripping with egotistical "I's" and "me's"—"Behold, here am *I*, send *me*, *I* will be thy son, and *I* will redeem all mankind, that one soul shall not be lost, and surely *I will do it*; *wherefore give me thine honor*" (Moses 4:1). And God replied, "I will send" "my Beloved Son, which was my Beloved and Chosen from the beginning." "And the second was angry, and kept not his first estate; and, at that day, many followed after him" (Abraham 3:27–28; Moses 4:2). Thus, from the beginning Heavenly Father determined that His Firstborn, Jehovah, "who verily was foreordained before the foundation of the world" (1 Peter 1:20), was and would be the center of the Father's plan of redemption of all His spirit children. These central spiritual truths are beautifully taught in the endowment.

Not coincidentally, it was also in a temple setting[14] in the land of Bountiful where the Savior taught these central spiritual truths or mysteries about His "doctrine" (3 Nephi 11:31) to the Nephites when He appeared after His resurrection. First, He called Nephi and eleven others forward and gave unto them "power to baptize" (3 Nephi 11:20–22).[15] In other words, He reconfirmed the importance of the first ordinance of the gospel, including detailed instructions on the manner of baptism and "the words which ye shall say" (3 Nephi 11:23–26). Next, He put this first ordinance in the context of His doctrine: "And this is my doctrine, and it is the doctrine which the Father hath given unto me" (3 Nephi 11:31). Christ's doctrine comes from the Father, the author of the plan of salvation, and centers on the Son: "Whoso believeth in me, and is baptized, the same shall be saved" (3 Nephi 11:33). Belief or faith in the Savior and His atoning sacrifice is the first principle of the Father's plan. In a later visit to His Nephite disciples, the Savior expanded on this spiritual truth: "This is the gospel which I have given unto you—that I came into the world to do the will of my Father, *because my Father sent me*. And my Father sent me that I might be lifted up upon the cross; and after that I had been lifted up upon the cross, that I might draw all men unto me" (3 Nephi 27:13–14). Moreover, as the Savior explained in the next verse, men are lifted up and drawn unto Him to be judged "by the *power of the Father*" (v. 15). In other words, Heavenly Father foreordained and sent Jehovah to be the Savior and Redeemer of the world, and the Father's power is and was essential to the Atonement wrought by the Lord through His suffering in Gethsemane and on the cross. He actively oversees the accomplishment of *His* plan.

President Nelson has emphasized repeatedly that our faith is and should be centered on the person of Jesus Christ and not merely abstract ideas or concepts sometimes described by "shortcut phrases, such as 'the Atonement' or 'the enabling power of the Atonement' or 'applying the Atonement' or 'being strengthened by the Atonement.' These expressions present a real risk of misdirecting faith by treating the event as if it had living existence and capabilities independent of our Heavenly Father and His Son, Jesus Christ." The Savior is the one, President Nelson teaches, "who suffered," "broke the bands of death," "paid the price for our sins and transgressions and blots them out on condition of our repentance," and "delivers us from physical and spiritual death," not any "amorphous entity called 'the Atonement.'" Thus, the Father's role in preparing, foreordaining and making possible His Firstborn's atoning sacrifice and the Son's accomplishment of that sacrifice, "the central act of all human history,"[16] are the first and foremost truths of the gospel of Jesus Christ. Indeed, as President Nelson affirmed in the statement quoted in the headnote to this chapter, these are the first and foremost truths and principles revealed in the temple.

Faith in God and His Only Begotten Son Leads Us to Follow or Obey Them

The Prophet Joseph Smith taught that "faith is a principle of action and of power."[17] Thus, the Savior taught the Nephites, as we believe and strengthen our faith in God and Jesus Christ, we will repent and be baptized (see 3 Nephi 11:32–33; 3 Nephi 27:16, 19–20). The prophets refer to this type of motivating faith as "faith unto repentance" (Alma 34:17). We will discuss temple connections to the principle of repentance and the ordinance of baptism in later chapters.

For now, it is sufficient to ponder all that the Father did to provide a Savior to bring to pass the immortality and potential eternal life of every member of His family who kept their first estate. From Jehovah's spiritual birth as the Firstborn; the Father's tutoring and training of His Firstborn (Doctrine and Covenants 93:21) as He grew in that premortal realm to become a member of the Godhead, standing at the right hand of God the Father (John 1:1–3; 1 John 5:7; Doctrine and Covenants 76:13); to Jesus's birth as the Only Begotten of the Father and the Savior's sinless life and atoning sacrifice on Earth—the Father presided over every aspect of His Beloved Son's spiritual and physical development and ministry, in heaven and on earth. In short, the Father did everything in His power—allowing the Savior His agency as He allows us ours (Doctrine and Covenants 29:36; 93:12–14, 20)—to prepare and help His "Beloved Son" to accept and be able to fulfill His foreordination to be our Savior and Redeemer. Jesus taught, "Verily, verily, I say unto you, The Son can do nothing of himself, but what he seeth the Father do: for what things soever he doeth, these also doeth the Son likewise;" "I seek not mine own will, but the will of the Father which hath sent me" (John 5:19, 30). "I do nothing of myself; but as my Father hath taught me, I speak these things" (John 8:28). Truly, "God so loved the world," that is, all the rest of His spirit children, "that he gave his only begotten Son, that whosoever believeth in him should not perish, but have everlasting life" (John 3:16). Moreover, Christ so loved the Father that He did "always those things that please him" (John 8:29).

Similarly, our faith in and love for God and His Son should motivate us to strive to obey Them in all things. Indeed, faith in and love for Heavenly Father and His Son, Jesus Christ, are the very heart of the law of obedience. Whenever we think of the law of obedience, we should instinctively link it in our minds to the first principle of the gospel: "We believe in God, the Eternal Father, and in His Son, Jesus Christ, and in the Holy Ghost" (Articles of Faith 1:1).

"Obedience is the first law of heaven," taught President Joseph F. Smith.[18] It is the foundation upon which all other covenants and blessings are built. This law, Bruce R. McConkie explained, which commands us "to live in harmony with the Lord's laws, to keep all his commandments," is received in the temple by covenant, a "solemn, sacred, holy [covenant], pledging ourselves before gods and angels." "With this in mind," he admonished, "hear this word from the Lord: 'If you will that I give unto you a place in the celestial world, you must prepare yourselves by *doing* the things which I have commanded you and required of you.' (Doctrine and Covenants 78:7.)"[19] In short, the *General Handbook* summarizes, in the endowment we covenant to "live the law of obedience and strive to keep Heavenly Father's commandments" (27.2).

As observed through His teachings and life, Jesus is the great exemplar of the law of obedience. Notice how the Savior, in explaining

His doctrine to the Nephites, not only set the example of obediently "doing" the Father's will but also asks us to do the same: "I came into the world to *do* the will of my Father" (3 Nephi 27:13). "Ye know the things that ye must *do* in my church; for the works which ye have seen me *do* that shall ye also *do*; for that which ye have seen me *do* even that shall ye *do*" (v. 21). "Therefore, if ye *do* these things blessed are ye, for ye shall be lifted up at the last day" (v. 22).

In essence, all other actions the Savior asks us to take to live His doctrine as He describes in 3 Nephi 27 flow from the first and central truth of the gospel and the temple—*faith* in Jesus Christ and His Atonement (no one can enter into God's "rest save it be those who have washed their garments in my blood, because of their faith" [v. 19]). These actions include *repentance* ("and the repentance of all their sins" [v. 19]); *baptism* (being "baptized in my name" [vv. 16 and 19]); receiving the *gift of the Holy Ghost* ("that ye may be sanctified by the reception of the Holy Ghost," [v. 20]); and enduring to the end ("their faithfulness unto the end" [vv. 16 and 19]).

Note, however, after teaching so emphatically the importance of the law of obedience, doing the will of the Father (repeated six times in verses 21 and 22), that in 3 Nephi 27:27 the Lord, in effect, reveals the spiritual treasure of all that doing and obeying—that we may *become* like our Heavenly Father and our Beloved Redeemer. Here the operative verb switches from *doing* to *being* or *becoming*. "Therefore, what manner of men ought ye to *be*? Verily I say unto you, even as *I am*" (v. 27). Elder Dale G. Renlund put this ultimate objective of the Father's plan this way:

> Our Heavenly Father's [ultimate] goal in parenting is not to have His children [merely] *do* what is right; it is to have His children *choose to do* what is right and ultimately become like Him. If He simply wanted us to be obedient, He would use immediate rewards and punishments to influence our behaviors. But God is not interested in His children just becoming trained and obedient "pets" who will not chew on His slippers in the celestial living room. No, God wants His children to *grow up spiritually* and join Him in the family business. God established a plan whereby we can become heirs in His kingdom, a *covenant*

path that leads us to *become like Him*, have the kind of life He has, and live forever as families in His presence.[20]

A Modern Parable of the Law of Obedience

In Doctrine and Covenants 101, the Lord gives a parable about the importance of obedience to God particularly for our day (see section 101 headnote), a time in which belief in God or moral virtues based upon His law are under attack in nations and cultures throughout the world. In the parable, the servants planted twelve olive trees "as their lord commanded them," built a hedge or wall around them, and assigned watchmen to protect and preserve the olive trees from being "broken down when the enemy should come." The servants also "began to build a tower" as their lord had directed on which to place a watchman (vv. 44–45). However, "while they were yet laying the foundation" of the work their lord had commanded them to do, they began to rationalize and then became "very slothful" and "hearkened not unto the commandment of their lord" (vv. 43–50). Then the enemy came by night and broke down the hedge. Frightened, the servants fled and the enemy "destroyed their works, and broke down the olive trees." The nobleman then called on his servants, asking them, "Why! What is the cause of this great evil? Ought ye not to have *done* even as I commanded you" (vv. 51–53)?

Thereafter, the lord of the vineyard sent one of his servants to gather the residue of his servants to go and redeem the vineyard so that the lord "by and by" could bring the "residue of [his] house and possess the land" (vv. 54–58). "And the servant said unto his lord: When shall these things be? And he said unto his servant: *When I will*; go ye straightway, and *do* all things whatsoever I have commanded you." In other words, it is not for you necessarily to know the end from the beginning or even the whys of the Lord's commandments. It is ours to obey.

In this parable, the central role obedience plays in the gospel is beautifully illustrated. The vineyard represents the people of the Lord; the watchmen (and the hedge), His authorized servants called to teach and administer the gospel, which is the ultimate protection against the "enemy" of all righteousness. The tower represents "the temple the Lord had commanded the Saints to build in Jackson County, Missouri."[21] In the next several verses following this parable, the Lord explains why obedience is so important to accomplishing His purposes, which is to continue "the gathering together of my saints, . . . according to the parable of the wheat and the tares, that the wheat may be secured in the garners to possess eternal life, and be crowned with celestial glory" (vv. 64–65).

"Garners in the scriptures," according to Elder Bednar, can represent "the holy temples."[22] As explained in the next chapter, the ultimate purpose of gathering is to build temples and prepare a people able to go into them and receive the ordinances of exaltation and then make those ordinances available to their kindred dead. But nothing happens—no repentance, no baptism or confirmation, no gathering, no protection against the enemy and storms of life, no temples, and no exaltation—until there is obedience. "And this shall be my seal and blessing upon" those who obey God, the Lord of the Vineyard—"a faithful and wise steward in the midst of mine house, a ruler in my kingdom." Our desire should be to emulate or liken ourselves to the servant in the parable, representing the Prophet Joseph Smith, who "went straightway, and *did all things whatsoever his lord commanded him;* and after many days all things were fulfilled" (vv. 59–61).

The Lord has said, "I am able to do mine own work" (2 Nephi 27:20) and that He would "show unto the children of men that I am able to do mine own work" (v. 21). The burden of the scriptures is proof of this statement. The words of the Lord are always fulfilled.[23] "What I the Lord have spoken, I have spoken, and I excuse not myself; and though the heavens and the earth pass away, *my word shall not pass away, but shall all be fulfilled*, whether by mine own voice or by the voice of my servants, it is the same" (Doctrine and Covenants 1:38).

While *God's* work is to "bring to pass the immortality and eternal life of man" (Moses 1:39), the first part of which He has already accomplished (through the Resurrection of Christ) and the rest of which He is abundantly able to complete, "behold, . . . *your work*," He tells us, is to obey—"to keep my commandments, yea, with all your might, mind and strength" (Doctrine and Covenants 11:20). Indeed, in the Grand Council in heaven the Father presented His plan of salvation—including the creation of the earth and the role of Jesus Christ as our Savior and Redeemer, to which we all consented enthusiastically (see Job 38:7)[24]— and simply and clearly revealed His purpose: to "prove them herewith, *to see if they will do all things whatsoever the Lord their God shall command them*" (Abraham 3:24–25).Why is doing all things God commands us to do so important? Because God knows better than we do how to bless and help us to achieve His (and our) purpose—to become like Him. And every blessing is predicated upon obedience to the law governing that blessing (Doctrine and Covenants 130:21), even those blessings that we in our present mortal condition are unable to fully appreciate. Thus, as we trust God's plan and individualized direction concerning our part in that plan, we inevitably will receive the blessings that He has in store for us. As Paul taught, "Eye hath not seen, nor ear heard, neither have entered into the heart of man, the things which God hath prepared for them that love him" (1 Corinthians 2:9; see also Doctrine and Covenants 133:45). "And they who keep their first estate," the Father explained to each of us in the beginning, "shall be added upon; and they who keep not their first estate shall not have glory in the same kingdom with those who keep their first estate; and they who keep their second estate shall have glory added upon their heads for ever and ever" (Abraham 3:26).

"Increased time in the temple," President Nelson affirms, accelerates this virtuous cycle of growing our faith in the Lord Jesus Christ, thus increasing our ability to apply the gospel in our lives, growing from one principle or Christlike attribute to the next, like "nothing else can."[25] On another occasion, he put it more explicitly: "Ordinances of the temple fill our lives with power and strength available in no other way."[26] In fact, we have come to expect that in all of the themes President Nelson uses in general conference to urge us onward and upward in our spiritual journeys—finding "*rest* from the intensity, uncertainty, and anguish of this world" "by *overcoming* the world through your covenants with God";[27] increasing our "spiritual momentum";[28] reinforcing and strengthening our spiritual foundations;[29] increasing our faith in Christ to move the mountains in our lives;[30] think[ing] celestial!"[31]—he will remind us that increased temple activity and understanding plays a key role. All of us can use added spiritual momentum, strengthening of our spiritual foundations, and increased faith to move the mountains of doubt, discouragement, bad habits, and self-defeating compulsions[32] as we overcome the natural man and become saintlier in our desires and personalities. As President Nelson assures us, the temple is one of the greatest spiritual treasures Heavenly Father has given us to enable these miraculous outcomes.

Endnotes

1. Russell M. Nelson, "Go Forward in Faith," *Ensign*, May 2020.
2. Temples, "Draw Nearer to the Savior," https://www.churchofjesuschrist.org/temples/nearer-christ-through-temples?lang=eng.
3. *General Handbook* 4.1.
4. Nelson, "Personal Preparation for Temple Blessings."
5. Alonzo L. Gaskill, *Temple Reflections: Insights into the House of the Lord* (Springville, Utah: Cedar Fort, Inc., 2016), 82. See also Madsen, *The Temple: Where Heaven Meets Earth*, 47, 51–53.
6. Anthony Sweat, referring to the use of "symbol, imagery, and ritual to communicate spiritual knowledge" in the endowment, gave this explanation of the Lord's use of these teaching techniques: "In addition, symbol and ritual cut across racial, ethnic, social, and generational divides. The endowment experience isn't meant to speak only to modern American Saints but to connect equally to Saints in diverse cultures across the earth, past and present. Thus, the experience will likely be foreign to your modern frame of reference. Mystery is another word for this lack of obvious familiarity. If the endowment experience felt like a typical sacrament meeting or regular church or school class (things you are used to), it would be severely lacking. Mystery is the revelatory vehicle to help transport your mind and heart to other realms—in this case, the realm of heaven. If at first you find yourself bewildered about some things, and that causes you to study, think, and pray, then the endowment ceremonies are effectively doing their job" (Anthony Sweat, *The Holy Invitation: Understanding Your Sacred Temple Endowment* [Salt Lake City: Deseret Book, 2017], 47–48).
7. *General Handbook* 27.2.
8. Guide to the Scriptures, "Mysteries of God."
9. See, for example, John W. Welch, *Illuminating the Sermon at the Temple & the Sermon on the Mount: An Approach to 3 Nephi 11–18 and Matthew 5–7* (1999), 33 (in the forty-day literature, Jesus blesses His apostles with "an initiation or endowment, generally called the 'mysteries,' which emphasized garments, marriage, and prayer circles"), 90 (in JST, Matthew 7:6 the Lord commanded His followers to keep such things "within yourselves"); Madsen, *The Temple: Where Heaven Meets Earth*, 30 ("the 'mysteries of godliness' are, we know from modern scholarship, the ordinances of godliness" found in the "House of God"); Amy Hardison, *Understanding the Symbols, Covenants and Ordinances of the Temple* (American Fork, Utah: Covenant Communications, Inc., 2016), 92 ("During His forty-day ministry, the period of time between Christ's resurrection and His Ascension to heaven in Acts 1, Christ continued to teach His Apostles about sacred ordinances. In fact, 'the major purpose of the forty-day ministry [was] to teach the nature of vicarious ordinances and to instruct the Apostles in the fulness of the temple ceremony,'" quoting Joseph Fielding McConkie and Robert Millet, *Life Beyond* [Salt Lake City: Bookcraft, 1986], 158).

The *Encyclopedia of Mormonism* contains this explanation of "mysteries" of God as it relates to the doctrines and ordinances received in the temple:

The knowledge alluded to in the phrases "mysteries of God" or "mysteries of Godliness" [referred to in Doctrine and Covenants 84 and 107] may be received in ways other than exclusively verbal. Throughout history, divine knowledge also has been communicated in ceremonies, rites, purifications, and so on. Such is the case in the temples of the Latter-day Saints, where faithful members of the Church gain knowledge and understanding of heavenly truths as they receive ordinances by covenant.

The broad meaning of "Godliness" embraces the state of being like God, of approximating God's nature or qualities. The possibility is suggested in the so-called Law of the Harvest. Just as apple seeds produce apple trees, so the offspring of deity, human beings, when they are fully mature—that is, holy, knowledgeable and virtuous—are like their divine parents.

Jesus' statement in John 17:3, uttered as he petitioned his Father, takes on a more profound meaning in light of the scriptural references to the mysteries of God: "And this is life eternal, that they might know thee the only true God, and Jesus Christ, whom thou hast sent." The "knowing" to which the Savior refers is that higher knowledge often designated "mysteries of God" or "the mysteries of Godliness." (Clark D. Webb, "Mysteries of God," *Encyclopedia of Mormonism,* https://eom.byu.edu/index.php/Mysteries_of_God).

10. "The Family: A Proclamation to the World."
11. Gospel Topics, "Council in Heaven," https://www.churchofjesuschrist.org/study/manual/gospel-topics/council-in-heaven?lang=eng (citations omitted). Under "Related Topics" under the entry "Council in Heaven" in Gospel Topics, dozens of scriptures under the following topics in the Topical Guide provide further insights and knowledge about the context, principles, and purposes of our preexistent life as spirit children leading up to and following this Grand Council—"Agency and Accountability"; "Jesus Christ Chosen as Savior"; "Mortality"; "Premortality"; "Satan"; "Spirit Children of Heavenly Parents"; and "War in Heaven."
12. Dallin H. Oaks, "Truth and the Plan," *Ensign,* November 2018 ("We accepted [the challenges of mortality] in reliance upon the plan's assurance that God our Father would provide a Savior, His Only Begotten Son, who would rescue us"); see also Dallin H. Oaks, "The Great Plan," *Ensign,* May 2020 ("To reclaim us from death and sin, our Heavenly Father's plan would provide a Savior"); Brian K. Ashton "The Doctrine of Christ," *Ensign,* November 2016 (The testimony of the Father, when He announced the Christ at His appearance to the Nephites, and the Savior's declaration that He had completed the Atonement "established without doubt that Jesus's Atonement was complete and that the Father had fulfilled His covenant to provide a Savior").
13. Isaiah 14:12; 2 Nephi 24:12; Doctrine and Covenants 76:26.
14. Welch, *Illuminating the Sermon at the Temple & the Sermon on the Mount,* 24 and note 1; 99 and note 126. In his study, Brother Welch explores some fifty elements of Christ's sermon at the temple to establish his thesis that it is a "temple text," that is a text "that contains allusions to the most sacred

15. John Welch notes that this refers to their ordination to "what Latter-day Saints normally associate with the Aaronic Priesthood." Later that day He confers upon the disciples the power to bestow the Holy Ghost, or the Melchizedek Priesthood (3 Nephi 18:37). See Welch, *Illuminating the Sermon at the Temple & the Sermon on the Mount*, 53.
16. Nelson, "Drawing the Power of Jesus Christ into Our Lives."
17. David A. Bednar, "Ask in Faith," *Ensign*, May 2008, 94 (Elder Bednar's attribution to the Prophet Joseph Smith comes from *Lectures on Faith*, 3: "Faith is not only the principle of action, but of power also, in all intelligent beings, whether in heaven or on earth").
18. Thomas S. Monson, "Obedience Brings Blessings," *Ensign*, May 2013, quoting Joseph F. Smith, "Discourse," *Deseret News*, November 12, 1873, 644.
19. Bruce R. McConkie, "Obedience, Sacrifice, and Consecration," *Ensign*, May 1975, 51.
20. Dale G. Renlund, "Choose You This Day," *Ensign*, November 2018.
21. "Lesson 39: Doctrine and Covenants 101," *Doctrine and Covenants Teacher Manual*, https://www.churchofjesuschrist.org/study/manual/doctrine-and-covenants-teacher-manual-2017/lesson-39–doctrine-and-covenants-101?lang=eng, citing Doctrine and Covenants 57:2–3; 84:1–5; 97:10–12.
22. Ibid., citing David A. Bednar, "Honorably Hold a Name and Standing," *Ensign*, May 2009, 97.
23. See, for example, 2 Nephi 5:19 ("Behold, the words of the Lord had been fulfilled unto my brethren"); Mosiah 20:21 ("Are not the words of Abinadi fulfilled, which he prophesied against us—and all this because we would not hearken unto the words of the Lord, and turn from our iniquities?"); Alma 3:14 ("Thus the word of God is fulfilled"); Alma 13:26 ("And [Christ's coming to the Nephites] shall be made known unto just and holy men, by the mouth of angels, at the time of his coming, that the words of our fathers may be fulfilled, according to that which they have spoken concerning him, which was according to the spirit of prophecy which was in them"); Helaman 16:13 ("The words of the prophets began to be fulfilled"); 3 Nephi 1:15 ("And it came to pass that the words which came unto Nephi were fulfilled, according as they had been spoken"); 3 Nephi 23:10 ("And his disciples answered him and said: Yea, Lord, Samuel did prophesy according to thy words, and they were all fulfilled"); Ether 15:33 ("The words of the Lord had all been fulfilled").
24. Quentin L. Cook, "Safely Gathered Home," *Liahona*, May 2023 ("During the Council in Heaven in the premortal existence, the plan of salvation was discussed and *sustained*" [emphasis in original]).
25. Nelson, "Focus on the Temple," 121.
26. Russell M. Nelson, "Christ Is Risen; Faith in Him Will Move Mountains," *Liahona*, May 2021.
27. Nelson, "Overcome the World and Find Rest," 97.

28. Nelson, "The Power of Spiritual Momentum." See also Russell M. Nelson, "Now Is the Time," *Liahona*, May 2022 ("Positive spiritual momentum increases as we worship in the temple and grow in our understanding of the magnificent breadth and depth of the blessings we receive there"; "I plead with you to counter worldly ways by focusing on the eternal blessings of the temple").
29. Nelson, "Temple and Your Spiritual Foundation" ("Seek—prayerfully and consistently—to understand temple covenants and ordinances"; "spiritual doors will open. . . . your diligent efforts to do so will reinforce and strengthen your spiritual foundation").
30. Nelson, "Christ Is Risen; Faith in Him Will Move Mountains" ("Partake of sacred ordinances worthily"; "ordinances unlock the power of God for your life").
31. In his October 2023 general conference message, President Nelson explained not only *why* it is so important to draw upon the power of God to effect seemingly impossible changes in our psyche and character, but also *how* frequent service in the temple can help us do so. "Any addiction" or compulsion, he taught, "be it gaming, gambling, debt, drugs, alcohol, anger, pornography, sex, or even food," which I would add could include seemingly innocent but compulsive over- or unhealthy eating, for example, "offends God. Why? Because your obsession becomes your god. You look to it rather than to *Him* for solace." "If you struggle with an addiction [or compulsive behaviors]," the prophet counsels, "seek the *spiritual* and professional help you need" (emphasis in origingal). Spiritual help, he reminded us in this message and virtually every conference message, includes, perhaps most importantly, availing ourselves as often as our circumstances allow of the temple, where "you are drawn closer to the Savior and given greater access to His power. There you are guided in solving the problems in your life, even your most perplexing problems" (Nelson, "Think Celestial!")
32. Nelson, "Think Celestial!" ("Spending more time in the temple builds faith. And your service and worship in the temple will help you to think celestial. . . . There you are shown how to progress toward a celestial life. There you are drawn closer to the Savior and given greater access to His power.")

CHAPTER 5

The Spiritual Treasure of Increased Power to Gather Israel through the Keys Restored by Moses

"The ultimate objective of the gathering of Israel is to bring the blessings of the temple to God's faithful children."[1]

—Russell M. Nelson

When I started this study, the spiritual treasure of power to gather Israel was not one of the blessings I would have immediately associated with regular temple service. Rather, the spiritual treasures of the temple that first came to mind were the blessings of receiving the endowment and sealing ordinances for myself and the treasures of knowledge, perspective, love, and the rich spiritual strengthening that can come through regular temple attendance. But the more I have reflected on and studied what the scriptures teach about the role and purposes of temples in our lives, the more I have come to see how central the power to gather Israel is to the covenants we make in the temple. After all, if the central purpose of our covenants is to help us grow up spiritually and join our Father in Heaven in the "family business," as Elder Renlund put it, what better way to train us than to call us to assist in His work?

God's work and glory, as He described it in his call to Moses, is "to bring to pass the immortality and eternal life of man" (Moses 1:39). Yes, we go to the temple to receive our own ordinances, to reinforce in ourselves who we are from an eternal point of view, to find respite and spiritual strength to resist the evils of the day. But, as newly called missionaries learn, the most important lesson of a mission (and the temple) is, "It's not about me." The temple's call to obey, to sacrifice, to live the higher law of the gospel, to consecrate all that we have and are to God is, in essence, the call to love and serve others as Christ did. As Christ said to Peter, "When thou are converted, strengthen thy brethren" (Luke 22:32). When the Lord commanded His early Saints to go to the Ohio and there "be endowed with power from on high," it was for them to then "go forth among all nations . . . for I have a great work laid up in store" (Doctrine and Covenants 38:32–33).[2] Likewise, generally all missionaries go to the temple to be endowed preparatory to their going to "teach all nations, baptizing them in the name of the Father, and of the Son, and of the Holy Ghost" (Matthew 28:19). This is, after all, as President Russell M. Nelson constantly reminds us, "the most important work taking place on earth today."[3] As we gather Israel "on both sides of the veil,"[4] we "are engaged in the greatest challenge, the greatest cause, the greatest work on earth today."[5]

On this side of the veil, the gathering occurs as we do missionary work.[6] Concerning the other side of the veil, President Nelson teaches, "We gather pedigree charts, create family group sheets, and do temple work vicariously to gather individuals unto the Lord and into their families (see 1 Corinthians 15:29; 1 Peter 4:6)."[7] Both aspects of this great work[8] culminate in the temple. The keys of this work of gathering were restored in this dispensation first by the great gatherer and lawgiver Moses, and then Elias and Elijah in the Kirtland Temple in April 1836. We will study more about how the keys of Elias and Elijah relate to the gathering in later chapters. But first it is important to understand not only Moses's ministry anciently, and its relationship to temple ordinances and doctrine, but his role in the restoration of latter-day temples and temple work.

The Keys that Moses Restored Enable Temple Work and Worship

> **Doctrine and Covenants 110:11**—After this vision [of the Savior] closed, the heavens were again opened unto us; and Moses appeared before us, and committed unto us the keys of

the gathering of Israel from the four parts of the earth, and the leading of the ten tribes from the land of the north.

Moses first appeared with Elijah on the Mount of Transfiguration, when Moses gave Peter, James, and John the keys of the gathering of Israel, and Elijah conferred upon them the sealing power.[9] Moses appeared, again with Elijah, to the Prophet Joseph Smith and Oliver Cowdery in the Kirtland Temple, restoring his keys of gathering in our dispensation. How do such keys relate to the temple? We discover as the life of Moses unfolds in the Old Testament that Moses fulfilled the prophecy of Joseph, who was sold into Egypt, that a "Moses" would bring the children of Israel out of Egypt and gather them to their promised lands. As important as that was, however, in the process he would "build unto the Lord a house" in the wilderness and do everything in his power to prepare the Lord's covenant people to receive the ultimate blessings of such house—even to "behold the face of God" (Doctrine and Covenants 84:23)—to be ultimately gathered to their eternal home. His keys enable that same process today.

As Joseph Smith explained, God gathers His people in our time for the same purpose, to build, operate, and worship in temples. "What was the object of gathering the Jews or the people of God in any age of the world? . . . The main object was to build unto the Lord a house whereby He could reveal unto His people the ordinances of His house and the glories of His kingdom, and teach the people the way of salvation."[10] Before temples can be built, dedicated, staffed with ordinance workers, and filled with patrons, such workers and patrons must be converted, baptized, befriended, nourished by the good word of God, and prepared through service in the Church to enter the Lord's holy house.[11] In short, they must be "gathered" to centers of strength. In the early days of the Church, those gathering places were in Kirtland, Ohio; Independence, Missouri; Nauvoo, Illinois; and Salt Lake City, Utah. In our day, members are gathered to the stakes of Zion throughout the world.[12] Why stakes?

Section 5 of the *General Handbook* explains that "the term *stake* comes from the prophecies of Isaiah, who described latter-day Zion as a tent or a tabernacle that would be secured by stakes (see Isaiah 33:20; 54:2)." Looking to our day, the Savior quoted Isaiah's call to

Israel, both ancient and modern, to "enlarge the place of thy tent, and let them stretch forth the curtains of thy habitations; spare not, lengthen thy cords and strengthen thy stakes" (3 Nephi 22:2; see also Isaiah 54:2).[13] Another way to look at these scriptures is that the tent or tabernacle represents modern-day temples and the cords and tent stakes that hold up the tent represent modern stakes of Zion.

When they are set apart by someone authorized in writing to do so by the First Presidency (usually a General Authority), stake presidents are given priesthood keys to preside "over those who hold the Melchizedek Priesthood" and direct "God's work of salvation and exaltation in the stake." The *General Handbook* breaks this work into four categories: the work of "Living the Gospel of Jesus Christ," "Caring for Those in Need," "Inviting All to Receive the Gospel," and "Uniting Families for Eternity."

As a common judge, the stake president is directed to personally interview and is ultimately responsible for determining the worthiness of those going to the temple to receive their own endowment. With his counselors, as well as the bishopric, these priesthood leaders determine the worthiness of all others to renew their temple recommends. The stake president and the bishop also must recommend any individual before they can be interviewed by a member of the temple presidency to serve in the temple as an ordinance worker. Thus, the keys of gathering given to bishops and stake presidents make possible the ongoing preparation and spiritual nourishment of both patrons who come to receive their temple ordinances and serve as proxies for our kindred dead and all of the temple workers who administer these ordinances in the temple. In summary, the Lord gives us stakes as places of gathering or strengthening for a "defense and for a refuge from the storm, and from wrath when it shall be poured out without mixture on the whole earth" (Doctrine and Covenants 115:6). Stakes, in turn, and the keys held by the bishop and stake president, "secure," "hold up," or make possible the tabernacle or temples of the Lord. And increasingly, in addition to our homes, temples have become the ultimate refuge from the storms of life. All of these considerations are included in the keys restored by Moses to the Prophet Joseph Smith in 1836.

Conferral of the Priesthood and Ordination to Offices Therein—Becoming the Sons of Moses and Aaron

Stake presidents also hold keys to direct the preparation of and interview candidates to receive the Melchizedek Priesthood. Ordination of men to various offices in the Aaronic and Melchizedek Priesthoods is essential to God's work of salvation and exaltation in the Church, without which Israel could not be gathered and exalted. The ordinance of priesthood ordination is as important or binding as baptism, confirmation, or the temple endowment. In fact, for a man, receiving the priesthood is a prerequisite to entering the holy temple and is performed vicariously for all males by proxy preceding the washing and anointing ordinances, which are part of the endowment. Those who receive the priesthood and are ordained to an office therein[14] promise to do the following:

- Desire and worthily obtain both the Aaronic and Melchizedek priesthoods;
- Magnify their callings in the priesthood, or in other words, whatever callings are extended to them in the Church, including the "calling" or assignment to be a ministering brother;
- Beware concerning themselves, give diligent heed to the words of eternal life, and live by every word that proceeds forth from the mouth of God (in other words, when we receive the Melchizedek Priesthood, we also covenant to keep the law of obedience), including by "receiving" the Lord's servants or sustaining and giving heed to the counsel of the living apostles and prophets.

In turn, God swears by an oath that such faithful priesthood holders will:

- Be sanctified by the Spirit unto the renewing of their bodies;[15]
- Become the sons of Moses and of Aaron and the seed of Abraham and the Church and kingdom, and the elect of God;
- Receive the Lord;
- Receive the Father, His kingdom and, in short, "all that [the] Father hath" (Doctrine and Covenants 84:18, 31–40, 43–44).

More will be said later about the important distinction between merely "holding" the priesthood, or having the priesthood conferred upon us, and obtaining and exercising "power in the priesthood." This principle of power in the priesthood applies equally to men and women, who do not have the priesthood *conferred* upon them and are not *ordained* to priesthood offices, but nevertheless receive priesthood authority when they are set apart to specific callings and when they are endowed and sealed in the temple. To participate in temple work, however, young men must worthily accept and keep the covenants associated with the Aaronic Priesthood and men the covenants of the Melchizedek Priesthood.[16] One of the blessings promised as we so do is that we become "the sons of Moses and Aaron"—and worthy sisters could say "daughters" of Moses and Aaron. In the same way that the Levites administered the ordinances of the tabernacle, both men and women, including young men and women, are authorized to officiate in sacred priesthood or temple ordinances, including serving as proxies on behalf of those who have not received these ordinances for themselves.[17]

Service as a Proxy in Temple Ordinances Is an "Offering in Righteousness"

As we serve as temple proxies, we fulfill Malachi's prophecy that at the time of His Second Coming the Savior would "purify the sons [and daughters] of Levi, and purge them as gold and silver, that they may offer unto the Lord an offering in righteousness" (Malachi 3:1–3; 3 Nephi 24:1–3; see also Doctrine and Covenants 13:1). As we, though our priesthood covenants, become sons and daughters of Moses and Aaron (who as brothers were direct descendants of Levi), we also become sons and daughters of Levi through our covenants. What is the prophesied offering we offer to the Lord in righteousness in our day? The Lord answered through the Prophet Joseph Smith when He encouraged us "as Latter-day Saints" to "offer unto the Lord an offering in righteousness" by presenting "in his holy temple . . . a book containing the records of our dead, which shall be worthy of all acceptation" (Doctrine and Covenants 128:24). Thus, each of us offers an "offering in righteousness" when we perform ordinances for anyone who has died. When that ordinance is recorded in the "book" (meaning, in our day, the computer database) that is kept of all completed temple ordinances, such offering becomes "worthy of all acceptation" (Doctrine and Covenants 128:24).[18] Because of the keys Moses restored, all of us can become participants in fulfilling this and other glorious prophecies that fill the scriptures about the gathering of Israel in these latter days. As we do, we receive the Lord's promise of increased power to gather Israel. As the Lord promised in the dedicatory prayer to the Kirtland Temple, He will put upon us through our temple service "the testimony of the covenant." When we "go out and proclaim [His] word" (or love, share, invite), He will prepare our hearts against "all those judgments [He] is about to send," and is sending, "in [His] wrath, upon the inhabitants of the earth," that we "may not faint in the day of trouble" (Doctrine and Covenants 109:38).

Endnotes

1. Nelson, "The Temple and Your Spiritual Foundation."
2. In Doctrine and Covenants 43:16 the Lord declared His purpose in endowing His Saints "with power" is "that ye may give even as I have spoken." For a description of instructions early leaders and missionaries received to "tarry at Kirtland" to be endowed before carrying the gospel to other nations, see Anderson, *The Savior in Kirtland*, 277–81.
3. Nelson, "The Everlasting Covenant." See also Nelson, *Heart of the Matter*, 191–200.
4. For a few of President Nelson's oft-repeated references to this theme, see Nelson, "Let God Prevail"; Nelson, "Hope of Israel," Worldwide Youth Devotional, June 3, 2018, HopeofIsrael.lds.org; Nelson, "Sisters' Participation in the Gathering of Israel," *Ensign*, November 2018; Nelson, "The Gathering of Scattered Israel," *Ensign*, November 2006. See generally scripture references under Guide to the Scriptures, "Israel—Gathering of Israel"; Topical Guide, "Israel, Gathering of."
5. Nelson, "The Everlasting Covenant."
6. "The Gathering of Israel," Church History Topics, https://www.churchofjesuschrist.org/study/history/topics/gathering-of-israel?lang=eng.
7. Nelson, "The Future of the Church."
8. Significantly, Elder David A. Bednar has taught that the work of gathering on this side of the veil, commonly referred to as missionary work, and on the other side of the veil, commonly referred to as temple and family history work, is actually "one work." See David A. Bednar, "Missionary, Family History, and Temple Work," *Ensign*, November 2014.
9. See chapter 17, "The Spiritual Treasures from the Mission and Keys of Elijah."
10. Wilcox, *House of Glory*, 110, citing *History of the Church* 5:423–24.
11. For an insightful discussion of the role of the temple in missionary work and "real growth" in the Church, see Hafen, *The Contrite Spirit*, chapter 15, "Missionary Work, the Temple, and Real Growth."
12. See Donald W. Parry and Jay A. Parry, *Understanding the Signs of the Times* (Salt Lake City, Utah: Deseret Book, 1999), 48–72 ("The gathering of Israel from many lands will be seen as a great miracle, surpassing even the impressive events that led to the deliverance of Israel from Egypt [Ex. 7–17]," quoting Jeremiah 16:14–15 ("Behold, the days come, saith the Lord, that it shall no more be said, The Lord liveth, that brought up the children of Israel out of the land of Egypt; But, The Lord liveth, that brought up the children of Israel from the land of the north, and from all the lands whither he had driven them").
13. See also Doctrine and Covenants 82:14 ("Zion must increase in beauty, and in holiness; her borders must be enlarged; her stakes must be strengthened; yea, verily I say unto you, Zion must arise and put on her beautiful garments").
14. *General Handbook* 20.7 (Before "ordaining" a man to an office in the Aaronic or Melchizedek Priesthood, the authorized priesthood holder performing the ordination "confers" the applicable priesthood "unless it has already been

conferred"). For a discussion of how sisters obtain all of the blessings promised in connection with the oath and covenant of the priesthood, see "How Do Faithful Women Receive and Exercise Priesthood Auhority and Power?" in chapter 18 below.
15. For a discussion of the oath and covenant of the priesthood and this particular promise, see Nelson, *Heart of the Matter*, 92–103.
16. See, for example, Henry B. Eyring, "Faith and the Oath and Covenant of the Priesthood," *Ensign*, May 2008; Marion G. Romney, "The Oath and Covenant Which Belongeth to the Priesthood," *Ensign*, November 1980.
17. See Nelson, "Spiritual Treasures" ("You [referring to the sisters] are authorized to perform and officiate in priesthood ordinances [as a proxy] every time you attend" the temple).
18. The Prophet Joseph Smith also explained that the "acceptable offering and sacrifice" to be offered in the temple to be built in Jackson County, Missouri (Doctrine and Covenants 84:31) will include certain animal sacrifices, "as well as every ordinance belonging to the Priesthood," which will, when the temple in Jackson County is built and the sons of Levi be purified, "be fully restored and attended to in all their powers, ramifications, and blessings. This ever did and ever will exist when the powers of the Melchizedek Priesthood are sufficiently manifest; else how can the restitution of all things spoken of by the Holy Prophets be brought to pass. It is not to be understood that the law of Moses will be established again with all its rites and variety of ceremonies; this has never been spoken of by the prophets; but those things which existed prior to Moses' day, namely, sacrifice, will be continued" (Joseph Smith, *Teachings of the Prophet Joseph Smith*, Joseph Fielding Smith, ed. [*The Deseret News Press*, 1946], 172–73). President Joseph Fielding Smith explained that as part of the restoration of "all things" "since the beginning," "the law of sacrifice will have to be restored, or all things which were decreed by the Lord would not be restored. It will be necessary, therefore, for the sons of Levi, who offered the blood sacrifices anciently in Israel, to offer such a sacrifice again to round out and complete this ordinance in this dispensation." Such "sacrifice of animals will be done to complete the restoration when the temple spoken of is built; at the beginning of the millennium, or in the restoration, blood sacrifices will be performed long enough to complete the fulness of the restoration in this dispensation. Afterwards sacrifice will be of some other character" (Joseph Fielding Smith, *Doctrines of Salvation*, compiled by Bruce R. McConkie [Salt Lake City, Utah: Bookcraft, 1955], 3:94; see also "Section 13, The Restoration of the Aaronic Priesthood," *Doctrine and Covenants Student Manual*, 2002, 28–29, https://www.churchofjesuschrist.org/manual/doctrine-and-covenants-student-manual/section-13–the-restoration-of-the-aaronic-priesthood?lang=eng).

CHAPTER 6

The Spiritual Treasure of Power to Build a People Prepared for a Temple

Lessons from Moses's Ministry

> *"Let us never lose sight of what the Lord is doing for us now. He is . . . increasing our ability to help gather Israel. He is also making it easier for each of us to become spiritually refined."*[1]
>
> —Russell M. Nelson

Building (and Being) a People Prepared for a Temple

As we examine more fully the sacred record of the Lord's call to Moses and the ways in which He directed his ministry to ancient Israel, consider how all of us can learn from and pattern our own ministries after Moses's ministry, as he "plainly taught" and "diligently" "sought" to sanctify those to whom he ministered "that they might behold the face of God" (Doctrine and Covenants 84:23). Who was Moses, and how did the Lord prepare and use him to establish the "first temple" or tabernacle in the wilderness? What can we learn from Moses's tireless efforts to prepare a people capable of receiving the highest temple ordinances? Moreover, after he completed his earthly ministry, consider how the Lord continued to use Moses as He directed him to restore the keys of the gathering, which are so critical to the priesthood keys restored by the prophets Elias and Elijah. What can we learn about the gathering in our day from Moses's tireless efforts to gather the saints of his day?

To begin with, Moses had a special heritage and foreordination. He was a pure Levite, the great-grandson of Levi through his father, Amran,[2] and grandson of Levi through his mother, Jochebed.[3] His great-uncle, Joseph, the seer and rescuer of the Egyptian civilization, prophesied of Moses's birth.[4] Likewise, each member of the Church, whether literally descended from or adopted into the house of Israel (it doesn't matter), also has a special heritage and foreordination. Each of us was foreordained to assist in fulfilling God's promise to Abraham, that through his seed "all the families of the earth [would] be blessed, even with the blessings of salvation, even of life eternal" (Abraham 2:11). To better understand the importance and purpose of the keys Moses was called to exercise and restore, of which all of us are beneficiaries in fulfilling our divine calling to help gather Israel, we review first his own account of his providential birth in Exodus 2, touch on his upbringing, and then focus on his sacred call to free Israel from bondage and prepare them for the spiritual treasures Jehovah awaited to give His people.

Moses's Early Years and Call to the Ministry

When Moses was born, the children of Israel were in bondage to the Egyptians, and Pharaoh had commanded the Hebrew midwives to kill every male child that they delivered. Jochebed hid Moses for three months. But "when she could [no] longer hide him," she made "an ark of bulrushes, and daubed it with slime and with pitch, and put the child therein; and she laid it in the flags by the river's brink." Moses's sister, Miriam, who later became a prophetess in Israel, watched from a distance to see what would happen. When Pharaoh's daughter providentially came to bathe in the river and discovered the ark and Moses inside, "she had compassion on him." Miriam offered to find her a "nurse of the Hebrew women," which Pharaoh's daughter accepted. When Miriam brought her mother, Jochebed, Pharaoh's daughter told her, "Take this child away, and nurse it for me, and I will give thee thy wages." Jochebed, no doubt ecstatically, "took the child, and nursed it. And the child grew, and she brought him unto

Pharaoh's daughter, and *he became her son*. And she called his name Moses" (Exodus 2:1–10).

Concerning his youth and early adult years, the scriptures record only that "the child grew" (Exodus 2:10). However, we know from other sources that Moses "was remarkable for his beauty and form"[5] and "exceeding fair."[6] Pharaoh's daughter, who by divine providence could not have children of her own, reared him to become the successor to Pharaoh's throne.[7] Unlike the telling in DreamWorks' fantasy,[8] Moses had "a generous mind"[9] and "was learned in all the wisdom of the Egyptians" (Acts 7:22). Moreover, he became famous as a military leader, with victories that Josephus says made him Egypt's "national hero."[10]

When Moses "was full forty years old, it came into his heart to visit his brethren the children of Israel" (Acts 7:23). Paul indicates that this fateful decision evidenced a conversion in which he "refused to be called the son of Pharaoh's daughter," that is, heir to the throne of Pharoah, "choosing rather to suffer affliction with the people of God, than to enjoy the pleasures of sin for a season; esteeming the reproach of Christ greater riches than the treasures in Egypt" (Hebrews 11:24–26). Looking "on their burdens," Moses saw "an Egyptian smiting" one of the Hebrew slaves. "And he looked this way and that way, and when he saw that there was no man, he slew the Egyptian, and hid him in the sand" (Exodus 2:11–12). Returning the next day, he saw two Hebrews fighting. "To him that did the wrong," he asked, "wherefore smitest thou thy fellow?" The man answered, "Who made thee a prince and a judge over us? intendest thou to kill me, as thou killedst the Egyptian?" (Exodus 2:11–14) Moses realized that his actions in defense of one of his brethren had been discovered. When word reached Pharaoh of Moses's treason, Pharaoh ordered Moses's death (Exodus 2:15). Moses fled for his life, leaving his life of luxury and power forever.[11]

Providentially, Moses was led to the home of Jethro, the high priest of Midian, who had seven daughters. Midian, which lay on the shores of the Red Sea, was founded by Midian, Abraham's fourth son by Keturah, the wife of Abraham's latter years (1 Chronicles 1:32).[12] Moses met Jethro's daughter Zipporah, his future wife, at the well, where he rescued her and her six sisters from marauders. When they returned to recount the tale of Moses's daring deed to their father, Jethro reminded them of their duty of hospitality, so valued among peoples of that time and place, which apparently in their excitement they had forgotten: "Where is he? why is it that ye have left the man? call him, that he may eat bread" (Exodus 2:20). Jethro welcomed Moses into his home, invited him into the family sheep business, offered his daughter in marriage, and eventually ordained Moses to the Melchizedek Priesthood (Doctrine and Covenants 84:6). No doubt he tutored him in the ways of the Lord and the covenant the Lord made with Jethro's progenitor, Abraham. Moses dwelt with Jethro for forty years and wrote that he was "content" (Exodus 2:21).

At the time Jehovah, the premortal Jesus Christ, called to Moses "out of the midst of the bush" at Horeb, "the mountain of God" (Exodus 3:1–2), Moses had been preparing for his divine call for eighty years.[13] "Moses, Moses," Jehovah called. Moses responded, "Here am I." And the Lord said, "Draw not nigh hither: put off thy shoes from off thy feet, for the place whereon thou standest is holy ground" (Exodus 3:3–5). Jehovah then introduced Himself as "the God of thy father, the God of Abraham, the God of Isaac, and the God of Jacob," the great "I AM THAT I AM,"[14] calling Moses to deliver His people out of Egypt in answer to "their cry by reason of their taskmasters." The Lord then revealed His motivation for helping them as He seeks constantly to help us: "For I know their sorrows; And I am come down to deliver them" (Exodus 3:6–8, 14).

Like other prophets before, when he understood the incredible mission God had given him, Moses balked. "Who am I, that I should go unto Pharaoh, and that I should bring forth the children of Israel out of Egypt?" The Lord, perfectly aware of his feelings of inadequacy, strengthened his faith through a series of three miraculous manifestations (Exodus 4:1–9). Moses remonstrated again to the omniscient Lord, excusing himself because he was "not eloquent" and was "slow of speech" (Exodus 4:10). To this the Lord reassured him, "Who hath made man's mouth? or who maketh the dumb, or deaf, or the seeing, or the blind? have not I the Lord? Now therefore go, and I will be with thy mouth, and teach thee what thou shalt say" (Exodus 4:11–12).

At this point, Moses simply asked the Lord to send someone else.[15] But the Lord again reasoned with Moses, assuaging his fears and reassuring him that his older brother, Aaron,[16] would help him (Exodus 4:14). "And thou shalt speak unto him, and put words in his mouth: and I will be with thy mouth, and with his mouth, and will teach you what ye shall do" (Exodus 4:15). Even then God was not done reassuring Moses, addressing his unspoken fear—that he might be slain if he returned to Egypt. "Go, return into Egypt: for all the men are dead which sought thy life" (Exodus 4:18–19). "And Moses . . . returned to the land of Egypt: and . . . took the rod of God in his hand."[17]

Jehovah Personally Tutors Moses to Prepare Him for His Forty-Year Ministry

After Jehovah's call to Moses from the burning bush but before Moses began his monumental calling to free the children of Israel and guide them to the promised land, the Lord divinely tutored Moses as he had prophets before him such as Enoch and Abraham. "Caught up into an exceedingly high mountain" by the power of the Spirit and seeing and talking with "God face to face" (Moses 1:1–2), Jehovah, speaking by "divine investiture," that is "as if he were God the Father,"[18] taught Moses the most important truths of all. As He did so, Heavenly Father described the intimate nature of their covenant relationship—the same relationship He desires for each of us: "Behold, I am the Lord God Almighty, and Endless is my name. . . . And, behold, *thou art my son*; . . . and *thou art in the similitude of mine Only Begotten*; and mine Only Begotten is and shall be the Savior, for he is full of grace and truth." He then reemphasized the divine nature of Moses's calling—"*I* have a work for thee, Moses, my son" (Moses 1:3–4, 6).

As He did for Enoch[19] and the brother of Jared,[20] the Savior gave Moses a panoramic vision of the earth and its inhabitants. When God's influence left him, Moses discerned man's true relation to God, that without Him and His strengthening power, "man is nothing, which thing I never had supposed" (Moses 1:7–10). The Lord then allowed Moses to learn from his own experience the difference between the influence of the Almighty and the influence of the Adversary (see Moses 1:12–19). When Satan appeared as an angel of light, crying and ranting in a loud voice, "I am the Only Begotten, worship me," Moses began to "fear exceedingly" and saw the bitterness of hell. "Calling upon God," he commanded Satan to depart "in the name of the Only Begotten" (vv. 20–21), as we are taught in the endowment. Moses then beheld God's glory and was tutored again in vision about the nature of God, His creations, and His purpose, beholding "the earth, yea, even all of it; and there was not a particle of it which he did not behold, discerning it by the Spirit of God. And he beheld also the inhabitants thereof, and there was not a soul which he beheld not; and he discerned them by the Spirit of God; and their numbers were great, even numberless as the sand upon the sea shore" (Moses 1:27–28). The Lord then proceeded to reveal to Moses truths about His work and glory—"to bring to pass the immortality and eternal life of man"[21]—and the creation of "this earth," which he was commanded to write. The Lord prophesied that in our day, "when the children of men shall esteem my words as naught and take many of them from the book which thou shalt write,"[22] He would "raise up another like unto thee; and they shall be had again among the children of men—among as many as shall believe" (Moses 1:36–41).

Just as Moses was prepared for his ministry through a temple-like experience on a high mountain that taught him who he was in relation to God, we also are prepared for our important callings through our temple experience. *How* the Lord prepared this great priesthood leader for his divinely appointed ministry is exactly how *we* should prepare ourselves for our divinely appointed assignments (including our most important callings as husbands and fathers and wives and mothers). We each need to know deeply within our soul who we are in relation to our divine Creator, even our Father in Heaven. Just as He did for Moses, He has a work for us to do. What we learn in the scriptures, and especially in the temple, is absolutely critical to our faithfully fulfilling each and every one of such "works" or divine appointments we received and accepted in our premortal life with our Father in Heaven.[23]

The Exodus

Upon arriving in Egypt, Aaron and Moses "did the signs in the sight of the people" as the Lord had instructed. When the people "heard that the Lord had visited the children of Israel, and that he had looked upon their affliction, then they bowed their heads and worshipped" the Lord (Exodus 4:31). As predicted, however, Pharaoh mocked God's prophets, asking, "Who is the Lord, that I should obey his voice?" (Exodus 5:2). Below are the familiar signs, wonders, and plagues recounted in Exodus 7 through 12:

1. Waters of Egypt, its streams, rivers, including the mighty Nile, ponds and all pools and vessels of water (Exodus 7:14–15, 19) turned to blood;
2. Plague of frogs (Exodus 8:1–6);
3. Plague of lice (Exodus 8:16–19);
4. Plague of flies or, as interpreted from the original Hebrew, insects, including wasps and hornets,[24] except in the land of Goshen where the Israelites dwelt, to put "a division between [God's] people and Pharaoh's people" (Exodus 8:20–24);
5. Plague of murrain or epidemic, which caused the death of Egypt's (not Israel's) cattle (Exodus 9:1–7);
6. Plague of boils and blains, painful inflammatory sores on men and cattle who were not killed by the murrain (Exodus 9:8–12);
7. Plague of hail "such as [had] not been seen in Egypt since the foundation thereof" and "fire mingled with the hail, very grievous" (Exodus 9:13–26), Goshen again escaping the plague;
8. Plague of locusts, filling the houses of the Egyptians and their servants, unlike any such plague "since the day they were upon the earth" so that "the land was darkened; and they did eat every herb of the land; and all the fruit of the trees which the hail had left; and there remained not any green thing in the trees, or in the herbs of the field" (Exodus 10:1–15);
9. Plague of darkness, through which for three days "they saw not one another; neither rose any from his place" (Exodus 10:21–29); and finally
10. The slaying of the firstborn, both of men and animals, so that "there was not a house where there was not one dead" (Exodus 12:29–30).

The Passover

"Speak ye unto all the congregation of Israel [to] take to them every man . . . a lamb for an house," the Lord commanded Moses. The lamb was to "be without blemish, a male of the first year." Each family was to take the lamb's blood "and strike it on the two side posts and on the upper door post" of their house, roast the lamb, and eat it with unleavened bread and bitter herbs. Upon seeing the "blood . . . upon [their] houses," the Lord promised He would "pass over" them "and the plague shall not be upon you to destroy you, when I smite the land of Egypt." The Lord designated that day as "a memorial; and ye shall keep it a feast to the Lord throughout your generations . . . by an ordinance for ever" (Exodus 12:3, 5, 7–8, 14).

President Howard W. Hunter observed, "Passover is without equal in the Jewish calendar of celebrations. It is the oldest of the Jewish festivals . . . remind[ing] every generation of the return of the children of Israel to the promised land and of the great travail in Egypt which preceded it." Passover teaches us that through Christ's Atonement and Resurrection, Jesus gave us "not just a passover from death, but a gift of eternal life by an infinite sacrifice."[25]

Only when his firstborn son was smitten did Pharoah finally (at least for a brief time) soften his heart and let the children of Israel go and "serve the Lord" (Exodus 12:31). "And the Egyptians were urgent upon the people, that they might send them out of the land in haste; for they said, We be all dead men" (Exodus 12:33). Some scholars have estimated that the total number of Israelites in the Exodus, plus the "mixed multitude" of non-Israelites who went with them, may have numbered in the millions (based on the report in Exodus 12:37 that 600,000 men over age twenty "journeyed from Ramses to Succoth"). The Church Education System notes, however, that other scholars estimate that the number was far fewer.[26] Regardless of the actual number, the magnitude of the task the Lord had given Moses, to shepherd what was no doubt a large congregation, becomes apparent.

Not surprisingly, Pharaoh again had a change of heart, taking "six hundred chosen chariots, and all the chariots of Egypt" to pursue the children of Israel. Full of fear, "the children of Israel cried out unto the Lord," complaining to Moses, "because there were no graves in Egypt, hast thou taken us away to die in the wilderness?" Moses's response was full of faith, as our leaders' counsel concerning all the fearsome adversities in contemporary society: "Fear ye not, stand still, and see the salvation of the Lord." Nonetheless, Moses privately pleaded with the Lord for strength, as we should and do. His response is as relevant now as then: "Wherefore criest thou unto me? speak unto the children of Israel, *that they go forward*." Faithfully, Moses lifted up his rod, stretching his "hand over the sea, and divide[d] it: and the children of Israel [went] on dry ground through the midst of the sea" in accordance with the word of the Lord (Exodus 14:7, 10–11, 13, 15–16). "And the waters returned, and covered the chariots, and the horsemen, and all the host of Pharaoh that came into the sea after them; there remained not so much as one of them" (Exodus 14:28).

The Covenant of Sinai

It took the body of Israel two months[27] to arrive at Mount Sinai, where Jehovah had first commanded Moses to take them (Exodus 3:12). During this time, the Lord continued to tutor His people, who for about 215 years had been conditioned by the culture of brutality and idolatry of Egyptian civilization. Not only were the Israelites eyewitnesses to the miraculous signs and plagues wrought by God through Moses and Aaron in the land of Egypt and their deliverance from the Egyptian armies through the Red Sea, but they also saw the Lord leading them "by day in a pillar of a cloud" and "by night in a pillar of fire" (Exodus 13:21). They witnessed miracle after miracle—Moses being directed how to heal the waters of Marah, enabling them to quench their thirst, being taught that "I am the Lord that healeth thee" (Exodus 15:23–26). Daily (except on the Sabbath) they gathered manna, "bread from heaven," and quail for meat (Exodus 16:2). The Lord indeed bore the children of Israel, as He does us, "on eagles' wings" (Exodus 19:4).

No doubt Moses used these miraculous signs and every other opportune moment during these months to prepare his people for the ordinances and covenants God desired to give them and hoped would enter into their hearts. As the presiding Melchizedek Priesthood holder,[28] Moses "preached" and "plainly taught" the gospel of Jesus

Christ to his people,[29] seeking "diligently to sanctify his people that they might behold the face of God" (Doctrine and Covenants 84:23). This means that he labored to qualify them to receive their temple blessings.[30] The Lord promised ancient Israel, as He promises us, "If ye will obey my voice indeed, and keep my covenant, then ye shall be a peculiar treasure[31] unto me above all people. . . . And ye shall be unto me a kingdom of priests, and an holy nation" (Exodus 19:5–6), meaning becoming a temple-worthy and temple-going people. The *Old Testament Student Manual* reveals that "if they had accepted all of the privileges offered them and followed the instructions which would have qualified them to receive the fulfillment of all God's promises, they could have been accorded the grandest of all revelations: He offered to come down in the sight of all the people and let them hear when He spoke to Moses that they might know for themselves about His will and His law." However, the people "were not fully ready to come up 'in the sight' of the Lord on the mount where Moses was, for the Lord told him to go down and warn them not to come up."[32] Rather than encourage them, God's voice and "the thunderings, the lightnings and the . . . mountain smoking" from the presence of the Lord frightened them and "they removed, and stood afar off" (Exodus 20:18). They told Moses, "Speak thou with us, and we will hear; but let not God speak with us, lest we die" (Exodus 20:19).

Even so, they were greatly blessed to hear "the voice and the words of God as the Ten Commandments were given."[33] The Ten Commandments God revealed to Moses, by His own voice to all the hosts of Israel (Exodus 20:1–19), "are an integral part of the restored gospel of the Lord Jesus Christ."[34] The people accepted the covenant and commandments of the Lord[35] "with one voice and said, All the words which the Lord has said will we do" (Exodus 24:3). Moses wrote these divine laws in a "book of the covenant," read them to the people, and offered burnt offerings to make their covenant binding, sprinkling the blood therefrom "on the people" in token of the covenant the people entered into with Jehovah (Exodus 24:4–8).

"Then went up Moses, and Aaron, Nadab, and Abihu, and seventy of the elders of Israel," where they received the consummate temple-related privilege of seeing "the God of Israel: and there was under his feet as it were a paved work of a sapphire stone, and as it were the body of heaven in his clearness" (Exodus 24:9–10). The Lord then asked Moses to come and be with Him in the mountain "and I will give thee tables of stone, and a law, and commandments which I have written; that thou mayest teach them" (v. 12). Moses did so, taking his minister, or junior companion, Joshua. In all, Moses communed with God 40 days. "He neither ate bread nor drank water" (Exodus 24:18; 34:28). Meanwhile, his faithful minister Joshua waited for him to return.

The Lord Reveals the Pattern for a Temple

"During his 40-day fast upon the Mount, Moses received every detail needed" to construct the tabernacle, a House of the Lord.[36] Indeed, Moses was shown the "fashion" or "pattern" of the tabernacle (Exodus 26:30; 25:40; 27:8). The Lord invited the children of Israel to bring Him offerings to help build the sanctuary, "that I may dwell among them" (Exodus 25:2, 8). To what end? That "Israel could come and receive the keys of salvation and exaltation."[37] "For this cause I commanded Moses that he should build a tabernacle, that they should bear it with them in the wilderness," the Lord explained to the Prophet Joseph Smith, "that those ordinances ["washings," "anointings," "endowment," and other temple ordinances] "might be revealed which had been hid," or kept sacred, "from before the world was" (Doctrine and Covenants 124:37–39).[38]

Church instructional materials note that "each item [in the tabernacle, including its design, layout, furniture, and priests' clothing] was specified by the Lord to bear witness, in typology, symbolism, and similitude, of Jesus Christ and his atoning sacrifice." Moreover, each aspect

The erection of the Tabernacle and the Sacred vessels, as in Exodus 40:17–19, "And it came to pass in the first month in the second year, on the first day of the month, that the tabernacle was reared up. And Moses reared up the tabernacle, and fastened his sockets, and set up the boards thereof, and put in the bars thereof, and reared up his pillars. And he spread abroad the tent over the tabernacle, and put the covering of the tent above upon it; as the Lord commanded Moses."

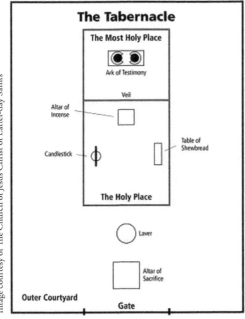

of ancient temple worship can be likened to first principles and ordinances of the gospel that point us to Christ. For example, at the altar of sacrifice the priest "symbolically offered his life," or figuratively speaking the life of the individual for whom the priest officiated. As discussed further in the next chapter, "the blood of the sacrificial animals . . . could be likened unto true repentance, in which the natural or sinful man gives up his life through a broken heart and a contrite spirit." Next, the priest went to the great laver, where the "ordinance of washing his hands and feet symbolized the cleansing power of baptism, the next step after true repentance." Receiving the Holy Ghost was symbolized by the olive oil and the burning of "the great candlestick which illuminated the chamber." Opposite the candlestick "stood the table of shewbread, upon which was the bread and the wine," "emblems of Jesus Christ and his sacrifice for mankind [which] were changed each Sabbath day." The incense that rose from the golden altar of incense "directly in front of the veil," "which the priests burned twice a day," represented prayer and the promise that temple worshippers may "part the veil" and commune with heaven. "The actual presence of God was symbolized by the ark of the covenant in the Holy of Holies. Thus we see how the layout of the tabernacle suggested a straight and narrow path leading to eternal life and also the steps that one must undertake if he is to return to the presence of God in the celestial kingdom."[39]

The Lord Reveals the Mosaic Law

As his forty-day communion with Jehovah was drawing to a close, the Lord gave Moses "two tables of testimony, tables of stone, written with the finger of God" (Exodus 31:18).[40] But even while revealing the ordinances that would allow the children of Israel to receive the greatest blessings available to God's children, the Lord told Moses to "get thee down" for the people "have corrupted themselves" (Exodus 32:7). Rejoining his faithful minister, who had waited a little lower on the mountain for over a month, Moses found the people "naked" (Exodus 32:5) and "dancing" (Exodus 32:19) before the golden calf in the most licentious and depraved of fertility rites.[41] After casting "the [stone] tables out of his hand," breaking them "beneath the mount" (Exodus 32:19), Moses fruitlessly sought an explanation from his older brother, whom he had left in charge of the people, as to how he could have become complicit in Israel's tragic apostasy (Exodus 32:21–24). "Then Moses stood in the gate of the camp, and said: Who is on the Lord's side? Let him come unto me" (Exodus 32:26). To their eternal credit, "all the sons of Levi" stepped forward and, in obedience to the command of the Lord, slew "about 3,000 rebels" (Exodus

32:27–28, 30, and headnote). Thus, because of their "stiffneckedness," the covenant people were relegated the lesser blessing of the ministering of angels, having forfeited the privilege offered them by a gracious and merciful God to "go up [personally] in the midst of thee" (Exodus 33:3).[42] Nevertheless, the Lord continued to minister personally to His chosen prophet, even as He does today—appearing and speaking to him again "face to face, as a man speaketh unto his friend" (Exodus 33:11) and again later, showing his "back parts" but not his face "as at other times" (JST, Exodus 33:23).

Possibly only a few days after his first miraculous forty-day fast,[43] the Lord commanded Moses, for another period of forty days and forty nights, to again summit Mount Sinai and commune with Him, bringing two new tablets of stone upon which the Lord engraved "the words of the law, according as they were written at the first" (but without the "words" and the "ordinances" of the "everlasting covenant of the holy priesthood," that is, the higher or temple ordinances that would have enabled all the hosts of Israel to enter the "rest" or presence of the Lord, or, in other words, to be endowed). For, the Lord declared, "I will take away the priesthood out of their midst . . . my holy order, and the ordinances thereof." Thus, they lost the promised blessing of having the Lord's presence "go up in their midst." "But I will give unto them the law as at the first, but it shall be after the law of a carnal commandment; for I have sworn in my wrath, that they shall not enter into my *presence*, into *my rest*, in the days of their pilgrimage" (JST, Exodus 34:1–2).[44]

Wandering in the Wilderness

Over the next six months,[45] under the direction of the prophet and men called of the Lord whom He "filled with the spirit of God," with "wisdom, . . . understanding and . . . knowledge, and in all manner of workmanship" (Exodus 35:31, 35), and through the consecrated offerings of the people, the tabernacle was completed. The Lord accepted His house by the visible token of the cloud that accompanied the hosts of Israel in their journeyings. "Then a cloud covered the tent of the congregation, and the glory of the Lord filled the tabernacle. And Moses was not able to enter into the tent of the congregation, because the cloud abode thereon, and the glory of the Lord filled the tabernacle" (Exodus 40:34–35).

Ten months or so after arriving at Mount Sinai,[46] the Lord commanded Israel to "go in and possess the land which the Lord sware unto your fathers, Abraham, Isaac, and Jacob" (Deuteronomy 1:8). Within three days of breaking camp, the chronic complaining and rebellion of certain members of the congregation "displeased the Lord" and "his anger was kindled" (Numbers 11:1). Moses's meekness[47] and long-suffering were tested to the breaking point: "Have I conceived all this people? have I begotten them, that thou shouldest say unto me, Carry them in thy bosom, as a nursing father beareth the sucking child, unto the land which thou swarest unto their fathers? . . . I am not able to bear all this people alone, because it is too heavy for me. And if thou deal thus with me, kill me, I pray thee, out of hand" (Numbers 11:12, 14–15).

In response to his seemingly well-deserved discouragement, the Lord, as He does today, called additional laborers to His vineyard to lighten Moses's load. In particular, Moses was directed to call "seventy men of the elders of Israel, whom thou knowest to be the elders [or leaders] of the people," a precursor to the General Authority and Area Seventies called to assist the Quorum of the Twelve and First Presidency today, "and bring them unto the tabernacle of the congregation." There, He promised to "take of the spirit which is upon thee, and . . . put it upon them; and they shall bear the burden of the people with thee, that thou bear it not thyself alone." The Lord then "came down in a cloud, and spake unto" Moses. As promised, when the seventy gathered to the tabernacle, "the spirit rested upon them, they prophesied, and did not cease." Eldad and Medad, two of the seventy who were unable to be at the tabernacle at the appointed time, also began to prophesy in the camp. A young man ran and informed Moses. Hearing this, Joshua counseled Moses to "forbid them." "And Moses said unto him, Enviest thou for my sake? *would God that all the Lord's people were prophets, and that the Lord would put his spirit upon them*!" (Numbers 11:16–17, 25–29) Here is a great lesson. The Lord is willing and anxious to personally tutor and bless all who are called to labor with Him in His vineyard.[48]

As they arrived at the promised land to fulfill the Lord's judgment on the peoples in Canaan,[49] the Lord's covenant people got cold feet. Except for faithful Caleb and Joshua, ten of the dozen spies (one from each tribe) sent to survey the land returned with an evil report, sowing doubt and rebellion among the congregation (to which many were predisposed in any event). Doubt and fear led to an open rebellion. "Let us make a captain, and let us return to Egypt," they cried "one to another" (Numbers 14:4). Words, as they will do, led to evil deeds "and in their rebellion" the traitorous Israelites went so far as to "[appoint] a captain to return to their bondage" (Nehemiah 9:17). "How long," the Lord lamented, "will it be ere they believe me, for all the signs which I have showed among them?" (Numbers 14:11).

What a lesson for modern Israel! Do we believe the Lord, Jehovah? Do we recognize and remember all the signs or miracles[50] that He has shown us, both in our individual lives and in the unfolding miracles of the restoration of the fulness of the gospel and the Church and kingdom of God on the earth in this last dispensation? Nevertheless, faithful, meek Moses continued to plead for his wayward people. "Pardon, I beseech thee," he prayed, "the iniquity of this people according unto the greatness of thy mercy, and as thou hast forgiven this people, from Egypt even until now" (Numbers 14:19). The Lord did pardon the unbelievers, "according to [Moses's] word." But He did not remove the natural and logical consequences of their faithless choices, declaring that those who "have not hearkened to my voice" "shall not see the land which I sware unto their fathers," but would be consigned to wander homeless "in the wilderness forty years." But His believing and faithful servants, who "had another spirit" and chose to follow the Lord "fully," He promised to "bring into the [promised] land" and that their "seed shall possess it" (Numbers 14:22–24, 33).

Imagine Moses's feelings when he learned that his "mission" was being extended not by months but decades. The Lord called him to bear for about forty more years[51] the burden of a people who had witnessed so many miracles that they "began to be," like the Nephites, "less and less astonished at a sign or a wonder from heaven, insomuch that they began to be hard in their hearts, and blind in their minds, and began to disbelieve all which they had heard and seen" (3 Nephi 2:1). During the ensuing decades Moses, notwithstanding the later loss of his older siblings, Miriam[52] and Aaron,[53] continued to provide miraculous leadership.

The Brazen Serpent, a Type of Christ

Later, the children of Israel were again "much discouraged because of the way." Rather than pray to the Lord for strength, they *"spake against God, and against Moses."* "Wherefore," they lamented, "have ye brought us up out of Egypt to die in the wilderness? for there is no bread, neither is there any water; and our soul loatheth this light bread." The Lord responded by sending "fiery serpents among the people, and they bit the people; and much people of Israel died." Thus chastened, "the people came to Moses, and said, We have sinned, for we have spoken against the Lord, and against thee; pray unto the Lord, that he take away the serpents from us. And Moses prayed for the people. And the Lord said unto Moses, Make thee a fiery serpent, and set it upon a pole: and it shall come to pass, that every one that is bitten, when he looketh upon it, shall live. And Moses made a serpent of brass, and put it upon a pole, and it came to pass, that *if a serpent had bitten any man, when he beheld the serpent of brass, he lived"* (Numbers 21:4–9).

Book of Mormon prophets who had the record of Moses in the brass plates drew lessons from this experience that apparently escaped the children of Israel. Alma declared that Moses taught of Christ and raised up "a type," or symbol, of Christ "that whosoever would look upon it might live." Some looked and lived, but many did not because they had no faith in Jesus Christ—"they did not believe that it would heal them" (Alma 33:19–20). "Few understood the meaning of those things" "because of the hardness of their hearts," just as they failed or refused to understand and accept the fulness of the gospel centering in Jehovah, the premortal Christ. The brazen serpent given to heal Israel from the venomous snake bites in the wilderness, which caused "fever, violent inflammation and thirst,"[54] is a type or metaphor for the healing power of Christ's Atonement. Jesus explained to Nicodemus, "As Moses lifted up the serpent in the wilderness, even so must the Son of man be lifted up: That whosoever believeth in him should not perish, but have eternal life" (John 3:14–15).

Moses Is Translated

After defeating the kingdoms encompassing all of the land east of Jordan and five kings of the Midianites, Israel had achieved its first permanent conquest, a vast territory that became the inheritance of the tribes of Reuben and Gad and half of the tribe of Manasseh. Moses finally was leading the hosts of Israel to cleanse the land promised to Abraham, Isaac, and Jacob.

In an exchange that illustrates the intimate relationship that Moses had developed with his Lord and Master, Jehovah, Moses then "besought the Lord," asking Him if the Lord would let him "go over, and see the good land that is beyond Jordan, that goodly mountain, and Lebanon." In other words, to continue to lead the people in their ultimate conquest of all of the land promised to Israel. But this was never Moses's calling, and he knew it. Moses recounted that "the Lord was wroth with me *for your sakes*, and would not hear me:[55] and the Lord said unto me, Let it suffice thee; speak no more unto me of this matter" (Deuteronomy 3:23–26), as if to suggest that Moses was so beloved of the Lord that He was loath to deny His servant all that he righteously desired. And surely Moses's desire to continue to lead and nurture his people was the fruit of a deep love borne of his tireless service and ministry to them over so many years.[56]

What the Lord did grant to Moses, however, was no small gift. "Get thee up into this mount Abarim, and see the land which I have given unto the children of Israel," He told Moses, "and when thou hast seen it, *thou also shalt be gathered unto thy people,* as Aaron thy brother was gathered" (Numbers 27:12–13). In other words, the Lord let him know that his ministry would soon end. But first, the Lord commanded Moses to take Joshua, "a man in whom is the spirit, and lay thine hand upon him; And set him before Eleazar the priest, and before all the congregation; and give him a charge in their sight. And thou shalt put some of thine honour upon him, that all the congregation of the children of Israel may be obedient" (Numbers 27:19–20, 22–23). Leaders are called, in part, to help us be obedient so that we might thereby qualify for the Lord's promises.

After ordaining Joshua, Moses finished the records of all the principles, laws, and commandments the Lord had given His people through him, as set forth in the first five books of the Bible, and gave the people his final blessing and charge,[57] the blessings and the cursings that would follow their choice to follow, or not follow, their Lord and Savior (see Deuteronomy 4–6, 28–29). In addition, he prophesied of both the scattering and eventual gathering of Israel in the last days, the keys of which the Lord had entrusted to him. The record then states that "Moses the servant of the Lord died there in the land of Moab, according to the word of the Lord. And *he* buried him in a valley in the land of Moab, over against Beth-peor: but no man knoweth of his sepulchre unto this day." Josephus describes that Moses "dismissed the elders, and then, as he was embracing [his son] Eleazer and Joshua, and still speaking to them, a cloud suddenly stood over him and he vanished in a deep valley."[58] Thus, Moses was translated when he was 120 years old so he could later return to confer upon Peter, James, and John the keys of the gathering of Israel in the meridian of time.[59] "His eye was not dim, nor his natural force abated" (Deuteronomy 34:1, 4–7). Joshua offered this inspired summary of the mission and ministry of this great prophet: "And there arose not a prophet since in Israel like unto Moses, whom the Lord knew face to face, In all the signs and the wonders, which the Lord sent him to do in the land of Egypt to Pharaoh, and to all his servants, and to all his land, And in all that mighty hand, and in all the great terror [footnote 12b: or awesome acts] which Moses shewed in the sight of all Israel" (Deuteronomy 34:10–12).

What is the overarching lesson that we can learn from a study of Moses's life and ministry? The Lord declared that "the redemption of Zion" in our day "must needs come by power." To accomplish this, He promised to "raise up unto my people a man, who shall lead [us] like as Moses led the children of Israel" (Doctrine and Covenants 103:15–16). That man, He declared, was and always will be His living prophet, beginning with Joseph Smith (see Doctrine and Covenants 103:21) and continuing (at the time this study was written) with President Russell M. Nelson and each of his duly ordained successors. Why? Because, the Lord declared, "Ye are the children of Israel, and of the seed of Abraham, and ye must needs be led out of bondage by power, and with a stretched-out arm. And as your fathers were led at the first, even so shall the redemption of Zion be" (Doctrine and Covenants 103:17–18). As we seek with all our hearts to gather Israel on "both sides of the veil," we will be led and directed by the power of God's Holy Spirit. In the process, we come to know the Lord. As the Lord declared, "I say *not* unto you as I said unto your fathers: Mine angel shall go up before you, but not my presence. But I say unto you: Mine angels shall go up before you, *and also my presence*, and in time ye shall possess the goodly land" (Doctrine and Covenants 103:19–21). With the Lord's help, we will accomplish all that is needful prior to His return. Indeed, as Moses knew and experienced repeatedly, through the ordinances of the temple we are promised the "power of godliness" and, ultimately in the Lord's own time and way, that we will "behold the face of God" (Doctrine and Covenants 84:20–21, 23)

Endnotes

1. Nelson, "Focus on the Temple," 121.
2. Exodus 6:16–20.
3. Exodus 2:1.
4. See JST, Genesis 50:24, 29, 34–35 ("The Lord God will raise up . . . unto thee, whom my father Jacob hath named Israel, a prophet; [not the Messiah who is called Shilo;] and this prophet shall deliver my people out of Egypt in the days of thy bondage"; "for a seer will I raise up to deliver my people out of the land of Egypt; and he shall be called Moses"; "I will raise up Moses, and a rod shall be in his hand, and he shall gather together my people, and he shall lead them as a flock, and he shall smite the waters of the Red Sea with his rod. And he shall have judgment, and shall write the word of the Lord. And he shall not speak many words, for I will write unto him my law by the finger of mine own hand. And I will make a spokesman for him, and his name shall be called Aaron"); 2 Nephi 3:10–17.
5. W. Cleon Skousen, *The Third Thousand Years* (Salt Lake City, Utah: Bookcraft, 1964), 161.
6. Acts 7:20.
7. Skousen, *Third Thousand Years*, 161–62. For a discussion of a wife's or matriarch's right under the patriarchal priesthood (which was the "manner of government" established in Egypt by Pharoah, the grandson of Ham [Abraham 1:25]) to identify the birthright son or heir to the throne, see appendix 2 below, note 4.
8. *The Prince of Egypt*, 1998, by DreamWorks animation division, a subsidiary of Universal Pictures.
9. Skousen, *Third Thousand Years*, 161, citing Josephus, Antiquities of the Jews, II:9:7.
10. Skousen, *Third Thousand Years*, 149, 162–65, 167–68. Note, in particular, in Skousen's account how the Lord prospered Moses, whose possible ascendancy to Egypt's throne was opposed by Egypt's priests because Moses was a Hebrew. These priests hoped that in proposing that Moses lead their armies against Egypt's enemies, the Ethiopians, who threatened to conquer Egypt, that Moses would be killed in battle. However, the Ethiopian king's daughter "fell deeply in love" with Moses as she watched him lead Egypt's army in the siege of Ethiopia's capital city and proposed a "duty marriage." By accepting her proposal, Moses ended the war, saving countless lives and bringing peace to the two kingdoms. While it is impossible to know for sure, the fact that Moses gave "thanks to God" for such a fortuitous end to this war, according to Josephus, suggests that the Lord had saved and watched over him not only at birth but throughout his life—as He does with all of His covenant children. Note also that this is the "Ethiopian woman" against whom Miriam and Aaron, Moses's brother and sister, railed in Numbers 12:11 (for which disloyalty to the Lord's anointed they were soundly punished).
11. In answer to the question "why did Moses slay an Egyptian?" in the *Old Testament Student Manual Genesis–2 Samuel*, the Church manual notes:

"'Smote' and 'slew' in King James English [from Exodus 2:11] are both translated from Hebrew *nakhah*, meaning 'to beat down'; it is the word used in describing the action taken by soldiers in combat against each other. It would be correct to say that Moses slew a man who was slaying another, or took a life in saving a life. His looking 'this way and that' before doing so, simply indicates that he was aware that the Egyptians would not condone his defense of a slave. [Rasmussen, *Introduction to the Old Testament*, 1:74.]"

"However, the historian Eusebius says that the slaying was the result of a court intrigue in which certain men plotted to assassinate Moses. In the encounter it is said that Moses successfully warded off the attacker and killed him. (Eusebius IX:27.) In the Midrash Rabbah, the traditional Jewish commentary on the Old Testament, it is asserted that Moses, with his bare fists, killed an Egyptian taskmaster who was in the act of seducing a Hebrew woman. This is confirmed in the Koran. Certainly, there must have been good reason for Moses' act, and most assuredly the Lord would not have called a murderer to the high office of prophet and liberator for his people Israel. [Petersen, *Moses*, 42.]" https://www.churchofjesuschrist.org/study/manual/old-testament-student-manual-genesis-2–samuel/exodus-1–10–let-my-people-go?lang=eng.

12. Skousen, *Third Thousand Years*, 168. Jethro received the Melchizedek Priesthood from Caleb, who was the great-, great-grandson of Esaias, who received the Melchizedek Priesthood "under the hand of God" and who "lived in the days of Abraham, and was blessed of him" (Doctrine and Covenants 84:7–14).

13. Exodus 7:7; Acts 7:23,30. See "Moses 1:1–11: God Revealed Himself to Moses," *The Pearl of Great Price Student Manual*, https://www.churchofjesuschrist.org/study/manual/the-pearl-of-great-price-student-manual-2018/the-book-of-moses/moses-1–1–11?lang=eng.

14. Compare JST, Exodus 6:3, which states, "I am the Lord God Almighty; the Lord JEHOVAH. Regarding Christ's declaration of His messiahship to the Jewish leaders in John 8:52–53, 56–59, in which He said, "Verily, verily, I say unto you, Before Abraham was, I am," Bruce R. McConkie states, "This is as blunt and pointed an affirmation of divinity as any person has or could make. 'Before Abraham was I Jehovah.' That is, 'I am God Almighty, the Great I AM. I am the self-existent, Eternal One. I am the God of your fathers. My name is: I AM THAT I AM'" ("Lesson 5: Jesus Christ Was Jehovah of the Old Testament," *Jesus Christ and the Everlasting Gospel Teacher Manual*, https://www.churchofjesuschrist.org/study/manual/jesus-christ-and-the-everlasting-gospel-teacher-manual/lesson-5–jesus-christ-was-jehovah-of-the-old-testament?lang=eng, quoting Bruce R. McConkie, *Doctrinal New Testament Commentary*, 3 vols. [Salt Lake City, Utah: Bookcraft, 1965–74], 1:464).

15. Exodus 4:13. See Skousen, *Third Thousand Years*, 175.

16. Aaron was three years older than Moses. See Exodus 7:7.

17. Enroute to Egypt, "in the way, by [an] inn," the Lord appears to Moses, angry because he had neglected the rite of circumcision as required by the

Abrahamic covenant for his sons, Gershom and Eliezer. Zipporah, realizing that perhaps her sons' lives are at stake, "took a sharp stone and circumcised her son" (JST, Exodus 4:25–26). Moses, naturally, is ashamed of his failure to obey the Lord's commandments, learning by experience, as we all do, from the things that he suffered. According to Bible commentators, Moses then determined that it was better to send Zipporah and the boys back to their grandfather, Jethro, while he proceeds to Egypt with Aaron. Skousen, *Third Thousand Years*, 184–85, quoting Clark's Bible Commentary, 1:34. According to Bruce Porter, Zipporah's action to ensure that her sons received the blessings of the ordinances required by the Lord is an example of her matriarchal authority and responsibility under the patriarchal priesthood. See appendix 2 below, note 4.

18. "Moses 1:1–11: God Revealed Himself to Moses," *The Pearl of Great Price Student Manual,* citing Moses 1:17, 25–26.
19. Moses 6:36; 7:21–23, 41–45, 47, 50–67.
20. Ether 3:25.
21. This may be one of the most oft-cited scriptures in all of the standard works, as evidenced by the many general conference speakers who cite it as summarized in the Scripture Citation Index, https://scriptures.byu.edu/#:t2102$136497:c1910139.
22. For a discussion of the factors that influence our ability to understand Moses's intent in his recounting of the revelation the Lord gave him about the creation of the earth and Adam and Eve, as they have come to us in the various translations of the Bible, see generally Melinda Wheelwright Brown, *Eve and Adam: Discovering the Beautiful Balance* (Salt Lake City, Utah: Deseret Book, 2020), 11–14.
23. According to the Prophet Joseph Smith, "Every man who has a calling to minister to the inhabitants of the world was ordained to that very purpose in the Grand Council of heaven before this world was. I suppose that I was ordained to this very office in that Grand Council" ("Chapter 26: Alma 13–16," *Book of Mormon Student Manual,* https://abn.churchofjesuschrist.org/study/manual/book-of-mormon-student-manual/chapter-26-alma-13-16?lang=eng, citing *History of the Church,* 6:364). Likewise, as President Kimball has taught, "In the world before we came here, faithful women were given certain assignments while faithful men were foreordained to certain priesthood tasks. While we do not now remember the particulars, this does not alter the glorious reality of what we once agreed to. You are accountable for those things which long ago were expected of you just as are those we sustain as prophets and apostles!" (Ibid., citing "The Role of Righteous Women," *Ensign,* November 1979, 102).
24. Skousen, *Third Thousand Years,* 196.
25. Howard W. Hunter, "Christ, Our Passover," *Ensign,* May 1985, 17, citing Alma 34:10 ("For it is expedient that there should be a great and last sacrifice; yea, not a sacrifice of man, neither of beast, neither of any manner of fowl; for it shall not be a human sacrifice; but it must be an infinite and eternal sacrifice").

26. See, for example, "Numbers 1–12 and Enrichment Section E: The Problem of Large Numbers in the Old Testament," *Old Testament Student Manual Genesis–2 Samuel*, https://www.churchofjesuschrist.org/study/manual/old-testament-student-manual-genesis-2-samuel/numbers-1-12–wilderness-wanderings-part-1?lang=eng. See also Jeffrey M. Bradshaw, "An Old Testament KnoWhy—Gospel Doctrine Lesson 13: Bondage, Passover, and Exodus (Exodus 1–3; 5–6; 11–14)," The Interpreter Foundation, April 4, 2018, https://interpreterfoundation.org/knowhy-otl13b-what-can-we-learn-about-the-historical-exodus-from-outside-the-scriptures/.
27. Compare Exodus 13:4 and Numbers 33:3 with Exodus 19:1. Skousen, *Third Thousand Years*, 210, 231.
28. Repeated references to "priests" prior to the establishment of the Aaronic or Levitical Priesthood among the Israelites suggests that there were other Melchizedek Priesthood holders among the tribes of Israel, although we do not know how worthy or active they were in magnifying their priesthood office of high priest. See, for example, Exodus 19:22, 24; Skousen, *Third Thousand Years*, 220. These pre-Levitical Priesthood references to "priests" by Moses in the Old Testament are similar to references to "priests" given by Book of Mormon prophets. "They were priests of the Melchizedek Priesthood, or as Alma expressed it, 'the Lord God ordained priests, after his holy order, which was after the order of his Son.' (Alma 13:1–20)" (Bruce R. McConkie, *Mormon Doctrine*, 2nd ed., 1966, 599).
29. 1 Corinthians 10:1–4; Hebrews 3:16; 4:2; see Skousen, *Third Thousand Years*, 218–20. Compare Doctrine and Covenants 84:19 and 84:23.
30. Skousen, *Third Thousand Years*, 232–34.
31. "The phrase 'peculiar treasure' was translated from the Hebrew *segullah*, meaning 'highly valued possession—a treasure'" (Nelson, *Heart of the Matter*, 40).
32. "Exodus 11–19: The Passover and the Exodus," *Old Testament Student Manual Genesis–2 Samuel*, quoting Rasmussen, Introduction to the Old Testament, 1:83.
33. Ibid.
34. Mark E. Peterson, *Moses: Man of Miracles* (Salt Lake City: Deseret Book, 1977), 110.
35. The laws outlined in Exodus 21–23 "were the laws for governing the nation," constituting the civil law of the land, albeit received as the divine law of God. "These [laws] do not constitute the 'law of Moses' which was 'added because of transgression' (Gal. 3:19)' and then taken away at the time of Christ. Paul makes it clear that the laws which were 'added' after Israel's apostasy were the dietary laws and the strict religious rites." Skousen, *Third Thousand Years*, 238. Note, however, that the *Old Testament Student Manual* refers to the "whole series of laws and commandments" outlined in these chapters as "the Mosaic law" ("Exodus 21–24; 31–35: The Mosaic Law: A Preparatory Gospel," *Old Testament Student Manual Genesis–2 Samuel*, 137).
36. "Exodus 25–30; 35–40: The House of the Lord in the Wilderness," *Old Testament Student Manual: Genesis–2 Samuel*, 147.

37. Ibid. Similarly the Lord reveals a "pattern" for the building and financing of Latter-day temples. For example, the Lord commanded the Prophet Joseph Smith to build the Kirtland Temple "after the manner which I shall show unto three of you, whom ye shall appoint and ordain unto this power" (Doctrine and Covenants 95:14). See Anderson, *The Savior in Kirtland* (describing how, after calling upon the Lord, "the Building," or a vision of the Kirtland Temple, "appeared within viewing distance. . . . After we had taken a good look at the exterior, the Building seemed to come right over us, and the Makeup of this Hall seemed to coincide with what I there saw to a minutia" (quoting "Truman Angell Autobiography," in *Our Pioneer Heritage*, comp. Kate B. Carter, 20 vols. [Salt Lake City: Daughters of Utah Pioneers, 1958–77]). See also Doctrine and Covenants 97:8–12 (temple to "be built unto me in the land of Zion" in Jackson County, Missouri according to "the pattern which I have given you" and to be financed by the "sacrifice" and "tithing of my people").

38. In the January 1972 *Ensign* devoted entirely to the subject of temples, Dr. Sidney B. Sperry, Professor of Old Testament Languages and Literature at Brigham Young University, wrote: "We do not know the extent to which ordinances pertaining to the Melchizedek Priesthood were performed in the tabernacle while in the wilderness and in Palestine up to the time of the building of Solomon's Temple, but that such ordinances were performed seems certain in the light of such statements as this: 'David's wives and concubines were given unto him of me, by the hand of Nathan, my servant, and others of the prophets who had the keys of this power. . . .' (Doctrine and Covenants 132:39.) It seems more reasonable to believe that Nathan and the other prophets would seal David's wives and concubines to him in a holy place such as the tabernacle than in any other structure." As the Lord revealed to the Prophet Joseph Smith, "in all ages of the world, whenever the Lord has given a dispensation of the priesthood to any man by actual revelation, or any set of men, this [sealing] power has always been given" (Doctrine and Covenants 128:9). "Just how endowment ceremonies [for the living] were arranged for in the tabernacle," Brother Sperry adds, "we can only conjecture. But within the Holy of Holies, where the ark of the covenant was located, the Lord made provision to commune with the leaders of his people" (Sidney B. Sperry, "Ancient Temples and Their Functions," *Ensign*, January 1972; see also Richard O. Cowan, *Temples Dot the Earth* [Cove Fort, 1997], 11–13).

39. "Exodus 25–30; 31:1–11; 35–40," *Old Testament Instructor's Guide, Religion 301–2* (Salt Lake City, Utah: Church Educational System The Church of Jesus Christ of Latter-day Saints, 1982, https://www.churchofjesuschrist.org/study/manual/old-testament-instructors-guide/exodus-25–30–31–1–11–35–40?lang=eng).

40. Note that the stone tablets engraven by the finger of God "were written on both sides" (Exodus 32:15).

41. Skousen, *Third Thousand Years*, 258.

42. See Skousen, *Third Thousand Years*, 262–63. The Lord, in response to Moses's pleading, assures His prophet that "my presence shall go with *thee*, and I will give *thee* rest" (Exodus 33:14), suggesting that Moses retained the ultimate

blessings of the covenant, to enter into the rest or presence of the Lord, which the people generally forfeited.
43. Skousen, *Third Thousand Years*, 265.
44. During his valedictory address to the children of Israel near the end of his ministry, Moses recounted how the Lord revealed that He would write on the second tables of stone "the words that were on the first tables, which thou brakest, save the words of the everlasting covenant of the holy priesthood, and thou shalt put them in the ark" (JST, Deuteronomy 10:2).
45. Skousen, *Third Thousand Years*, 272.
46. Ibid., 303.
47. Numbers 12:3 ("Now the man Moses was very meek, above all the men which were upon the face of the earth").
48. Jacob 5:72 ("And it came to pass that the servants did go and labor with their mights; and the Lord of the vineyard labored also with them").
49. See Deuteronomy 7:1–6; Skousen, *Third Thousand Years*, 340–41.
50. Oxford Languages defines "miracle" as "a surprising and welcome event that is not explicable by natural or scientific laws and is therefore considered to be the work of a divine agency." https://www.google.com/search?q=miracle+definition&rlz=1C1CHBF_enUS873US873&oq=miracle+definition&aqs=chrome..69i57j0i512l9.5720j1j15&sourceid=chrome&ie=UTF-8. The Guide to the Scriptures describes a "sign" as "an event or experience that people understand to be evidence or proof of something. A sign is usually a *miraculous manifestation* from God" (emphasis added). The Bible Dictionary reminds us that members of the Church "should seek for the gifts of the Spirit but should not seek for signs to satisfy curiosity or sustain faith. Rather, the Lord will give signs as He sees fit to those who believe (Doctrine and Covenants 58:64)." However, in my experience, the Lord often answers our prayers in such an obvious way that the answer becomes a personal sign for us. This especially can be the case for youth and even young children when they are beginning to nurture their testimonies, for example, asking God to help them find something that is lost and then praying again after an unsuccessful exhaustive search and finding it, perhaps in unexpected ways. God has used such faith-promoting signs to strengthen faith in His leaders from the beginning. See, for example, "Sign," International Standard Bible Dictionary, https://www.biblestudytools.com/encyclopedias/isbe/sign.html (citing the signs the Lord showed Moses, including the burning bush, the rod turning into a serpent, the leprous hand, etc.; to Gideon and the fleece of wool (Judges 6:36–40); signs Jesus did in training the Twelve, eg. Luke 5:1–11 and John 20:30 ("Jesus performed many other signs in the presence of his disciples, which are not recorded in this book"); and "the visions by which Peter and Paul were led to the evangelization of the Gentiles were interpreted by them as signs of the divine purpose").

When President Nelson promises "that the Lord will bring the miracles He knows you need as you make sacrifices to serve and worship in His temples," he often does so in the context of admonitions to "act in faith" (Nelson, "Becoming Exemplary Latter-day Saints.") For example, in his April 2021 general conference message, he reminded us that Christ "took upon himself" our individual "misery, [our] mistakes, [our] weakness, and [our] sins. He paid the compensatory price and provided the power for you to move every mountain you will ever face. You obtain that power with your faith, trust, and willingness to follow Him." He then suggested that overcoming our "mountains" of misery, mistakes and weaknesses "may require a miracle. Learn about miracles. Miracles come according to your faith in the Lord. Central to that faith is trusting His will and timetable—how and when He will bless you with the miraculous help you desire. Only your unbelief will keep God from blessing you with miracles to move the mountains in your life" (Nelson, "Christ Is Risen; Faith in Him Will Move Mountains").

51. Skousen notes that "up to this time, the Israelites had been in the desert only a little over a year. This sentence from the Lord therefore meant that they were condemned to wander another 38 ½ years." Notably, as happened with those who had worshipped the golden calf, the ten spies who were responsible for the "insidious spirit of insurrection" that cursed Israel "died by the plague before the Lord" (Numbers 14:37). Skousen, *Third Thousand Years*, 321.
52. Numbers 20:1.
53. Numbers 20:25–26. Indeed, the Lord told Moses and Aaron when they arrived at Mount Hor to ascend the mountain with Eleazar, where Moses was commanded to "strip Aaron of his garments, and put them upon Eleazer his son: and Aaron shall be gathered unto his people, and shall die there."
54. Skousen, *Third Thousand Years*, 345.
55. Here Moses may have been referring to the miracle of the water from the rock at Meribah, when again "there was no water for the congregation" and the people complained to Moses. Moses and Aaron went to the Lord, who instructed Moses to "take the rod, and gather thou the assembly together . . . and *speak ye unto the rock* before their eyes; and it shall give forth his water . . . out of the rock" (Numbers 20:2–4, 6–8). Rather than "speak" to the rock, as the Lord commanded, Moses, shouting in exasperation to his ever-complaining and faithless people ("hear now, ye rebels; must *we* fetch you water out of this rock") "smote the rock twice" with his rod. Then, the record notes, "water came out abundantly, and the congregation drank, and their beasts also" (Numbers 20:10–11). In effect, Moses failed to credit or "sanctify [the Lord] in the eyes of the children of Israel," suggesting that he had power, rather than acting, as all priesthood bearers must, in the name of Jesus Christ, or Jehovah. "Therefore," the Lord declared, "ye shall not bring this congregation unto the land which I have given them" (Numbers 20:11–12). Priesthood holders must always remember that their most important role is to point the people to the Lord, not themselves. As Jesus taught His Nephite disciples, "I am the light which ye shall hold up" (3 Nephi 18:24).

However, as the *Old Testament Student Manual* suggests, the statement that the Lord was "wroth" with Moses and would not allow him to lead Israel into the promised land "for your," that is Israel's, sake could also "imply that there were reasons other than the error of Moses for the prohibition. Two other facts strengthen this supposition. First, both Moses and the higher priesthood were taken from Israel because of the people's unworthiness, not Moses' (see

Doctrine and Covenants 84:23–25). Second, Moses was translated when his mortal ministry was finished (see Alma 45:19). In other words, Moses was privileged to enter a land of promise far greater than the land of Canaan. He had finished his calling in mortality, and a new leader was to take Israel into the promised land. And, Moses was translated—hardly a punishment for sinning against God" ("Numbers 13–36: Wilderness Wanderings, Part 2," *Old Testament Student Manual Genesis–2 Samuel*, https://www.churchofjesuschrist.org/study/manual/old-testament-student-manual-genesis-2-samuel/numbers-13-36-wilderness-wanderings-part-2?lang=eng).

56. Elder Bruce R. McConkie urged that we "not lose sight of the high and exalted place of Moses in the divine program. He ranks with Adam and Enoch; he has the spiritual stature of Noah and Abraham; and he stands with Melchizedek and Moriancumer in faith and devotion" (*The Mortal Messiah: From Bethlehem to Calvary*, Book 1 (Salt Lake City: Deseret Book, 1981), 81, note 1.

57. See Deuteronomy 33, which sets forth the Lord's blessing on each of the tribes of Israel, including Joseph, from whom many members of the Church are descended and of whom the Lord said: "And of Joseph he said, Blessed of the Lord be his land . . . let the blessing come upon the head of Joseph, and upon the top of the head of him that was separated from his brethren. His glory is like the firstling of his bullock, and his horns are like the horns of unicorns [fn. 17b: Heb the wild ox]: with them he shall push the people together to the ends of the earth [fn. 17c cites Doctrine and Covenants 58:44–45, which refers to the gathering of Israel]: and they are the ten thousands of Ephraim, and they are the thousands of Manasseh" (Deuteronomy 33:13, 16–17).

58. Skousen, *Third Thousand Years*, 381, citing Josephus, Antiquities of the Jews, IV:8:48. President Joseph Fielding Smith explained that both Moses and Elijah "had to have tangible bodies" when they conferred their keys upon Peter, James and John, "who stood at the head of the dispensation of the meridian of time." "For that reason Moses disappeared from among the people and was taken up into the mountain, and the people thought he was buried by the Lord" (Joseph Fielding Smith, *Doctrines of Salvation*, 2:110–11). In our dispensation, the Lord revealed that Moses and other of the ancient prophets, including Elijah, "were with Christ in his resurrection" (Doctrine and Covenants 133:55), meaning that they were resurrected at the time of Christ's resurrection. Thus, when they appeared to Joseph Smith and Oliver Cowdery in the Kirtland Temple, they appeared as resurrected beings.

59. Book of Mormon writers apparently had access to information in the brass plates that clarified this point, since Helaman, describing Alma's disappearance, explains that he "was taken up by the Spirit, or buried by the hand of the Lord, even as Moses. But behold, the scriptures saith the Lord took Moses unto himself; and we suppose that he has also received Alma in the spirit, unto himself; therefore, for this cause we know nothing concerning his death and burial" (Alma 45:19).

CHAPTER 7

The Spiritual Treasure of Sacrifice or Daily Repentance

"Experience the strengthening power of daily repentance—of doing and being a little better each day. When we choose to repent, we choose to change! We allow the Savior to transform us into the best version of ourselves. We choose to grow spiritually and receive joy—the joy of redemption in Him. When we choose to repent, we choose to become more like Jesus Christ."[1]

—Russell M. Nelson

Sacrifices in the First Temple

Mosiah 13:29–30—And now I say unto you that it was expedient that there should be a law given to the children of Israel, yea, even a very strict law; for they were a stiffnecked people, quick to do iniquity, and slow to remember the Lord their God; Therefore there was a law given them, yea, a law of performances and of ordinances, a law which they were to observe strictly from day to day, to keep them in remembrance of God and their duty towards him.

One of the greatest lessons from Moses's life and ministry to the children of Israel is that God always meets us where we are. According to the *Old Testament Student Manual*, when God sent Moses to free the enslaved Israelites, they were "in poor spiritual condition," "steeped" for centuries "in Egyptian tradition and idol worship." Notwithstanding repeated pleas from God to abandon "their abominations and idols," they were simply unwilling or unable to do so (Ezekiel 20:6–8). Thus, the Lord "blessed them with a law suited to help them grow spiritually, starting from where they were. . . . It was a far greater challenge to get Egypt out of Israel than it was to get Israel out of Egypt." Viewed from the standpoint of the reality of their spiritual condition, then, the law of Moses was not a "step backward" but "a great step forward"; "not as great as Israel could have taken, but a great step nevertheless."[2] To assist them in the process of their spiritual growth and conversion, Father in Heaven devised a system of "principles, rules, ceremonies, rituals, and symbols to remind the people of their duties and responsibilities" to God.[3] Likewise, the laws or covenants of the temple and the gospel generally are designed to bring about our spiritual growth and conversion. As we apply the universal principles included in the law of sacrifice, we find increased power to keep all of our other covenants with God, through which we attain our desires of everlasting life with Him.

Appendix 1 summarizes the names, emblematic objects used, purposes, and times of administration for each of the sacrifices and offerings required under the law of Moses, which included burnt offerings; sin offerings; trespass offerings; meal or meat offerings; and heave offerings (a separated portion of an animal sacrifice, which was ceremonially raised and lowered in dedication to God and was afterward reserved for use by the priests). In addition to the sacrifices and other performances established by the law of Moses, which were administered by the Priesthood of Aaron (see Doctrine and Covenants 107:13), the law was based upon and helped the spiritually perceptive understand and live the first principles and ordinances of the gospel. For example, though the principle of faith is "never referred to directly" among the long lists of carnal commandments in the book of Leviticus, the principle of faith "is implied since faith is absolutely necessary in all acts" and ordinances administered by the lesser priesthood. Moreover, Book of Mormon prophets, such as Amulek, who lived and administered the ordinances required under the law of Moses, "clearly taught that faith was a prerequisite to the law bringing one to repentance" (see Alma 34:15). Similarly, the "sacrificial systems of Israel were expressly designed to help" the people live the principle of repentance by pointing Israel to the "atoning sacrifice of Christ." As witnessed among the descendants of Lehi, but no doubt faithful Israelites in the Old World also experienced, as individuals exercised faith in Christ and repented, "their sins were remitted, not by the law of Moses but through their faith in the future Messiah, which was demonstrated by their obedience to the law of Moses" (see Mosiah 13:28). Finally, while references to the ordinance of "baptism in the Old Testament have been lost, from other sources we learn that it was part of the Mosaic law (see 1 Corinthians 10:1–4; 1 Nephi 20:1; Doctrine and Covenants 84:26–27)."[4] Thus, as faithful prophets and priests taught these first principles and administered the ordinances of the Mosaic law,[5] the law served as a "schoolmaster" to bring the children of Israel to Christ (Galatians 3:24), preparatory, in the fulness of God's time, to their receiving the ordinances of the Melchizedek Priesthood, even the ordinances of exaltation.

The Mosaic Law's Dietary Restrictions and the Word of Wisdom

In addition to various sacrifices, the Mosaic law contained strict rules about food that was "clean" and should be eaten and food that was "unclean" and should be avoided. For example, Israelites could eat beasts that "parteth the hoof, and is clovenfooted, and cheweth the cud," except for camels, hares, and swine. Fish that had "fins and scales" (Leviticus 11:3–4, 9–10) were clean, but those without were unclean, and so forth. Likewise, in our day the Lord has counseled that wine or "strong drink" are "not good, neither meet in the sight of your Father." In addition, "tobacco . . . is not good for man" and "hot drinks are not for the body" (Doctrine and Covenants 89:4–5, 9).

In Daniel 1 we learn how the faithfulness of Daniel and his three Jewish friends—Hananiah, Mishael, and Azariah—to the dietary codes of the Mosaic law brought them not only "into favour and tender love with the prince of the eunuchs" (Daniel 1:9), who was charged with preparing them for service in the court of King Nebuchadnezzar, but ultimately brought them spiritual treasures from God of "knowledge and skill in all learning and wisdom" (Daniel 1:17). "And in all matters of wisdom and understanding, that the king enquired of them, he found them ten times better than all the magicians and astrologers that were in all his realm" (Daniel 1:20). The *Old Testament Seminary Teacher Manual* points out that while there may have been "some practical health reasons" for the strict dietary code from Leviticus 11 that Daniel and his friends appeared to follow so faithfully," more importantly, "this part of the law of Moses was given as an outward, physical sign that conveyed spiritual truths."[6] By voluntarily abstaining from certain foods or by cooking them in a special way, obedient Israelites made a daily, personal commitment to their faith, choices that generated "quiet self-discipline," promoted "personal identity" with God's covenant people, setting them apart from "the world," and kept them "in remembrance of Jehovah."[7] Likewise, the important dietary restrictions and counsel contained in the Word of Wisdom, which we are asked to obey to qualify for a temple recommend, not only protect against "actual health dangers and [give] nutritional counsel" but serve "as a symbolic reminder of our covenant status, [set] us apart from much of the world, and [are] a test of our obedience."[8]

Exactly what does it mean to "obey" the Word of Wisdom? The *General Handbook* gives this explanation: "Prophets have clarified that the teachings in Doctrine and Covenants 89 include abstinence from tobacco, strong drinks (alcohol), and hot drinks (tea and coffee). Prophets have also taught members to avoid substances that are harmful, illegal, or addictive or that impair judgment." Finally, the *Handbook* notes, "There are other harmful substances and practices that are not specified in the Word of Wisdom or by Church leaders. Members should use wisdom and prayerful judgment in making choices to promote their physical, spiritual, and emotional health" (38.7.14). How grateful we should be for prophets who not only teach us correct principles—reminding us, as President Nelson has done, that our bodies are temples (John 2:19; 1 Corinthians 3:16–17) and that as we treat them as such, we will be less inclined to "overeating," undue "physical indulgence of any kind," and "more self-discipline"— but show us what that looks like.[9]

Sacrifice and the Ancient Law of Tithing

The *General Handbook* describes the two main principles or elements that are included in the law of sacrifice: first, "repenting with a broken heart and contrite spirit," which is discussed in the next section, and, second, "sacrificing to support the Lord's work" (27.2). The principal financial sacrifice the Lord has asked of us to qualify for temple blessings is to live the law of tithing.

> **Malachi 3:8–10**—Will a man rob God? Yet ye have robbed me. But ye say, Wherein have we robbed thee? In tithes and offerings. Ye are cursed with a curse: for ye have robbed me, even this whole nation. Bring ye all the tithes into the storehouse, that there may be meat in mine house, and prove me now herewith, saith the Lord of hosts, if I will not *open you the windows of heaven and pour you out a blessing, that there shall not be room enough to receive it.*

The law of tithing is ancient. Abram gave Melchizedek "tithes of all" (Genesis 14:20) or, as rendered in many translations, "a tenth of everything,"[10] as did Jacob (see Genesis 28:20–22). The Lord included it in the law given to Moses: "And all the tithe of the land, whether of the seed of the land, or of the fruit of the tree, is the Lord's: it is holy unto the Lord" (Leviticus 27:30). Indeed, "tithing is a commandment that has always been given to God's faithful followers since the creation of the earth."[11]

In this dispensation the Lord again revealed this ancient law, commanding "my people" to "pay one-tenth of all their interest annually; and this shall be a standing law unto them forever" (Doctrine and Covenants 119:3–4).[12] As described in the *General Handbook* 34.3.1, "tithing is the donation of one-tenth of one's income to God's Church (see Doctrine and Covenants 119:3–4; *interest* is understood to mean income). All members who have income should pay tithing." Tithes, the *General Handbook* observes, "are sacred. They represent the sacrifice and faith of members of the Church" (34.0).

President Oaks also expressly ties the law of tithing to the law of sacrifice, quoting the Prophet Joseph Smith's statement from the sixth Lecture on Faith, which "can be applied," he said, "not only to whatever small sacrifice we might make in paying our tithing, but also to every sacrifice we are called upon to make in keeping the commandments of God":

Let us here observe that a religion that does not require the sacrifice of all things, never has power sufficient to produce the faith necessary unto life and salvation; for from the first existence of man, the faith necessary unto the enjoyment of life and salvation never could be obtained without the sacrifice of all earthly things. . . . Those, then, who make the sacrifice, will have the testimony that *their course is pleasing in the sight of God*; and those who have this testimony will have faith to lay hold on eternal life, and will be enabled, through faith, to endure unto the end, and receive the crown that is laid up for them that love the appearing of our Lord Jesus Christ.[13]

Thus sacrifice, including tithing, is all about increasing our faith in Jesus Christ.

President Nelson taught that temple recommend requirements like being "a full-tithe payer" and "understand[ing] and obey[ing] the Word of Wisdom" are "spiritual separators."[14] As such, the specific material and spiritual blessings promised in connection with these commandments are indeed among the precious "spiritual treasures" of the temple of which President Nelson has testified. Both from my own experience and from countless testimonies of others, I know that as we qualify to enter the Lord's holy house, He does and will "open you the windows of heaven and pour you out a blessing, that there shall not be room enough to receive it." While it may seem like a sacrifice, especially for new converts when first introduced to these standards, the Lord has promised all "who remember to keep and do [the Lord's] sayings, walking in obedience to the commandments," including these temple worthiness standards, shall receive, spiritually and also temporally, "health in their navel and marrow to their bones; And shall find wisdom and great *treasures* of knowledge, even hidden *treasures*; And shall run and not be weary, and shall walk and not faint" (Doctrine and Covenants 89:18–20).

The Law of Sacrifice and Its Relationship to the Principle of Daily Repentance

What is the law of sacrifice? Anciently, as explained in the *Guide to the Scriptures*, "the law of sacrifice . . . included offering the firstborn of their flocks. This sacrifice symbolized the sacrifice that would be made by the Only Begotten Son of God (Moses 5:4–8). This practice continued until the death of Jesus Christ, which ended animal sacrifice as a gospel ordinance (Alma 34:13–14)."

> **Moses 5:4–8**—And Adam and Eve, his wife, called upon the name of the Lord . . . and he gave unto them commandments, that they should worship the Lord their God, and should offer the firstlings of their flocks, for an offering unto the Lord. And Adam was *obedient* unto the commandments of the Lord. And after many days an angel of the Lord appeared unto Adam, saying: Why dost thou offer sacrifices unto the Lord? And Adam said unto him: I know not, save the Lord commanded me. And then the angel spake, saying: This thing is a similitude of the *sacrifice* of the Only Begotten of the Father, which is full of grace and truth. Wherefore, thou shalt do all that thou doest in the name of the Son, and thou shalt *repent* and call upon God in the name of the Son forevermore.

In obedience to the commandment of the Lord, after being driven out of the Garden of Eden, Adam and Eve "called upon the name of the Lord" and worshipped Him. Prayer is a form of worship, perhaps the most fundamental of all gospel practices.[15] "And they heard the voice of the Lord from the way toward the Garden of Eden, speaking unto them" (Moses 5:4). As fundamental as the commandment to pray is the truth that God hears and answers our prayers. As the experience of Adam and Eve teaches us, the law of obedience, which Adam and Eve so ably typify, is prerequisite to and followed by the law of sacrifice.

Like the law of obedience (and, in fact, all the laws of God), the law of sacrifice points to and strengthens our faith in Jesus Christ. Faith leads to repentance. "Repentance is an act of faith in Jesus Christ—an acknowledgment of the power of His Atonement. Remember that you can be forgiven only on His terms. As you gratefully recognize His Atonement and His power to cleanse you from sin, you are able to 'exercise your faith unto repentance' (Alma 34:17)."[16]

3 Nephi 9:19–22—And ye shall offer up unto me no more the shedding of blood; yea, your sacrifices and your burnt offerings shall be done away, for I will accept none of your sacrifices and your burnt offerings. And ye shall offer *for a sacrifice* unto me *a broken heart and a contrite spirit*. And whoso cometh unto me with a broken heart and a contrite spirit, him will I baptize with fire and with the Holy Ghost. . . . Therefore, *whoso repenteth* and cometh unto me as a little child, him will I receive, for of such is the kingdom of God. Behold, for such I have laid down my life, and have taken it up again; *therefore repent*, and come unto me ye ends of the earth, and be saved.

As the Savior taught when He appeared to the Nephites, to come to know God, the greatest offering we can place on the altar of sacrifice is our own sins.[17] Thus, while it may not always be obvious, the second principle of the gospel, repentance, is at the heart of temple doctrine and temple covenants. Elder D. Todd Christofferson describes how anciently when the children of Israel went to the temple, they often took an animal to sacrifice on the altar in the form of a "burnt offering." After His death the Savior asked us to bring a broken or "repentant" heart and a contrite or "obedient" spirit. "In reality," Elder Christofferson teaches, God is asking us to give ourselves, "what you are and what you are becoming."

"Is there something in you or in your life," he asks, "that is impure or unworthy? When you get rid of [or sacrifice] it, that is a gift to the Savior. Is there a good habit or quality that is lacking in your life? When you adopt it and make it part of your character, you are giving a gift [an offering] to the Lord. Sometimes this is hard to do, but would your gifts of repentance and obedience be worthy gifts if they cost you nothing? Don't be afraid of the effort required. And remember, you don't have to do it alone. *Jesus Christ will help you make of yourself a worthy gift.*"[18]

What Does the Temple Teach Us about the Principle of Repentance?

In the dedicatory prayer for the Kirtland Temple, Joseph Smith said, "Do thou grant, Holy Father . . . that all those who shall worship in this house . . . may *grow up* in thee" (Doctrine and Covenants 109:14–15). And "when [we] transgress" may we "speedily repent and return unto thee, and find favor in thy sight, and be restored to the blessings which thou hast ordained to be poured out upon those who shall reverence thee in thy house" (verse 21). In other words, the Lord knows that we as good-faith temple patrons will *not* be perfect but are and will continue to be in the process of "growing up" or changing.

In his message about the "power of spiritual momentum," President Russell M. Nelson encourages all to "get on the covenant path and stay there." He shares a "vivid dream" he had in which he taught a "large group of people" about the covenant path. In that dream a woman asked "how someone who has broken his or her covenants can get back on that path." His answer? "Discover the joy of daily repentance." In essence, the covenant path is the path of repentance, a path "designed to test and teach us," "refine our natures,"[19] help us "to change" and to "grow spiritually," "doing and being a little better each day." "When coupled with faith," President Nelson teaches, the process of change or "repentance opens our access to the power of the Atonement of Jesus Christ."[20] Thus, the greatest tool the Lord has given us to receive His divine help in returning to the Father is the principle of repentance. Moreover, as President Nelson explains, daily repentance leads to an improved quality of life and helps us realize the purpose of our mortal (and spiritual) creation—to "grow up" to become like our Heavenly Parents: "Nothing is more liberating, more ennobling, or more crucial to our individual progression than is a regular, daily focus on repentance. Repentance is not an event; it is a process. It is the key to happiness and peace of mind."[21]

Many of the myriad practices and rituals the Lord gave ancient Israel to keep them in remembrance of their covenant relationship with Him seem strange and foreign to us today. Lest we yield to the temptation to think that we are somehow "better" than our early Israelite brothers and sisters, however, President Nelson has reminded us that "in some respects, it is easier to build a temple than it is to build a people prepared for a temple."[22] Sometimes, perhaps even much of the time, we may rightly wonder if we are up to the task of achieving the "total conversion" President Nelson calls for, the personal holiness and spiritual maturity the children of Israel in Moses's day seemed to be unable to achieve. In this regard, then, their experience is instructive—even in their weakness, the Lord succored and carried them. Could He do any less for us in our weakness? As will become increasing clear in this study, the great lesson of the temple is that God is *"able* to make [us] holy" (Doctrine and Covenants 60:7). The temple and the ordinances administered therein are a key part of how He does this.

Endnotes

1. Nelson, "Becoming Exemplary Latter-day Saints."
2. "Leviticus 1–10: A Law of Performances and Ordinances, Part 1: Sacrifices and Offerings," *Old Testament Student Manual: Genesis–2 Samuel*, 159, https://abn.churchofjesuschrist.org/study/manual/old-testament-student-manual-genesis-2-samuel/leviticus-1-10-a-law-of-performances-and-ordinances-part-1-sacrifices-and-offerings?lang=eng.
3. "Law of Moses," Guide to the Scriptures, https://www.churchofjesuschrist.org/study/scriptures/gs/law-of-moses?lang=eng. The chapter in the *Old Testament Student Manual* referenced in note 2 above contains an illuminating discussion of various aspects of the principles, rituals, practices, and ordinances included in the law of Moses (as do other chapters therein that focus on the Mosaic law). See also McConkie, *Mortal Messiah*, Book 1, 67–82.
4. "Leviticus 1–10: A Law of Performances and Ordinances, Part 1: Sacrifices and Offerings," *Old Testament Student Manual: Genesis–2 Samuel*, 159–60, https://www.churchofjesuschrist.org/study/manual/old-testament-student-manual-genesis-2-samuel/leviticus-1-10-a-law-of-performances-and-ordinances-part-1-sacrifices-and-offerings?lang=eng.
5. Unlike baptism, which is an Aaronic Priesthood ordinance (see Doctrine and Covenants 13), confirmation is a Melchizedek Priesthood ordinance. Thus, the role of this ordinance under the Mosaic law is less obvious after Moses than, for example among the early patriarchs and Book of Mormon peoples, who had the Melchizedek Priesthood. See generally Lynne Wilton Wilson, "The Holy Spirit Creating, Anointing, and Empowering throughout the Old Testament," in *The Gospel of Jesus Christ in the Old Testament*, eds. D. Kelly Ogden, Jared W. Ludlow, and Kerry Muhlestein (Provo, Utah: BYU Religious Studies Center, 2009), https://rsc.byu.edu/gospel-jesus-christ-old-testament/holy-spirit.
6. "Leviticus 1–16," *Old Testament Teacher Resource Manual*, 90, https://www.churchofjesuschrist.org/study/manual/old-testament-seminary-teacher-resource-manual/the-book-of-leviticus/leviticus-1-16?lang=eng.
7. "Leviticus 11–18: A Law of Performances and Ordinances, Part 2: The Clean and the Unclean," *Old Testament Student Manual Genesis–2 Samuel*, 173, https://www.churchofjesuschrist.org/study/manual/old-testament-student-manual-genesis-2-samuel/leviticus-11-18-a-law-of-performances-and-ordinances-part-2-the-clean-and-the-unclean?lang=eng.
8. "Leviticus 1–16," *Old Testament Seminary Teacher Resource Manual*, 90.
9. See Nelson, *Heart of the Matter*, 133–35 ("Years of treating patients with heart maladies," he has noted, "convinced me that the most important number to watch is one's weight. . . . Keeping your weight within a healthy range for your body type is important for long-term health." His secret (which many of us, including the author, sometimes only hope to emulate)? "I have been blessed with good health, and I have been conscientious about taking care of my body. I have weighed myself every day for decades, and if I put on a pound or two, I cut back my intake for a few days" [Ibid., 129]).

10. Bible Gateway, Genesis 14:20, https://www.biblegateway.com/verse/en/Genesis%2014:20.
11. Allen D. Haynie, "God's Law to Bless Individuals and Nations," https://ph.churchofjesuschrist.org/payment-of-tithes.
12. President Howard W. Hunter traces the history of tithing in the Bible, stating that it "existed from the beginning and continues today." "It was basic in the Mosaic law." Even the Levites, he noted, who received the people's tithes, were commanded to tithe, citing Numbers 18:6 ("Thus speak unto the Levites, and say unto them, When ye take of the children of Israel the tithes which I have given you from them for your inheritance, then ye shall offer up an heave offering of it for the Lord, even a tenth part of the tithe") (Howard W. Hunter, "Chapter 9: The Law of Tithing," *Teachings of Presidents of the Church: Howard W. Hunter* [Salt Lake City, Utah: The Church of Jesus Christ of Latter-day Saints, 2015], 134–35, https://www.churchofjesuschrist.org/study/manual/teachings-of-presidents-of-the-church-howard-w-hunter/chapter-9–the-law-of-tithing?lang=eng). (See, for example, Leviticus 27:30, 32; Numbers 18:26; Deuteronomy 12:17; 14:22, 23, 28; 2 Chronicles 31:5, 6; Nehemiah 10:38; 13:12; Luke 11:42; Doctrine and Covenants 85:3.)
13. Dallin H. Oaks, "The Blessing of Commandments," BYU Speeches, citing Joseph Smith, *Lectures on Faith*, 60–61, https://speeches.byu.edu/talks/dallin-h-oaks/blessing-commandments/.
14. Nelson, "Personal Preparation for Temple Blessings."
15. See chapter 14, "The Spiritual Treasure of Communing with Heaven," for a discussion of "true prayer."
16. "Repentance," *True to the Faith* (Salt Lake City, Utah: The Church of Jesus Christ of Latter-day Saints, 2004), 132.
17. As King Lamoni's father prayed, "I will give away all my sins to know thee" (Alma 22:18).
18. D. Todd Christofferson, "When Thou Art Converted," *Ensign*, May 2004, 11.
19. Nelson, "The Power of Spiritual Momentum."
20. Nelson, "We Can Do Better and Be Better," citing 2 Nephi 9:23 (Christ "commandeth all men that they must repent, and be baptized in his name, having perfect faith in the Holy One of Israel, or they cannot be saved in the kingdom of God"); Mosiah 4:6 ("The atonement . . . has been prepared from the foundation of the world, that thereby salvation might come to him that should put his trust in the Lord, and should be diligent in keeping his commandments, and continue in the faith even unto the end of his life"); 3 Nephi 9:22 ("Whoso repenteth and cometh unto me as a little child, him will I receive, for of such is the kingdom of God. Behold, for such I have laid down my life, and have taken it up again; therefore repent, and come unto me ye ends of the earth, and be saved"); 27:19 ("No unclean thing can enter into his kingdom; therefore nothing entereth into his rest save it be those who have washed their garments in my blood, because of their faith, and the repentance of all their sins, and their faithfulness unto the end").
21. Ibid.
22. Nelson, "Closing Remarks," *Ensign*, November 2019.

CHAPTER 8

The Spiritual Treasure of Proxy Baptisms and Confirmations

"We encourage [our youth] to qualify for limited-use temple recommends. . . . We are very grateful for your worthiness and willingness to participate in that sacred temple work. We thank you!"[1]

—Russell M. Nelson

The Savior Invites Youth, and Adults, to Prepare for and Participate in Temple Ordinances

When the Savior appeared to the Nephites at the temple in Bountiful, He taught men, women, and children "in number about two thousand and five hundred souls" (3 Nephi 17:25). Undoubtedly, among the children were youth of the ages of young men and young women in the Church today. For example, Jesus commanded the adults to bring "their little children" and set "them down on the ground [in a circle] round about Him," Jesus standing "in the midst" (3 Nephi 17:12). From His statement at the conclusion of His instruction that the multitude should "go ye unto your homes" (3 Nephi 17:3), and to the men and women "to behold your little ones" as He prayed for and took each child, "one by one" (3 Nephi 17:21, 23), we can infer that the multitude consisted of families, parents and their children, presumably of all ages, including youth.

If, as a number of gospel scholars have shown, Jesus's teachings in 3 Nephi are seen as "a sacred, ancient temple experience," as "teachings, instructions, doctrines and commandments" given "in connection with or in preparation for" the types of ceremonies we associate with our temple experience,[2] it is noteworthy to me that the Savior would speak to and teach not only the adults, but also the youth and even young children, including inviting each of them to be physical witnesses of His resurrection. The Lord's confidence in the ability of these young people to understand and live temple doctrines is reminiscent of the focus of our current prophet and apostles, who have invited the youth to offer "the gospel of Jesus Christ to God's children on both sides of the veil,"[3] and to "search out your ancestors and to prepare yourselves to perform proxy baptisms in the house of the Lord for *your* kindred dead."[4] These invitations to focus on temple and family history work in their personal goals has been reinforced in the program for youth and children introduced in 2019.[5]

In this chapter, we first examine doctrines related to the ordinances of baptism and confirmation for the living and the dead. We then turn to how, through proxy baptisms and confirmations, the Lord is making the spiritual treasures of the temple more accessible, particularly to strengthen and prepare our youth and recent converts for the higher ordinances of the temple and protect them "against the intensifying influence of the adversary."[6]

Baptism, the First Ordinance and Covenant of the Gospel and the Temple

Baptism is the first ordinance of the gospel of Jesus Christ and the first ordinance of the temple, following, as it does, the first principles, faith in the Lord Jesus Christ and repentance. The fourth article of faith states: "We believe that the first principles and ordinances of the gospel are: first, Faith in the Lord Jesus Christ; second, Repentance; third, Baptism by immersion for the remission of sins; fourth, Laying on of hands for the gift of the Holy Ghost." Baptism is essential for salvation.[7] As Jesus taught Nicodemus, "Except a man be born of water and of the Spirit, he cannot enter into the kingdom of God" (John 3:5). When Alma the Younger first established the "church of God, or the church of Christ" (Mosiah 18:17) in the land of Helam "having authority from the Almighty God" (Mosiah 18:13), he provided "the most complete scriptural statement as to what the newly baptized commit to do and be."[8] Putting the elements of the covenant of baptism that Alma taught his converts at the waters of Mormon in the first person helps us visualize what we promise to do when we are baptized, as well as the promises God makes to us personally as we do so:

Promises I Make:

1. I desire to "come into the fold" or Church of God, which, as named by the Lord today, is The Church of Jesus Christ of Latter-day Saints (Doctrine and Covenants 115:4) and
2. To "be called [one of] His people";
3. I am "willing to bear [others'] burdens, that they may be light,"
4. "Mourn with those that mourn" and
5. "Comfort those that stand in need of comfort";
6. I will "stand as [a witness] of God at all times and in all things, and in all places that I may be in, even until death";
7. I will "serve" God and my neighbor; and
8. "Keep his commandments" (in other words, every baptized member of the Church covenants at baptism to keep the law of obedience, a covenant that we renew each time we partake of the sacrament).

Blessings I Receive if I Keep My Covenants:

1. I will "be redeemed of God";
2. "Be numbered with those of the first resurrection";
3. "Have eternal life"; and
4. God will "pour out his Spirit more abundantly upon" me (Mosiah 18:9–13).

The sacramental prayers include these promises and blessings, although in more summary fashion. When we repeat these prayers with the priests who administer the sacrament, we express weekly our *willingness* "to take upon [us] the name of thy Son," "always remember Him," and "keep His commandments which he has given" us. In turn, the Lord promises that as we do so, we "may always have his Spirit to be with" us (Doctrine and Covenants 20:77, 79).

Adam Was Taught the Importance of Baptism and Confirmation in the Context of the Plan of Salvation

Enoch, a contemporary and the third great-grandson of Adam (Genesis 5:7–18), explained to his people that Adam was taught the necessity of baptism in the context of the plan of salvation. God called upon Adam "by his own voice, saying: I am God; I made the world, and men before they were in the flesh"—that is, He created or begot us spiritually before we were born physically. What has God taught man from the beginning? That because of the Fall, "Satan hath come among the children of men, and tempteth them to worship him"; and when they yield to temptation, the "natural man" (Mosiah 3:19) becomes "carnal, sensual, and devilish, and [is] shut out from the presence of God" (Moses 6:48). "But God hath made known unto our fathers that all men must repent," "be baptized . . . in the name of mine Only Begotten Son," and "receive the gift of the Holy Ghost."

"Why is it," Adam asked the Lord, "that men must repent and be baptized in water? And the Lord said unto Adam: Behold I have forgiven thee thy transgression in the Garden of Eden" (Moses 6:50–53). Here the Lord teaches an important principle "that the Son of God hath atoned for original guilt, wherein the sins of the parents cannot be answered upon the heads of the children, for they are whole from the foundation of the world" (Moses 6:54). In our dispensation, the Lord explained this important truth to Joseph Smith in these words: "Every spirit of man was innocent in the beginning; and God having redeemed man from the fall, men became again, in their infant state, innocent before God. And that wicked one cometh and taketh away light and truth, through *disobedience*, from the children of men, and because of the *tradition of their fathers*" (Doctrine and Covenants 93:38–39).

"Little children," as Mormon taught, "are alive in Christ, [redeemed] from the foundation of the world" (Moroni 8:12). Thus, like Adam and Eve, each of us brings about our own "fall" as we yield to temptation, through disobedience, and because of the bad examples or cultural and other false traditions of our fathers. Likewise, each of us has access to the scriptures and words of the living prophets, who teach us truth, including correct traditions based upon the gospel. Most importantly, we each have access to God's power through the atoning blood of Christ by applying the doctrine of Christ—the first principles and ordinances of the gospel.

Continuing to place the ordinance and covenant of baptism in the context of the plan of salvation, Enoch explains that Adam was taught from the beginning and taught his children, as Lehi also explained to his children,[9] that without the opportunity to experience sin, thus "tasting the bitter," they could not "know to prize the good. And it is given unto them to know good from evil; wherefore, they are agents unto themselves" (Moses 6:55–56). Being agents, we can, through Christ's atoning power, repent, be baptized, weekly renew our baptismal covenants through the ordinance of the sacrament (see discussion below), and thus be cleansed and delivered from all of the negative consequences of our mistakes. As we do this sincerely and faithfully from week to week, we can "always retain a remission of [our]sins" and "grow in the knowledge of the glory of him that created you" (Mosiah 4:12), which, as we explore in chapter 19, is the ultimate promise or spiritual treasure of the temple.

Confirmation, the Second Ordinance

Confirmation, as instructed in the Church's *General Handbook*, includes the admonition to "receive the Holy Ghost."[10] This, in essence, is a covenant—God promises the companionship of the Holy Ghost *if* we "receive" it. As discussed in the introduction, we show what we are "willing to receive" from God by the laws we are willing to obey, whether celestial, terrestrial, or telestial (see Doctrine and Covenants 88:21–32). God no doubt desires, with all His heart, to bestow upon each of His children the gift of eternal life, but if we "receive not the gift," He will not force it on us (Doctrine and Covenants 88:33). The doctrine of receiving, or being willing to receive, the blessings God desires to give His children, by keeping the laws associated with such blessings, is central to all ordinances and covenants.

As both Nephi and Christ explained in their summary of the Doctrine of Christ, to receive the full blessings of the Atonement, we must be "born of water *and of the Spirit*" (John 3:5). This the Lord further explained to Adam: "Wherefore teach it unto your children, that all men, everywhere, must *repent*, or they can in nowise inherit the kingdom of God, for no unclean thing can dwell there, or dwell in his presence; for, in the language of Adam, *Man of Holiness is his name*, and the name of his Only Begotten is the Son of Man, even Jesus Christ, a righteous Judge" (Moses 6:57). The Lord then teaches by imagery, as He does in the temple, symbolic similarities between our physical birth and the spiritual rebirth we can experience through baptism and confirmation. "Inasmuch as ye were born into the world by water [the amniotic fluid in which we were carried in our mothers' wombs as our physical bodies developed] and blood, and the spirit . . . even so ye must be born again into the kingdom of heaven, *of water, and of the Spirit*, and be cleansed by *blood*, even the blood of mine Only Begotten; that ye might be sanctified from all sin, and enjoy . . . eternal life in the world to come, even immortal glory" (Moses 6:59). Concluding his summary of these basic gospel doctrines taught to Adam by revelation, Enoch summarizes, "For by the water ye keep the commandment; by the Spirit ye are *justified*, and by the blood ye are *sanctified*" (Moses 6:60). Thus, through baptism and confirmation, we can be both justified[11] and sanctified.[12] In other words, after receiving a remission of our sins through baptism, and receiving a witness of the Spirit that we are *justified* (or pardoned from the punishment of our sins and declared guiltless), we need to press on, repenting daily and receiving the enabling power of Christ to become like Him, available through the shedding of His blood, which comes to us by the power of the Holy Ghost, to become "pure, clean and holy" or sanctified, new creatures in Christ. Of course, as President Nelson has repeatedly taught, this is a process, not an event.

The Role of the Sacrament in the Process of Sanctification

Moroni beautifully explains this process of sanctification, becoming like or acquiring the attributes of Christ, which comes by exercising sufficient faith in Jesus Christ to follow Him or keep His commandments, receiving His ordinances, continuously repenting, and regularly renewing our covenants with Him:

> **Moroni 8:25–26**—And the first fruits of repentance is baptism; and baptism cometh by faith unto the fulfilling the commandments; and the fulfilling the commandments bringeth remission of sins; And the remission of sins bringeth meekness, and lowliness of heart; and because of meekness and lowliness of heart cometh the *visitation of the Holy Ghost*, which Comforter filleth with hope and perfect love, which love endureth by diligence unto prayer, until the end shall come, when all the saints shall dwell with God.

How do we know when we are justified or have received a remission of our sins? One way we know is described in the experience of King Benjamin's people who, after pleading for forgiveness in the process of renewing their baptismal covenants,[13] as "the Spirit of the Lord came upon them . . . were filled with *joy*, having received a remission of their sins, and having *peace of conscience*, because of the exceeding faith which they had in Jesus Christ who should come" (Mosiah 4:3). The Lord used similar words to explain to Oliver Cowdery how he could know that He had heard his prayers for direction and spiritual confirmation of his standing before the Lord, reminding him, "Did I not speak peace to your *mind*" (Doctrine and Covenants 6:23)? In other words, sometimes we just "know" in our mind, not just our heart, that God knows and has answered our pleadings for forgiveness or direction. Another description of this spiritual feeling was given by Enos who, after praying intensely for forgiveness, said that his "guilt was swept away" (Enos 1:6).

King Benjamin also explained to his people what they needed to do to *retain* the confirmation they had received that they were clean before the Lord, walking with confidence, "guiltless before God" or being "justified," as they moved forward in their lives. He counseled them to "remember . . . the greatness of God, and your own nothingness," be *humble* and to *call* "on the name of the Lord *daily*," and *stand* "steadfastly in the faith." As we do so, the Lord promises, we can "always rejoice," "be filled with the love of God, and *always retain a remission*" of our sins (Mosiah 4:11–12, 26).

Why is having the Holy Ghost with us always so important? Because His specific mission is to testify of and convey to us every reassurance, answer, gift, Christlike attribute, and blessing from Heavenly Father, all of which come because of Christ's Atonement (Moses 6:61). After Adam was taught these essential truths about "the plan of salvation unto all men," which is made possible "through the blood of [the] Only Begotten" (Moses 6:62), the Lord, through the power of the Holy Ghost, baptized and confirmed him. Adam "was caught away by the Spirit of the Lord, and was carried down into the water, and was laid under the water, and was brought forth out of the water. And thus he was baptized, and the Spirit of God descended upon him, and thus he was born of the Spirit, and became quickened in the inner man. And he heard a voice out of heaven, saying: Thou art baptized with fire, and with the Holy Ghost" (Moses 6:64–66).

The record also indicates that Adam was ordained to the holy priesthood: "And thou art after the order of him who was without beginning of days or end of years, from all eternity to all eternity." Thus, the Lord taught from the very beginning the process by which we become sons and daughters of God: "Behold, thou art one in me, a son of God; and thus may all become my sons" (Moses 6:67–68), meaning, of course, all men and women may become His sons and daughters by receiving the essential ordinances of the gospel.

Baptism and Confirmation for the Dead

As our youth (and others) go to the temple to perform proxy baptisms and confirmations, they have the opportunity to begin, as President Nelson described, to be "taught in the Master's way," which "differs from the modes of others. His way is ancient and rich with symbolism."[14] Michael Wilcox describes three possible symbols suggested by the ordinance of baptism, which youth may want to ponder as they officiate in this ordinance:

- **Bath or cleansing:** "The font reminds of a bath where our sins are washed away. As we are immersed in the water, we become pure. This is taught in the scriptures."
- **Birth:** "The font represents the womb. As a newborn baby

emerges from the water of the mother's womb, so too are we 'born again' through the waters of baptism into a new and innocent life. This also is affirmed in the scriptures."

- **Burial:** "The font suggests to the mind a grave. The old man of sin, the natural man, is buried in the water so that a new man of Christ may be resurrected. This we do in similitude of the Savior's death and resurrection. This interpretation is also suggested in the scriptures."

"Is baptism a bath, a birth, or a burial? It is all of them. Because such symbols convey multiple meanings, they will, if we continue to ponder them, constantly edify and instruct us throughout our lives."[15]

The Lord Himself described how baptisms for the dead remind us of death and resurrection, basic elements of the plan of salvation. "To be immersed in the water and come forth out of the water," He teaches in Doctrine and Covenants 128, "is in the likeness of the resurrection of the dead in coming forth out of their graves; . . . Consequently, the baptismal font was instituted as a similitude of the grave, and was commanded to be in a place underneath where the living are wont to assemble, to show forth the living and the dead, and that all things may have their likeness" (vv. 12–13). In other words, as we observe baptismal fonts being filled with water in chapels before each baptismal service and as we enter the baptistry in the temple where the font is always filled with water, we are reminded of the rich symbolism of this ordinance—burial or immersion in water and coming up out of the water each time we are baptized as a proxy for someone waiting in the spirit world, reminding us that death and resurrection made possible through Christ's Atonement are fundamental aspects of the plan of salvation.

The Lord further teaches that as our youth serve as proxies in these ordinances, particularly for their kindred dead, their hearts shall turn to their fathers, as prophesied by the prophet Malachi, and, in the process, "be made perfect" (Doctrine and Covenants 128:17, quoting Malachi 4:5–6). Elder David A. Bednar was very specific about the blessings or spiritual treasures our precious youth (and converts) can receive as they respond to the prophetic invitations to (1) "learn about and experience the Spirit of Elijah"; (2) "study, to search out your ancestors"; (3) "prepare yourselves to perform proxy baptisms in the house of the Lord for your kindred dead"; and (4) "help other people identify their family histories":

> As you respond in faith to this invitation, your hearts shall turn to the fathers. The promises made to Abraham, Isaac, and Jacob will be implanted in your hearts. Your patriarchal blessing, with its declaration of lineage, will link you to these fathers and be more meaningful to you. Your love and gratitude for your ancestors will increase. Your testimony of and conversion to the Savior will become deep and abiding. And I promise you . . . [a]s you participate in and love this holy work, you will be safeguarded in your youth and throughout your lives.[16]

Changes in Temple Ordinances Evidence the Ongoing Nature of the Restoration and the Lord's Desire to Make the Spiritual Treasures of the Temple More Accessible

Another important lesson learned from the history of the restoration of temple doctrine and practices as related to proxy baptisms, which was one of the first temple ordinances performed in this dispensation,[17] is the principle of continuing revelation. The Lord adapts the *practices* related to the ordinances, through which the unchanging *principles* or covenants of the gospel are administered, to the circumstances of the people, as evidenced by the varied ways in which the ordinances have been administered over the dispensations. President Wilford Woodruff offered the following reflections on this process: "All was not revealed at once, but the Lord showed the Prophet [Joseph Smith] a principle, and the people acted upon it according to the light which they had. All the perfection and glory of it was not revealed at first; but, as fast as it was revealed, the people endeavored to obey."[18]

As noted on the Church's website, "Between 1840 and 1845, in the absence of more specific direction, men sometimes acted as proxies for women, and women for men. In 1845, after Joseph Smith's death, Brigham Young" discontinued this practice, explaining that "Joseph in his lifetime did not receive everything connected with the doctrine of redemption" but that the Lord continued to lead the Church by revelation, "giving them here a little and there a little."[19] Of this change,

President Woodruff recorded, "We obtained more light upon the subject, and President Young taught the people that men should attend to those ordinances for the male portion of their dead friends, and females for the females. This showed the order in which those ordinances should be administered, which ordinances had before been revealed, and shows us that we are in a school where we shall be constantly learning."[20]

The Lord revealed to the Prophet Joseph Smith in September 1842, after a period in which proxy baptisms performed in the Mississippi River were not always witnessed and recorded, "Let there be a recorder, and let him be eye-witness of your baptisms; let him hear with his ears, that he may testify of a truth, saith the Lord" that the ordinance has been performed correctly. Thus, when a brother holding the Melchizedek Priesthood serves as recorder for proxy baptisms and signifies that the baptismal prayer was said correctly and the proxy totally immersed, and when the ordinance is later recorded, the Lord declared that such ordinance will "be recorded in heaven" and, more importantly, "bound in heaven" (Doctrine and Covenants 127:6–7).

We have also seen examples of the Lord's hand in adjusting temple ordinances to circumstances in our day. For example, in response to the COVID-19 pandemic beginning in March 2020, the First Presidency announced a number of changes related to the administration of temple ordinances, including the closure and then phased reopening of temple operations.[21] In a letter dated January 17, 2020, the First Presidency announced adjustments in temple ceremonial clothing.[22] Other examples of changes relating to baptisms for the dead evidence the Lord's desire to make the spiritual treasures of the temple more accessible to youth and recent converts:

- The organization of ward youth groups, and, more recently, encouragement for recent converts to prepare family names and to attend the temple within weeks of their baptism, making "regular excursions to temples to be baptized for the dead, giving young Church members an opportunity to attend the temple years before they were endowed";[23]
- "In 2017, Church leaders announced that young men holding the Aaronic Priesthood office of priest could perform baptisms for the dead";[24]

- In November 2019 in connection with general conference leadership meeting, the First Presidency announced that "any member holding a current temple recommend, including [young women and young men holding] limited-use recommend[s], may serve as a witness to a proxy baptism" and "any baptized member of the Church, including children and youth, may serve as a witness to the baptism of a living person."[25]

The First Presidency has explained that the purpose of all such inspired changes to "the methods of instruction" and other adjustments in the temple experience, which have been made "many times, even in recent history," is "to help members better understand and live what they learn in the temple."[26]

I thrill each week as I watch our grandsons and other worthy Aaronic Priesthood holders in sacrament meeting administer the sacrament to me and others in the congregation. Likewise, I thrill in my temple service each time I see eager, radiant young men and young women come to the temple and serve in the baptistry. Our challenge and constant prayer as leaders, parents, and grandparents is to help them understand the "power of godliness" that is available to them and to each of us through these ordinances and the simple yet powerful principles of faith and repentance that lead us to experience this power.

Sometimes—perhaps even much of the time—neither they nor we may feel that there is all that much that is especially "godly" about our lives. But how much faith is demonstrated in their (and our) sincere participation in this sacred weekly ordinance and in the baptism and confirmation ordinances our youth officiate in in the Lord's holy house! As they bring with them (and we bring with us) our offering of a "broken heart and a contrite spirit," manifest through our *desire* to repent and to be clean, we can realize the Lord's promise to *know*, then and from day to day and week to week, that the "course" we are pursuing, the "covenant path" we are on and the *direction* of our life's journey, is *"pleasing in the sight of God."*[27] Such "assurance[s] of faith" and "hope" (Hebrews 10:22; 6:11) are, without doubt, among the spiritual treasures God was referring to when He promised to "manifest [Himself] to my people in mercy in [my] house" (Doctrine and Covenants 110:6–7).

Endnotes

1. Nelson, "Closing Remarks," *Ensign*, November 2019.
2. Welch, *Illuminating*, 5. See also Welch's description of the Savior's blessing of the children on the occasion of His first visit to the Nephites on pages 97–99 and his conclusion that "while it cannot be said exactly what transpired at this time on this extraordinary afternoon," when He told the parents to "behold your little ones" (3 Nephi 17:23), "the children apparently now somehow belonged to the parents through the Lord's blessing in a way they had not belonged to them before."
3. "Hope of Israel," Worldwide Devotional with President Russell M. Nelson and Wendy W. Nelson.
4. David A. Bednar, "The Hearts of the Children Shall Turn," *Ensign*, November 2011, 26 (emphasis added).
5. See, for example, "Ideas for Growing in All Areas of Life," in the *Personal Development: Youth Guidebook*, https://www.churchofjesuschrist.org/study/manual/personal-development-youth-guidebook/ideas-for-growing-in-all-areas-of-life?lang=eng (suggested spiritual goals include "worthily receive and hold a temple recommend" and "work on your family history and serve in the temple") and "Activity: The Plan of Happiness and the Covenant Path" among the "Service and Activity Ideas—Spiritual Activity Ideas" found in the Children and Youth Program at https://www.churchofjesuschrist.org/youth/childrenandyouth/for-youth?lang=eng.
6. Bednar, "The Hearts of the Children Shall Turn," 27.
7. "Baptisms for the Dead," Gospel Topics, https://www.churchofjesuschrist.org/study/manual/gospel-topics/baptisms-for-the-dead?lang=eng.
8. Jeffrey R. Holland, *Christ and the New Covenant* (Salt Lake City, Utah: Deseret Book, 1997), 106.
9. 2 Nephi 2:11 ("For it must needs be, that there is an opposition in all things. If not so, my first-born in the wilderness, righteousness could not be brought to pass, neither wickedness, neither holiness nor misery, neither good nor bad. Wherefore, all things must needs be a compound in one; wherefore, if it should be one body it must needs remain as dead, having no life neither death, nor corruption nor incorruption, happiness nor misery, neither sense nor insensibility").
10. *General Handbook* 18.8.2.
11. "To be pardoned from punishment for sin and declared guiltless. A person is justified by the Savior's grace through faith in Him. This faith is shown by repentance and obedience to the laws and ordinances of the gospel. Jesus Christ's Atonement enables mankind to repent and be justified or pardoned from punishment they otherwise would receive" Guide to the Scriptures, https://www.churchofjesuschrist.org/study/scriptures/gs/justification-justify?lang=eng; see also Isa. 45:25 ("in the Lord shall all Israel be justified"); Romans 2:13 ("not the hearers but the doers of the law shall be justified"); Romans 5:1–2, 9 ("man is justified through the blood of Christ"); 1 Corinthians 6:11 ("ye are justified in the name of the Lord Jesus"); Titus 3:7 ("being justified by

his grace, we shall be made heirs"); James 2:21 ("was not Abraham our father justified by works"); James 2:14–26 ("by works a man is justified, and not by faith only"); 2 Nephi 2:5 ("by the law no flesh is justified"); Mosiah 14:11 ("my righteous servant shall justify many, for he shall bear their iniquities"; see also Isaiah 53:11); Alma 5:27 ("could ye say that your garments have been cleansed through Christ"); Doctrine and Covenants 20:30–31 ("justification through the grace of Jesus Christ is true"; see also Doctrine and Covenants 88:39); Moses 6:60 ("by the Spirit ye are justified").

12. "The process of becoming free from sin, pure, clean, and holy through the Atonement of Jesus Christ (Moses 6:59–60)." Guide to the Scriptures; see also 2 Thessalonians 2:13 ("God hath chosen you to salvation through sanctification of the Spirit"); Hebrews 10:10 ("we are sanctified through the offering of the body of Jesus"); Hebrews 13:12 ("Jesus suffered that he might sanctify the people with his own blood"); Alma 13:10–12 ("high priests were sanctified and their garments were washed white through the blood of the Lamb"); Helaman 3:33–35 ("sanctification cometh to those who yield their hearts unto God"); 3 Nephi 27:20 ("repent that ye may be sanctified by the reception of the Holy Ghost"); Doctrine and Covenants 20:31 ("sanctification through the grace of Jesus Christ is just and true"); Doctrine and Covenants 76:41 ("Jesus came to sanctify the world"); Doctrine and Covenants 88:68 ("sanctify yourselves that your minds become single to God").

13. As noted in chapter 6, although lost to the Old Testament, the Book of Mormon makes clear that baptism was part of the gospel taught and observed under the law of Moses, as Alma and other prophets taught so forcefully.

14. Nelson, "Personal Preparation for Temple Blessings."

15. Wilcox, *House of Glory*, 18–19. See also Alonzo L. Gaskill, *Sacred Symbols: Finding Meaning in Rites, Rituals, & Ordinances* (Springville, Utah: Bonneville Books, 2011), 38 (baptism "is commonly associated with both the womb and the grave").

16. Bednar, "The Hearts of the Children Shall Turn," 26–27.

17. See Mackley, 372–73. The earliest temple ordinances performed in this dispensation were the initial washings and anointings performed in connection with the completion of the Kirtland Temple between March 1836 and April 1837. See Mackley, 41–42 and note 141; *Saints*, vol. 1, 232–33, 453. The first baptisms for the dead were performed in 1840. See Mackley, 47–50, 372; *Saints*, vol. 1, 421–22.

18. Mackley, 52, quoting Wilford Woodruff, *Journal of Discourses*, 26 vols. (London: Latter-day Saints' Book Depot, 1854–56), 5:84, April 9, 1857.

19. "Baptism for the Dead," Church History Topics, https://www.churchofjesuschrist.org/study/history/topics/baptism-for-the-dead?lang=eng.

20. Mackley, 53.

21. See, for example, "The Latest News on Temple Reopenings," News Release, March 15, 2022, https://newsroom.churchofjesuschrist.org/article/first-presidency-limited-reopening-temples; Letter from the First Presidency dated May 7, 2020 re "Phased Reopening of Temples," https://newsroom.churchofjesuschrist.org/multimedia/file/0507–Phased-Reopening-of-Temples.pdf. For a

timeline of news releases related to the coronavirus's impact on temple work through August 2020, see "The Church and Coronavirus: A Timeline of News Releases and Media Coverage," *LDS Living*, October 1, 2020, https://www.ldsliving.com/coronavirus/s/92512.

22. Letter from the First Presidency dated January 17, 2020 re "Adjustments in Temple Ceremonial Clothing," https://newsroom.churchofjesuschrist.org/multimedia/file/first-presidency-letter-temple-clothing-2020-january.pdf.
23. "Baptism for the Dead," Church History Topics, https://www.churchofjesuschrist.org/study/history/topics/baptism-for-the-dead?lang=eng.
24. Ibid.
25. "Church Adjusts Policy for Witnessing Ordinances," *Ensign*, November 2019, https://www.churchofjesuschrist.org/study/*Ensign*/2019/11/news-of-the-church/church-adjusts-policy-for-witnessing-ordinances?lang=eng.
26. "A Message from the First Presidency on Changes to the Temple Endowment," Official Statement, July 20, 2020, https://newsroom.churchofjesuschrist.org/article/first-presidency-temple-message-july-2020. See, for example, Sweat, *The Holy Covenants*, 11–12 ("While learning God's ways and making exalted priestly covenants is part of the 'ancient order' of things, how this ancient order and its associated covenants are presented in the temple has been adjusted over time by those with prophetic authority. Remember, there is a difference between endowment [the power and capacity to enter the presence of God and receive a fulness of His exalted blessings] and the presentation of the endowment [a teaching tool]") (footnotes omitted). Discussing the "gradual refining" of temple ordinances over time, President Nelson testifies that such adjustments "signal how eager the Lord is for us to center our lives on Him and on the ordinances of His holy house" (Nelson, *Heart of the Matter*, 179–81).
27. Smith, *Lectures on Faith*, 60–61 (as quoted in Oaks, "The Blessing of Commandments").

CHAPTER 9

The Spiritual Treasures of Washings and Anointings

"Temple blessings include our washings and anointings that we may be clean before the Lord."[1]

—Russell M. Nelson

The Washing Ordinance Anciently

Among the objects the Lord instructed Moses to prepare to be used in administering ordinances in the tabernacle was a laver of brass, or basin, to be used for washings. Moses was instructed to "put water" in the laver "for Aaron and his sons [to] wash their hands and their feet" before entering the tabernacle "that they die not" (Exodus 30:18 and note 18a, 19–21). Thus, to "hallow" Aaron and others who would administer the temple ordinances of that day, the Lord commanded Moses to bring "Aaron and his sons . . . unto the door of the tabernacle of the congregation, and . . . *wash them with water*," clothe them in priestly robes, which we will discuss in the next chapter, and "anoint" them (Exodus 29:4–7; see also Exodus 40:12). "And Moses brought Aaron and his sons, and *washed them with water*" (Leviticus 8:6). Similarly, for Solomon's temple, Hiram from Tyre of the tribe of Naphtali[2] "made a molten sea, ten cubits from the one brim to the other," which "was round all about," and five cubits[3] high. "It stood upon twelve oxen, three looking toward the north, and three looking toward the west, and three looking toward the south, and three looking toward the east: and the sea was set above upon them, and all their hinder parts were inward" (1 Kings 7:23–26).

The *Old Testament Student Manual*, quoting Bruce R. McConkie, explains that the "12 brazen oxen," upon whose backs the "large molten sea of brass" rested symbolized "the 12 tribes of Israel." "This brazen sea was used for performing baptisms for the living. There were no baptisms for the dead until after the resurrection of Christ." Elder McConkie reminds us, as noted earlier, that "all direct and plain references to baptism have been deleted from the Old Testament (1 Ne. 13) and that the word baptize is of Greek origin. Some equivalent word, such as wash, would have been used by the Hebrew peoples. In describing the molten sea the Old Testament record says, 'The sea was for the priests to wash in.' (2 Chron. 4:2–6.) This is tantamount to saying that the priests performed baptisms in it."[4]

Whether the washings performed anciently to enable priests to officiate in the ordinances of the tabernacle and later Solomon's temple are deemed to be "baptisms" or ritual washings or ablutions, the effect is the same—cleanliness and worthiness are necessary both to officiate in Christ's earthly kingdom and to enter His heavenly kingdom. Moreover, such cleanliness or holiness is impossible without the cleansing and sanctifying power of the Atonement. Thus, just as "the ritual washings required by the law of Moses (prior to service in the temple) were associated with the cleansing power of the Atonement," so too today the temple washing ordinance, which involves a symbolic washing, represents "the cleansing and covering power of the Atonement."[5]

Other commentators note the symbolism of the twelve oxen and the four cardinal directions of the compass. For example, "Oxen are established types for God and His righteous followers. To the ancients, they represented power, patience, and sacrifice, as well as Christ or deity. . . . Thus, as the initiate was washed in the font or laver, symbolically he was taught who it was that supported him in this new relationship—namely God and His righteous disciples."[6] Another commentator explained that as "the baptismal font rests securely on the strong backs of twelve oxen [representing] the tribes of Israel," to which we belong, "the saving ordinances for the world rest on backs made strong by the blessings of the Restoration. That weight will not be removed until *every child* of God is found. With our heads directed to the four points of the compass, we desire and invite all to receive the ordinances that open the sanctifying power of the Atonement."[7]

The number twelve also represents priesthood authority, suggesting that the ordinance performed in the font is being done by proper authority. Moreover, the number four is said to represent geographic completeness or totality, suggesting that the ordinance is necessary for all and will in effect cover the earth. Anciently, kings' thrones similarly sat on the back of oxen facing the four cardinal directions, suggesting that those who keep their covenants "will be given the right to preside over all things. Thus, symbolically speaking, [temple washings mirror] the initiate's entrance onto the path leading to enthronement, exaltation, and deification." Oxen under the Mosaic law were "clean" or "kosher" animals, thus suggesting that those washed and cleansed in connection with temple rites covenanted to "live as God and His Christ would live—as faithful followers of the Messiah should live."[8]

Ancient Practice of Anointing

Exodus 40:13—"And thou shalt put upon Aaron the holy garments, and *anoint him*, and sanctify him; that he may minister unto me in the priest's office" (see also Exodus 28:41; Exodus 29:7).

According to the Bible Dictionary, to "anoint" means "to apply oil or ointment to the head or the person. . . . Anciently anointing was done for reasons both secular and sacred." For example, guests were anointed as "a sign of hospitality in Luke 7:46 and of routine personal grooming in 2 Sam. 12:20 and Matt. 6:17. The maimed or sick were anointed with wine, oil, or ointment as medicine (Isa. 1:6; Luke 10:34; Rev. 3:18). The sick were also anointed with oil as part of the sacred procedure in healing of the sick by faith and the laying on of hands (Mark 6:13; James 5:14–15)." In summary, "although the scriptures do not specifically so state, we may confidently assume that anointing with oil has been part of true, revealed religion ever since the gospel was first introduced on this earth to Adam."[9]

"The holy anointing oil" that was used in the ancient temple "was composed of olive oil mixed with spices and was to be restricted in use to certain specified ceremonies (Ex. 30:22–33; 37:29)." In temples today olive oil is also used in the anointing ordinance, which has been consecrated solely for this sacred purpose. Before beginning and in preparation for their sacred service, Amy Hardison notes, priests "were required to remove any profane items (such as their shoes) from their persons, to ritually wash their hands and feet to further remove any traces of the profane world, to be sanctified through the anointing with oil, and finally to be clothed in the vestments of the priesthood. Only after these gestures were completed could they approach God."[10] In preparation for the dedication of the tabernacle, the Lord commanded Moses to "take the anointing oil, and anoint the tabernacle . . . and all the vessels thereof: and it shall be holy" (Exodus 40:9). The principal purpose of these anointings was to set apart the priests and vessels "for divine service. Once anointed with oil, the object or person was considered to be in a state of holiness and thus worthy to stand before God in a sacred setting." Anointings, in effect, signaled "an elevation in official status," while imparting "something of the holiness of God to the person" called to such divine service (for example, when Samuel anointed Saul as the first king of Israel). "The endowment of grace, power, and Spirit that came with this anointing was not for Saul alone. It was to enable him, and all kings of Israel, to bless God's people."[11] The washing, anointing, and clothing ordinances similarly enable us to bless others in and out of the Church, but especially in our homes.

Initiatory Ordinances Today

In the link under "Temples" on the Church's website, the Church introduces the topic "About the Endowment" by explaining that when we join the Church, we receive "two ordinances—baptism and confirmation. Likewise, the temple endowment is received in two parts: In the first part, you will privately and individually receive preliminary ordinances called the *initiatory ordinances*."[12] The Church's temple preparation manual explains that these "initiatory ordinances" ("initiatory" because they begin the endowment) include three specific ordinances—"the ordinances of washing and anointing," which include promises of "definite, immediate blessings as well as future blessings," and being "authorized to wear" or "officially clothed in the garment and promised marvelous blessings in connection with it."[13] With respect to the blessing pronounced in these initiatory ordinances, President Boyd K. Packer offered this counsel to patrons receiving their own endowment: "It is important that you listen carefully as these ordinances are administered and that you try to remember the blessings promised and the conditions upon which they will be realized."[14] We would all do well to follow this counsel.

To those who officiate today in priesthood ordinances, which in the temples include women as well as men, the Lord has said, as He did anciently, "Be ye clean, that bear the vessels of the Lord" (Isaiah 52:11; see also 3 Nephi 20:41; Doctrine and Covenants 38:42; 133:5).[15] When we think of officiating, we naturally think of called and set apart temple ordinance workers. However, as President Nelson teaches us, patrons also "officiate" as proxies for the deceased.[16]

As we strive to be faithful to all of our gospel covenants, including the all-important principle of daily repentance, we can have confidence in the Lord's promise that we will "always have His Spirit to be with" us (Doctrine and Covenants 20:77), as we are reminded each week when we partake of the sacrament. If we have the Lord's spirit with us, we can also be assured that we are entitled to the promise to "always retain a remission of [our] sins" (Mosiah 4:12). This confidence can be strengthened each time we officiate as proxies on behalf of those awaiting their temple ordinances in the spirit world if we review in our minds the powerful promises we received when we were washed and anointed. As President Nelson noted, "Temple blessings include our washings and anointings *that we may be clean* before the Lord."[17] Our confidence is further strengthened as we recall, as President Nelson described them, the extraordinarily "special blessings regarding your divine heritage and potential" that we receive when we are or were anointed. That potential includes, as John the Beloved described, the spiritual treasure of not only being "washed" by Jesus Christ "from our sins in his own blood," but being "made" "kings and priests" and queens and priestesses "unto God and his Father" (Revelation 1:5–6; 5:10), and becoming a "peculiar treasure unto" the Lord, "a kingdom of priests" (Exodus 19:5–6), even "kings and queens," priests and priestesses, "who can someday become a holy nation and dwell in the presence of God."[18]

Laws Relating to Cleanliness in the Old Testament

The Lord has said, "Wherefore, verily I say unto you that all things unto me are spiritual, and not at any time have I given unto you a law which was temporal; neither any man, nor the children of men; neither Adam, your father, whom I created" (Doctrine and Covenants 29:34). Thus, not only the specific washing, anointing, and clothing practices that Jehovah revealed to Moses for the administration of ancient temple ordinances had the spiritual purpose of sanctifying His people, but also the so-called "carnal" commandments had similar spiritual purposes. Among these were the dietary restrictions relating to clean and unclean foods discussed in chapter 7, as well as instructions relating to treating certain diseases and health conditions. What spiritual lessons can we discern from such commandments the Lord gave ancient Israel? How were the people blessed as they thought constantly about what is "clean" and should be embraced and what is "not clean" and should be shunned? Similarly, what things in our culture, including social and other media, has the Lord, through His prophets, declared to be "unclean" and avoided at all costs and what things has He encouraged us to embrace?

Speaking of what our Heavenly Father encourages us to embrace reminds me of an *Ensign* article entitled "Our Refined Heavenly Home" by Douglas L. Callister of the Seventy. I shared this article in my final interview with our departing missionaries when my wife and I were mission leaders of the Portugal Lisbon Mission. Elder Callister gives us a beautiful "word picture" of the clean, "virtuous, lovely, and refined" things that the temple, with its carefully groomed landscaping, furnishings, artwork, and other appointments, teaches us characterize a celestial life. He invites us, as does each ordinance administered in the temple, to "peek behind the veil that temporarily separates us from our heavenly home" and consider how our language and tastes in literature, music, and art compare with "the language, literature, music, and art of heaven." For example, he invites us to compare the

"85 channels and uncountable DVDs" (today it would be hundreds of cable channels and uncountable streaming services), "computer games or Internet surfing" with "richer experiences of great reading, conversations, and enjoyment of music." Elder Callister recalled President David O. McKay's love for literature. He "could quote 1,000 poems from memory" and said that "we may choose [books] which will make us better, more intelligent, more appreciative of the good and the beautiful in the world, or we may choose the trashy, the vulgar, the obscene, which will make us feel as though we've been 'wallowing in the mire.'" I appreciate Elder Callister's insight that "there could not be a heaven without music of surpassing beauty," as well as his invitation to each of us, in the "maturing process of [our] eternal journey" home, to consider whether we diet primarily on, as it were, "musical French fries" or primarily "grand" music "which uplifts and inspires."[19] The same question could be asked of other forms of media we "feast upon,"[20] remembering Jacob's admonition not to "spend money," or more relevant perhaps to our day, time, "for that which is of no worth [or] cannot satisfy." Rather, he counsels, "feast upon that which perisheth not, neither can be corrupted" (2 Nephi 9:51), or, in other words borrowed from Joseph Smith, "let your soul delight" in "honesty," "truth," "chastity," "benevolence," "virtue," "doing good," "loveliness," and all that is "of good report or praiseworthy" (Articles of Faith 1:13). In this regard, President Nelson's example, which has otherwise been so powerful for me personally, as it has been to so many throughout the Church and the world, is outright stunning when he shared in a Worldwide Young Adults broadcast in May 2022, that at his age and experience, "I have stopped spending time on things that don't matter."[21]

Temples allow us, for the relatively brief moments we are in them, to step outside the confines of this telestial existence and imagine what it is like to live in a celestial realm in our Heavenly Parents' home. Every ordinance we receive for ourselves and in behalf of others reminds us of this reality, of what the Lord invites us to embrace, to treasure, and to enjoy. Like Naaman of old, who went in faith to Elisha to be cleansed of his leprosy (2 Kings 5:1–14), by serving in proxy baptisms and confirmations and "worship[ping] in the temple as often as [our] circumstances allow,"[22] we too can be washed, cleansed, and healed.

Endnotes

1. Nelson, "Personal Preparation for Temple Blessings."
2. 1 Kings 7:12–14.
3. "Originally the distance from the elbow to the tip of the fingers. It varied in length, from 17½ inches in the 8th century B.C. to 21½ inches in the time of our Lord" (Bible Dictionary, "Cubit"). In other words, the laver or font was from 14–1/2' to almost 18' wide and from 7.3' to almost 9' high.
4. "Solomon: Man of Wisdom, Man of Foolishness: 1 Kings 1–11," *Old Testament Student Manual*, https://www.churchofjesuschrist.org/study/manual/old-testament-student-manual-kings-malachi/chapter-1?lang=eng, quoting Bruce R. McConkie, *Mormon Doctrine*, 103–104.
5. Gaskill, *Sacred Symbols*, 38, quoting Mark H. Green III, *The Scriptural Temple* (Springville, Utah: Horizon, 2004), 61. In support of Elder McConkie's observation, David Fluckiger notes the importance, even today, among orthodox Jews of a ritual washing ordinance performed in a "'mikveh' or 'mikvah' (Hebrew: הָקְמ / הווקמ׳. . .) [or] bath used for the purpose of ritual immersion . . . to achieve ritual purity." See "Mikveh," *Wikipedia, the free encyclopedia*, https://en.wikipedia.org/wiki/Mikveh. See also "Ritual Washing in Judaism," *Wikipedia*, https://en.wikipedia.org/wiki/Ritual_washing_in_Judaism; Sara Malka, "Inside a Mikvah |Tour of a Jewish Ritual Bath |What is a Mikveh?" Frum it Up, https://www.youtube.com/watch?v=p7WIE3kBERM. "One forceful argument for the 'traditional' temple mount location," Brother Fluckiger notes, "is the uncovering of a large host of Mikveh pools by archeologists near the 'entrance' of the traditional temple mount." Commenting on the relationship between baptism, an Aaronic Priesthood ordinance, and the temple washing ordinance, a Melchizedek Priesthood ordinance, Brother Fluckiger observes that "Aaronic Priesthood baptism releases one from the transgression of Adam (and little children are already free as they are not morally culpable) and is a Washing of Grace. The consequence allows salvation in the celestial kingdom (based on worthiness through repentance throughout one's life). On the other hand, the Melchizedek Priesthood washing is conditional based on works (obedience). Melchizedek Priesthood washing is preparatory to exaltation and is a Washing of Obedience (works)" (Email to author from David Fluckiger, May 1, 2023 [used by permission]).
6. Gaskill, *Sacred Symbols*, 33 (footnotes omitted).
7. Wilcox, *House of Glory*, 124 (emphasis in original).
8. Gaskill, *Sacred Symbols*, 34–35.
9. Bible Dictionary, "Anoint."
10. Hardison, 96 (footnote omitted).
11. Ibid., 95–96. For a discussion of anointing practices in the ancient world, which carried over to early Christianity, see Gaskill, *Sacred Symbols*, 40–48.
12. "About the Temple Endowment," https://www.churchofjesuschrist.org/temples/what-is-temple-endowment?lang=eng (emphasis in original).
13. *Preparing to Enter the Holy Temple*, 32; see also Doctrine and Covenants 124:39.

14. Boyd K. Packer, *The Holy Temple* (Salt Lake City, Utah: Bookcraft, Inc., 1980), 155.
15. See discussion of priesthood authority exercised by sisters generally, as well as sister ordinance workers, below under "How do Faithful Women Receive and Exercise Priesthood Authority and Power?" in chapter 18.
16. Nelson, "Spiritual Treasures" ("In the holy temple you [speaking to women in the Church] are authorized to perform and officiate in priesthood ordinances every time you attend. Your temple endowment prepares you to do so").
17. Nelson, "Personal Preparation for Temple Blessings."
18. "Lesson 12—Temple Ordinances and Covenants," *The Eternal Family Teacher Manual—Religion 200* (Salt Lake City, Utah: The Church of Jesus Christ of Latter-day Saints, 2016), https://www.churchofjesuschrist.org/study/manual/the-eternal-family-teacher-manual/lesson-12-temple-ordinances-and-covenants?lang=eng; "Marriage for Eternity," *Eternal Marriage Student Manual; Preparing for an Eternal Marriage—Religion 234; Building an Eternal Marriage—Religion 235* (Salt Lake City, Utah: Church Educational System of The Church of Jesus Christ of Latter-day Saints, 2003), https://www.churchofjesuschrist.org/study/manual/eternal-marriage-student-manual/marriage-for-eternity?lang=eng ("We understand that we are to be made kings and priests unto God"); see also Doctrine and Covenants 76:55–56. Anciently Egyptians performed similar rituals, beginning with the first Pharaoh, the grandson of Noah, who Abraham described as "a righteous man" who sought "earnestly to imitate that order established by the fathers in the first generations, in the days of the first patriarchal reign, even in the reign of Adam" (Abraham 1:26). In his extensive study of records describing these ancient practices, Sister Hardison noted, Hugh Nibley observed that "ordinances are more than just symbols—they go beyond that. . . . They always have a double nature: they are or mean something that is real." In other words, quoting Heber C. Kimball, our temple initiatory ordinances "are signs of things in the heavens. Everything we see here is typical of what will be hereafter," including the heavenly anointing referred to in the verses in Doctrine and Covenants 76 cited above and in other scriptures (Hardison, 99, quoting Heber C. Kimball in Linda Aukschun, "The Ordinances and Performances That Pertain to Salvation," *Riches of Eternity: 12 Fundamental Doctrines from the Doctrine and Covenants* [Salt Lake City: Aspen Books, 1900], 135).
19. Douglas A. Callister, "Our Heavenly Home," *Ensign*, June 2009.
20. Other scriptural suggestions of things to "feast upon" include "the words of Christ" (2 Nephi 32:3), God's love (2 Nephi 32:3) and the fruit, or word of God, specifically the doctrine of the Atonement of Jesus Christ, which we plant in our hearts by acting upon such doctrine and "which is most precious, which is sweet above all that is sweet, and which is white above all that is white, yea, and pure above all that is pure." This fruit fills us "that [we] hunger not, neither . . . thirst" (Alma 32:42), even the fruit of eternal life.
21. Nelson, "Choices for Eternity."
22. *General Handbook* 10.2.4, 11.2.4, 25.1, 25.3.1.

CHAPTER 10

The Spiritual Treasure of "Beautiful Garments"

"Each adult temple patron . . . wear[s] the sacred garment of the priesthood under their regular clothing. This is symbolic of an inner commitment to strive each day to become more like the Lord. It also reminds us to remain faithful each day to covenants made and to walk on the covenant path each day in a higher and holier way."[1]

—Russell M. Nelson

In this chapter we consider the spiritual treasure associated with temple clothing or garments, including current prophetic guidance about the symbolic and practical significance of the garments that faithful endowed members wear day and night. We also briefly describe the articles of temple clothing worn anciently and the symbolism Old Testament peoples may have associated with each such item, which helps us better appreciate temple clothing worn today.

Isaiah 52:1—Awake, awake; put on thy strength, O Zion; put on thy beautiful garments, O Jerusalem, the holy city. (See also 2 Nephi 8:24; 3 Nephi 20:36; Moroni 10:31; Doctrine and Covenants 82:14.)

Doctrine and Covenants 113:7–8—Questions by Elias Higbee: What is meant by the command in Isaiah [52:1], which saith: *Put on thy strength, O Zion*—and what people had Isaiah reference to? He had reference to those whom God should call in the last days, who should hold the power of priesthood to bring again Zion, and the redemption of Israel; and *to put on her strength is to put on the authority of the priesthood*, which she, Zion, has a right to by lineage; also to return to that power which she had lost.

These verses provide the doctrinal backdrop to an important feature of temple ordinances and doctrine—putting on the "strength" of the holy priesthood represented by our "beautiful" temple garments. Isaiah's call to ancient and modern Israel to "awake, awake; put on thy strength, O Zion; *put on thy beautiful garments*" (Isaiah 52:1) is nothing less than receiving the power and authority conferred upon men and women in the holy endowment and through the garment of the holy priesthood, which is granted to those who honor and faithfully keep their covenants. As we see "wrath" being "poured out without mixture" in our day (Doctrine and Covenants 115:6), as the Lord prophesied, we can be comforted in knowing that the vision of Isaiah, Nephi, Moroni and, indeed, all of the holy prophets is being realized through the ordinances and covenants available to each of us in God's holy house.

Simple white clothing is used in the temple, including the baptistry, which is similar for men and women.[2] "During the endowment and sealing ordinances, members put on additional [articles of] ceremonial clothing over their white clothing," which are referred to as the "robes of the holy priesthood." In addition, in the clothing portion of the initiatory ordinance, individuals who are receiving their own endowment are officially clothed in, or authorized to wear, the temple garment, consisting of "modest underclothing," which "comes in two pieces" and is "worn under the outer clothing day and night." A link to a video showing temple garments and ceremonial clothing, which beautifully explains the sacred nature of such clothing, can be found under "Sacred Temple Clothing" on the Church's Temples website.[3]

Prophetic Instruction Related to the Wearing of Temple Garments

The *General Handbook* sets forth the most current, definitive statement by Church leaders about the purpose and meaning of temple garments and the covenant we gladly receive and accept as part of the initiatory ordinances of the endowment, as described in the preceding chapter. Church leaders remind us that "it is a sacred privilege to wear the temple garment." Relatively few individuals were authorized to wear the garments of the holy priesthood as they administered temple ordinances anciently, which puts in wonderful perspective the privilege we have to wear the garment and the robes of the holy priesthood with which we officiate on behalf of our kindred dead and others. Wearing the garment "is an outward expression of an inner commitment to follow the Savior Jesus Christ." It is also "a reminder of covenants made in the temple." Most importantly, the *General Handbook* and prophets past and present help us understand the specific blessing or spiritual treasure promised by the Lord as we keep our covenant to wear the garment "properly throughout life." We are promised that "it will serve as a protection."[4]

The *General Handbook* also provides instruction on how the garment should be worn, that is, "beneath the outer clothing." However, "it is a matter of personal preference whether other undergarments are worn over or under the temple garment." The *General Handbook* also instructs that "the garment is sacred and should be treated with respect." Finally, and most importantly, Church leaders help us understand what it means to wear the garment "throughout our lives": "*The garment should not be removed for activities that can reasonably be done while wearing the garment. It should not be modified to accommodate different styles of clothing.*"[5] In years past, the First Presidency, and even President Nelson prior to his ordination as prophet,[6] provided more detailed instructions on this issue. But, consistent with the "principle-based" revisions the Church adopted in 2022 to *For the Strength of Youth*,[7] more detailed instructions are not necessary. Because all endowed members have the supernal gift of the Holy Ghost, they can and should, as the *General Handbook* states, "seek [His] guidance to answer personal questions about wearing the garment."[8]

Symbolic Nature of Temple Clothing

The *Temple Preparation Seminar Teacher's Manual* notes that, along with "the characters depicted, the physical setting, the signs given, and all [other] events," each of which has or will be covered in other chapters of this study, the clothing worn in the temple is symbolic. When the symbolism in each of these aspects of our temple worship is understood, the manual adds, such understanding "will help each person recognize truth and grow spiritually."[9]

One symbol associated with the white clothing everyone wears in the temple is purity. That all patrons and workers dress in the same simple but sacred white clothing also symbolizes our equal worth before God. President James E. Faust, quoting from Acts 10:34 that "God is no respecter of persons," commented: "Within the hallowed walls of the temples, there is no preference of position, wealth, status, race, or education. All dress in white. All receive the same instruction. All make the same covenants and promises. All receive the same transcendent, eternal blessings if they live worthy to claim them. All are equal before their Creator."[10] The temple garment also symbolizes our deep respect for and commitment to keep the law of chastity. "The garment represents sacred covenants. It fosters modesty and becomes a shield and protection to the wearer. . . . The garment, covering the body, is a visual and *tactile reminder* of [covenants made in the temple]. For many Church members the garment has formed a barrier of protection when the wearer has been faced with temptation. Among other things it symbolizes our deep respect for the laws of God—among them the moral standard."[11] In this sense, the garment's physical or "tactile" nature is both real and symbolic, forming a "barrier of protection" against temptation and, in many cases as members have experienced and testified, physical protection as well.[12]

Symbolism Associated with Scriptural Apron of Fig Leaves

> **Genesis 3:7**—And the eyes of [Adam and Eve] were opened, and they knew that they were naked; and they sewed fig leaves together, and made themselves aprons.

After partaking of the forbidden fruit, Adam and Eve discovered their nakedness. They then attempted to cover themselves, in essence to hide their transgression. Sister Hardison notes that the apron of fig leaves "is one of those rich symbols that can be interpreted on several levels." First, not only is hiding "inferior" to having a sin atoned, but also attempting "to take care of the transgression through their own efforts . . . denies the Savior's role." Moreover, when Jehovah made "coats of skin" to "clothe" Adam and Eve (Genesis 3:21) after they discovered their nakedness, He did so through the sacrifice of an animal, which scholars suggest was likely a lamb, "teaching them that the true cost of covering one's sins is the blood of the Lamb."[13] Second, the fig and apron both "symbolize fertility and reproduction." "Adam and Eve put on aprons of figs because they could now bear seed." Third, "leaves of fig trees . . . detached from the branches . . . won't live long. Thus, fig-leaf aprons represent death and mortality."

Finally, "when Adam and Eve covered themselves with leaves, they became, in a sense, trees. Trees frequently represent mankind [for example, the tall cedars of Lebanon represent proud men or Israel an olive tree]. . . . But Adam and Eve aren't to be just any trees. They are to be trees planted by a river, the trees described in Ezekiel 47 [or Revelation 22]. These trees bear fruit continuously and have leaves that never fade and have the power to heal. They represent righteous men and women whose roots are deep and who drink in the divine knowledge, power, and attributes of Living Water. So nourished, they bear the fruit of righteous works, and they heal themselves and others. . . . Adam and Eve are also expressing their spiritual destiny of becoming like Christ, the Tree of Life."[14]

Symbolism Associated with Articles of Ancient Temple Clothing

Exodus 28:2–4, 39—And thou shalt make *holy garments* for Aaron thy brother for glory and for beauty . . . that he may minister unto me in the priest's office. And these are the garments which they shall make; a breastplate, and an *ephod*, and a *robe*, and a *broidered coat*, a *mitre*, and a *girdle*. . . . And thou shalt make them *linen breeches* to cover their nakedness; from the loins even unto the thighs they shall reach.

Leviticus 8:13—And Moses brought Aaron's sons, and put *coats* upon them, and girded them with *girdles*, and put *bonnets* upon them; as the Lord commanded Moses.

In his study of *Sacred Symbols*, Alonzo Gaskill helps us understand the perspective members of the ancient house of Israel brought to their temple experience, as they furnished their consecrated offerings for the temple ordinances administered by the priests and witnessed them officiate in the robes of the holy priesthood. "Throughout the ancient world—when temples still had their place as the central component of religious life—'the candidate begins on his arrival' at the temple or holy place 'by removing his dusty clothes' and then he gets 'dressed in white robes and slippers.'"[15] Significantly, changing into white clothes "meant that the individual engaging in the ceremony or ordinance was aware that he or she was about to enter into a covenant to be new or different than he or she had previously been. It was a public statement about an inner transition—a transition of heart, mind and desires."[16] It certainly would not be appropriate to conclude, from studies by Brother Gaskill and other scholars about the symbolism ancient Israelites and other peoples of Old Testament eras may have associated with each article of clothing the Lord commanded Moses to have made for Aaron and his sons, that such symbols or associations apply to analogous articles of temple clothing we use today. Rather, as the Church's Temples pages declare, the articles of ceremonial clothing, or robes of the Holy Priesthood, used in the endowment and sealing ordinances are intended to "[evoke] religious symbolism reminiscent of temple practices described in the Old Testament."[17] In other words, as we learn more about how ancient Israelites viewed and hallowed all aspects of temple worship and rites the Lord revealed for their day, it helps us better appreciate the deep and eternal significance of each element of temple worship in our day. Some of the associations ancients may have made with the clothing the Lord commanded Moses to have prepared in Exodus 28 include:

- **Coat or undergarment** (Exodus 28:39; Leviticus 8:7; 16:4): The priestly clothing referred to in these verses, "a cotton undershirt of sorts, to be worn by the temple (or tabernacle) high priest," Gaskill suggests, derives from a Hebrew word translated "coat" or "Kethoneth," "the root meaning of [which] is twofold—'To cover' or 'to hide'." When, as noted above, Jehovah clothes Adam and Eve in a Kethoneth or garment made of the skin of an animal slain on their behalf, such garment becomes a type or symbol for the high priest—and for us—of "the atonement of Christ, and his willingness to 'cover' our sins, thereby 'hiding' our shame."[18]

- **"Linen breeches"** (Exodus 28:42; Leviticus 6:10): These verses "tell us that the priests were to wear, in conjunction with their undershirt, 'linen breeches' that extended 'from the loins even unto the thighs' (Exodus 28:42). Of the combination of this white cotton/linen shirt and pant set, one commentator wrote: 'The subject of holiness . . . is seen typified in each of the garments made of the fine twined linen, giving us an appreciation of the term *Holy Garments*. The coat [or undershirt] that clad his person would signify an holiness of the heart that beat beneath it . . . whilst these linen breeches [or underpants] that covered his nakedness declare an holiness of the flesh' or 'desires and passions.'"[19]

- **Mitres or hats and bonnets** (Exodus 28:4, 37, 39; 29:6; 39:28; Leviticus 8:9; 16:4): "Caps worn by the Mosaic priests, during their priestly service in the temple, symbolized 'holiness and righteousness'—two attributes . . . of . . . Jesus Christ, our Great High Priest . . . [which are important] to all who lead or serve in the kingdom." "The word 'bonnet' is derived from a word which means 'to elevate' or 'lift up.' . . . Thus, when the temple priests donned their priestly 'bonnets' or 'caps' the act implied that they were entering into a covenant to walk up to the promises made and the calling received."[20]

- **Veils** (1 Corinthians 11:4–7; 13–15): Paul's admonition that a "woman's head should be covered in prayer" in these verses, and that she "ought . . . to have power on her head" in verse 10, which is translated in the Greek to read "the woman should have Authority on her head," suggests that her temple "head-covering is what Paul calls it—authority: in prayer and prophecy she, like the man, is [acting] under the authority of God."[21]

- **Robes** (Exodus 28:4, 31, 34; 29:5; 39:22–26; Leviticus 8:7): "In priestly tradition, special outerwear depicted power. . . . Robes are standard symbols for the 'power of heaven' or priesthood, and the wearer is to be viewed as the 'earthly representative' of God."[22]
- **Girdles or sashes** (Exodus 29:9; Leviticus 8:7): "In the Hebrew Bible the Mosaic priests were to wear a sash or girdle . . . around their waist when working in the tabernacle. This sash or belt was worn on top of the priestly robe, tied, with the ends hanging down." Symbols associated with the sash include "chastity or virginity." With the sash there is also the implication that it is tied with a bow, reminding Old Testament priests, or us, as we tie a bow in the ceremonial clothing of the "covenant process," binding or tying ourselves "to God, which, of course, is exactly what covenants do."[23]

Much has been written about temple symbols, including the act of putting on priestly robes and other sacred gestures used in the endowment.[24] Such symbolic actions in the endowment, like other ordinances, help us learn by doing. As we deepen our understanding of the ancient contexts and meanings associated with these actions, our understanding and appreciation for the truths these symbols point to also deepens.

Endnotes

1. Nelson, "Closing Remarks," *Ensign*, November 2019.
2. *General Handbook* 38.5.1 describes this white clothing as follows: "Women wear . . . a long-sleeve or three-quarter-sleeve dress (or a skirt and long-sleeve or three-quarter-sleeve blouse), socks or hosiery, and shoes or slippers. Men wear . . . a long-sleeve shirt, necktie or bow tie, pants, socks, and shoes or slippers."
3. "Sacred Temple Clothing," https://www.churchofjesuschrist.org/temples/sacred-temple-clothing?lang=eng. See also Gospel Topics, "Garments," https://www.churchofjesuschrist.org/study/manual/gospel-topics/garments?lang=eng.
4. *General Handbook* 38.5.5.
5. Ibid. (emphasis added).
6. In 2002 President Nelson gave the following counsel about how we should treat the temple garment: "The First Presidency prepared a letter to the Church [about wearing the garment]. They wrote: 'Practices frequently observed among the members of the Church suggest that some members do not fully understand the covenant they make in the temple to wear the garment in accordance with the spirit of the holy endowment. Church members who have been clothed with the garment in the temple have made a covenant to wear it throughout their lives. This has been interpreted to mean that it is worn as underclothing both day and night. . . . The promise of protection and blessings is conditioned upon worthiness and faithfulness in keeping the covenant. The fundamental principle ought to be to wear the garment and not to find occasions to remove it. Thus, members should not remove either all or part of the garment to work in the yard or to lounge around the home in swimwear or immodest clothing. Nor should they remove it to participate in recreational activities that can reasonably be done with the garment worn properly beneath regular clothing. When the garment must be removed, such as for swimming, it should be restored as soon as possible'" (Russell M. Nelson, "Prepare for Blessings of the Temple," *Ensign*, March 2002).
7. See Dieter F. Uchtdorf, "Jesus Christ Is the Strength of Youth," *Liahona*, November 2022; *For the Strength of Youth: A Guide for Making Choices*, "Make inspired choices" (Salt Lake City, Utah: The Church of Jesus Christ of Latter-day Saints, 2022), https://www.churchofjesuschrist.org/study/manual/for-the-strength-of-youth/02–choices?lang=eng.
8. General Handbook 38.5.5.
9. *Endowed from on High: Temple Preparation Seminar Teacher's Manual*, chapter 5, "Learning from the Lord Through Symbols" (Salt Lake City, Utah: The Church of Jesus Christ of Latter-day Saints, 2003), 24, https://abn.churchofjesuschrist.org/study/manual/endowed-from-on-high/lesson-5?lang=eng. For more information about temple symbolism, see, for example, Donald W. Parry, *Temple Symbols and Their Meanings* (Salt Lake City, Utah: Deseret Book, 2020), 175; Christopher Kimball Bigelow, *Temples of the Church of Jesus*

Christ of Latter-Day Saints (San Diego, California: Thunder Bay Press, 2108), especially "The Rich Symbolism in Stone of the Salt Lake Temple," 5–12.
10. *Endowed from on High: Temple Preparation Seminar Teacher's Manual*, chapter 5, "Learning from the Lord Through Symbols," quoting James E. Faust, "Eternity Lies before Us," *Ensign*, May 1997, 10.
11. *Endowed from on High: Temple Preparation Seminar Teacher's Manual*, chapter 5, "Learning from the Lord Through Symbols," quoting *Preparing to Enter the Holy Temple*, 20, 23.
12. In an April 2002 *Ensign* article about parallels between ancient and modern Israel, President Nelson noted that the Lord wants "obedient Saints of modern Israel to receive physical and spiritual protection just as He had provided for His faithful followers centuries before." While he was speaking specifically about the physical protection promised in the Word of Wisdom (Doctrine and Covenants 89:21), the same principle applies to obedience to the covenants made in the temple, including in the initiatory ordinances (Russell M. Nelson, "The Exodus Repeated," *Ensign*, April 2002).
13. Hardison, 110; see also discussion below of the priestly "coat or undergarment."
14. Hardison, 108–11.
15. Gaskill, *Sacred Symbols*, 139.
16. Ibid., 140–41.
17. "Sacred Temple Clothing," https://www.churchofjesuschrist.org/temples/sacred-temple-clothing?lang=eng.
18. Gaskill, *Sacred Symbols*, 161 and note 146.
19. Ibid., 162. See also Gaskill, *Temple Reflections*, chapter 3, "Clothed Upon with Glory," 36–54.
20. Gaskill, *Sacred Symbols*, 148.
21. Ibid., 151, 153 (footnotes and citations omitted).
22. Ibid., 154 (footnotes and citations omitted).
23. Ibid., 157–58 (footnotes and citations omitted).
24. In addition to Alonzo Gaskill's work cited above, see, for example, Gerald E. Hansen Jr., *Sacred Walls: Learning from Temple Symbols* (American Fork, Utah: Covenant Communications, Inc., 2009); Kim Gibbs, *Understanding the Sacred Symbolism of Temple Clothing* (American Fork, Utah: Covenant Communications, Inc., 2019); Hardison, "Glossary of Symbols," 207–23.

CHAPTER 11

The Spiritual Treasure of Being Given and Called by Sacred Names

> *"Study everything Jesus Christ is by prayerfully and vigorously seeking to understand what each of His various titles and names means personally for you."*[1]
>
> —Russell M. Nelson

Increasing our understanding of the importance and use of names and titles in the scriptures will prepare us better to receive, understand, and appreciate the spiritual treasures associated with the sacred names received and used in the endowment. From the beginning, when God has had a work for any of His sons or daughters to do, He has called them by name. In this chapter we seek to understand the spiritual treasure of being called by God by our own given name. Next, we examine the importance of the name of Jesus Christ and what it means to take His name upon us, as we do at baptism, express a willingness to do in the sacrament, and ultimately do in the endowment and sealing ordinances. Finally, we review briefly how names were used and understood anciently and how this ancient understanding helps us prepare ourselves to understand and better appreciate sacred names received in the endowment.

God Knows Us and Calls Us to His Holy Work by Our Names

From the very beginning, when God had a work for His prophets and servants to do, He called them by name. He "called Adam"

(Genesis 3:9; Moses 4:15). He called "Enoch, my son" (Moses 6:27). To Moses He said, "I have a work for thee, Moses, my son" (Moses 1:6). Likewise, He called Abraham (Abraham 1:16) and Samuel (1 Samuel 3:6, 10) to the ministry by name. I have no doubt that He used the given names of all other prophets in His sacred calls and communications with them.

To the Prophet Joseph Smith, the first word Heavenly Father spoke in opening this dispensation was "Joseph." Joseph Smith wrote: "When the light rested upon me I saw two Personages, whose brightness and glory defy all description, standing above me in the air. One of them spake unto me, *calling me by name*" (Joseph Smith—History 1:17). The Savior, in a later revelation, declared, "Behold, thou art Joseph, and thou wast chosen to do the work of the Lord" (Doctrine and Covenants 3:9). Likewise, He spoke to Oliver Cowdery, "Thou art Oliver" (Doctrine and Covenants 6:20), "Oliver Cowdery" (Doctrine and Covenants 8:1; 18:1, 9), and "my son" (Doctrine and Covenants 9:1, 3, 6); to David Whitmer, "thou art David, and thou art called to assist" (Doctrine and Covenants 14:11); to John Whitmer, "my servant John" (Doctrine and Covenants 15:1); to Peter Whitmer, "my servant Peter" (Doctrine and Covenants 16:1); to Thomas B. Marsh, "Thomas, my son" (Doctrine and Covenants 31:1); and so forth throughout the Doctrine and Covenants. The Lord makes no distinction by gender—women are called by name the same as men as we learn in scripture from current and past dispensations: "Hearken unto the voice of the Lord your God, while I speak unto you, Emma Smith, my daughter; for verily I say unto you, all those who receive my gospel are sons and daughters in my kingdom" (Doctrine and Covenants 25:1). The first word addressed to the first individual called to be eyewitness of the Lord's resurrection was her name, "Mary" (John 20:16).[2]

As one commentor explains, "Being called [by God] by one's name is a special privilege and means 'divine selection for a task,'" as when the Father calls Joseph Smith by his name or the Lord raised Lazarus from death by calling his name. "Each of these is either a call to a special mission or a call to discipleship. As such, being called by name also suggests a special relationship and intimacy. Therefore, it is not surprising that God says to the whole house of

Israel, 'I have called thee by thy name; thou art mine' (Isaiah 43:1)."[3] In encouraging members of the Church to learn more about Christ's many names as a way "to better understand His divine mission and His selfless character" and thus be inspired "to become more like Him," Elder Jonathan S. Schmitt of the Seventy pointed out that God revealed a divine pattern by giving some of his prophets and disciples "new names," which "were indicative of their nature, capacity, and potential." For example, as discussed in more detail in the supplementary reading in appendix 2, "Jehovah gave Jacob the new name of Israel, which means 'one who prevails with God' or 'let God prevail.'" Other examples include Jesus giving "James and John the name of Boanerges, which meant the 'sons of thunder'" and, "Simon the name of Cephas or Peter, which means a rock," symbolic of "his future leadership."[4]

The *General Handbook* instructs that when administering an ordinance, we always use the individual's full name (see, for example, 18.7.7; 18.8.2; 18.10.5). Likewise, when setting apart to a calling in the Church, the authorized Melchizedek Priesthood holder "calls the person by his or her full name" (*General Handbook* 18.11.2).

While God calls laborers to His work by using their individual names, in the scriptural record of prophetic calls He also often solemnly introduces Himself by some of His scared names and titles. For example, to Moses, Jehovah declares, "Behold, I am the Lord God Almighty, and Endless is my name" (Moses 1:4). To John and Peter Whitmer, He said, "Hearken, my servant John, and listen to the words of Jesus Christ, your Lord and your Redeemer" (Doctrine and Covenants 15:1; 16:1). To the Prophet and six elders in 1830, He declared, "Listen to the voice of Jesus Christ, your Redeemer, the Great I AM" (Doctrine and Covenants 29:1).

When God called Moses to bring the children of Israel out of Egypt, Moses was concerned that he might be asked on whose behalf or by what authority he acted. "And Moses said unto God, Behold, when I come unto the children of Israel, and shall say unto them, The God of your fathers hath sent me unto you; and they shall say to me, What is his name? what shall I say unto them? And God said unto Moses, I AM THAT I AM: and he said, Thus shalt thou say unto the children of Israel, I AM hath sent me unto you" (Exodus 3:13–14).

The *Old Testament Student Study Guide* explains that "'I Am That I Am' is a form of 'Jehovah,' one of the names of Jesus Christ. Moses and the Israelites understood the name to mean that God is eternal and not created by man, as were other gods of the day. This name was a way for the Lord to identify himself as the all-powerful true and living God. The Israelites came to *greatly reverence this name* and declared that speaking it was blasphemy."[5]

What Does It Mean to Take upon Yourself the Name of Jesus Christ?

The significance and ultimate power of the name of Heavenly Father—"in the language of Adam, Man of Holiness is his name" —"and the name of his Only Begotten [which] is the Son of Man, even Jesus Christ, a righteous Judge" (Moses 6:57), cannot be overstated. As did ancient Israelites, we get a glimpse of the power of Christ's name and voice from the account in Mark of the man with an unclean spirit, who unwittingly became a testator of Christ's name when he cried out, "Let us alone; what have we to do with thee, thou Jesus of Nazareth? art thou come to destroy us? I know thee who thou art, the *Holy One of God*" (Mark 1:23–27; see also Mark 5:17; Luke 4:33–37). Later He commissioned His twelve disciples to do the same by the power of His name, the "name of Jesus Christ of Nazareth," and His authority (Matthew 10:1–8; Acts 3:6).

At the time King Benjamin's people renewed their baptismal covenants, were spiritually reborn, and experienced a mighty change of heart as they took upon themselves the name of Christ, King Benjamin reminded them that "there is no other name given whereby salvation cometh" (Mosiah 5:8). He also taught that taking upon themselves the name of Christ was not a one-time event but a lifetime process: "I would that ye should *take upon you the name of Chr*ist, all you that have entered into the covenant with God that ye should be obedient unto the end of your lives." This suggests that taking upon themselves the name of Christ included the choice to obey Him until the end of their lives.

In response to the question by what name the Nephites should call the Church, Jesus reminded His disciples, "Have they [the members of the Church in that day] not read the scriptures, which say ye must take upon you the name of Christ, which is my name?" Perhaps they failed to understand the scope of King Benjamin's teachings. "For by this name shall ye be called at the last day," Jesus continued, "and whoso taketh upon him my name, and endureth to the end, the same shall be saved at the last day. Therefore, *whatsoever ye shall do, ye shall do it in my name*; therefore ye shall call the church in my name" (3 Nephi 27:5–7). Calling the Church by its proper name is a commandment that President Nelson has reiterated in our day.[6] Significantly, ordinances are performed "in the name of . . . Jesus Christ," as with the sacrament (Doctrine and Covenants 20:77, 79), or "in the name of the Father, and of the Son, and of the Holy Ghost," as with the ordinance of baptism (Doctrine and Covenants 20:73) and certain temple ordinances, which members of the Godhead, the Savior said, "are one" (3 Nephi 11:27).

What does it mean to take upon ourselves the name of Christ? As King Benjamin taught, in entering into the covenant of the gospel at baptism, we are spiritually begotten by Christ, becoming His sons and daughters. Thus, we are called by His name. When we renew our baptismal covenant in the sacrament, however, President Dallin H. Oaks taught, "It is significant that . . . we do not witness that we *take upon us* the name of Jesus Christ. We witness that we are *willing* to do so. (See Doctrine and Covenants 20:77.) The fact that we only witness to our willingness suggests that something else must happen before we actually take that sacred name upon us."[7]

President Oaks then describes two sacred events that our promise anticipates—taking upon us the authority of God in the temple and being exalted in the celestial kingdom. Both Old Testament and Latter-day scriptures describe the temple as "a place where the Lord their God would 'cause his name to dwell' (Deut. 12:11; see also Deut. 14:23–24; Deut. 16:6)," "as a house for 'the name' of the Lord God of Israel" (citing 1 Kings 9:3; 2 Chr. 7:16; Doctrine and Covenants 124:39; 105:33; 109:2–5), and a place where His name would "be put" upon His people (Doctrine and Covenants 109:26). President Oaks explains:

All of these references to ancient and modern temples as houses for "the name" of the Lord obviously involve something far more significant than a mere inscription of his sacred name on the structure. The scriptures speak of the Lord's putting his name in a temple because he gives authority for his name to be used in the sacred ordinances of that house. That is the meaning of the Prophet's reference to the Lord's putting his name upon his people in that holy house. (See D&C 109:26.)

Willingness to take upon us the name of Jesus Christ can therefore be understood as willingness to take upon us the authority of Jesus Christ. According to this meaning, by partaking of the sacrament we witness our willingness to participate in the sacred ordinances of the temple and to receive the highest blessings available through the name and by the authority of the Savior when he chooses to confer them upon us.[8]

Thus, an important part of our baptismal covenant, as it is renewed in the ordinance of the sacrament, involves a willingness to prepare ourselves to go to the temple and receive the sacred ordinances that are only administered there and keep the covenants made in those ordinances. In short, "we are signifying our commitment to do all that we can to achieve eternal life in the kingdom of our Father. We are expressing our candidacy—our determination to strive for—exaltation in the celestial kingdom." As explained in greater detail in chapter 19, as we continue on the covenant path and "keep the commandments of God," in due time we can receive the "fulness" and be "partakers of the glory" of the Father, becoming members of "the church of the Firstborn." "This is the ultimate significance of taking upon us the name of Jesus Christ."[9]

The Role of Names or Key Words and Signs or "Gestures of Approach" in Antiquity

Amy Hardison describes various ways in which biblical peoples viewed names. For example, "children's names often recorded the parents' experience," as when Joseph names his son "Manasseh," meaning "he who causes to forget." In other words, becoming a father allowed

Joseph to forget, to a degree, the pain of being rejected by his brothers and sold into Egypt. Likewise, "it was common in ancient Israel for parents to give their child a name that expressed their testimony and devotion to God," as when the parents of Elijah chose his name, meaning "my God is Yaweh" (in Hebrew, the conjunction of *ēl*, God, and the divine name *Yahweh*, shortened to "*Yaw/Yā*"). "Such names expressed devotion but were also used in both Egypt and Israel to petition a deity to place a person under His protection." "Parents might also choose a particular name because of its associations with others who bore that name. Helaman, the son of Helaman, named his sons Nephi and Lehi, hoping they would remember and emulate their righteous forebears,"[10] as do many parents today. In the ancient world names reflected "the essence of a person, one's very nature. 'The name and the personality were so closely associated in Hebrew thought that they were considered almost identical.'" "This was an age that 'tended to identify words and realities.' God spoke, and the world came into existence."[11]

Truman G. Madsen describes how ancient saints or members of God's early-day church believed that when God placed His name in the temple, His presence was there. Thus, "prayers were directed to the temple in the belief that God's presence was there as it was in heaven." Think of Daniel, living in Babylonian captivity, praying toward the temple in Jerusalem. In summary, Brother Madsen concludes, three key ideas about the role and importance of sacred names in ancient temple rites helps us appreciate the role of sacred names used in the endowment: "(1) in names, especially divine names, is concentrated divine power; (2) through ritual processes one may gain access to these names and take them upon oneself; (3) these ritual processes are often explicitly temple related. . . . In the temple ritual setting, names are not seen as mere labels. They mark degrees or attributes or roles in one's transformation process. They are symbolic of new births or beginnings. Thus, an individual, while retaining his identity, may take on several names as he moves through stages toward the divine."[12]

"Who shall ascend into the hill of the Lord? or who shall stand in his holy place?" the Psalmist asked. "He that hath clean hands, and a pure heart; who hath not lifted up his soul unto vanity, nor sworn deceitfully." These are they who "receive the blessing from the Lord, and righteousness from the God of his salvation . . . that *seek thy face* [in His holy temple] (Psalm 24:3–6). Thus, the temple becomes a place where we can "ascend" to God and "stand in his holy place," even His presence, because He put His name there.[13]

The existence of sacred names or key words in the temple ceremony is intimated in Joseph Smith's inspired description of several figures or drawings replicated in Facsimile No. 2 in the book of Abraham in the Pearl of Great Price. For example, Facsimile No. 2, Figure 3, the Prophet revealed, is a representation of "God, sitting upon his throne, clothed with power and authority; with a crown of eternal light upon his head; representing also the grand *Key-words of the Holy Priesthood*, as revealed to Adam in the Garden of Eden, as also to Seth, Noah, Melchizedek, Abraham, and all to whom the Priesthood was revealed." Likewise, in Figure 7 is another representation of "God sitting upon his throne, revealing through the heavens the grand *Key-words of the Priesthood*." The comment relating to Figure 8 tells us that what these key words are and what they mean "cannot be revealed unto the world; but [are] to be had in the Holy Temple of God." As President Nelson taught, such scriptural references to elements of the endowment not only underscore the "antiquity" of temple ordinances,[14] but remind us of the unchanging nature of the essential truths or covenants associated with the ordinances of the gospel.[15]

In a vision of the heavenly temple in the book of Revelation, the Lord declares to John the Beloved that He would make each of us who receives the ordinances of the temple and who "overcomes" the world "a pillar" in that heavenly temple, and "he [or she] shall go no more out: and I will write upon him [or her] the name of my God . . . and I will write upon him [or her] *my new name*" (Revelation 3:12). Brigham Young, in an often-quoted statement, explains that an important part of our "endowment is to receive [in the] ordinances in the House of the Lord" the special knowledge "which [is] necessary for [us], after [we] have departed this life, to enable [us] to walk back to the presence of the Father, passing the angels who stand as sentinels, being able to give them the *key words*, the *signs* and *tokens*, pertaining to the holy Priesthood, and gain [our] eternal exaltation in spite of earth and hell."[16]

In their extensive study of how symbols can deepen our understanding of the Atonement, Donald and Jay Parry describe how religious rituals include "sacred actions or 'ceremonial movements.'

Some scholars refer to these rites of transition as 'gestures of approach' because they are religious gestures (or acts or movements) that worshipers make as they approach God during sacred worship. The ancient temple, especially, included sacred gestures that enabled and empowered worshipers to move from the outer gate inward to the most holy place of all, the holy of holies." Such ritual actions are integral to modern temple ordinances as well because "they symbolically cleanse and prepare worshipers for entry into and movement through sacred space as they transition from the profane world into the sacred temple."[17]

Lessons learned from the ancients, which have filtered down through the millennia in many religious traditions, can help us as we mature in our own efforts to receive through the ultimate teacher in the temple, the Holy Ghost, all that the Lord desires for us to know and feel in our own personal temple worship. After reviewing the use of certain names, gestures, handclasps, signs, or "tokens of recognition" in the Old Testament, in early Christianity, Catholicism and Judaism, and even Islam, Professor Gaskill summarizes the meaning and importance of these practices in religious rituals generally: "Frequently accompanying [these] signs and tokens," which were and still are used in ritual practices in these various religious traditions, "are certain 'secret' words or phrases," which, if kept secret, "symbolized fidelity to covenants. . . . They represented to the recipient an endowment or gift, as they were considered symbols of God's holy words. Thus to receive them implied both that God had endowed you, but also that God had *entrusted* you. Consequently, they were also symbols of divine friendship and acceptance."[18]

What the Names and Key Words of the Endowment Enable Us to Become—One with Our Father

Isaiah saw in vision that "in the last days" the temple, "the mountain of the Lord's house," would "be established in the top of the mountains" and that "all nations shall flow unto it" (Isaiah 2:2). As many have pointed out, this is an apt description of the Salt Lake Temple. But more importantly, in his visions of the miraculous gathering of the last days, Isaiah reveals much more about the role of temple ordinances in blessing in our day all people of the earth who would accept God's invitation to "come unto" Him.[19] In the side-by-side translations of Isaiah 56:4–8 below by Church scholar Avraham Gileadi (in the left column) and the King James Version (in the right column), we read how the temple endowment, with its "key words, signs and tokens," blesses not only the seed of Abraham who "are lawful heirs, according to the flesh" (Doctrine and Covenants 86:9), but "the eunuchs" and "strangers," those of all nations, races, kindreds, tongues, and peoples, regardless of lineage, who accept the gospel and keep the Lord's sabbaths or commandments.

Isaiah 56:4–8

For thus saith the Lord:	For thus saith the Lord
As for the eunuchs who keep my Sabbaths	unto the eunuchs that keep my sabbaths,
and choose to do what I will—	and choose the things that please me,
holding fast to my covenants—	and *take hold of my covenant*;
to them I will give a handclasp and a name within the wall of my house	Even unto them will I give in mine house and within my walls a place and *a name better than of sons and of daughters*:
that is better than sons and daughters;	*I will give them an everlasting name,*
I will endow them with an everlasting name	that shall not be cut off.
that shall not be cut off.	Also the sons of the stranger, that join themselves to the Lord, to serve him,
And the foreigners who adhere to the Lord	and to love the *name of the Lord*,
to serve him,	to be his servants,
who love the *name of the Lord*,	everyone that keepeth the sabbath from polluting it, and taketh hold of *my covenant*;
that they may be his servants—	
all who keep the Sabbath without profaning it,	Even them will *I bring to my holy mountain*,
holding fast to *my covenant*—	and make them joyful in my house of prayer:
these I will bring to my holy mountain	
and gladden in my house of prayer.	their burnt offerings and their sacrifices shall be accepted upon mine altar;
Their offerings and sacrifices shall be accepted on my altar,	for mine house shall be called an house of prayer for all people.
for my house shall be known as a house of prayer for all nations.	The Lord GOD which gathereth the outcasts of Israel saith,
Thus says my Lord the Lord, who gathers up the outcasts of Israel:	Yet will I gather others to him, beside those
I will gather others to those already gathered.	that are gathered unto him.[20]

The *Old Testament Student Manual* commentary on this passage states that "to understand Isaiah's meaning" in this temple text, "one must understand the significance of three words and their meaning to ancient Israel. The words are *Sabbath, strangers,* and *eunuchs.*"

- *Sabbath*—"For ancient Israel *Sabbath*" meant "more than simply working or playing on Sunday (Saturday for the Jews)," but observing all holy days ("including Passover, Pentecost, Tabernacles, and the Day of Atonement, which were also called sabbaths"), indeed keeping "the whole law of Moses."
- A *stranger* "was not a full citizen," but someone who "had recognized rights and duties" and "was under the protection of God," someone "the Israelites were charged to treat kindly."
- *Eunuchs*—"Under the Mosaic law, anyone who had been sexually mutilated was not allowed into full fellowship in the house of Israel (see Deuteronomy 23:1–2)," "wholeness of body" typifying or symbolizing "spiritual wholeness." "A priest or Levite who was a eunuch could not function in the priesthood offices (see Leviticus 21:17–23)."

With the meaning of these three words in mind, "one can see the beauty of Isaiah's promise given in Isaiah 56. Strangers (Gentiles) and eunuchs (those previously excluded from full fellowship with the covenant people, and who felt they could produce no fruit in the covenant, being 'a dry tree' [v. 3]), would now find the full blessings of God extended to them if they kept the sabbaths (epitomizing the law of God). Not only will the 'outcasts of Israel' (those who were scattered) be gathered in the last days, but so will 'others' (v. 8). Whether one is a literal descendant of Israel will not matter as much as whether one will make and keep the covenant with God. In the age of restoration, the house of God will be '*an house of prayer for all people*'" (v. 7)."[21] In both translations above, Isaiah teaches the importance of "tak[ing] hold of my covenant" and receiving the "name of the Lord," that is, Jesus Christ, through the ordinances of the gospel, especially baptism and confirmation as King Benjamin described,[22] and ultimately, as President Oaks taught, the ordinances of the temple. Through the covenant of baptism, Brother Madsen observes, a person "not only pledges allegiance to Jesus [Christ], but is also established or born 'into fellowship with him' and with the Father in whose name he acts."[23] During the periods of the temples of Solomon (often referred to as the "First" temple) and Zerubbabel (or the "Second" temple), Brother Madsen writes, "receiving the name [of God, YHWH or Yahweh] was a privilege of obedience. It was to be 'inscribed' on and inside the person—in the hands (see Isaiah 56) and on the 'inward parts,'"[24] as Jeremiah prophesied:

> **Jeremiah 31:31–34**—Behold, the days come, saith the Lord, that I will make a new covenant with the house of Israel, and with the house of Judah: Not according to the covenant that I made with their fathers in the day that I took them by the hand to bring them out of the land of Egypt; which my covenant they brake. . . . But *this shall be the covenant that I will make with the house of Israel*; [In the latter] days, saith the Lord, *I will put my law in their inward parts, and write it in their hearts*; and will be their God, and they shall be my people. And they shall teach no more every man his neighbour, and every man his brother, saying, Know the Lord: for they shall all know me, from the least of them unto the greatest of them, saith the Lord.

Through frequent temple worship and keeping our temple covenants, we allow God to write His law in our "inward parts," our hearts and souls. In the process, we become His people and we come to know Him. As Brother Madsen expressed, the "highest spiritual aspiration" of the ordinance of the endowment, particularly as it relates to the sacred names received as part of the endowment, is "that there will one day be full harmony of nature between the One who names, the name, and the named. This is the vision of the temple" that Isaiah describes in chapter 56.[25] The ultimate promise of the house of the Lord is that, in entering into the "rest" or presence of the Lord, we will both know Him and be one with Him.

Endnotes

1. Nelson, "Drawing the Power of Jesus Christ into Our Lives."
2. See Jonathan S. Schmitt, "That They Might Know Thee," *Liahona*, November 2022, 104.
3. Hardison, 135 (footnotes omitted). Frequently in scripture the Lord's call to an individual by name is followed by Him identifying Himself by name. For example, in Abraham 1:16, the Lord calls "Abraham, Abraham, behold, my name is Jehovah." (See also note 19 in chapter 16; Genesis 15:1, 7 [the Lord "came unto Abram in a vision, saying Fear not, Abram. . . . I am the LORD that brought thee out of Ur"]). Such "exchange of names," scholars note, was one element of ancient covenant-making. (See "The Great Exchange: Understanding More About Covenants," Growing Graceful, https://growinggraceful.com/2018/05/15/the-great-exchange-understanding-more-about-covenants/; Jared T. Parker, "Cutting Covenants," in *The Gospel of Jesus Christ in the Old Testament*, eds. D. Kelly Ogden, Jared W. Ludlow, and Kerry Muhlestein, (BYU Religious Studies Center, 2009), https://rsc.byu.edu/gospel-jesus-christ-old-testament/cutting-covenants#:~:text=Covenants%20are%20a%20key%20aspect,curse%20for%20violating%20the%20covenant [discussing how the covenant Jehovah made with Abraham in Genesis 15 may be viewed as a "temple text"]). As one Bible ministry points out, "the giving or the exchange of names is one of the most powerful aspect[s] of any Covenant making process. It is what validates the Covenant itself. It makes it authentic and genuine." Bible Vision International Ministries, https://biblevisionintministries.org/christian-living/covenant/his-name-identifies-you-with-the-covenant-use-it/.
4. Schmitt, "That They Might Know Thee," 104.
5. "Exodus 3: The Burning Bush," *Old Testament Student Study Guide* (Salt Lake City, Utah: Church Educational System, The Church of Jesus Christ of Latter-day Saints, 2002), https://www.churchofjesuschrist.org/study/manual/old-testament-seminary-student-study-guide-obs/the-book-of-exodus/exodus-3-the-burning-bush?lang=eng (emphasis added). See also chapter 6, note 14.
6. Russell M. Nelson, "The Correct Name of the Church," *Ensign*, November 2018; Nelson, "Opening the Heavens for Help," *Ensign*, May 2020.
7. Dallin H. Oaks, "Taking upon Us the Name of Jesus Christ," *Ensign*, May 1985, 81 (emphasis in original).
8. Ibid. (citation omitted).
9. Ibid. (certain citations omitted).
10. Hardison, 131–32.
11. Ibid., 133 (footnotes omitted).
12. Madsen, *The Temple: Where Heaven and Earth Meet*, 138–39.
13. Ibid., 142.
14. Nelson, "Becoming Exemplary Latter-day Saints," 114 ("These sacred temple rites are ancient"); Nelson, "Personal Preparation for Temple Blessings."
15. Nelson, "Come, Follow Me" (All "devoted disciples of Jesus Christ—since the world was created—have made the same covenants with God" and "have received the same ordinances that we as members of the Lord's restored

Church today have made: those covenants that we receive at baptism and in the temple"). Elder David B. Haight of the Quorum of the Twelve similarly observed: "Saints of all ages have had temples in one form or another. There is evidence that temple worship was customary from Adam to Noah and that after the Flood the holy priesthood was continued; therefore, we have every reason to believe the ordinances of the temple were available to those entitled to receive them" (Haight, "Personal Temple Worship," citing Widtsoe, "Temple Worship," 53–54).

16. *Preparing to Enter the Holy Temple*, 31, quoting *Discourses of Brigham Young*, comp. John A. Widtsoe (Salt Lake City: Deseret Book, 1971), 416 (emphasis added).
17. Gaskill, *Sacred Symbols*, 189, quoting Donald W. Parry and Jay A. Parry, *Symbols & Shadows: Unlocking a Deeper Understanding of the Atonement* (Salt Lake City: Deseret Book, 2009), 22.
18. Gaskill, *Sacred Symbols*, 198 (emphasis added).
19. See Mark 1:17 ("And Jesus said unto [his newly called apostles], Come ye after me"); 2 Nephi 26:25 (Christ "saith: Come unto me all ye ends of the earth, buy milk and honey, without money and without price"); Alma 5:34 ("Yea, he saith: Come unto me and ye shall partake of the fruit of the tree of life; yea, ye shall eat and drink of the bread and the waters of life freely").
20. Madsen, *The Temple: Where Heaven and Earth Meet*, 155. The translation in the left column is from *The Apocalyptic Book of Isaiah: A New Translation with Interpretive Key*, trans. Avraham Gileadi (Provo, Utah: Hebraeus Press, 1982), 142, while the version in the right column is the King James Version of the Bible.
21. "The Last Days and the Millennium: Isaiah 55–66," *Old Testament Student Manual—Kings–Malachi*, https://www.churchofjesuschrist.org/study/manual/old-testament-student-manual-kings-malachi/chapter-18.html?lang=eng (certain citations omitted).
22. Mosiah 1:11–12 ("And moreover, I shall give this people a name, that thereby they may be distinguished above all the people which the Lord God hath brought out of the land of Jerusalem; and this I do because they have been a diligent people in keeping the commandments of the Lord. And I give unto them a name that never shall be blotted out, except it be through transgression"); Mosiah 5:7 ("And now, because of the covenant which ye have made ye shall be called the children of Christ, his sons, and his daughters; for behold, this day he hath spiritually begotten you; for ye say that your hearts are changed through faith on his name; therefore, ye are born of him and have become his sons and his daughters. . . . And . . . this is the name that I said I should give unto you that never should be blotted out, except it be through transgression; therefore, take heed that ye do not transgress, that the name be not blotted out of your hearts").
23. Madsen, *The Temple: Where Heaven and Earth Meet*, 149 (citation omitted).
24. Ibid., 145.
25. Ibid., 155.

CHAPTER 12

The Spiritual Treasures in the Endowment Instruction

Coming to Know Who God Is and Who We Are in Relation to Him

"You were chosen by our Father to come to earth at this crucial time because of your premortal spiritual valor. You are among the finest, most valiant men [and women] who have ever come to the earth."[1]

—Russell M. Nelson

From the earliest days of the Restoration, the Lord made clear His intention to follow the pattern and promise of every gospel dispensation, which includes making available the crowning ordinances of the gospel. These ordinances can only be received in places or buildings consecrated and appointed by the Lord. As early as September 21, 1823, years before the organization of the Church, Moroni quoted the Lord's promise through Malachi that He would "reveal unto you the [sealing power of the] Priesthood, by the hand of Elijah" (Joseph Smith—History 1:38).[2] In December 1830, less than a year after the formal organization of the Church, the Lord declared, "I will come suddenly to my temple" (Doctrine and Covenants 36:8). In January 1831, He promised His obedient Saints that He would endow them "with power from on high" (Doctrine and Covenants 38:32,

38), a promise he repeated in February 1831 (Doctrine and Covenants 43:16) and June 1834 (Doctrine and Covenants 105:11). On July 20, 1831, in answer to the Prophet Joseph Smith's question, "Where will thy Temple stand, unto which all nations shall come in the last days?" the Lord responded, "A spot for the temple is lying westward, upon a lot which is not far from the courthouse" (Doctrine and Covenants 57:3) in Independence, Missouri. Less than a month later, on August 3, 1831, the Prophet dedicated that site for the construction of "a complex or campus of two dozen temples—twelve Aaronic and twelve Melchizedek."[3] In December 1832 the Lord commanded the Saints to build a "house of God" in Kirtland, Ohio (Doctrine and Covenants 88:119).[4] After great sacrifice, this temple in Kirtland, the first in this dispensation, was dedicated on March 27, 1836 (see Doctrine and Covenants 109). In essence, from the beginning of the Restoration the Lord was seeking to prepare His people to receive the ordinances of the temple so that they could be endowed with heavenly power.

What is this endowment of heavenly power the Lord promises us? One answer I have gleaned from my temple experience is that this endowment of priesthood power begins with gaining a deep and abiding testimony about who God is and who I am in relation to Him. This spiritual treasure can be obtained in the instruction received in the endowment[5] *and* in scriptures that expand on and explain this instruction as we earnestly seek and search for it.

For example, as Elder James E. Talmage and others have explained, the endowment gives us an overview of the "whole plan of salvation," including the Grand Council in Heaven, during which Heavenly Father presented His plan for the redemption and exaltation of His children and the creation of the earth pursuant to that plan and foreordained the Savior to work out the infinite Atonement. As we consider in this chapter what the scriptures teach us about this Grand Council, and particularly what they suggest about our role and identity in that council and in our premortal experiences, ponder how this knowledge empowers you and provides powerful perspective to guide your day-to-day decisions.

Next, Elder Talmage notes, we learn about Adam and Eve's role in and the importance and purposes of the Fall and the role and importance of apostles and prophets in teaching and administering the doctrines, covenants, and ordinances that make access to Christ's enabling power possible, including the consequences of apostasy when they are rejected.[6] Again, as we examine in this chapter a few illustrative scriptures and teachings of the apostles and prophets about these themes, consider how likening Adam and Eve's experiences to ourselves empowers us with knowledge about how to draw upon God's power to spiritually strengthen ourselves and our families.

What the Scriptures Teach about Our Role and Identity in Premortality and the Grand Council in Heaven

To review the events surrounding what Abraham and Moses described about the Grand Council when Heavenly Father asked, "Whom shall I send?" and the Savior, the premortal Jehovah, answered, "Here am I send me" (Abraham 3:27), the entry "Council in Heaven" under Gospel Topics explains that the purpose of this council was for our Father "to present His plan for our progression," which, if followed, would enable us to become like Him. "We would be resurrected; we would have all power in heaven and on earth; we would become heavenly parents and have spirit children just as He does."[7] This plan, Elder Quentin L. Cook of the Quorum of the Twelve has taught, "included certain laws and ordinances of the priesthood instituted before the foundation of the world."[8] Thus, the role of covenants and ordinances is not only central to the gospel plan in this life, but has been from the beginning.

During this council, and no doubt during the eons of time during which we progressed spiritually in the presence of our Heavenly Parents, "we also learned that because of our weakness, all of us except little children would sin (see Doctrine and Covenants 29:46–47)" (Gospel Topics). I would add that "weakness" here can be understood two ways. "Weakness," in the singular, can mean the weakness inherent in our mortal condition as contemplated by the Father's plan—that in order to "know to prize the good" we must "taste the bitter" (Moses 6:55), that is we must be subject to Satan's temptations, comforted by the truth that "God is faithful" and "will not suffer [us] to be tempted above that [we] are able" (1 Corinthians 10:13). It also could refer to our individual weaknesses, that is, the deficiencies in our character that we bring with us from the premortal life as a result of our individual spiritual development that began ever since, and even before, we were spiritually begotten by Heavenly Parents.[9] For example, we learn that Satan "was a liar from the beginning" (Doctrine and Covenants 93:25), meaning from before the creation of the earth. We were taught, no doubt long before the convening of this Grand Council, that the Atonement would not only allow us to overcome through repentance the sins we would inevitably commit as a result of our weakness, but it would also give us strength to continue our spiritual progression, overcoming our weaknesses and acquiring the Christlike virtues we had only partially developed in our sojourn in the spirit world.

While, as noted in chapter 4, the accounts in Moses and Abraham about the Grand Council tell us much about the character and identity of Jehovah and Lucifer, other scriptures, as well as the teachings of living prophets, also hint at our own divine identities, echoes of which we feel as we participate in the endowment. For example:

- In his vision of the redemption of the dead, President Joseph F. Smith saw that before they were born latter-day prophets, together "with many others," which can be read to include each of us, "received their *first lessons* in the world of spirits and were *prepared* to come forth in the due time of the Lord to labor in his vineyard for the salvation of the souls of men" (Doctrine and Covenants 138:56). While the extent of these "lessons" and "preparations" is not revealed, we can be assured that over the eons we lived with our Heavenly Father, there was likely very little about His perfect plan for our progression that we did not understand.[10]
- In his vision of the events attending the Grand Council, John the Beloved reveals that as a result of Satan's rebellion, "there was war in heaven: Michael [the premortal Adam] and his angels fought against the dragon [Lucifer]; and the dragon fought and his angels. . . . And the great dragon was cast out, that old serpent, called the Devil, and Satan, which deceiveth the whole world: he was cast out into the earth, and his angels

were cast out with him" (Revelation 12:7, 9). How was this great battle won? John sees that "they overcame him by the blood of the Lamb, and by the word of their testimony; and they loved not their lives unto the death" (Revelation 12:10). Who were the angels who fought with Michael? Those who were valiant in their testimonies of "the Lamb," meaning the Lamb of God or Jehovah (who even then we looked to as our Exemplar and Redeemer), which would include no doubt members of Christ's Church today. The phrase "loved not their lives unto the death" suggests to me that all of us exercised a high degree of faith in Jesus Christ and faithfulness to His and our Father's teachings.

Finally, Alma tells us a lot about the high and holy station faithful sisters and priesthood holders attained in our premortal existence as he describes what we each did then to qualify for the sacred callings we were foreordained to fulfill in this life—"being called and prepared from the foundation of the world according to the foreknowledge of God, on account of their *exceeding faith* and *good works*; in the first place being left to choose good or evil; therefore they having chosen good, and exercising exceedingly great faith, are called [foreordained] with a holy calling" (Alma 13:3).[11] With these and other doctrinal statements about our divine origins and potential destiny in our minds, we can leave each session with greater power or capacity to confront the day-to-day challenges in our lives.[12]

The Creation and Fall

As the three pillars of the plan of salvation—the Creation, the Fall, and the Atonement[13]—unfold to each of us as patrons in the endowment, consider how these doctrines relate to you personally and your family or to that individual for whom you are serving as proxy and his or her family. Lehi taught, "Adam fell that men might be; and men are, that they might have joy" (2 Nephi 2:25). President Russell M. Nelson declared that "the earth was created that families might be" and that "the spirit children of God" might have the opportunity "to progress toward an eternal exaltation."[14] Malachi prophesied that without the return of the prophet Elijah before the Second Coming of the Lord to restore the sealing power, the earth would be "cursed" (Malachi 4:5–6; 3 Nephi 35:5–6; Doctrine and Covenants 110:15) or "utterly wasted" (Doctrine and Covenants 2:3; 138:48; J. Smith-History 1:39). In other words, we learn through the beautiful presentation of the majestic and miraculous creation of the earth, the subsequent depiction of the Fall, and the solemn presentation and acceptance of holy covenants that bind us to God through the Atonement of His Son that all of these events—the Creation, Fall, and Atonement—were accomplished so that we each might come to earth, be sealed to our families, and grow spiritually to one day return to the glorious presence of our Heavenly Parents and with Them receive a fulness of joy.

With this overarching observation in mind, divining the sequence and substance of what President Nelson referred to as the various "phases" (or "periods," each variously described as a "a day, a time or an age") of the spiritual and temporal creations described in Genesis, the books of Moses and Abraham, and even in the endowment, "culminating with the creation of Adam and Eve,"[15] becomes far less important than how we can maintain an eternal perspective in our lives so that we can stay focused on keeping our covenants in order to continue, and not halt, the incredible progress we made in our first estate. As Elder Bruce R. McConkie taught, the scriptural and temple "accounts of the Creation . . . enable us to understand" first, "the nature of our mortal probation, a probation in which all men are being tried and tested 'to see if they will do all things whatsoever the Lord their God shall command them' (Abraham 3:25), and, second, the all-important role of 'the atoning sacrifice of the Lord Jesus Christ.'"[16] The blessings of the Atonement, of course, including Christ's redeeming and perfecting power, are only available on the terms He and the Father have prescribed, which center on receiving and keeping the covenants entered into through the ordinances of the gospel, including most importantly temple ordinances.

Who directed and assisted in the Creation? "The Living Christ: The Testimony of the Apostles" states: "Under the direction of His Father, [Jesus Christ] was the creator of the earth."[17] In Genesis 1:26 and Moses 2:26 God said, "Let us make man in our image, after our likeness." The "us" refers to God the Father and Jehovah. Abraham 4:26, however, states that "the Gods took counsel among themselves and . . . went down to organize man in their own image, in the image of the Gods to form they him, male and female to form they them." This verse suggests that possibly other "noble and great ones" may have been involved in the creation in addition to the Father and the Son.[18]

Did God Give Adam and Eve Conflicting Commandments and, if so, Why?

> **Moses 2:28**—And I, God . . . said unto [Adam and Eve]: Be fruitful, and multiply, and replenish the earth.

> **Moses 3:16–17**—And I, the Lord God, commanded the man, saying: Of every tree of the garden thou mayest freely eat, But of the tree of the knowledge of good and evil, thou shalt not eat of it, *nevertheless, thou mayest choose for thyself,* for it is given unto thee; but, remember that I forbid it, for in the day thou eatest thereof thou shalt surely die.

"To bring the plan of happiness to fruition," President Nelson taught, "God issued to Adam and Eve the first commandment ever given to mankind. It was a commandment to beget children. A law was explained to them. Should they eat from 'the tree of the knowledge of good and evil' (Genesis 2:17), their bodies would change; mortality and eventual death would come upon them. But partaking of that fruit was prerequisite to their parenthood."[19]

"But," many have asked, "can God be kind and good if He is placing them in [a] predicament" where to keep one commandment (to have children) they must break another commandment (to not eat of the tree of knowledge of good and evil)?[20] Elder McConkie explains, "The whole plan of salvation, including both immortality and eternal life for all the spirit hosts of heaven, hung on [Adam and Eve's] compliance with this [first] command." Thus, Adam and Eve choose to obey, to fall. "Adam fell as fall he must. But he fell by breaking a lesser law—an infinitely lesser law—so that he too, having thereby *transgressed*, would become subject to sin and need a Redeemer and be privileged to work out his own salvation, even as would be the case with all those upon whom the effects of the fall would come."[21]

Moreover, as Melinda Brown argues, by giving contradictory commandments, or "opposing alternatives," Adam and Eve are given "the perfect impetus for action." "They've been given the privilege of choice [*thou mayest choose for thyself, for it is given unto thee*], but they must have options to nudge them forward. As President Boyd K. Packer explained, 'There was too much at issue to introduce man into mortality by force. That would contravene the very law essential to the plan.'"[22] Sister Brown adds that the choice put to Adam and Eve should also be viewed in the context of Heavenly Father's character, His perfect love and truthfulness, as He advises them that their choice to disobey the commandment not to eat of the tree of knowledge of good and evil will have consequences, namely it will bring pain and suffering "for [their] sake[s]" (Moses 4:28). Indeed, Eve clearly understood that her choice would necessarily result in her expulsion from the paradisaical Eden, consistent with Heavenly Father's plan. "If I have to leave and you choose to stay," she in effect lovingly counsels with Adam, so that he also might make this all-important choice, "how can we 'multiply and replenish the earth'?" The Father later confirms Eve's understanding when He says to Jehovah: "Therefore I, the Lord God, will send him forth from the Garden of Eden, to till the ground from whence he was taken," or, in other words, begin the process of "working out" his own salvation (Philippians 2:12; Alma 34:37). "So I drove out the man" (Moses 4:29, 31), meaning, of course, the man Adam and his wife, Eve. Most importantly, however, the Father never intended that they, or we, should have to do this alone, but provided a Redeemer from the beginning, even from the "foundation of the world," to provide an escape from both sin and death—and all of the consequences that flow therefrom.[23]

Recall also that after God created Adam and Eve, He spoke and interacted with and, indeed, taught them (see, for example, Genesis 2:19 ("the Lord God . . . brought [every beast of the field and every fowl of the air] unto Adam to see what he would call them"). Sister Brown details how, beginning with the Prophet Joseph Smith, prophets and apostles have testified that Heavenly Father tutored Adam and Eve, preparing them temporally and spiritually for their divine mission to bring about the all-important Fall and lead the first gospel dispensation.[24] Elder Jeffrey R. Holland has also observed that Adam and Eve, like each of us who also chose to come to earth and "fall" (see Doctrine and Covenants 93:38–39), "were willing to transgress knowingly and consciously (the only way they could 'fall' into the consequences of mortality, inasmuch as Elohim certainly could not force innocent parties out of the garden and still be a just God) *only because they had a full knowledge of the plan of salvation*, which would provide for them a way back from their struggle with death and hell."[25]

While prophetic and other insights on what Adam and Eve knew or might have known when confronted by Satan in the Garden of Eden may be helpful, the fact is, as President Oaks has taught, "*For reasons that have not been revealed*," the "transition, or 'fall,'" from paradisiacal immortality to mortality, "could not happen without a transgression—an exercise of moral agency amounting to a willful breaking of a law (see Moses 6:59)."[26] More importantly, each of us is repeatedly reminded in the endowment how we can apply the lessons learned by Adam and Eve to our own lives. Restating these lessons, Adam said: "Blessed be the name of God, for because of my transgression [or in the case of each one of us, 'because of my mistakes and sins'] my eyes are opened, and [because of the Atonement] in this life I shall have joy, and again in the flesh I shall see God. And Eve, his wife, heard all these things and was glad, saying: Were it not for our transgression, we never should have had seed, and never should have known good and evil, and the joy of our redemption, and the eternal life which God giveth unto all the obedient" (Moses 5:10–11). According to God's infinite wisdom, He created a plan whereby we could learn by our own "experience" (Doctrine and Covenants 105:10; 122:7) the "difference between holy and unholy" (Leviticus 10:10), "clean and unclean" (Leviticus 11:47), "good and evil" (Genesis 3:22), and, through obedience to the laws and ordinances of the gospel, be rescued and redeemed from the negative consequences of our difficult learning experiences.

The Atonement of Jesus Christ

The heart of Heavenly Father's plan, of course, is the Atonement, which has not only been taught from the beginning of mortality, from the days of Adam and Eve, but from the beginning of premortality or our spiritual existence as begotten spiritual sons and daughters of Heavenly Parents. Christ is "the Lamb slain from the foundation of the world" (Revelation 13:8; Moses 7:47). Paul also taught that "before the foundation of the world," God "predestinated us unto the adoption of children by Jesus Christ . . . in whom we have redemption through his blood" (Ephesians 1:4–5, 7). "Although no one is predestined or predetermined to receive exaltation or eternal condemnation before being born into mortality," Andrew Skinner writes, "the vehicle of our exaltation, the Atonement, *was* predestined. That is to say, all who are eventually exalted, based on choices they make in mortality, are predestined to be exalted through the atonement of Jesus Christ and in no other way." Thus, "the temple ceremony teaches . . . that the redemption provided by the Savior was no afterthought but rather the core of our Heavenly Father's plan for his children."[27]

Because of their willingness to accept the consequences of their choice to bring about the Fall, Adam and Eve "brought about the required changes in their bodies, including the circulation of blood and other modifications. . . . They were now able to have children."[28] As Lehi taught, "If Adam [and Eve] had not transgressed . . . they would have had no children" (2 Nephi 2:22–23). They also became mortal. President Nelson observes, however, that "mortal life, glorious as it is, was never the *ultimate* objective of God's plan. Life and death here on planet Earth were merely *means* to an end—not the end for which we were sent." That end, of course, includes the certainty of the resurrection, enabling our bodies to "function without blood, just as Adam's and Eve's did in their *paradisiacal* form,"[29] and the possibility of eternal life.

Likening Adam and Eve's Symbolic Role in the Endowment Instruction to Ourselves

As noted in *Endowed from on High*, virtually everything in the endowment, including the "characters depicted," is symbolic.[30] In other words, the principal purpose of the symbolic depiction of Adam and Eve's creation and fall in the endowment instruction is not necessarily for us to learn a history lesson about Adam and Eve. Rather, we should consider how the great themes presented in this part of the instruction about the Creation, Fall, and Atonement apply to us. We are, in effect, to consider ourselves as if we were Adam and Eve. Thus, we should ask ourselves as the instruction about Adam and Eve unfolds, what insights can we gain from this symbolic narrative, as well as the insights we gain from the selective facts revealed in the scriptures about their actual lives, that might help us appreciate more fully the instructions or doctrine taught in both the endowment and sealing ordinances?

Much can be gained from studying the few details found in the scriptures about the premortal and mortal life and role of Adam, or Michael,[31] and Mother Eve. Suffice it to say, as Elder Bruce R. McConkie summarized, "Adam, a male spirit, then called Michael, stood next in power, might, and dominion to the Lord Jehovah. Eve, a female spirit, whose premortal name has not been revealed, was of like stature, capacity, and intelligence."[32] Adam and Eve, our ultimate grandparents, stand next to Christ in exemplifying faithful adherence to God's plan of salvation for His children. Their story is our story. We should consider constantly, as we ponder the endowment instruction, "How can I apply the lessons taught by their experiences and emulate their example in my life?" One of the most important lessons they teach us, perhaps, is that husband and wife should be equal partners. "In the day that God created man, in the likeness of God made he him; Male and female created he them; and blessed them, and *called their name Adam*, in the day when they were created" (Genesis 5:1–2). "Man" as it appears in Genesis 1:27 and Genesis 5:1 refers to humankind, male and female, Adam and Eve collectively. And God called "their" name "Adam." As President Kimball explained, "Man here is always in the plural. It was plural from the beginning," referring "not [to] a separate man, but a complete man, which is husband and wife."[33] Thus, in Adam and Eve's story we are beautifully taught the truth that marriage, especially eternal marriage, is a divinely instituted partnership in which husband and wife are "equal partners."[34]

Properly understood, the Genesis account of Eve being made out of Adam's rib also teaches this lesson.

> **Genesis 2:21–23**—And the Lord God caused a deep sleep to fall upon Adam and he slept: and he took one of his ribs, and closed up the flesh instead thereof; And the rib, which the Lord God had taken from man, made he a woman, and brought her unto the man. And Adam said, This is now bone of my bones, and flesh of my flesh: she shall be called Woman, because she was taken out of Man.

The Hebrew word *tsela*, from which the word "rib" is derived, is often translated as "side." The word "made," in the phrase "made he a woman," is frequently translated as "built" or "constructed." With these meanings in mind, Melinda Brown suggests that a word picture emerges of "the Master Builder taking one side of Adam (humanity) and constructing a separate, complementary human, with the two individuals now symbolizing the inherent, sacred interconnectedness between male and female, man and woman."[35] As President Nelson taught, "From the rib of Adam, Eve was formed. . . . The rib signifies neither dominion nor subservience, but a lateral relationship as partners, to work and to live, side by side."[36]

Understanding the Creation account's description of Eve as a "helpmeet" to Adam similarly adds to our appreciation of the high and holy calling of wife and mother. "And the Lord God said, It is not good that the man should be alone; I will make him *an help meet for him*" (Genesis 2:18). In her study of lessons we can learn from the story of Adam and Eve, Sister Brown analyzes the Hebrew phrase *'ezer kenegdo*, which is translated in our Bible as "an help meet for him": "*'Ezer* refers to the kind of help the Lord gives—divine assistance that succors, delivers, and rescues. . . . [The word] originated from two roots, 'to save' and 'to be strong,' which over time merged into one, rendered 'to help.' . . . A more accurate and complete term might be 'rescuer' or 'deliverer.' . . . *Kenegdo* is . . . translated as 'equal to.'" In summary, Brown concludes, the Hebrew words *'ezer kenegdo*, referring to Eve, suggests a rescuer or deliverer meet for, meaning "worthy of" or "equal" to, her husband, Adam.[37]

Another important lesson we learn from Eve is the sanctity of the divine calling of motherhood. "And Adam called his wife's name Eve, because she was *the mother of all living*; for thus have I, the Lord God, called the first of all women, which are many" (Moses 4:26). To Eve's name in Hebrew, *Chavvah*, meaning "life," God added a glorious title, "Mother of all living." Her divine mission "to co-create and nurture life, that the great plan of the Father might achieve fruition"[38] was uniquely hers, equal in importance to Adam's. Eve, then, is the great type of motherhood, teaching by example the divine calling of wife and mother, as the Lord explained in the sublime revelation about the new and everlasting covenant of marriage, which is discussed in greater detail in chapter 17: "For they [wives] are given unto [their husbands in the new and everlasting covenant of marriage] to *multiply and replenish the earth*, according to my commandment, and to fulfil *the promise which was given by my Father before the foundation of the world*, and for their exaltation in the eternal worlds, that they may *bear the souls of men*; for herein is the work of my Father continued, that he may be glorified" (Doctrine and Covenants 132:63). By providing tabernacles for the spirit children of God, even bearing "the souls of men," mothers fulfill the promise Heavenly Father made to all of us in our premortal life with Him and our Heavenly Mother, that we would receive the opportunity to become as They are and enjoy what They enjoy, even eternal life or "exaltation in the eternal worlds." In so doing, wives and mothers, as co-creators with God, assist in bringing to pass the work and glory of God, even the immortality and eternal life of each of His children who choose to follow Him and His beloved Son, Jesus Christ. In short, it is difficult to overstate the grandeur from an eternal perspective of the calling of motherhood.

The book of Moses contains other important lessons we can learn from Adam and Eve:

Moses 5:1–2, 4–5, 9–12—And it came to pass that after I, the Lord God, had driven them out, that Adam began to till the earth, and to have dominion over all the beasts of the field, and to eat his bread by the sweat of his brow, as I the Lord had commanded him. *And Eve, also, his wife, did labor with him.* And Adam knew his wife, and *she bare unto him sons and* *daughters*, and they began to multiply and to replenish the earth. . . . And *Adam and Eve, his wife, called upon the name of the Lord*, and they heard the voice of the Lord from the way toward the Garden of Eden, speaking unto them, and they saw him not; for they were shut out from his presence. And he gave unto them commandments. . . . And Adam and Eve blessed the name of God, and they *made all things known unto their sons and their daughters*.

The lessons our first parents teach us include the following:

1. They labored together.
2. Obedient to the first commandment Father gave them in the Garden, "to multiply and replenish the earth," Eve bore children whom they raised together.
3. They called upon the name of the Lord, worshipping Him together.
4. Together they kept the covenants of obedience and sacrifice (see chapters 4 and 7), indeed, all the laws of the gospel.
5. They taught their children the gospel.[39]

The scriptures relate that three years previous to his death, Adam called his righteous posterity, including the patriarchs Seth, Enos, Cainan, Mahalaleel, Jared, Enoch, and Methuselah, "into the valley of Adam-ondi-Ahman, and there bestowed upon them his last blessing." No doubt, if Mother Eve were alive at the time, she would have been at his side. "And the Lord appeared unto them, and they rose up and blessed Adam, and called him Michael, the prince, the archangel. And the Lord administered comfort unto Adam, and said unto him: I have set thee to be at the head; a multitude of nations shall come of thee, and thou art a prince over them forever." Adam then stood, "being full of the Holy Ghost," and prophesied "whatsoever should befall his posterity unto the latest generation" (Doctrine and Covenants 107:53–56). How blessed we are by the examples of these divinely called, prepared, and chosen great-grandparents who were true and faithful in all things, including the covenants we receive in the endowment.

What Appropriately Can and Cannot Be Said Regarding the Temple Experience Outside of the Temple?

In his 2001 general conference address, President Nelson stated that "because the ordinances and covenants of the temple are sacred, we are under solemn obligation not to speak outside the temple of that which occurs in the temple. There are, however, some principles we can discuss." He then listed topics and scriptures that teach about temple doctrines and practices that he recommends be studied, not only by first-time temple attenders but also by seasoned Church members.[40]

Elder David A. Bednar has similarly observed, "Because of its sacredness we are sometimes reluctant to say anything about the temple to our children and grandchildren. As a consequence, many do not develop a real desire to go to the temple, or when they go there, they do so without much background to prepare them for the obligations and covenants they enter into. I believe a *proper understanding or background will immeasurably help prepare our youth for the temple* . . . [and] will foster within them a desire to seek their priesthood blessings just as Abraham sought his." He then urges parents to "share with [your] children the spiritual feelings [you] have in the temple. And let us teach them more earnestly and more comfortably the things we can appropriately say about the purposes of the house of the Lord."[41] In so doing, Elder Bednar provides two guidelines:

> Guideline #1. Because we love the Lord, we always should speak about His holy house with reverence. We should not disclose or describe the special symbols associated with the covenants we receive in sacred temple ceremonies. Neither should we discuss the holy information that we specifically promise in the temple not to reveal.

> Guideline #2. The temple is the house of the Lord. Everything in the temple points us to our Savior, Jesus Christ. We may discuss the basic purposes of and the *doctrine and principles associated with temple ordinances and covenants.*[42]

The Endowment in Church History

The Prophet Joseph Smith administered the endowment to his wife, Emma, in the Nauvoo Mansion on September 28, 1843. "Soon after, Emma had washed and anointed Jane Law, Rosannah Marks, Elizabeth Durfee, and Mary Fielding Smith. It was the first time a woman had officiated in a temple ordinance in the latter days."[43] After Joseph Smith's martyrdom, work on the Nauvoo Temple continued. On November 30, 1845, it had advanced sufficiently for Brigham Young to dedicate the upper floor of the temple. The apostles, with the help of other members, "hung heavy curtains to divide the large hall into several rooms decorated with plants and murals. At the east end of the attic, they partitioned off a large space for the celestial room, the most sacred place in the temple, and adorned it with mirrors, paintings, maps, and a magnificent marble clock."[44] Men and women who had previously been endowed under the direction of Joseph Smith "participated again in the washings, anointings and endowment ceremony" and then began officiating in these ordinances on behalf of others in December 1845. "On some days more than 100 people received their endowment and by the end of the month 1,000 individuals had been endowed."[45] "During the eight weeks prior to the exodus [from Nauvoo], approximately 5,500 were endowed."[46]

Other early milestones mentioned in *Saints* include the dedication on January 1, 1877, of the baptistry in the basement of the partially completed St. George Temple by Elder Wilford Woodruff and the assembly hall by Elder Erastus Snow. A sealing room was also dedicated, evidencing the urgency Church leaders felt to be able to move the work of redeeming the dead forward. "Wilford and Brigham supervised the first endowments for the dead performed in any temple. Wilford then spent nearly every day afterward doing temple work. He began wearing a white suit, the first time someone had worn white clothes rather than normal dress clothes as part of the temple ceremonies. [Brigham Young's wife,] Lucy, who likewise dedicated herself to temple work, wore a white dress as an example for women."[47]

One of the most important assignments Wilford Woodruff, as the newly called president of the St. George Temple, and others received from the prophet was to write down the temple ordinances, which previously had been conveyed word of mouth. President Young then finalized them. "In standardizing the ordinances, Brigham was fulfilling a charge Joseph Smith had given him after the first endowments in Nauvoo. 'This is not arranged right, but we have done the best we could under the circumstances,' Joseph had told him then. 'I wish you to take this matter in hand and organize and systematize all these ceremonies.'"[48]

On the occasion of the initial dedication of portions of the St. George Temple, the first since the Nauvoo Temple, President Brigham Young gave forceful voice to the urgency the Saints felt, declaring, "When I think upon this subject, I want the tongues of seven thunders to wake up the people. Can the fathers be saved without us? No. Can we be saved without them? No. And if we do not wake up and cease to long after the things of this earth, we will find that we as individuals will go down to hell." "Supposing we were awake to this thing, namely the salvation of the human family," he said, "this house would be crowded, as we hope it will be, from Monday morning until Saturday night."[49] Likewise, President Nelson has pled and worked tirelessly to teach members of the Church about, and encourage us to gather, covenant Israel, inviting each of us, as the main object of such gathering, to prepare for and "experience" or receive "fully" the Lord's "sacred [temple] ordinances."[50] This ministry, as was the Prophet Joseph Smith's, is reminiscent of the ministry of Moses to the covenant people of Israel anciently and no doubt inspired by the keys of gathering he restored in 1836 to the Prophet Joseph Smith, which keys are held by the living prophet today.

Endnotes

1. Nelson, "We Can Do Better and Be Better," 69.
2. Mackley, 32–33.
3. Richard E. Bennett, *Temple Rising: A Heritage of Sacrifice* (Salt Lake City, Utah: Deseret Book, 2019), 4–5.
4. Ibid., 7–8.
5. In "About the Endowment" in the link to "Temples" on the Church website, the Church explains that the first part of the endowment or initiatory ordinances are received individually. The second part of the endowment is received "in a group setting along with others who are attending the temple," some of which is "presented through video" and includes "instruction on the way all people can return to the presence of the Lord" ("About the Temple Endowment," https://www.churchofjesuschrist.org/temples/what-is-temple-endowment?lang=eng).
6. James E. Talmage of the Quorum of the Twelve Apostles lists the following important themes comprising the instruction in the endowment: "A recital of the most prominent events of the creative period, the condition of our first parents in the Garden of Eden, their disobedience and consequent expulsion from that blissful abode, their condition in the lone and dreary world when doomed to live by labor and sweat, the plan of redemption by which the great transgression may be atoned, the period of the great apostasy, the restoration of the Gospel with all its ancient powers and privileges, the absolute and indispensable condition of personal purity and devotion to the right in present life, and a strict compliance with Gospel requirements" (*The House of the Lord: A Study of Holy Sanctuaries Ancient and Modern* [Salt Lake City, Utah: The Church of Jesus Christ of Latter-day Saints, 1912], chapter 4, "Modern Temple Ordinances").
7. "Council in Heaven," Gospel Topics, https://www.churchofjesuschrist.org/study/manual/gospel-topics/council-in-heaven?lang=eng.
8. Cook, "Safely Gathered Home." Andrew Skinner suggests, "Probing reflection on the temple ceremony teaches us that in our premortal existence we possessed an extensive knowledge" of the Savior's redemptive mission, including the ordinances established "from the foundation of the world" to enable us to receive exaltation, including the "symbolism and specific tokens centering on the bodily sacrifice of Christ" (Skinner, *Temple Worship*, 50, 52).
9. See chapter 1, note 4. President Nelson's perspective on the duration of our mortal existence relative to our premortal (not to mention postmortal) existence is apt—"mortal lifetime is hardly a nanosecond compared with eternity" (Nelson, "Choices for Eternity").
10. In a footnote in his address to young adults in May 2022, President Nelson quotes Orson Hyde, then serving as President of the Quorum of the Twelve Apostles, to the effect that "'we understood things better [in the premortal world] than we do in this lower world.' [Elder Hyde] continued, surmising about promises we likely made there: 'It is not impossible that we signed [agreements accepting our callings or foreordinations to perform specific labors in this life] with our own hands, which articles may be retained in the archives above, to be presented to us when we rise from the dead, and be judged out of our own mouths, according to that which is written in the books'" (Nelson, "Choices for Eternity," note 15, quoting Orson Hyde,

"Remarks," *Deseret News*, December 21, 1859, 322). See also Hardison, 86 (quoting Neal A. Maxwell: "The degree of detail involved in the covenants and promises participated in [during our premortal existence] may be a more highly customized thing than many of us surmise" [*But for a Small Moment*, (Salt Lake City, Utah: Bookcraft, 1986), 99]).

11. See chapter 6, note 23; "Chapter 26: Alma 13–16," *Book of Mormon Teacher Manual* (Salt Lake City, Utah: Seminaries and Institutes of Religion Curriculum Services, The Church of Jesus Christ of Latter-day Saints, 2009), https://www.churchofjesuschrist.org/study/manual/book-of-mormon-teacher-manual/chapter-26?lang=eng; "Chapter 7: Recognizing and Developing Talents and Abilities," *The Gospel and the Productive Life Student Manual Religion 150* (Salt Lake City, Utah: Church Educational System, The Church of Jesus Christ of Latter-day Saints, 2004), 45–46, https://www.churchofjesuschrist.org/study/manual/the-gospel-and-the-productive-life-student-manual/chapter-7?lang=eng (Elder Bruce R. McConkie wrote: "All the spirits of men, while yet in the Eternal Presence, developed aptitudes, talents, capacities, and abilities of every sort, kind, and degree. During the long expanse of life which then was, an infinite variety of talents and abilities came into being. . . . When we pass from preexistence to mortality, we bring with us the traits and talents there developed. True, we forget what went before because we are here being tested, but the capacities and abilities that then were ours are yet resident within us. Mozart is still a musician; Einstein retains his mathematical abilities; Michelangelo his artistic talent; Abraham, Moses, and the prophets their spiritual talents and abilities. . . . And all men with their infinitely varied talents and personalities pick up the course of progression where they left it off when they left the heavenly realms" (*The Mortal Messiah*, 4 vols. [1979–81], 1:23, 25).

12. See Nelson, *Heart of the Matter*, 47 ("The way you think about who you are [beloved son or daughter of heavenly parents] affects every decision you will ever make").

13. See Russell M. Nelson, "The Creation," *Ensign*, May 2000, 85; Bruce R. McConkie, "Christ and the Creation," *Ensign*, June 1982; Gaskill, *Temple Reflections*, 81–85.

14. Nelson, "The Creation," 85, 84. "Lesson 2: Heavenly Father's plan of salvation" from *Preach My Gospel* describes the purposes of the creation as follows: "Heavenly Father's plan provided for the creation of the earth, where His spirit children would receive physical bodies and gain experience. Our life on earth is necessary for us to progress and become like God" (*Preach My Gospel: A Guide to Sharing the Gospel of Jesus Christ*, https://www.churchofjesuschrist.org/study/manual/preach-my-gospel-2023/04–chapter-3/09–chapter-3–lesson-2?lang=eng).

15. President Nelson takes his summary of the creative periods from Genesis, Moses, and Abraham (Nelson, "The Creation"). For other interpretations of the scriptural creation accounts, for example, compare Rodney Turner, *This Eternal Earth: A Scriptural and Prophetic Biography* (Orem, Utah: Granite Publishing and Distribution, 2000), 107–20 with Eric N. Skousen, *Earth in the Beginning* (Orem, Utah: Verity Publishing, 1996), including especially appendix C, "Deciphering the Creation Code Books."

16. McConkie, "Christ and the Creation." Commenting on the three accounts of creation, Elder McConkie notes:

    The Mosaic and Abrahamic accounts place the creative events on the same successive days. We shall follow these scriptural recitations in our analysis. The temple account, for reasons that are apparent to those familiar with its teachings, has a different division of events. It seems clear that the "six days" are one continuing period and that there is no one place where the dividing lines between the successive events must of necessity be placed.

    The Mosaic and the temple accounts set forth the temporal or physical creation, the actual organization of element or matter into tangible form. They are not accounts of the spirit creation. Abraham gives a blueprint as it were of the Creation. He tells the plans of the holy beings who wrought the creative work. After reciting the events of the "six days" he says: "And thus were their decisions at the time that they counseled among themselves to form the heavens and the earth." (Abr. 5:3.)

    Then he says they performed as they had planned, which means we can, by merely changing the verb tenses and without doing violence to the sense and meaning, also consider the Abrahamic account as one of the actual creation.

17. "The Living Christ: The Testimony of the Apostles," https://www.churchofjesuschrist.org/study/scriptures/the-living-christ-the-testimony-of-the-apostles/the-living-christ-the-testimony-of-the-apostles?lang=eng#p2.

18. Melinda Brown points out that "the parallels across these [three] versions support and bear witness to our belief that at least two and quite possibly more than two divine beings participated in this critical step of the plan of salvation." Further, she suggests when Genesis 1:27 states that "God created man in his own image . . . male and female created he them," "we might deduce that the Divine Council included both male and female deity." In fact, she adds, if Elohim is plural, as Joseph Smith taught ("the word Eloiheam ought to be in the plural all the way through [the scriptures]"), "perhaps the name Elohim represents our Heavenly Parents" (*Eve and Adam*, 57–58).

    Hugh Nibley quotes from various apocryphal writings that along with Elohim and Jehovah, Michael also, or Adam, "was active in the council of the creation, and was one of the three who participated in directing the whole operation" (Hugh Nibley, *Temple and Cosmos: Beyond This Ignorant Present*, ed. Don E. Norton, *The Collected Works of Hugh Nibley*, vol. 12 [Salt Lake City, Utah: Deseret Book, 1992], 306).

    Elder McConkie observed: "This we know: Christ, under the Father, is the Creator; Michael, his companion and associate, presided over much of the creative work; and with them, as Abraham saw, were many of the noble and great ones. Can we do other than conclude that Mary and Eve and Sarah and myriads of our faithful sisters were numbered among them? Certainly these sisters labored as diligently then, and fought as valiantly in the war in heaven, as did the brethren, even as they in like manner stand firm today, in mortality, in the cause of truth and righteousness" (Bruce R. McConkie, "Eve and the Fall," *in Woman* [Salt Lake City, Utah: Deseret Book, 1979], 57–68. See also Turner, 89–91).

19. Russell M. Nelson, "Constancy Amid Change," *Ensign*, November 1993, as quoted in Russell M. Nelson, *Teachings of Russell M. Nelson* (Salt Lake City, Utah: Deseret Book, 2018), 110.
20. Brown, *Adam and Eve*, 84.
21. McConkie, *The Promised Messiah: The First Coming of Christ* (Salt Lake City: Deseret Book, 1978), 220–21 (emphasis added). President Dallin H. Oaks noted that "some acts, like murder, are crimes because they are inherently wrong. Other acts, like operating without a license, are crimes only because they are legally prohibited. Under these distinctions, the act that produced the Fall [eating the fruit of the tree of knowledge of good and evil] was not a sin—inherently wrong—but a transgression—wrong because it was formally prohibited. . . . It was Eve who first transgressed the limits of Eden in order to initiate the conditions of mortality. Her act, whatever its nature, was formally a transgression but eternally a glorious necessity to open the doorway toward eternal life" (Dallin H. Oaks, "The Great Plan of Happiness," *Ensign*, November 1993, as quoted in Brown, *Adam and Eve*, 85–86).

For a succinct overview of how the doctrines about the Fall and the Atonement restored by the Prophet Joseph Smith—including the "nature of man," "original sin," "the doctrine of moral agency," "the problem of evil," the "grace of God and the agency of man," and these "conflicting commandments"—differ from, and are similar to, conflicting views espoused by various Christian theologians over the centuries and today, see Daniel K Judd, "The Fortunate Fall of Adam and Eve," in *No Weapon Shall Prosper: New Light on Sensitive Issues*, Robert L. Millett, ed., BYU Religious Studies Center, 2011, https://rsc.byu.edu/no-weapon-shall-prosper/fortunate-fall-adam-eve (quoting President Joseph Fielding Smith, who commented about Moses 3:16–17 that "if we had the original record, we would see the purpose of the fall clearly stated and its necessity explained;" further, in effect, "the Lord said to Adam that if he wished to remain as he was in the garden, then he was not to eat the fruit, but if he desired to eat it and partake of death he was at liberty to do so. *So really it was not in the true sense a transgression of a divine commandment.* Adam made the wise decision, in fact the only decision that he could make")(emphasis added).
22. Brown, *Adam and Eve*, 83–84, quoting Boyd K. Packer, "Atonement, Agency and Accountability," *Ensign*, May 1988, 70.
23. Ibid., 84–85.
24. Ibid., 74–78. Among other prophets and apostles who Sister Brown cites as testifying that Adam and Eve's all-important decision to partake of the forbidden was informed by an understanding of the plan of salvation include the following: (1) Elder James E. Talmage described the Garden of Eden as the "first sanctuary" or temple, "for therein did the Lord first speak unto man and make known the Divine law" (Brown, *Adam and Eve*, 75 note 5, quoting Talmage, *The House of the Lord*, 17); (2) The Prophet Joseph Smith taught that "God conversed with [Adam] face to face: in his presence he was permitted to stand, and from his own mouth he was permitted to receive instruction—he heard his voice, walked before him and gazed upon his glory—while intelligence burst upon his understanding" (Brown, *Adam and Eve*, 76–77). See also Brown, *Adam and Eve*, 75 and note 6, where Joseph Smith was recorded as teaching that Adam "received revelations, commandments and ordinances at the beginning," https://www.

josephsmithpapers.org/paper-summary/history-1838–1856–volume-c-1–2–november-1838–31–july-1842/551, and that "God had revealed all the saving ordinances to Adam" "and set Adam to watch over them" and promised "'to send Angels to reveal them' in the event of their loss," quoting Joseph Smith (*The Words of Joseph Smith: The Contemporary Accounts of the Nauvoo Discourses of the Prophet Joseph Smith*, ed. Andrew F. Ehat and Lyndon W. Cook [Salt Lake City, Utah: Bookcraft, 1999], 38–44). (3) Joseph Fielding Smith testified: "When Adam was in the Garden of Eden he was in the presence of the Father and was taught by him. He learned his language. He was as familiar with our Eternal Father in that garden as we are with our fathers in mortal life" (Brown, *Adam and Eve*, 77, quoting *Doctrines of Salvation* 1:26).

25. Brown, *Adam and Eve*, 77–78, quoting Holland, *Christ and the New Covenant*, 203.
26. Oaks, "The Great Plan of Happiness," 73 (emphasis added). One commentator reads Moses 2:28 and 5:10–11 as suggesting that God's command that Adam and Eve "multiply and replenish the earth" was not understood or effective until after the Fall and that at the time of their choice to partake of the forbidden fruit they did not fully understand the "Gospel plan of salvation" (https://www.bhporter.net/_files/ugd/c71091_0280a332bbfe436b8811a588a7f6c2e9.pdf). We can look forward to that day when "those things which never have been revealed from the foundation of the world, but have been kept hid from the wise and prudent," including all of the whys and wherefores of the Fall, "shall be revealed unto babes . . . in this, the dispensation of the fulness of times" (Doctrine and Covenants 128:18).
27. Skinner, 48–50.
28. Russell M. Nelson, "The Atonement," *Ensign*, November 1996, 33.
29. Ibid., 34; emphases in original. In conjunction with his plea to each of us to seek to "better understand temple covenants and ordinances," President Nelson, quoting Elder John A. Widtsoe, then of the Quorum of the Twelve Apostles, emphasized the importance of seeking the guidance of the Holy Ghost: "The endowment is so richly symbolic that only a fool would attempt to describe it; it is so packed full of revelations to those who exercise their strength to seek and see, that no human words can explain or make clear the possibilities that reside in temple service. The endowment which was given by revelation can best be understood by revelation" (*Heart of the Matter*, 182 [citing John A. Widtsoe, "Symbolism in the Temples," in Archibald F. Bennett. ed., *Saviors on Mount Zion*, 1950, 163]).
30. *Endowed from on High*, 24, https://www.churchofjesuschrist.org/study/manual/endowed-from-on-high/lesson-5?lang=eng. Alonzo Gaskill states, "Adam and Eve are our pattern. Their story is ours. Symbolically speaking, you and I are to consider ourselves as if we were Adam and Eve" (*Sacred Symbols*, 109).
31. See, e.g., Robert L. Millett, "The Man Adam," *Ensign*, January 1994. See also Daniel 12:1 ("And at that time [the last days] shall Michael stand up, the great prince which standeth for the children of thy people," meaning, as the headnote to Daniel 12 states, "In the last days Michael shall deliver Israel from their troubles"); JST, Revelation 12:6–8 ("There was war in heaven; Michael

and his angels fought against the dragon; and the dragon and his angels fought against Michael; And the dragon prevailed not against Michael").

32. McConkie, "Eve and the Fall," in *Woman*, 57–68, as quoted in Brown, *Adam and Eve*, 35. See also Doctrine and Covenants 138:38–39 (President Joseph F. Smith saw, in his vision of the spirit world, "our glorious Mother Eve, with many of her faithful daughters who had lived through the ages and worshiped the true and living God").
33. Spencer W. Kimball, "The Blessings and Responsibilities of Womanhood," *Ensign*, March 1976, as quoted in Brown, Adam and Eve, 62.
34. "The Family: A Proclamation to the World."
35. Brown, *Adam and Eve*, 62–63.
36. Russell M. Nelson, "Lessons from Eve," *Ensign*, November 1987, 86.
37. Brown, *Adam and Eve*, 65–68.
38. Nelson, "Lessons from Eve," 87. Nelson, "Lessons from Eve," 87. A woman's divine mission (and eternal capability—even to those who through no fault of their own do not have this opportunity or ability in mortality) to "co-create" life with God, as President Nelson teaches, not only fulfills the purposes and promise of the Father to provide mortal tabernacles to all of His children who kept their first estate (as revealed in Doctrine and Covenants 132:63 cited below), but opens the door to one of the central blessings promised the faithful in the Abrahamic covenant and sealed upon couples in the sealing ordinance. As the Lord promised Abraham, Isaac, and Jacob: "In blessing I will bless thee, and in *multiplying I will multiply thy seed as the stars of the heaven, and as the sand which is upon the sea shore*" (Genesis 22:17; see also Genesis 26:4, 24; Genesis 28:3; Exodus 32:13; Leviticus 26:9; Deuteronomy 7:13; Hebrews 6:14). The Lord revealed further what this spiritual treasure entails in Doctrine and Covenants 132, where He sets forth the conditions and blessings of the new and everlasting covenant of marriage (described in greater detail in chapter 18), that faithful recipients of this covenant "shall pass by the angels, and the gods, which are set there, to their exaltation and glory in all things, as hath been *sealed* upon their heads, which glory shall be a fulness *and a continuation of the seeds forever and ever*" (v. 19). Why is the promise of posterity ("continuation of the seeds") in the sealing ordinance so important? Among other reasons, because it fulfills God's purpose to bring about the immortality and eternal life of man (and all those who in the eternities have the potential to become spirit offspring of the gods and, eventually, men and women). As stated in the terms of the Abrahamic covenant, through the seed of His covenant people God will "bless all the nations of the earth" who accept His covenant (Genesis 18:18; 22:18; 26:4; Abraham 2:11)—both in time and in eternity. What greater blessing or happiness (even "joy and rejoicing" [Doctrine and Covenants 52:43]) comes to a covenant-keeping couple than to raise up their posterity unto the Lord and to see that posterity being instruments in His hands to bless others? This joy is assured not only now *but hereafter*.

In 1841, just two years before section 132 was recorded, the Lord again commanded His people "to build a house to my name." This house would become the Nauvoo Temple, where many of the faithful Saints were sealed. Why build a temple again at such cost and sacrifice? The Lord answered, "that I may *bless* you, and crown you with honor, immortality, and eternal life" (Doctrine and Covenants 124:55). After instructing the Prophet in the next verse to build the Nauvoo House for the "boarding of strangers," in which Joseph and "his house" or "posterity" were promised they would "have place" "from generation to generation," the Lord returns, in verses 57 and 58, to the theme of "blessing" (specifically temple blessings) mentioned in verse 55: "For this *anointing* have I put upon his head [referring to Joseph Smith's anointing, which reference, of course, would be equally applicable to all others so anointed], that his *blessing* shall also be put upon the head of his posterity after him. And as I said unto Abraham concerning the kindreds of the earth, even so I say unto my servant Joseph: In *thee and in thy seed* shall the kindred of the earth be blessed." While it cannot be stated with certainty, it may be that the Lord was reminding Joseph and those other Saints who were "endowed" in the Kirtland Temple, which endowment consisted principally of the initiatory ordinances of the temple, that they (and we) are both *commanded* and *blessed* in the initiatory as well as the sealing ordinances, as were Adam and Eve, Abraham and Sarah, and all faithful disciples of Christ, to be fruitful and "to multiply and replenish the earth" (Doctrine and Covenants 132:63), that thereby they and others—even all "the kindred of the earth"—might be "blessed" with "the blessings of the Gospel, which are the blessings of salvation, even of eternal life" (Abraham 2:11). For a detailed description of the endowment or initiatory ordinances administered in the Kirtland Temple, see Anderson, *The Savior in Kirtland*, 249–65.

39. Ibid.
40. See Nelson, "Personal Preparation for Temple Blessings" and discussion in the introduction above.
41. Bednar, "Prepared to Obtain Every Needful Thing," 103 (footnotes omitted) (one of the things Elder Bednar includes among the things parents may "appropriately" teach their children is how we learn in the temple to follow "the Savior by receiving and honoring covenants to keep the law of obedience, the law of sacrifice, the law of the gospel [of Jesus Christ], the law of chastity, and the law of consecration").
42. Ibid. See also Sweat, *The Holy Covenants*, 52–58 ("If the Lord is going to reveal unto us His reserved mysteries for the faithful, then keeping covenants to not reveal special symbols and specific teachings from the temple ceremony reflects our readiness in character, maturity, and spirituality to receive those 'hidden things, which no man knew' that are 'most precious' (Doctrine and Covenants 101:33); those things that the Lord 'delights' to reveal 'to those who serve me in righteousness and in truth unto the end' (Doctrine and Covenants 76:5)").
43. *Saints: The Story of The Church of Jesus Christ in the Latter Days* (Salt Lake City, Utah: The Church of Jesus Christ of Latter-day Saints), vol. 1, *The Standard of Truth*, 510. See also Mackley, 83.
44. *Saints*, vol. 1, 579.
45. Mackley, 102.
46. Cowan, 60–61.
47. *Saints, vol. 2, No Unhallowed Hand—1846–1893*, 427.
48. Ibid., 427–28. See also Nelson, *Heart of the Matter*, 179.
49. Ibid., 426.
50. Nelson, "The Temple and Your Spiritual Foundations," 95.

CHAPTER 13

The Spiritual Treasure of Living God's "Higher Laws"

The Laws of the Gospel, Chastity, and Consecration

> *"Those who live the higher laws of Jesus Christ have access to His higher power. . . . As we strive to live the higher laws of Jesus Christ, our hearts and our very natures begin to change. The Savior lifts us above the pull of this fallen world by blessing us with greater charity, humility, generosity, kindness, self-discipline, peace, and rest."*[1]
>
> —Russell M. Nelson

The object of our learning in and outside of the temple is not just intellectual "knowing" but applying what we know to become more like the Savior. In this regard, it is noteworthy that "the word *endow* as used in the New Testament comes from the Greek word *enduein*, meaning 'to dress, clothe, put on garments, put on attributes, or receive virtue.'"[2] Receiving "virtue," in the context of the endowment, means receiving the "capacity to act" or "potency," meaning "the ability or capacity to achieve or bring about a particular result."[3] The results we strive for through the ordinances of the gospel, the revelations declare, and specifically the ordinances of the temple, are two-fold. First, "the power of godliness is manifest" (Doctrine and Covenants 84:19) in our lives over time as we continue to grow spiritually. Second, we are assured that ultimately we will "see" or "behold the face of God" and "enter into the rest" or "fulness of his glory" (Doctrine and Covenants 84:22–24).

Specifically how we achieve these results, President Nelson advised, is not "spelled out in any manual." It will require tutoring from the Holy Ghost as you "seek to understand what the Lord would have you know and do."[4] But to begin with we know it involves understanding and then striving to keep the covenants we make in the gospel and the endowment. Thus, following on our previous discussion in this study about the specific covenants associated with the ordinances of baptism, confirmation, the sacrament,[5] and ordination to the priesthood,[6] as well as temple covenants to live the laws of obedience[7] and sacrifice,[8] in this chapter we examine covenants to live the higher law of the gospel of Jesus Christ and the laws of chastity and consecration. By thinking a little more deeply about the covenants we have made or will make in the temple, the understanding and keeping of which are vital to receiving the Lord's promised endowment of power, we can better appreciate President Nelson's observation that "each temple ordinance 'is not just a ritual to go through, it is an act of solemn promising.'"[9]

What Is the Law of the Gospel of Jesus Christ?

The *General Handbook* (27.2) teaches that "the law of the gospel of Jesus Christ . . . is the higher law that [Jesus] taught while He was on the earth." As prophets have so often reminded us in general conference,[10] the Lord summarized this "higher" law when asked, "Master, which is the great commandment in the law?" Jesus responded, "Thou shalt love the Lord thy God with all thy heart, and with all thy soul, and with all thy mind. This is the first and great commandment. And the second is like unto it, Thou shalt love thy neighbour as thyself. On these two commandments hang all the law and the prophets" (Matthew 22:36–40). In its most fundamental iteration, the "law of the gospel of Jesus Christ" is the law of love, which, indeed, is a "higher" law. Without the motivation of love, as Paul taught, everything else is "sounding brass," "tinkling cymbals," and "profiteth [us] nothing." Indeed, though we have and exercise all other spiritual gifts, without charity, we are "nothing" (1 Corinthians 13:1–3).

As reviewed in chapter 4, Christ's "gospel" (3 Nephi 27:9, 13, 21) encompasses most importantly the "first principles and ordinances of the gospel" (Articles of Faith 1:4)—faith in the Lord Jesus Christ and His Atonement, repentance, baptism for the remission of our sins, and being sanctified by receiving the Holy Ghost, which process of sanctification continues as we endure faithfully to the end of our lives, weekly renewing our baptismal and other covenants in the sacrament. This process involves seeking to live all of Christ's teachings.[11] As Elder Bruce R. McConkie defined it, the "gospel of Jesus Christ . . . embraces all of the laws, principles, doctrines, rites, ceremonies, acts, powers, authorities, and keys necessary to save and exalt men in the highest heaven hereafter."[12] The fundamental purpose of the Savior's gospel is to enable God's children to spiritually progress through the power of Christ's Atonement to be or become like Him. As Christ summarized, "What manner of men ought ye to be? Verily I say unto you, even as I am" (3 Nephi 27:27).

Notably, the phrase "law of the gospel" appears in the scriptures twice. First, in preparation for the blessings promised for establishing "a house" (Doctrine and Covenants 88:119), or building the Kirtland Temple, including being endowed "with power from on high" (Doctrine and Covenants 38:32; see also Doctrine and Covenants 88:68; 95:8–9),[13] the elders were commanded to teach one another and "be instructed more perfectly" "in the law of the gospel" and "in all things that pertain unto the kingdom of God, that are expedient for you to understand" (Doctrine and Covenants 88:78). This same instruction, which began in January 1833 in the School of the Prophets in Newell K. Whitney's store and continued in formal and informal settings thereafter, goes on today most importantly in our homes (through *Come, Follow Me*, among other instructional resources provided by the Church) and in the Church through Primary, Sunday School, Priesthood, Relief Society, seminary, institute, and temple preparation classes. It also occurs in the temple.

The second reference to "law of the gospel" occurs in Doctrine and Covenants 104, a revelation about caring for the poor. In this context the phrase is less about instruction or "book-learning" *about* the gospel and more about the *application* of gospel principles, in particular the higher law of love, which is embodied in the welfare and self-reliance principles revealed in section 104. These principles include the truth that everything temporal that we rely on to sustain our lives, "all things" in the earth belong to God who created them. To fulfill His divine purposes in the law of agency, which Elder Boyd K. Packer clarified refers to "moral agency,"[14] God gives us a sacred stewardship and makes us accountable to Him for all our blessings. To provide for His Saints, the Lord commands that the "rich be made low" by sharing what they have so that the "poor [may] be exalted" (Doctrine and Covenants 104:16). This means that those in need are helped, most importantly by teaching them principles of self-reliance that the Lord has revealed, and the Church generously provides, to individuals in and out of the Church to life themselves out of poverty and distress.[15] The Lord declared that the consecrated offerings of members of the Church and others, through fast offerings and Humanitarian Fund donations, be administered in the Lord's "own way" (Doctrine and Covenants 104:16), meaning consistently with the self-reliance principles He has revealed. These principles, which are central to the "law of the gospel" and include the principles of sacrifice and consecration, have remained constant through the ages, even as their application has varied according to the circumstances of God's people.[16]

King Benjamin taught these same principles related to the law of the gospel in his sermon at the temple. "In the first place," he noted, God "hath created you, and granted unto you your lives" (Mosiah 2:23). Further, He "is preserving you from day to day, by lending you breath, that ye may live and move and do according to your own will, and even supporting you from one moment to another" (Mosiah 2:21). "And behold, all that he requires of you is to keep his commandments" (Mosiah 2:22).

Which commandment specifically? In essence, the law of the gospel of Jesus Christ. "Ye should impart of your substance to the poor, every man according to that which he hath, such as feeding the hungry, clothing the naked, visiting the sick and administering to their relief, both spiritually and temporally, according to their wants." What specific blessing does the Lord promise us if we do so? That we will "[retain] a remission of [our] sins from day to day." Finally, "all these things are [to be] done in wisdom and order; for it is not requisite that a man should run faster than he has strength" (Mosiah 4:26–27).

The ways in which we are asked today to apply these principles "in wisdom and order" are succinctly summarized under section 22 of the *General Handbook*, including to "build self-reliance" and "minister to those with temporal and emotional needs." President J. Reuben Clark Jr. taught that "the real long-term objective" of all these and similar efforts "is the building of character in the members of the Church [and other recipients], givers and receivers, rescuing all that is finest down deep inside of them and bringing to flower and fruitage the latent richness of the spirit."[17]

In addition, "the Lord has established the law of the fast and fast offerings to bless His people and to provide a way for them to serve those in need." When members fast, they go "without food and drink for a 24-hour period (if physically able)"[18] and give a generous fast offering, "at least equal to the value of the meals not eaten. Members are encouraged to give more than the value of these meals if they can" (*General Handbook* 22.2.2). Thus, the paying of generous fast (and other) offerings and being faithful in our ministering assignments are two "small and simple things" (Alma 37:6) the Lord has given us to fulfill our covenant to live the law of the gospel of Jesus Christ. Further, we are all encouraged "to serve others as the Savior did," "strive to become aware of each other's strengths and needs," and "minister to one another with love and understanding." "Where JustServe.org is available, members and others can use it to identify service opportunities in the community. Members and others can also provide disaster relief or community service through Church-sponsored projects, donations to the Church's Humanitarian Fund or assisting in disaster relief through Helping Hands (where applicable)"(*General Handbook* 22.2.3, 22.2.4).

What Is the Law of Chastity?

The *General Handbook* teaches that "the law of chastity . . . means that a member has sexual relations only with the person to whom he or she is legally and lawfully wedded according to God's law."[19] Priesthood leaders will ask in our temple recommend interview whether we "obey the law of chastity."[20] To the "old" law ("thou shalt not commit adultery") the Savior added in the Sermon on the Mount a higher law—"whosoever looketh on a woman, to lust after her, hath committed adultery already in his heart. Behold, I give unto you a commandment, that ye suffer none of these things to enter into your heart" (3 Nephi 12:27–29; Matthew 5:27–30). Thus, the Church teaches, "The law of chastity encompasses more than sexual intercourse."[21] *For the Strength of Youth* describes this higher standard as follows: "Keep sex and sexual feelings sacred. They should not be the subject of jokes or entertainment. Outside of marriage between a man and a woman, it is wrong to touch the private, sacred parts of another person's body even if clothed. In your choices about what you do, look at, read, listen to, think about, post, or text, avoid anything that purposely arouses lustful emotions in others or yourself. This includes pornography in any form."[22]

If, as noted in the discussion about the Word of Wisdom, our bodies are literally "temples" in which our spirits reside, then it follows that, as President Nelson reminds us, we should treat them "with the care we give every house of the Lord." "We came to this earth that we might have a body and present it pure before God in the celestial kingdom. The great principle of happiness consists in having a body. . . . [Because he was denied a body,] Satan is determined to have us misuse our bodies. . . . [We give Satan power] every time we abuse our body in any way."[23]

"It is better that ye should deny yourselves of these things," the Savior taught, "wherein ye will take up your cross, than that ye should be cast into hell" (3 Nephi 12:30). "And now for a man to take up his cross, is to deny himself all ungodliness, and every worldly lust, and keep my commandments" (JST, Matthew 16:26). Notably, the temple recommend question that touches on this aspect of the law of chastity asks, "Do you *strive* for moral cleanliness in your thoughts and behavior?"[24]

Just as important as focusing on the "don'ts" or "vices" associated with the law of chastity should be a focus on the "do's" or virtues of this law. *Preach My Gospel* wisely observes that "virtue originates in [our] thoughts and desires." By focusing "on righteous, uplifting thoughts" and putting "unworthy thoughts out of [our minds] rather than dwell[ing] on them, this wonderful missionary guide counsels, we can grow into this Christlike attribute. As James taught, when we "resist the devil," he flees from us (James 4:7). Because we have a body, "our will—especially when fortified by the Spirit—is stronger than the devil's."[25] Drawing upon the powers of heaven to become more like the Savior "is a gradual, lifelong process," requiring that we "be patient with [ourselves]. God knows that change and growth take time. He is pleased with your sincere desires and will bless you for every effort you make." The Church's (and the gospel's) emphasis on becoming pure and striving for moral cleanliness, like our earlier discussion about worthiness, is hopeful and helpful as we strive to become more like the Savior in all aspects of our lives.[26]

The spiritual treasures associated with keeping the law of chastity, which involve repenting completely when any aspect of it is violated, include (1) qualifying "yourself to make and keep sacred covenants in the temple"; (2) preparing "yourself to build a strong marriage and to bring children into the world as part of an eternal and loving family"; (3) avoiding "the spiritual and emotional damage that come from sharing sexual intimacy outside of marriage"; (4) protecting "yourself from harmful diseases"; (5) gaining confidence, as promised in Doctrine and Covenants 121, and true happiness; (6) improving "your ability to make good decisions now and in the future";[27] (7) "great treasures of knowledge" (a promise that applies to both the Word of Wisdom and the Law of Chastity);[28] and (8) "God's approval and personal spiritual power."[29]

What Is the Law of Consecration?

Doctrine and Covenants 42:30–33—And behold, thou wilt remember the poor, and consecrate of thy properties for their support that which thou hast to impart unto them. . . . And inasmuch as ye impart of your substance unto the poor, ye will do it unto me. . . . Every man shall be made accountable unto me, a steward over his own property, or that which he has received by consecration.

To "consecrate," according to the Guide to the Scriptures, means "to dedicate, to make holy, or to become righteous. The law of consecration is a divine principle whereby men and women voluntarily dedicate their time, talents, and material wealth to the establishment and building up of God's kingdom." As the temple preparation booklet *Preparing to Enter the Holy Temple* makes clear, the law of consecration involves not only what we *have*, but what we *are*: "We covenant to give of our resources in time and money and talent—*all we are* and all we possess—to the interest of the kingdom of God upon the earth."[30] Similarly, the *General Handbook* states that "the law of consecration . . . means that members dedicate their time, talents, and everything with which the Lord has blessed them to building up Jesus Christ's Church on the earth" (27.2).

The *Doctrine and Covenants Student Manual* (Enrichment L) gives a wonderful summary of "The Law of Consecration and Stewardship" introduced by the Lord in Doctrine and Covenants 42 as a part of the "law of the Church," including the scriptural principles underlying the law. In some periods the applications of these principles meant that members were to have "all things in common," including the people of Enoch (Moses 7:17–18), Melchizedek (JST, Genesis 14:27), the early-day Saints after Christ's crucifixion (Acts 4:32), the Nephites (3 Nephi 26:19 and 4 Nephi 1:3) and, in a measure, Latter-day Saints who lived the United Order for about three-and-a quarter years, when it was discontinued by the Lord.[31]

In our day, such principles are no less relevant. As Bruce R. McConkie taught, "Sacrifice and consecration are inseparably intertwined. The law of consecration is that we consecrate our time, our talents, and our money and property to the cause of the Church; *such are to be available to the extent they are needed to further the Lord's interests on earth.*" Elaborating on when and how much of our time, money, and property are needed to further the Lord's work, Elder McConkie taught, "We are not always called upon to live the whole law of consecration and give *all* of our time, talents, and means to the building up of the Lord's earthly kingdom. Few of us are called upon to sacrifice much of what we possess, and at the moment there is only an occasional martyr in the cause of revealed religion. But what the scriptural account means is that to gain celestial salvation we must be able to live these laws to the full *if we are called upon to do so.* Implicit in this is the reality that we must in fact live them *to the extent we are called upon so to do.*" In conclusion, he counselled, "I think it is perfectly clear that the Lord expects far more of us than we sometimes render in response. We are not as other men. We are the saints of God and have the revelations of heaven. Where much is given much is expected. We are to put first in our lives the things of his kingdom."³²

Accepting calls to serve in the Church, especially when seemingly inconvenient, is certainly a small but important part of our consecration. Having been taught these principles by the example of faithful parents who accepted calls no matter the inconvenience or sacrifice required in their lives, I had the opportunity to learn for myself the power of these principles both during my formal education and early career. Soon after returning from my mission, I decided to transfer from Brigham Young University to a very demanding program at a so-called "Ivy League" university back East at the beginning of my junior year of undergraduate studies. Shortly after beginning my program, I was called to serve in the elders quorum presidency, which at the time involved a time commitment far greater than I had previously experienced in my young adult life (in addition to the demands of working to provide for our growing family, which numbered four by the time I graduated two years later). Likewise, soon after beginning an even more demanding professional career at a major law firm after completing BYU law school and a one-year post-graduate judicial clerkship, I was called to serve as bishop of a large and socio-economically diverse ward. The small sacrifices required to magnify those callings pale beside the tremendous blessings our young family (which then numbered six) received through those years of service. Truly the Lord, from that day to this, has opened the "windows of heaven" and "poured out blessings" that we have not fully had room to receive (see 3 Nephi 24:10), as He does to everyone who consecrates their lives to Him.

Comparing the laws of sacrifice and consecration and putting the latter in context with all of the other laws received by covenant in the temple, Anthony Sweat explained: "Some struggle to see a difference between the law of sacrifice and the law of consecration." While there may be overlap, he notes that "sacrifice is to give things up; consecration is to dedicate them to God, but often we retain them. Sacrifice is the release of the unholy; consecration retains to make holy." He concludes, "Sacrifice, chastity, obedience, and the gospel each contribute and prepare us to fully implement the law of consecration."³³

Endnotes

1. Nelson, "Overcome the World and Find Rest," 96, 97.
2. Pinegar, 225.
3. Merriam-Webster, "Virtue," https://www.merriam-webster.com/dictionary/virtue and "Potency," https://www.merriam-webster.com/dictionary/potency.
4. Nelson, "Spiritual Treasures," 77.
5. See "The Role of the Sacrament in the Process of Sanctification" in chapter 8.
6. See "Ordination to the Priesthood—Becoming the Sons of Moses and Aaron" in chapter 6.
7. See "Faith in God and His Only Begotten Son Leads us to Follow or Obey Them" in chapter 4.
8. See "How Does the Law of Sacrifice Relate to the Principle of Repentance?" in chapter 7.
9. Nelson, "Personal Preparation for Temple Blessings," 33, quoting Gordon B. Hinckley, *Teachings of Gordon B. Hinckley*, 1997, 638.
10. See, for example, Russell M. Nelson, "What We Are Learning and Will Never Forget," *Ensign*, May 2021, 78 ("Has this shared trial [during the COVID -19 pandemic] drawn you closer to your neighbors—to your brothers and sisters across the street and around the world? In this regard, the two great commandments can guide us: first, to love God and, second, to love our neighbor. (Mark 12:30–31).").
11. See Evan A. Schmutz, "Trusting the Doctrine of Christ," *Ensign*, May 2021, 48–49 (The doctrine of Christ "is much more profound than a mere summary repetition of its five key elements. It encompasses the law of the gospel").
12. Bruce R. McConkie, *Mormon Doctrine* (Salt Lake City, Utah: Bookcraft, 1966), 331.
13. "Lesson 34: Doctrine and Covenants 88:70–141," *Doctrine and Covenants Teacher Manual—Religion 324 and 325* (Salt Lake City, Utah: Seminaries and Institutes of Religion Curriculum Services The Church of Jesus Christ of Latter-day Saints, 2017, https://www.churchofjesuschrist.org/study/manual/doctrine-and-covenants-teacher-manual-2017/lesson-34–doctrine-and-covenants-88–70–141?lang=eng).
14. Boyd K. Packer, "These Things I Know," *Ensign*, May 2013, 8 ("Agency is defined in the scriptures as "moral agency," which means that we can choose between good and evil."); Boyd K. Packer, "Our Moral Environment," *Ensign*, May 1992, 67 ("The phrase 'free agency' does not appear in scripture. The only agency spoken of there is moral agency, 'which,' the Lord said, 'I have given unto him, that every man may be accountable for his own sins in the day of judgment" [citing Doctrine and Covenants 101:78 (emphasis in original)]).
15. See, for example, Caring for Those in Need: 2021 Annual Report, 22–24, 34–35, https://www.churchofjesuschrist.org/bc/content/shared/english/charities/pdf/2021/PD60013504–CaringForThoseInNeed-Annual-Report-2021–mobile-eng.pdf?lang=eng ("anyone—regardless of their religious belief—is welcome to participate"); "Church Rolls out 'My Path to

Self-Reliance' in Uganda," News Release, April 21, 2015, https://news-ug.churchofjesuschrist.org/article/church-rolls-out-my-path-to-self-reliance-in-uganda.

16. See, for example, "Lesson 14: The Law of Consecration," *Doctrine and Covenants and Church History: Gospel Doctrine Teacher's Manual* (Salt Lake City, Utah: The Church of Jesus Christ of Latter-day Saints, 1999), https://www.churchofjesuschrist.org/study/manual/doctrine-and-covenants-and-church-history-gospel-doctrine-teachers-manual/lesson-14–the-law-of-consecration?lang=eng; Welch, *Illuminating the Sermon at the Temple*, 73–74.

17. *Our Heritage: A Brief History of The Church of Jesus Christ of Latter-day Saints* (Salt Lake City, Utah: The Church of Jesus Christ of Latter-day Saints, 1996), 109, https://www.churchofjesuschrist.org/study/manual/our-heritage/chapter-nine?lang=eng.

18. See Nelson, "Opening the Heavens for Help," 74 ("How do we fast? Two meals or a period of 24 hours is customary. But you decide what would constitute a sacrifice for you, as you remember the supreme sacrifice the Savior made for you").

19. *General Handbook* 27.2. The Lord's law of chastity is described in the Gospel Principles manual as having "sexual relations only with our spouse to whom we are legally married. No one, male or female, is to have sexual relations before marriage. After marriage, sexual relations are permitted only with our spouse" (*Gospel Principles* [Salt Lake City, Utah: The Church of Jesus Christ of Latter-day Saints], 2011, https://www.churchofjesuschrist.org/study/manual/gospel-principles/chapter-39–the-law-of-chastity?lang=eng.

20. See question 8 in temple recommend questions listed under "Worshipping and Worthiness—What is Required to Participate Worthily in Priesthood Ordinances?" in chapter 2.

21. *Gospel Principles*, "Chapter 39: The Law of Chastity."

22. *For the Strength of Youth: A Guide for Making Choices*, "Your Body is Sacred—Invitations," https://site.churchofjesuschrist.org/study/manual/for-the-strength-of-youth/06–body?lang=eng.

23. Nelson, *Heart of the Matter*, 133–34 (quoting Joseph Smith, "Church History," *Times and Seasons*, March 1, 1842, 707). For President Nelson's enlightening perspective as "a former physician, surgeon, and medical researcher" on the importance of honoring our bodies and his observation that *most sins involve the body*," including "abuse, of others or ourselves; violations of the law of chastity, or the misuse of the sacred power of procreation; addiction, whether it be to alcohol, drugs, pornography, food, sex, tobacco, or any other substance or practice that violates divine law" (even tattooing), see Nelson, *Heart of the Matter*, 132, 134 (emphasis in the original).

24. See question 7 in temple recommend questions listed under "Worshipping and Worthiness—What is Required to Participate Worthily in Priesthood Ordinances?" in chapter 2.

25. Nelson, *Heart of the Matter*, 134.

26. "Seek Christlike Attributes," *Preach My Gospel: A Guide to Sharing the Gospel of Jesus Christ*, The Church of Jesus Christ of Latter-day Saints, 2023, https://site.churchofjesuschrist.org/study/manual/

preach-my-gospel-2023/14-chapter-6?lang=eng. The 2023 update to *Preach My Gospel* carries over a practical suggestion President Packer first made in general conference: "Your mind is like a stage in a theater. If you allow unwholesome thoughts to linger on the stage of your mind, you are more likely to sin. If you actively fill your mind with wholesome things, you are more likely to embrace what is virtuous and shun what is evil. Be wise about what you allow to enter and remain on the stage of your mind" (see Boyd K Packer, "Inspiring Music—Worthy Thoughts," *Ensign*, November 1973, 28).

27. "Prophetic Teachings on Temples—Law of Chastity—For the Strength of Youth," https://www.churchofjesuschrist.org/temples/prophetic-teachings-on-temples?lang=eng.
28. Doctrine and Covenants 89:19; 121:45.
29. *For the Strength of Youth*, "Your Body is Sacred—Promised Blessings."
30. "Preparing to Enter the Holy Temple," 35, https://media.ldscdn.org/pdf/lds-manuals/preparing-to-enter-the-holy-temple/2011-01-00-preparing-to-enter-the-holy-temple-eng.pdf.
31. "The Law of Consecration and Stewardship—L-7 The History of Consecration," *Doctrine and Covenants Student Manual—Religion 324–325* (Salt Lake City, Utah: Seminaries and Institutes of Religion Curriculum Services, The Church of Jesus Christ of Latter-day Saints, 2018), https://www.churchofjesuschrist.org/manual/doctrine-and-covenants-student-manual/enrichment-l-the-law-of-consecration-and-stewardship?lang=eng. See also Sweat, *The Holy Covenants*, 91–100 ("Consecration is not merely monetary and cannot be reduced to communal economics. Consecration involves our very beings—our breath, our bodies, our abilities, our opportunities").
32. Bruce R. McConkie, "Obedience, Consecration, and Sacrifice," *Ensign*, May 1975, 50–51. In explaining that the law of consecration involves being able to give whatever of our time, talents, and means that the Lord through His servants requires, Elder McConkie was echoing what Presidents Marion G. Romney and J. Reuben Clark, each counselors in the First Presidency, had previously taught: "The basic principle and the justification for the law of consecration 'is that everything we have belongs to the Lord; therefore, the Lord may call upon us for any and all of the property which we have, because it belongs to Him. . . . (Doctrine and Covenants 104:14–17, 54–57)'" (Marion G. Romney, "Living the Principles of the Law of Consecration," *Ensign*, February 1979, 3, quoting J. Reuben Clark Jr., Conference Report, October 1942, 55, as quoted in "The Law of Consecration and Stewardship," *Doctrine and Covenants Student Manual*).

   Leaders of the Church have cautioned against a common misinterpretation of revelations equating the secular principle of "equal outcomes" or "equality-in-fact" with the Lord's statements relative to the law of consecration that men are to be "equal in earthly things" (Doctrine and Covenants 78:5); see also Doctrine and Covenants 70:14 ("Nevertheless, in your temporal things you shall be equal, and this not grudgingly, otherwise the abundance of the manifestations of the Spirit shall be withheld"). The Lord clarified what He meant by being "equal in earthly things" in Doctrine and Covenants 82:17

where He said, "You are to be equal, *or in other words, you are to have equal claims on the properties,* for the benefit of managing the concerns of your stewardships, every man according to his wants and his needs, inasmuch as his wants are just." As President Clark put it, "One of the places in which some of the brethren are going astray is this: There is continuous reference in the revelations to equality among the brethren, but I think you will find only one place where that equality is really described, though it is referred to in other revelations. That revelation (D. & C. 51:3) affirms that every man is to be 'equal according to his family, according to his circumstances and his wants and needs.' (See also D. & C. 82:17; 78:5–6.) Obviously, this is not a case of 'dead level' equality. It is 'equality' that will vary as much as the man's circumstances, his family, his wants and needs may vary."

Building on President Clark's teachings, President Marion G. Romney warned against forced or government-mandated "counterfeits" or "imitations" of the Lord's laws and programs for caring for the poor and needy: "I suggest we consider what has happened to our agency with respect to . . . government welfare services. . . . The difference between having the means with which to administer welfare assistance taken from us and voluntarily contributing it out of our love of God and fellowman is the difference between freedom and slavery. . . . When we love the Lord our God with all our hearts, might, mind, and strength, we will love our brothers as ourselves, and we will voluntarily, in the exercise of our free agency, impart of our substance for their support. . . . President [J. Reuben] Clark. . . referring to government gratuities, said: 'The dispensing of these great quantities of gratuities has produced in the minds of hundreds of thousands—if not millions—of people . . . a love for idleness, a feeling that the world owes them a living. It has made a breeding ground for some of the most destructive political doctrines that have ever found any hold, . . . and I think it may lead us into serious political trouble. . . . Society owes to no man a life of idleness, no matter what his age. I have never seen one line in Holy Writ that calls for, or even sanctions this. In the past no free society has been able to support great groups in idleness and live free.' (CR, Apr. 1938, pp. 106–7.)"

"Both history and prophecy—and I may add, common sense," President Romney continued, "bear witness to the fact that no civilization can long endure which follows the course charted by bemused manipulators and now being implemented as government welfare programs all around the world. Babylon shall be destroyed, and great shall be the fall thereof. (See Doctrine and Covenants 1:16.) But do not be discouraged. Zion will not go down with her, because Zion shall be built on the principles of love of God and fellowman, work, and earnest labor, as God has directed" ("Church Welfare Services' Basic Principles," *Ensign*, May 1976, 120–21, 123, as quoted in "The Law of Consecration and Stewardship," *Doctrine and Covenants Student Manual*).
33. Anthony Sweat, The Holy Covenants, 95.

CHAPTER 14

The Spiritual Treasure of Communing with Heaven

"[In] the house of the Lord . . . we learn how to part the veil and communicate more clearly with heaven."[1]

—President Nelson

Having the Heavens Opened to Us

All gospel truths are important and together form one great whole. However, possibly no practice is more fundamental or more important than prayer. As in all things, the Savior set the example. In order to have sufficient time to commune with His Father, He would often sacrifice time that could otherwise have been used for needed rest, "rising up a great while before day" (Mark 1:35) or continuing "all night in prayer to God" (Luke 6:12). For His communion to be intimate and uninterrupted, He "would withdraw to desolate places and pray" (Luke 5:16) or go "up into a mountain apart to pray" (Matthew 14:23; Mark 6:46; Luke 6:12). To further emphasize this important practice, the Lord includes in the scriptures and the temple supernal truths about how to pray, including as President Nelson has taught, praying "to our Heavenly Father, in the name of Jesus Christ, by the power of the Holy Ghost," which he described as "the 'true order of prayer,' in contrast to 'vain repetitions' or recitations given to 'be seen of men.'"[2] As one temple commentator noted, "The act of prayer and the principle on which it is based permeate the temple and the scriptures; in prayer we draw upon the powers of heaven. It is the foundational principle of a loving Heavenly Father who invites His children to seek Him. This concept is taught with great clarity and by example in the temple."[3]

In this chapter, we focus on one of the greatest spiritual treasures we receive in the temple—learning how, and being able consistently, "to part the veil and communicate more clearly with heaven."[4] The power and authority of the higher, or Melchizedek Priesthood, is . . . *to have the heavens opened unto them*, to *commune* with the general assembly and church of the Firstborn, and to enjoy the *communion and presence* of God the Father, and Jesus the mediator of the new covenant" (Doctrine and Covenants 107:18–19). To learn how "to have the heavens opened unto" us and how to "commune" with heaven is a spiritual blessing or treasure received in the temple, the keys to which knowledge and power were restored by Peter, James, and John and the prophets Moses, Elias, and Elijah in connection with the restoration of the Melchizedek Priesthood and the authority to administer all of the ordinances thereof, especially the ordinances of the temple.

Ancient Prophets Prayed to God at Altars Consecrated for Sacred Purposes

From the beginning, in response to the commandment of God, "Adam and Eve . . . called upon the name of the Lord, and they heard the voice of the Lord from the way toward the Garden of Eden, speaking unto them." In addition to the commandment to pray, they were commanded to build an altar where "they should worship the Lord their God, and should offer the firstlings of their flocks, for an offering unto the Lord" (Moses 5:4–5). As reviewed in chapter 7, because of their obedience over "many days," an angel appeared to Adam and Eve and gave them further light and knowledge, explaining the law of sacrifice, by which we sacrifice the things of this world in "similitude of the sacrifice of the Only Begotten of the Father." This we do, as we do with all of our thanks and petitions to God, "in the name of the Son forevermore" (Moses 5:6–7). The practice of offering a sacrifice upon an altar built and consecrated for that purpose and praying to or worshipping God in connection therewith continued through the generations of the patriarchs. "Noah builded an altar unto the Lord, and took of every clean beast, and of every clean fowl, and offered burnt offerings on the altar; and gave thanks unto the Lord, and rejoiced in his heart" (JST, Genesis 9:4). Abraham likewise "built an altar . . . and made an offering unto the Lord, and prayed" (Abraham 2:17; see also Genesis 12:8).

Altars have also been associated from the beginning with making covenants. When Noah built his altar, he said, "I will call on the name of the Lord, that he will not again curse the ground any more for man's sake, for the imagination of man's heart is evil from his youth; and that he will not again smite any more every thing living, as he hath done, while the earth remaineth" (JST, Genesis 9:6). In response to his prayer, God set the rainbow as a "token of the covenant which I have established between me and thee" (JST, Genesis 9:21–25). Similarly, Abraham, Isaac, and Jacob built altars in the places where God appeared to them and administered sacred temple ordinances and covenants.[5] Likewise, the Lord commanded Aaron and his sons to offer sacrifices "at the door of the tabernacle of the congregation before the Lord: where I will meet you, to speak there unto thee" (Exodus 29:42).[6] Reading repeatedly how altars are built, used, and revered in the Old Testament, Amy Hardison notes, "allows us a deeper understanding of the altars in the temple. For both ancient and Latter-day Saints, the altar is the place for making and sealing covenants, the place of God's presence, the place of prayer, and the place of sacrifice. The altar is the place where we offer up our whole souls to God as we strive for greater intimacy and devotion. . . . It is where the sacred ordinance of marriage is performed, reminding us that a successful marriage must include personal sacrifice and the putting to death of the natural man."[7]

The Temple Is a House of Prayer

The Lord refers to the temple, His houses both ancient and modern, as a "house of prayer." To Isaiah, the Lord promises to make His faithful Saints "joyful in my house of prayer: their burnt offerings and their sacrifices shall be accepted upon mine altar; for mine house shall be called an house of prayer for all people" (Isaiah 56:7).

When the Lord commanded the prophet Joseph Smith to "establish [His] House," He called it, first and foremost, "a house of prayer" (Doctrine and Covenants 88:119). In His revealed dedicatory prayer of the Kirtland Temple, the Lord directs the Prophet to pray, "Do thou grant, Holy Father, . . . that this house may be a house of prayer" (Doctrine and Covenants 109:14, 16), what we should hope and pray each of His temples would be to us.

While cleansing the temple, Christ cites Isaiah in affirming that the temple was not only His house,[8] but rightly "called of all nations the house of prayer" (Mark 11:17; see also Matthew 21:13; Luke 19:46). After Christ had finished "praying in a certain place," which might have been at the temple in Jerusalem, "one of his disciples said unto him, Lord, teach us to pray, as John also taught his disciples" (Luke 11:1). "When thou prayest," the Savior responded, "enter into thy closet, and when thou hast shut thy door, pray to thy Father who is in secret. . . . Use not vain repetitions, as the heathen, for they think that they shall be heard for their much speaking" (Matthew 6:6–7; see also 3 Nephi 13:6–7). Professor Welch has observed that in these verses the Savior is teaching us about individual, secret prayer. Then, in the Lord's Prayer that He offers next, He teaches how to pray in a group, which Welch affirms "was undoubtedly intended as a pattern or model for group prayers."[9] He and other commentators[10] characterize this group prayer as part of a "temple text." Regarding the temple-oriented nature of Christ's prayer, Elder Bruce R. McConkie wrote: "Jesus himself 'was praying in a certain place.' Prayers may be offered in all places and at all times, but we are dealing here with a particular prayer. . . . Clearly it was a prayer in marked contrast to those customarily offered by the Jews in general. . . . Jesus now [taught] the *true order of prayer* . . . [as] he had done in Galilee."[11]

In His prayers of dedication for temples, we learn much about the Lord's feelings about prayers offered in, and in memory or remembrance of, His temples and our covenants made therein. The scriptures contain two such dedicatory prayers—the dedicatory prayer offered by Solomon on the First Temple, which is found in 1 Kings and 2 Chronicles, and the dedicatory prayer of the Kirtland Temple found in Doctrine and Covenants 109. Note especially where and how Solomon prays: "And Solomon stood before the altar of the Lord in the presence of all the congregation of Israel" (1 Kings 8:22) "and kneeled down upon his knees before all the congregation of Israel, and spread forth his hands toward heaven" (2 Chronicles 6:13). In his prayer of dedication on the Kirtland Temple, the Lord teaches the importance of seeking Him earnestly in our prayers: "O Lord God Almighty, hear us in these our petitions, and answer us from heaven, thy holy habitation, where thou sittest enthroned, with glory, honor, power, majesty, might, dominion, truth, justice, judgment, mercy, and an infinity of fulness, from everlasting to everlasting. O hear, O hear, O hear us, O Lord! And answer [our] petitions" (Doctrine and Covenants 109:77–78).

Early Christian and Jewish Texts Reflect the Role of Prayer in Temple Rituals from the Beginning

Hugh Nibley, one of the Church's preeminent scholars on the role of temples in the ancient world, describes the "sensational finds" of ancient texts that "have completely changed our pictures of the early Christian and Jewish world"—texts such as "the Dead Sea Scrolls, Chenoboskion (Nag Hammadi), the earliest Christian library discovered the same year . . . and then the Papyri Bodmer, which includes the *Letters of Paul,* far older than anything we have ever known before."[12] What makes these discoveries significant, he notes, is that they "were buried for the purpose of being found in the later dispensation. . . . That is remarkable—they have been preserved in their purity," just as was the Book of Mormon.[13] In short, Dr. Nibley argues, cumulatively these many texts confirm that temple doctrines and rituals restored by the Lord through the Prophet Joseph Smith coincide remarkably with the doctrines and practices that these sources report the Lord taught His apostles in the original or "primitive" Church of Jesus Christ. Among these, Nibley explains, are three "heretical" (at least in the eyes of nineteenth century Christianity) ideas revealed through the Restoration: (1) the creation involved an organization and animation of existing matter (think of it as the means by which matter "obeys" God, as Abraham describes),[14] not out of nothing (*creato ex nihilio*); (2) Christ was the Only Begotten of Heavenly Father in the flesh, that is, born of a mortal mother, Mary, with a physical body capable of death and an immortal Father, with power to overcome death; and (3) Christ was resurrected with a physical (glorified but tangible) body.[15] Most importantly, however, Nibley observes, is the central focus, in all these documents, on the ordinances of the gospel—and significantly the ordinances of the temple.

> Very nearly all of the early Christian documents (and there are over 200 of them) have to do with what the Lord taught the apostles after the resurrection. What was said in the forty days? The New Testament does not tell us. What did he tell the apostles? According to these documents, he gave them the ordinances of the temple—but only to the apostles, to be held in secret. They would last only two generations, he explains, then they would be taken away. So they were not to pass beyond the general authorities, but were given to them as a special blessing to make that dispensation complete. They would be restored later on (in our dispensation). The ordinances are described in great detail. You could almost go through the temple using these documents, for so much is there.[16]

After receiving these ordinances, Professor Nibley writes, the apostles—just as our own missionaries today—"were able to go out and preach the gospel."[17]

In one text, the *Ginza*, Christ is reported to teach the importance of prayer in the context of the temple when He revealed, "I taught Adam and Eve . . . the order of prayer, and the ordinances which would help one to return to the presence of the Father."[18] One of the first and most important things the Lord taught Adam and Eve, as noted above from the book of Moses and in these apocryphal works, "was that they should always call upon God, in whatever they did, in the name of the Son."[19] "One text says that these ordinances which Adam received in his dispensation have always been the same. They were taught to Adam and his posterity by three angels. His descendants were required to call upon God even as he had, and thereafter to do everything as he had done."[20]

One important takeaway from all of the scholarship that is emerging about the "history and significance of the temple in ancient Israel, in the early Christian church, and among Latter-day Saints"[21] is simply the observation made by President Nelson that such studies "underscore the antiquity of temple work."[22]

Prophets Teach Us What They Have Learned about How to Part the Veil

In general conference, prophets have counselled repeatedly about principles of more effective prayer.[23] Two of the most memorable, for me, were Elder David A. Bednar's duet of talks on meaningful prayer. In his April 2008 talk, "Ask in Faith," he counselled that "meaningful prayer requires both holy communication and consecrated work" and that we should persevere through the trial of our faith, "recognizing and accepting the will of God in our lives."[24] This message was followed by his October 2008 sermon, "Pray Always," in which he focused on using our morning prayers as a "spiritual creation" for attributes we are striving to develop in our character and then our evening prayers to review how we did and express gratitude for God's help during the day. In addition, he counselled that our prayers "become more meaningful as we pray for others with real intent and a sincere heart."[25]

As we seek to understand more deeply what the Lord teaches in the endowment ceremony, including about how to pray more effectively, President Nelson promised, "Spiritual doors will open. You will learn how to part the veil between heaven and earth, how to ask for God's angels to attend you, and how better to receive direction from heaven." The principles of "true" prayer are key elements in the process of drawing upon the endowment of priesthood power (Christ's power) given in the temple. "The Lord has declared that despite today's unprecedented challenges, those who build their foundations upon Jesus Christ, and have learned how to draw upon His power, need not succumb to the unique anxieties of this era."[26] Admonishing us, in effect, to "step up" our prayer lives, President Nelson in the April 2022 general conference counselled, "Seek and expect miracles. . . . Do the spiritual work to seek miracles. *Prayerfully ask God* to help you exercise that kind of faith. I promise that you can experience for yourself that Jesus Christ 'giveth power to the faint; and to them that have no might he increaseth strength.' Few things will accelerate your spiritual momentum more than realizing the Lord is helping you to *move a mountain in your life*."[27]

I was impressed that following this remarkable talk, in leadership councils area presidencies and area seventies followed President Nelson's counsel. They spoke often about principles of asking and receiving and expecting miracles, especially the Lord's extraordinary question to his disciples, "What will ye that I should do unto you?" (3 Nephi 28:4) and other Book of Mormon examples of "mighty prayer" (see, for example, Enos 1:4 ["I cried unto (my Maker) in *mighty prayer and supplication* for mine own soul; and all the day long did I cry unto him"]; Alma 6:6 ["the children of God were commanded that they should gather themselves together oft, and join in fasting and *mighty prayer* in behalf of the welfare of the souls of those who knew not God"]; Alma 8:10 ["Nevertheless Alma labored much in the spirit, wrestling with God in *mighty prayer*, that he would pour out his Spirit upon the people who were in the city"]; 3 Nephi 27:1–2 ["the disciples were gathered together and were united in *mighty prayer* and fasting" and "Jesus again showed himself unto them"]).

Finally, in learning and appreciating this key temple doctrine, recall that the first keynote address President Nelson delivered in general conference after his ordination as prophet was "Revelation for the Church, Revelation for Our Lives." As the headnotes to each section of the Doctrine and Covenants testify, revelation most often comes in response to prayer. In that address President Nelson shares some of his own experiences with prayer, including how in an operating room he "stood over a patient—unsure how to perform an unprecedented procedure—and experienced the Holy Ghost diagramming the technique in [his] mind";[28] praying "daily for revelation" as a member of the Quorum of the Twelve; praying about his marriage to Wendy Watson after his wife of sixty years passed away;[29] and experiences with revelation and prayer after his calling as President of the Church. For example, he shared "how willing the Lord is to reveal His mind and will" to him since his call to lead the

Church.³⁰ One of the suggestions he gave in that address about how to "grow into the principle of revelation," or, in other words, to "part the veil" and "commune" with heaven, was this: After you pray, take time to listen to the promptings of the Spirit. Then "write the thoughts that come to your mind. Record your feelings and follow through with actions that you are prompted to take." Doing so, he promised, would bring the spiritual treasure promised by the Lord of receiving "revelation upon revelation, knowledge upon knowledge, that thou mayest know the mysteries and peaceable things—that which bringeth joy, that which bringeth life eternal" (Doctrine and Covenants 42:61).³¹ President Nelson repeated this counsel in his October 2022 conference address: "Record the thoughts that come to you as you pray; then follow through diligently."³²

It is clear from the personal experiences President Nelson has so generously shared (or allowed others to share) about his own spiritual growth is that he follows his own counsel! For example, we are indebted to Sister Wendy Nelson for giving us a glimpse into the revelatory process that President Nelson experiences regularly, and urges us to develop in our own lives, which we learn about in the temple. After her marriage to President Nelson in 2006, Sister Nelson recounted how she often was a witness to the revelatory process President Nelson engaged in, especially in preparation for general conference. But, she noted, this process accelerated after his ordination as President of the Church. On one occasion, she said, "[I woke up and] could feel the prompting to 'move out of bed now.' So I went downstairs and did some family history research and then puttered with some other things. Two hours later, my husband emerged from our bedroom and said, 'Wendy, you won't believe what has been happening for two hours. The Lord has given me detailed instruction about a process I am to follow.'" On other occasions she did not feel the need to get up but would observe quietly when President Nelson told her, "OK, dear, it is happening." Soon she would see him "sitting up on the side of the bed writing." Sister Nelson reported that while she never read the sacred messages the Lord had for her husband, she testified that she was "a witness by being present and . . . a witness by being absent that the Lord indeed instructs His prophet."³³ More important than how President Nelson personally (or any of us) communicates with heaven is his admonition for us to improve our own prayers. "Routine recitations of past and upcoming activities, punctuated with requests for blessings," he notes, do not "constitute the kind of communing with God that brings enduring power. Pray to know how to pray with power." Citing the example of Enos referred to above, who clearly "learned how" to "part the veil and communicate . . . with heaven," President Nelson encourages, "each one of us can do the exact same thing [as Enos]. God will teach anyone who sincerely wants to communicate with Him how to pray."[34]

The Keys to Ask and Receive Blessings

> **Doctrine and Covenants 124:94–95, 97**—And from this time forth I appoint unto [Hyrum Smith] that he may be a prophet, and a seer, and a revelator unto my church, as well as my servant Joseph; That he may act in concert also with my servant Joseph; and that he shall receive counsel from my servant Joseph, *who shall show unto him the keys whereby he may ask and receive.* . . . Let my servant William Law also receive the keys by which he may *ask and receive blessings.*

Andrew Ehat and Lyndon Cook, editors of a collection of Joseph Smith's discourses given during the Nauvoo period, point to a number of documented references that explain that the "keys to ask and receive" refer to the "order of God for receiving revelations."[35] On October 5, 1840, three months before he received Doctrine and Covenants 124, the Prophet Joseph Smith gave a discourse on the priesthood in which he connected the concept of the "keys of the priesthood," or the "keys to ask and receive," to the principle of revelation received through prayer. When God spoke with Noah, the Prophet taught, revealing that because the earth was "filled with violence" He would destroy the wicked, Noah was in effect exercising the keys of the priesthood he held. In other words, through prayer Noah "[obtained] the voice of Jehovah" and "talked with him in a familiar and friendly manner," the same way that He had "blessed Adam at the beginning." The Prophet further taught that these same same principles and powers to receive revelation, which were taught through priesthood or temple ordinances "under the direction and commandments of the Almighty [in previous dispensations] . . . shall all be had in the last dispensation."[36] Six days before the endowment was first given in 1842, the Prophet told the Relief Society "that he was about to deliver 'the keys of the Priesthood to the Church, and said that the faithful [sisters] should receive them with their husbands, that the Saints whose integrity has been tried and proved faithful, might know how to ask the Lord and receive an answer.'" Keys of the priesthood, in this context, mean teachings, instruction, or sacred knowledge revealed through priesthood ordinances, including, most importantly, temple ordinances. Bathsheba W. Smith similarly recorded that "when speaking in one of our general fast meetings, [Joseph Smith] said that we did not know how to pray to have our prayers answered. But when I and my husband [were endowed by Joseph Smith], he taught us the order of prayer."[37]

We would all do well, in our personal pondering and study about how we can each improve our personal and family prayers[38] and better receive the promises or spiritual treasures of parting the veil and communing with heaven, to consider the "keys" or sacred instructions we each receive in the endowment. For me personally, it is always a continuing source of comfort to know that in the leadership councils of the Church held in the temple, these keys are exercised, whereby our Prophet and all the General Authorities who assist him in implementing the divine direction he receives from the Lord "ask and receive blessings."[39]

Reconciliation and Prayer

In the Sermon on the Mount, the Lord teaches an important application of Lehi's statement (oft-quoted by Elder Bednar[40]) that certain of God's creations (human beings, who were created in His image) were created to act, while other things (such as the matter that responded to Jehovah's commands during the creation) were created to be acted upon. "God . . . hath created all things, both the heavens and the earth, and all things that in them are, both *things to act* and *things to be acted upon*" (2 Nephi 2:14). For example, the Savior taught the importance of controlling our anger and not letting it control us. "Whosoever is angry with his brother shall be in danger of his judgment. And whosoever shall say to his brother, Raca, shall be in danger of the council; and whosoever shall say, Thou fool, shall be in danger of hell fire" (3 Nephi 12:21). President Nelson echoed this teaching: "Contention reinforces the false notion that confrontation is the way to resolve differences; but it never is. Contention is a choice. Peacemaking is a choice. You have your agency to choose contention or reconciliation. I urge you to choose to be a peacemaker, now and always."[41]

Thus, the Savior taught, before we come to Him in prayer and approach Him as it were at His altar, as Adam prayed, with our "offering" or "gift," we should "act" to be reconciled to anyone who we feel may have hurt us or who we may have offended in any way. This is particularly important in our marriages and families as we pray as couples and before family prayer. "Therefore if thou bring thy gift to the altar, and there rememberest that thy brother hath ought against thee; Leave there thy gift before the altar, and go thy way; first be reconciled to thy brother, and then come and offer thy gift" (Matthew 5:22–24; compare 3 Nephi 12:23–24).

Acting to apologize, to forgive, to be reconciled before we pray makes our prayers so much more powerful and effective! If we cannot bring ourselves to do so, perhaps we could follow President Brigham Young's counsel, confessing our offense and asking His forgiveness *and* the forgiveness of our spouse or family member, as the case may be, as we pray so that our prayer *will* reach heaven. "It matters not whether you or I feel like praying [or feel like making reconciliation before we pray], when the time comes to pray, pray. If we do not feel like it, we should pray till we do. . . . You will find that those who wait till the Spirit bids them pray, will never pray much on this earth."[42]

The Savior repeated this principle of reconciliation before (or even in) prayer in the Lord's prayer: "Forgive us our debts, *as we forgive our debtors*" (3 Nephi 13:11). As we forgive, we receive forgiveness. "For if ye forgive men their trespasses, your heavenly Father will also forgive you: But if ye forgive not men their trespasses, neither will your Father forgive your trespasses" (Matthew 6:14–15). The Lord also said,

"Wherefore, I say unto you, that ye ought to forgive one another; for he that forgiveth not his brother his trespasses standeth condemned before the Lord; for there remaineth in him the greater sin. I, the Lord, will forgive whom I will forgive, but of you it is required to forgive all men" (Doctrine and Covenants 64:9–10).

This principle, taught so powerfully in the endowment,[43] prepares us symbolically to enter the presence of the Lord. In the Lord's presence, who suffered that all might receive forgiveness and be reconciled with God, it would be ironic, even intolerable, if we were to come bearing a grudge or having failed to be reconciled to anyone in that circle of prayer—or as it were in God's kingdom—whom we may have offended or by whom we may have chosen to be offended.

Endnotes

1. Nelson, "Hear Him," 90. See also Pinegar, 191–92.
2. Nelson, "Sweet Power of Prayer," 7 (footnotes omitted), citing Bruce R. McConkie, *A New Witness for the Articles of Faith* (Salt Lake City, Utah: Deseret Book, 1985), 380.
3. Pinegar, 191.
4. Nelson, "Hear Him," 90.
5. See chapter 16 below and appendix 2.
6. See Hardison, 33.
7. Ibid., 37.
8. Later He ominously refers to the temple as your house (see Matthew 23:38 ["Behold, your house is left unto you desolate"]; Luke 13:35).
9. Welch, 80.
10. Welch states that "Hugh Nibley has seen in the structure of the Lord's Prayer more than a polite request or a legal petition" (Ibid., 80 and note 86).
11. Gaskill, *Sacred Symbols*, 17 and note 39, quoting McConkie, *Mortal Messiah*, Book 3, 186–87.
12. Nibley, *Temple and Cosmos*, 264.
13. Ibid., 265.
14. See, for example, Abraham 4:10, 12, 21.
15. See generally Nibley, *Temple and Cosmos*, 270–71, 287.
16. Ibid., 295–96.
17. Ibid., 297.
18. Ibid., 302.
19. Ibid. 307.
20. Ibid., 308. In these ancient texts, in fact, the Lord is reported to have implicitly taught the importance of prayer by instructing His apostles and their wives on the higher ordinances while in the act of praying: "Standing with the apostles in the prayer circle, the Lord tells them, 'I will teach you all the ordinances necessary that you may be purged by degrees and progress in the next life.' In many of these forty-day stories (and there are several), after the Lord is about to leave the apostles, he says, 'I have taught you all these things. Now we will stand in a circle, and you will repeat after me this prayer, and we will go through all the ordinances again'" (Ibid., 309; see also ibid., 313–14). Truman Madsen adds in this vein that "the idea of the temple as a house of prayer and fasting has roots in the ancient order of prayer in which God's name prevails (see 1 Kings:28–29). The orthodox Jewish prayer quorum or minyan is traceable at least as far back as the Babylonian captivity. And the book of Daniel (see 6:10) spoke of his praying toward the temple three times daily, a practice later encouraged by Joseph Smith" (Madsen, *The Temple: Where Heaven Meets Earth*, 131).
21. Pinegar, "Appendix: The History and Significance of Temples" (containing a "lightly annotated list of books" on this subject). For a far more comprehensive bibliography, see Daniel W. Bachman, with Donald W. Perry, Stephen D. Ricks, John W. Welch, "A Temple Studies Bibliography" (updated September

25, 2015), in *Mormonism and the Temple: Examining an Ancient Religious Tradition* (Logan, Utah: Academy for Temple Studies, 2013), 127–129 with 8,797 citations to books, articles, chapters in books, pamphlets, talks, and entries in various reference works. "At present the scope is limited to the following areas of temple studies: (1) Near Eastern and Mediterranean temples in general. That includes pre-Israelite temples in the Near East, and Greek, Roman, and Egyptian temples. (2) Israelite temple in the Old and New Testament periods. (3) Mormon Temples." See https://www.templestudies.org/bibliography-a-f/ and https://www.templestudies.org/bibliography-o-z/.
22. Nelson, "Personal Preparation for Temple Blessings."
23. See, for example, Nelson, "Sweet Power of Prayer"; Russell M. Nelson, "Lessons from the Lord's Prayers," *Ensign*, May 2009, 46.
24. Bednar, "Ask in Faith," 94–97.
25. David A. Bednar, "Pray Always," *Ensign*, November 2008, 41.
26. Nelson, "The Temple and Your Spiritual Foundation."
27. Nelson, "The Power of Spiritual Momentum" (emphasis added). See also Nelson, *Heart of the Matter*, 168–73.
28. For a more detailed description of this experience, which, he testified, came because of "people praying" for him and "praying [him]self," see Spencer J. Condie, *Russell M. Nelson: Father, Surgeon, Apostle* (Salt Lake City, Utah: Deseret Book, 2003), 151.
29. In sharing details about President Nelson's courtship with Wendy L. Watson, Sheri Dew describes how, upon reading a brief note of encouragement to him signed by Sisters Dew and Watson, which he received and read while seated on the stand before the beginning of one of the meetings held in connection with his assignment to organize the first stake in Rome, Italy, Elder Nelson "had a strong, immediate, and clear spiritual impression about" Sister Watson after reading her name on the card. Illustrative of how the process of revelation works together with prayer, Sister Dew recounts that "once home from Europe, [Elder Nelson] took the note with him to the Salt Lake Temple to seek confirmation about that impression. What he learned was that when it was time for him to consider remarriage, he needed to meet this woman" (Sheri Dew, *Insights from a Prophet's Life: Russell M. Nelson* [Salt Lake City, Utah: Deseret Book, 2019], 240.
30. Nelson, "Revelation for the Church, Revelation for Our Lives."
31. Ibid.
32. Nelson, "Overcome the World and Find Rest," 98.
33. Sarah Jane Weaver, "Sister Wendy Nelson Shares Her Personal Witness of President Nelson's Prophetic Calling and Ministry," *Church News*, March 15, 2019, https://www.churchofjesuschrist.org/church/news/sister-wendy-nelson-shares-her-personal-witness-of-president-nelsons-prophetic-calling-and-ministry?lang=eng. See also "Sister Wendy Nelson on President Nelson's Revelations," Youtube video clip, https://www.youtube.com/watch?v=cDd-9I4GRhc. Read President Nelson's testimony about how the Lord directs His Church through His prophets at Nelson, *Heart of the Matter*, 150 ("Now, as I serve as President of the Church, I can speak from my own experience. I

testify that our Savior always has instructed and inspired His prophets, and He always will. . . . Jesus Christ actively guides His prophets, seers, and revelators. Of this I bear personal witness.")

34. Nelson, *Heart of the Matter*, 102.
35. *The Words of Joseph Smith: The Contemporary Accounts of the Nauvoo Discourses of the Prophet Joseph*, "5 October 1840 (Monday Morning)," note 19, Andrew F. Ehat and Lyndon W. Cook, eds., https://rsc.byu.edu/words-joseph-smith/5–october-1840–monday-morning, referring to Orson Hyde's explanation of Doctrine and Covenants 124:95 and 97 in the 1870 edition of the Doctrine and Covenants.
36. "5 October 1840 (Monday Morning)" discourse by Joseph Smith, reported in *Words of Joseph Smith*. In note 19 of their annotations to the foregoing discourse, Ehat and Cook noted: "There is evidence that prior to 19 January 1841 the Prophet had thought long on the question of keys of access to God. For example, in 1833 the Prophet taught the brethren of the School of the Prophets 'how to get revelation.' Also in 1835, Joseph Smith taught the Father of Lorenzo Young how to get the spiritual power to heal his son. 'Join in prayer,' the Prophet said, 'one be mouth and the others repeat after him in unison . . . [then] continuing the administration in this way until you receive a testimony that he will be restored' ("Biography of Lorenzo Dow Young," Utah Historical Quarterly 14:45). But three months after these instructions were given, the Prophet received the keys of the sealing power from Elijah. Apparently based on a maturing appreciation of the authority Elijah bestowed upon him, the Prophet six years later stated that 'For him to whom these keys [of Elijah] are given there is no difficulty in obtaining' revelation (see Doctrine and Covenants 128:10–11). Thus, based on the authority he received of Elijah, Joseph Smith conferred the keys of the priesthood in the endowment 4 May 1842" (citations omitted).
37. Ibid. note 19.
38. An experience shared in the *Ensign* by Richard D. Anthony about his own struggle to improve his personal prayers has inspired and stayed with me for over forty-four years. To me it is a homely, but powerful, parable of the possibilities we are introduced to in the temple, as we seek to apply what we learn about prayer and so much more. (See Richard D. Anthony, "I Was a Bishop before I Really Learned to Pray," *Ensign*, January 1976).
39. President N. Elson Tanner, who was serving as first counselor in the First Presidency at the time of President Harold B. Lee's passing in 1973, shares that in the meeting of apostles held to consider the reorganization of the First Presidency, the brethren "dressed in the robes of the holy priesthood," "held a prayer circle; President Kimball asked me to conduct it and Elder Thomas S. Monson to offer the prayer." Afterward, "each member of the quorum in order of seniority" shared their feelings, all agreeing that "we should organize [the First Presidency] now." Elder Ezra Taft Benson then nominated Spencer W. Kimball to be the President of the Church. This was seconded by Elder Mark E. Petersen and unanimously approved. President Tanner goes on to explain that these revelatory and sacred procedures are followed in regularly

The Spiritual Treasure of Communing with Heaven

scheduled presiding councils of the Church. (See N. Eldon Tanner, "The Administration of the Church," *Ensign*, November 1979. See also *Teachings of the Living Prophets Student Manual—Religion 333*, "Chapter 4: The Quorum of the First Presidency" [Salt Lake City, Utah: Seminaries and Institutes of Religion Curriculum The Church of Jesus Christ of Latter-day Saints, 2010]). For a description of events in the Salt Lake Temple related to President Nelson's ordination as President of the Church, see "A Message from the First Presidency, January 16, 2018," https://www.churchofjesuschrist.org/bc/content/ldsorg/church/news/2018/01/19/2018-01-1000-a-message-from-the-first-presidency.pdf.

40. See, for example, David A. Bednar, "And Nothing Shall Offend Them," *Ensign*, November 2006 ("In the grand division of all of God's creations, there are things to act and things to be acted upon [see 2 Nephi 2:13–14]. . . . To believe that someone or something can make us feel offended, angry, hurt, or bitter diminishes our moral agency and transforms us into objects to be acted upon. As agents, however, you and I have the power to act and to choose how we will respond to an offensive or hurtful situation").
41. Nelson, "Peacemakers Needed."
42. Marvin J. Ashton, "Know He Is There," *Ensign*, February 1994, quoting from *Discourses of Brigham Young*, John A. Widtsoe, ed., 1941, 44.
43. In her temple study (*The Temple Experience: Passage to Healing and Holiness* [Springville, Utah: CFI, 2017], 42), Wendy Ulrich places the all-important principle of forgiveness in the context of a different part of the temple experience—baptism for the dead: "Forgiving others is what gives us access to the storehouse of the Redeemer, from which all debts can be finally and fully repaid. As we grant mercy, we gain the right to reclaim our lost blessings from Jesus Christ himself. . . . When we forgive others, Christ assumes their debt to us, and we can then look to him for the healing, peace, security, hope, trust, well-being, and self-image he alone can restore. He is willing to take this debt if we are willing to release the original debtor to him to deal with on his terms and with his infinite wisdom and perspective on all the factors involved in their choices."

CHAPTER 15

The Spiritual Treasure of Passing through the Veil

Symbolically Entering into the Presence of the Lord

"In the temple we take a 'step-by-step ascent into the Eternal Presence.'"[1]

—Russell M. Nelson

Scriptural Term "Veil"

In this chapter we focus on the special significance, in essence the spiritual treasures and some of the symbolism, associated with the culminating experience of the endowment ordinance, which the Church's "Temples" page describes as "symbolically return[ing] to the Lord's presence as [temple patrons complete the veil ceremony and] enter the celestial room."[2] The veil described in the Old Testament was used in the ancient tabernacle and First and Second Temples to separate the Holy Place from the Holy of Holies (see Exodus 26:33). There, above the mercy seat upon the Ark of the Covenant, God declared to Moses, "I will meet with thee, and I will commune with thee" (Exodus 25:22). Only the high priest was permitted to pass through the veil, once a year, on the Day of Atonement.

Hardison described the veil in Old Testament times as follows: "The veil was made of a blend of blue, purple, and red wools and fine-twined linen. According to Josephus, the four colors represented the four elements from which the earth was created: air (blue), fire (red or scarlet), water or the sea (purple, a color made from seashells), and earth (white, the color of the linen which had grown from the earth). These colored threads were used to either embroider or weave designs of cherubim into the fabric of the veil. Cherubim are attested in the [ancient near east] as the 'guardians of the sacred and of the threshold.' The Talmud says that this veil was sixty feet long, thirty feet high, and the thickness of the palm of the hand, making it extremely heavy."[3]

The Guide to the Scriptures provides several additional meanings to the scriptural term "veil" that are instructive when thinking about the physical veil of the temple: "A symbol for a separation between God and man," for example, "the veil shall be rent and you shall see me" (Doctrine and Covenants 67:10; 38:8)[4] and "a God-given forgetfulness that blocks people's memories of the premortal existence."[5] Other scriptural uses of the term "veil" include the brother of Jared's experience, who could not be kept from beholding "within the veil," that is beholding things beyond or through the veil into the spirit world when communing with the Lord in Ether 3:19 and 12:19, and the Prophet Joseph Smith's description of how the "veil was taken from our minds" when the Lord appeared to him and Oliver Cowdery in Doctrine and Covenants 110:1. Similarly, the headnote to Doctrine and Covenants 129 describes the "keys" the Lord gave the Prophet "whereby messengers from *beyond the veil* may be identified."

The Veil as the Entrance to Heaven or the Presence of the Father and the Son

When Christ, at the conclusion of His agonizing ordeal on the cross, uttered His final words in mortality, "It is finished" (John 19:28) and "Father, into thy hands I commend my spirit" (Luke 23:46), He "bowed his head, and gave up the ghost" (John 19:28, 30). At that moment, three of the Gospel writers report, "the veil of the temple was rent in twain from the top to the bottom; and the earth did quake, and the rocks rent" (Matthew 27:51; see also Mark

15:38; Luke 23:45). Recall that under the Mosaic law, once each year on the Day of Atonement, the high priest would pass through the veil of the temple into the Holy of Holies "as part of the cleansing rites which freed Israel from sin (Leviticus 16)."[6] In acknowledgment that His Only Begotten had accomplished that which He had been foreordained to do, to work out the infinite Atonement so that all of us could be cleansed from sin and return to our Father in Heaven whence we came, God the Father rent the temple's veil. This was done, as Elder Bruce R. McConkie taught, as a sign to Israel and all the world that "the privilege to enter into the Holy of Holies was no longer restricted to the high priest of Israel or even to those who adhered to the Mosaic ordinances. Now believers of all nations could enter 'into the highest and holiest of all places, that kingdom where eternal life is found.'"[7] Symbolically, Jesus Christ "had passed through the veil of death," President Nelson testified, "would soon enter the presence of His Father, and had opened to all the opportunity of likewise passing through the veil into God's eternal presence."[8]

Paul similarly taught that being the first to pass through the veil, Christ, as He was in all things, was our "forerunner" or Exemplar, the ultimate "anchor" to our souls: "That . . . we might have a strong consolation, who have fled for refuge to lay hold upon the hope set before us: Which hope we have as an anchor of the soul, both sure and steadfast, and which *entereth into that within the veil*; Whither *the forerunner is for us entered, even Jesus,* made an high priest for ever after the order of Melchisedec" (Hebrews 6:18–20). Thus, in the ultimate instruction received in the endowment ordinance, we have the privilege again, as we did at baptism, of following the example of the Savior, our forerunner, who entered into that holy presence "within the veil," even the presence of God, the Eternal Father. How wonderful that Church leaders have made available to all, by clicking on the "Photo Gallery" on the "Temples" page of the Church website,[9] so many photos not only of temple endowment or instruction rooms, where the veils of modern temples are located, but also temple celestial rooms, which patrons enter as they pass through the veil, symbolically entering into the presence of God the Father and Jesus Christ, or returning to our heavenly home.

The Veil as a Symbol of Christ's Flesh or Atonement

Hebrews 10:19–20—Having therefore, brethren, boldness to enter into the holiest by the blood of Jesus, By a new and living way, which he hath consecrated for us, *through the veil*, that is to say, his flesh.

Passing through the veil of the temple symbolizes and reminds us that we can enter God the Father's presence with "boldness" and confidence *only* "by the blood of Jesus." In short, the veil symbolizes His "flesh," His Atonement, encompassing His entire life's example, a "new and living way" of doing, living, and becoming.

When as patrons we conclude the endowment, whether for ourselves or as proxy for the dead, we would do well to ponder President Nelson's explanation of the literal meanings of the word "atonement" in various languages. "In the English language," he taught, "the components are *at-one-ment*, suggesting that a person is at one with another." Other derivatives include "expiation," which "means 'to atone for,'" and "reconciliation," which "comes from Latin roots *re*, meaning 'again'; *con*, meaning 'with'; and *sella*, meaning 'seat,'" or read literally, "to sit again with." "In Hebrew, the basic word for atonement is *kaphar*, a verb that means 'to cover' or 'to forgive.' Closely related is the Aramaic and Arabic word *kafat*, meaning 'a close embrace'—no doubt related to the Egyptian ritual embrace," references to which can be found in the Book of Mormon. For example, "'the Lord hath redeemed my soul . . . ; I have beheld his glory, and I am encircled about eternally in the arms of his love.' Another [Book of Mormon reference] proffers the glorious hope of our being 'clasped in the arms of Jesus.'"[10]

With President Nelson, I, at times, "weep for joy when I contemplate the significance of it all." Each time we participate in a sacred endowment ceremony, as we "symbolically return to the Lord's presence" or are symbolically "redeemed" or "atoned," as President Nelson teaches, we are "received in the close embrace of God [the Father] with an expression not only of His forgiveness, but of our oneness of heart and mind. What a privilege!"[11]

Endnotes

1. Nelson, "Overcome the World and Find Rest," note 14, quoting President David O. McKay in Madsen, *The Temple: Where Heaven Meets Earth*, 11.
2. "About the Temple Endowment," https://www.churchofjesuschrist.org/temples/what-is-temple-endowment?lang=eng.
3. Hardison, 39 (citation omitted).
4. Rodney Turner, in describing the effects of the Fall, notes the following statement by Brigham Young: "When the earth was framed and brought into existence and man was placed upon it, it was near the throne of our Father in heaven. . . . but when man fell, the earth fell into space, and took up its abode in this planetary system, and the sun became our light." He then adds the following insight about a possible explanation about the nature of the veil that separates us from the spirit world:
    > When Earth fell, so did its counterpart heaven ["the indivisible character of the earth and its heaven is affirmed by the fact that 'heaven and earth shall pass away,' only to be followed by 'new heavens and a new earth.'" (See Matthew 24:55; Doctrine and Covenants 29:23–24; Ether 13:9)]. Since the original firmament or atmosphere enveloping the planet was compatible with the bloodless, immortal natures of man [Adam and Eve] and beast, it is likely that the "air" they breathed was more refined than the blood-transmitted oxygen which is the basis of mortal life. It may have been a life-sustaining element akin to, if not identical with, the Spirit of the Lord. The placing of Earth in this solar system led to the necessary modification of its atmosphere so as to make it compatible with the oxygen-breathing requirements of the earth's then-mortal denizens. In any event, both Earth and man are cut off from the presence of the Lord by a very real veil of element. The Savior's return will be attended by an unveiling of those glories which now lie hidden behind a gross curtain of materiality (Turner, 138–39 [footnotes and citation omitted]. See also ibid., 154 notes 28, 29, 31 and 32).
5. "Veil," Guide to the Scriptures, https://www.churchofjesuschrist.org/study/scriptures/gs/veil?lang=eng.
6. McConkie, *Doctrinal New Testament Commentary*, 3:165.
7. Hardison, 40, quoting McConkie, *Doctrinal New Testament Commentary*, 1:830. Hardison notes that "just as the veil of the temple was rent, even so Roman soldiers rent or pierced Christ's flesh with a spear. As a resurrected being, Christ retained these marks of violent death. They became tokens to prove to disciples on both hemispheres that He was the risen Christ. These marks evidence the immense cost of entering into God's presence" (Hardison, 40. See also Acts 1:3, referring to the marks of Christ's crucifixion as "infallible proofs" or "sure signs and tokens.")
8. Russell M. Nelson, "Jesus Christ Is Our Savior," *Liahona*, April 2023.
9. "Media Gallery—All Temples," https://www.churchofjesuschrist.org/temples/photo-gallery?lang=eng. Indeed, as we saw in the virtual tour led by Elder and Sister Renlund given in connection with the Washington, D.C. temple open

house, the Brethren are eager to make available to all, through the ubiquitous access available through the internet, glimpses of the beauty and purposes of these sacred temple precincts. (See Washington D.C. Temple Visitors' Center, "360 Degree Virtual Tour of the Washington, D.C. Temple," https://dctemple.org/open-house/.
10. Nelson, "The Atonement" (footnotes omitted [emphasis in original]).
11. Ibid.

CHAPTER 16

The Spiritual Treasures from the Dispensation of the Gospel of Abraham

The Promises Made to and Lessons Learned from the Lives of Abraham and Sarah

> *"For the more than 36 years I've been an Apostle, the doctrine of the gathering of Israel has captured my attention. Everything about it has intrigued me, including the ministries and names of Abraham, Isaac, and Jacob; their lives and their wives; the covenant God made with them and extended through their lineage."*[1]
>
> —Russell M. Nelson

Without a doubt one of the most important events of the Restoration occurred on April 3, 1836, when Moses, Elias, and Elijah conferred on the Prophet Joseph Smith and Oliver Cowdery in the Kirtland Temple the respective keys of the holy priesthood with which each were entrusted. In chapter 5 we reviewed the significance of the keys restored by Moses, which are so important to gathering Israel and creating a body of covenant-keeping members of the Church, without which there could be no work of salvation and exaltation[2] or temples. In this chapter and chapter 18 we focus on the meaning and importance of the keys of the dispensation of the gospel of Abraham. In the next chapter, we focus on the keys to the sealing power Elijah restored.

After Moses conferred the keys of the gathering of Israel, Elias appeared to the Prophet and Oliver Cowdery and conferred upon them the "dispensation of the gospel of Abraham." Elias then prophesied that "in them and their seed"—meaning all who have or will become the covenant seed of Abraham—"all generations after [them] should be blessed" (Doctrine and Covenants 110:12). According to the Abrahamic covenant discussed later in this chapter, this means that "all generations" would be "blessed with the blessings of the gospel, which are the blessings of salvation, even of life eternal" (Abraham 2:11).

Who Was Elias?

> **Doctrine and Covenants 27:5–10**—For the hour cometh that I [Jesus Christ] will drink of the fruit of the vine with you [Joseph Smith] on the earth, and with Moroni . . . ; And also with *Elias, to whom I have committed the keys of bringing to pass the restoration of all things spoken by the mouth of all the holy prophets since the world began*, concerning the last days; And also John [the Baptist,] the son of Zacharias, which Zacharias he (Elias) visited and gave promise that he should have a son, and his name should be John, and he should be filled with the spirit of Elias; Which John [the Baptist] I have sent unto you, my servants, Joseph Smith, Jun., and Oliver Cowdery, to ordain you unto the first priesthood which you have received, that you might be called and ordained even as Aaron.

> **Luke 1:19**—And the angel answering said unto [Zacharias], I am Gabriel, that stand in the presence of God.

According to the Bible Dictionary, the term "Elias" can (1) refer to the prophet Elijah; (2) be a title for someone who is a "forerunner," such as John the Baptist; (3) be a title for other divine messengers assigned to "specific missions or restorative functions that they are to fulfill," such as "John the Revelator (Doctrine and Covenants 77:14) and Noah or Gabriel," who appeared to Zacharias as noted in Doctrine and Covenants 27:6–7 quoted above; and (4) the Elias "who committed the dispensation of the gospel of Abraham" to Joseph Smith and

Oliver Cowdery in the Kirtland Temple, who "lived in mortality in the days of Abraham."

The Bible Dictionary goes on to describe the Church's current answer to the question, "Who was the Elias who restored the keys of the dispensation of Abraham?" In short, we do not yet know for sure.[3] Some believe, however, including President Joseph Fielding Smith, that "Elias was Noah, who came and restored his keys."[4] This belief is based on the verses in Doctrine and Covenants 27 cited above, in which the Lord revealed that he had committed to Elias "the keys of bringing to pass the restoration of all things." This Elias, the Lord further reveals, visited Zacharias "and gave promise that he should have a son, and his name should be John" (Doctrine and Covenants 27:7), even John the Baptist, who would prepare the way for the Savior of the world. We know that Elias who visited Zacharias was none other than the angel Gabriel, as revealed in Luke 1:19. The Prophet Joseph Smith taught that Gabriel was Noah.[5] President Joseph Fielding Smith declared that the Lord committed to Noah "the keys of bringing to pass the restoration of all things spoken by the mouth of all the holy prophets since the world began" (Doctrine and Covenants 27:6). Therefore, he concludes, the Elias who restored the keys of the dispensation of Abraham must have been Noah.[6] Religion professor Monte S. Nyman, citing President Joseph Fielding Smith, agrees, stating that Noah's mission following the flood was similar to Adam's. Noah and his sons (and their wives) were commanded, as were Adam and Eve, "to be fruitful, and multiply, and replenish the earth" and to have dominion over "every beast of the earth" (Genesis 9:1–2, 7). God told Noah that He would "establish my covenant with you, and with your seed after you" (Genesis 9:9), which, most importantly, would include the covenant of the gospel. Moreover, Professor Nyman states, "Noah's tie with Abraham would possibly be that Abraham's life overlapped the life of Noah, and the covenant with Abraham was an extension of Noah's mission to restore all things."[7] Indeed, as we shall see, Abraham not only taught or restored the fulness of the gospel (in essence, "all things") throughout his life, as Noah and Shem no doubt did throughout their long lives, but Abraham's seed are called and promised that they would do the same in our day. Whether Elias was Noah or his protégé Abraham (or another of their contemporaries), however, is of less importance to us than understanding the nature and importance of the dispensation or "gospel of Abraham" that he restored.

What Was the "Dispensation" or "Gospel of Abraham"?

> **Galatians 3:6–9, 13–14, 16, 29**—Abraham believed God, and it was accounted to him for righteousness. Know ye therefore that they which are of faith, the same are the children of Abraham. . . . *God . . . preached before the gospel unto Abraham,* saying, In thee shall all nations be blessed. . . . And if ye be Christ's, then are ye Abraham's seed, and heirs according to the promises.

The "gospel of Abraham," as Paul teaches in Galatians, is nothing more than the fulness of the gospel of Jesus Christ, including most importantly "the patriarchal order of the priesthood and the eternal marriage covenant."[8] President Russell M. Nelson, teaching about the importance and meaning of covenants, declares that because of the Abrahamic covenant, which is at the center of Christ's gospel and which He renewed through the prophet Elias in this last dispensation, members of the Church "have the right to receive the fulness of the gospel, enjoy the blessings of the priesthood, and qualify for God's greatest blessing—that of eternal life."[9] Such supernal blessings beg the question, "Who were Abraham and Sarah and what is the nature of the covenant God made with them that can so influence the outcome of *our* lives?"

How Do the Lives of Abraham and Sarah Reflect the Influence of Temple Ordinances They Received?

Thanks to the Restoration, we have a rich source of information answering these questions in the Pearl of Great Price, which contains a revelation to Joseph Smith (which the Prophet describes as a "translation") of "the writings of Abraham while he was in Egypt, called the Book of Abraham, written by his own hand," which were discovered in "the catacombs of Egypt."[10] As one looks closely at the scriptural record of the lives of both Abraham and Sarah (discussed in this chapter), as well as their son Isaac and his wife, Rebekah, and their grandson Jacob and his wife, Rachel (discussed in appendix 2), one can discover and learn much not only about the instruction in the endowment, but, more importantly, about the promises and ultimate effect that God designed such instruction to have in our lives, to give us "power from on high" to do and be good, to "grow spiritually," as President Nelson often encourages us to do[11] and to receive the "power of godliness" in our lives.

The Bible Dictionary tells us that Abraham, meaning "Father of a multitude," was "originally called Abram, 'exalted father' (Gen. 11:26; 17:5),"[12] and was the "son of Terah, born in Ur of the Chaldees (Gen. 11:26–28)."[13] "Abraham is always regarded in the Old Testament as founder of the covenant race," the "father of the faithful" (Doctrine and Covenants 138:41). From "latter-day revelation," the Bible Dictionary continues, "we learn that [Abraham] was greatly blessed with divine revelation concerning the planetary system, the creation of the earth, and the premortal activities of the spirits of mankind. One of the most valiant spirits in the premortal life, he was chosen to be a leader in the kingdom of God before he was born into this world (Abr. 1–5)."[14] Jesus taught that "Abraham rejoiced to see my day: *and he saw it*, and was glad" (John 8:56), indicating just how intimately acquainted Abraham was with the Savior and His gospel. "Sarai," according to the Bible Dictionary, "possibly means 'contentions,' or more probably is another form of Sarah." The Lord gave her a new name, "Sarah," meaning "princess" (Genesis 17:15).[15]

Abraham began his personal history with a key event in the life of every son of God—his ordination to the holy priesthood. "Finding there was greater happiness and peace and rest for me, I *sought* for the blessings of the fathers, and the right whereunto I should be ordained to administer the same" (Abraham 1:2). The revelations tell us that Abraham "received the priesthood from Melchizedek" (Doctrine and Covenants 84:14)[16] and was ordained "a High Priest" (Abraham 1:2). The phrase "the right whereunto I should be ordained to administer the same" also suggests that Abraham, as a high priest, received the right to administer ordinances of salvation and exaltation to his posterity.[17] Significantly, Abraham told us he was "a follower of righteousness" but desired "also to be one who possessed great knowledge, and to be a greater follower of righteousness, and to possess a greater knowledge and to be a . . . prince of peace" (Abraham 1:2), a title attributed to Melchizedek. It would appear from this, and the fact that Melchizedek ordained him, that Melchizedek had a greater influence on Abraham than either his father, Terah, or his grandfather, Nahor, who had each "turned from their righteousness" (Abraham 1:3; see also Genesis 12:1).[18]

Abraham, with missionary zeal, sought to bring the people of Ur to repentance, just as Melchizedek sought to bring the people of Salem to repentance. In the process, Abraham prophesied that if the people would not repent, there would be a "famine in the land" (Abraham 1:5, 29). However, as wicked peoples have throughout time, the Chaldeans rejected Abraham's words and even sought his life, with the consent of his father, offering him up as a human sacrifice to their idols. (See Facsimile 1; Ab. 1:5–15, 30.) In answer to his prayer for deliverance, Abraham was "filled with a vision of the Almighty," who sent an angel to deliver him from the altar to which he was bound.

The Lord, calling him to the ministry by name—"Abraham, Abraham, behold, my name is Jehovah" (Abraham 1:16)[19]—promises, "Behold, I will lead thee by my hand, and I will take thee, to put upon thee my name, even the Priesthood of thy father,[20] and my power shall be over thee. . . . Through thy ministry my name shall be known in the earth forever, for I am thy God" (Abraham 1:18–19). In connection with his calling, Abraham, like Nephi and the Book of Mormon prophets after him, obtained "the records of the fathers, even the patriarchs," which recounted no doubt God's dealings with men from the days of Adam down to the ministry of Noah and Shem, including the fulness of the gospel as taught to Adam and Enoch (most likely in much more detail than we have in the Pearl of Great Price), as well as information about "the right of Priesthood" and "a knowledge of the . . . creation, and also of the planets, and of the stars, as they were made known unto the fathers" (Abraham 1:31). He also received the Urim and Thummim (Abraham 3:1), through which he received some of his revelations (see Abraham 3:7).

Before leaving Ur in response to the Lord's call, however, Abraham made one of the most important decisions of his life—marrying a worthy companion. A "princess of the royal lineage of Shem,"[21] Sarai, who was Abraham's older brother's daughter, was ten years younger than Abraham. When her father passed away due to the severity of the famine, she was legally adopted by Terah, Sarai's grandfather and Abraham's father, thus becoming Abraham's foster "sister," as he claimed and as the Lord directed him to say when he later sojourned in Egypt.[22]

In obedience to the Lord's command, Abraham and Sarai left Ur with Abraham's foster brother, Lot, and his wife (Sarai's sister, Milcah) and establish what became a prosperous settlement named Haran.[23] There he continued his missionary labors, this time with some success.[24] Later, after praying for guidance, the Lord again appeared unto Abraham and commanded him to continue on to the land previously promised to him, where God would make of him "a minister to bear my name in a strange land which I will give unto thy seed after thee for an everlasting possession, when they hearken to my voice" (Abraham 2:6).

In this face-to-face visit with Jehovah, the Lord again taught Abraham who He was (as He does whenever He calls a new prophet): "I am the Lord thy God; I dwell in heaven; the earth is my footstool; I stretch my hand over the sea, and it obeys my voice; I cause the wind and the fire to be my chariot; I say to the mountains—Depart hence—and behold, they are taken away by a whirlwind, in an instant, suddenly. *My name is Jehovah*, and I know the end from the beginning; therefore my hand shall be over thee" (Abraham 2:7–8). The Lord then made eight additional promises, which together comprise the Abrahamic covenant: (1) "I will make of thee a great nation";[25] (2) "I will bless thee above measure";[26] and (3) "make thy name great among all nations";[27] (4) "thou shalt be a blessing unto thy seed after thee, that in their hands they shall bear this ministry and Priesthood unto all nations; And I will bless them through thy name"; (5) "for as many as receive this Gospel shall be called after thy name, and shall be accounted thy seed, and shall rise up and bless thee, as their father"; (6) "I will bless them that bless thee, and curse them that curse thee"; (7) "I give unto thee a promise that this right [to the priesthood] shall continue in thee, and in thy seed after thee"; (8) in Abraham's "literal seed, or the seed of the body . . . shall all the families of the earth be blessed, even with the blessings of the Gospel, which are the blessings of salvation, even of life eternal" (Abraham 2:9–11). After his supernal visit with Jehovah, Abraham exclaimed in his heart, "Thy servant has sought thee earnestly; now I have found thee" (Abraham 2:12). Then, in his characteristic fashion, Abraham "hearkened" to the will of the Lord. He was sixty-two years old (Abraham 2:14).[28]

To summarize, "the covenant God made with Abraham," President Nelson taught, "and later reaffirmed with Isaac and Jacob is of transcendent significance." He explained how both Bible and Book of Mormon peoples were referred to as the *children of the covenant*, meaning, as the Savior explained, descendants and inheritors of the promises God made with Abraham: "Behold, ye are the children of the prophets; and ye are of the house of Israel; and ye are of the covenant which the Father made with your fathers, saying unto Abraham: And in thy seed shall all the kindreds of the earth be blessed" (3 Nephi 20:25).[29] President Nelson highlights several of the promises in the Abrahamic covenant outlined above, including:

- "Jesus the Christ would be born through Abraham's lineage.
- Abraham's posterity would be numerous, entitled to an eternal increase, and also entitled to bear the priesthood.
- Abraham would become a father of many nations.
- Certain lands would be inherited by his posterity.
- All nations of the earth would be blessed by his seed.
- This covenant would be everlasting—even through 'a thousand generations.'"

"Some of these promises," President Nelson noted, "have been fulfilled; others are still pending. [Book of Mormon] prophets knew that the Abrahamic covenant would be finally fulfilled only in the latter days." Through Elias's conferral of priesthood keys on Joseph Smith, God renewed the Abrahamic covenant in our day. "With this renewal," President Nelson declared, "we have received, as did they of old, the holy priesthood and the everlasting gospel. . . . Some of us are the literal seed of Abraham; others are gathered into his family by adoption. The Lord makes no distinction."[30]

Abraham's Repeated and Intimate Interactions with Jehovah Illustrate What It Means to Be "Endowed with Power from on High"

Other events in Abraham's life help us visualize how the promises or spiritual treasures of the temple can be fulfilled in our lives. For example, on his way to Canaan and upon his arrival, Abraham stops to build altars, offer sacrifice, and pray "devoutly" for his extended family in Ur (Abraham 2:17) and for protection from the "idolatrous nation[s]" in the area (v. 18). In response to this prayer, the Lord appears to him again, renewing His promise to give the land to his seed (v. 19; see also v. 20). Abraham is guided and protected by the Lord, who counsels him to go to Egypt because the famine in Canaan is so "grievous" (v. 21) and to tell the Egyptians that Sarai is his sister, so they do not kill him because of her beauty (vv. 22–25; compare Gen. 12:14–20). Abraham receives another visitation from the Lord, who speaks to him "face to face, as one man talketh with another," and puts His hand on Abraham's eyes and shows him the stars and other celestial bodies in the universe that He has created, even to Kolob, which is "set nigh unto the throne of God" and governs "all those planets" that "belong to the same order" as the planet earth (ie., it appears, the Milky Way Galaxy), which knowledge he is then commanded to "declare" to the Egyptians (see Abraham 3:1–16). In this revelatory experience, Jehovah teaches Abraham about the premortal life, including the existence of independent, eternal "intelligences that were organized before the world was" (v. 22), that is, as the Family Proclamation states, organized as begotten spirit sons and daughters of Heavenly Parents.[31] He also teaches Abraham about the spirit creation of all other material things—mineral, plant, and animal—which "obey" as they are organized by God during the six creative periods of the temporal or physical creation as explained in the endowment and in the scriptural accounts in Abraham 4 and 5, Moses, and Genesis.[32] The Lord also teaches Abraham the principle of foreordination in the Grand Council in heaven, including the foreordination of the Son of Man; the purpose of life, to "prove them herewith, to see if they will do all things whatsoever the Lord their God shall command them" (vv. 23–27); and the fall of Lucifer, who "was angry" when not chosen to "redeem" man on his own, self-aggrandizing terms and "kept not his first estate" (v. 28).

Upon his return from his mission to Egypt to the altar he had built in Bethel, near Jerusalem (ancient Salem, Melchizedek's kingdom), Abraham "called on the name of the Lord." He magnanimously offered his nephew Lot the choice of whichever part of the countryside he preferred for his flocks to graze (Genesis 13:3–11). The Lord reassured Abraham that notwithstanding the "sacrifice" he made to keep the peace with Lot (or, more accurately, for their herdsmen to keep the peace with each other), "all the land which thou seest," "northward, and southward, and eastward, and westward" (Genesis 13:14–15) would be his. Later, the scriptural record recounts, Abraham moved to Hebron, located about twenty miles south of Jerusalem, where he again built an "altar unto the Lord" (Genesis 13:18).

Abraham rescued Lot and others, who had been taken prisoner in a war waged by King Chedorlaomer and his allies when the city of Sodom and its ally cities refused, after twelve years of subjugation to King Chedorlaomer, to continue to pay tribute. In this chapter of his life, we gain another glimpse of Abraham's ongoing communication and relationship with Melchizedek, "the priest of the most high God," who "brought forth bread and wine," blessed Abraham, and to whom Abraham gave "tithes of all" he had gained in battle (except the property recovered from Sodom and Gomorrah, which Abraham refused to keep, considering it tainted because of the wickedness of the "inhabitants of those cities") (Genesis 14).[33] The Lord appeared again to Abraham "in a vision," renewing His promises to and covenant with Abraham (Genesis 15).

When he was eighty-six, "God commanded Abraham, and Sarah gave Hagar to Abraham" as a plural wife. "Why did she do it?" the Lord asked in Doctrine and Covenants 132. "Because this was the law," or the will of the Lord, "and from Hagar sprang many people" (Doctrine and Covenants 132:34–35; see also Genesis 16:1–4). This tells us more about Sarah than all of the movies ever made about Abraham. She was not a "handmaid" to Abraham, or "subservient partner." She was an equal partner in her understanding of the plan of salvation and her desire and ability to keep the high and glorious covenants that she had made with Jehovah.[34] Last, but not least in this summary list of Abraham and Sarah's temple-like encounters with the Almighty, in an act reminiscent of the endowment, the Lord gave Abram and Sarai new names, Abraham and Sarah.[35] Equally important, He promised them that Sarah, who, at age ninety, was beyond child-bearing years, would miraculously bear a son, whom they should call Isaac and with whom God would establish and renew His covenant (Genesis 17:5, 15–16, 21).

Covenant of Circumcision and Trial of Faith

Two other events highlight the important role ordinances played in the lives of this illustrious patriarch and matriarch, whose lives are so closely associated with the crowning blessings of the gospel received in the temple.

> **JST, Genesis 17:1, 3–7**—My people have gone astray from my precepts, and have not kept mine ordinances, which I gave unto their fathers; And they have not observed mine anointing, and the burial, or baptism wherewith I commanded them; But have turned from the commandment, and taken unto themselves the washing of children, and the blood of sprinkling; And have said that the blood of the righteous Abel was shed for sins; and have not known wherein they are accountable before me.

The first event, referred to in the foregoing inspired verses of Genesis, occurred thirteen years after Ishmael's birth, when Abraham was ninety-nine years old. In one of Jehovah's frequent face-to-face visits with His friend, Abraham, the Lord expressed sadness that His covenant people were not baptizing their children at age eight, the first ordinance established by the Lord from the beginning with Adam in similitude of the burial and resurrection of Christ, and had turned instead to heathen practices akin to infant baptism. To help His covenant people remember the all-important doctrine underlying baptism, that "little children are alive in Christ, even from the foundation of the world" (Moroni 8:12), the Lord instituted the "covenant of circumcision," that Abraham and his posterity who observed the covenant would remember "forever that children are not accountable before me until they are eight years old" (JST, Genesis 17:1, 3–7, 11). In his characteristic fashion, after God "left off from talking with him" and "went up from him, . . . Abraham took Ishmael his son, and all that were born in his house, and all that were bought with his money, every male among the men of Abraham's house; and circumcised the flesh of their foreskin *in the selfsame day*, as God had said unto him" (Genesis 17:22–23).

The second pivotal event was Abraham's trial of faith,[36] when Jehovah commanded him to offer what Paul referred to as his "only begotten son" (Hebrews 11:17), Isaac, in similitude of the offering by God the Father of His Only Begotten Son.

> **Genesis 22:1–2**—And it came to pass . . . that God did tempt [Hebrew for *test* or *prove*] Abraham, and said unto him, Abraham: and he said, Behold, here I am. And he said, Take now thy son, thine only son Isaac, whom thou lovest, and get thee into the land of Moriah; and offer him there for a burnt offering upon one of the mountains which I will tell thee of.

Who can imagine his feelings as he surely recalled that his own father had offered him up as a human sacrifice? Moreover, was not this the son in whom the Lord had promised that the covenant promises would be fulfilled? Yet, in childlike humility, Abraham made the preparations required and early the next day "saddled his ass, and took two of his young men with him, and Isaac his son, and clave the wood for the burnt offering" and began their three-day journey to do as the Lord had commanded (Genesis 22:3). President Spencer W. Kimball hints at the feelings and thoughts that might have passed through Abraham's mind as "his undaunted faith carried him with breaking heart toward the land of Moriah with [his son,] who little suspected the agonies through which his father must have been passing."[37] Moriah is located in the area of Jerusalem, the same area in which Melchizedek and his people had lived who were not long before translated and the site of Golgotha, where the Father would momentarily withdraw His sustaining influence as His Only Begotten Son was sacrificed for all creation.

On the third day, seeing "the place afar off... Abraham said unto his young men, Abide ye here with the ass; and I and the lad will go yonder and worship, and come again to you. And Abraham took the wood of the burnt offering, and [laid it upon Isaac's back]; and he took the fire in his hand, and a knife; and they went both of them together." Isaac, observing that they had "the fire and the wood," asked his father, "but where is the lamb for a burnt offering? And Abraham said, My son, God will provide himself a lamb for a burnt offering" (Genesis 22:4–7). Without further question, Isaac went with his father to the divinely appointed sacrificial site. The seminary *Old Testament Student Manual* points out that one of the important but often overlooked parallels between Abraham's experience and the sacrifice of the Savior is that Isaac, who may have been in his thirties ("as was the Savior at the time of His Crucifixion"), submitted voluntarily to Abraham. "Abraham was well over a hundred years old, and Isaac was most likely a strong young man who could have put up a fierce resistance had he chosen to do so. In fact, Isaac submitted willingly to what his father intended, just as the Savior would do."[38]

Arriving at the appointed place on the mount, Abraham, probably with Isaac's assistance, found and carried the large stones to build an altar and "laid the wood in order." Abraham then "bound Isaac his son, and laid him on the altar upon the wood. And Abraham stretched forth his hand, and took the knife to slay his son." We know the rest of the story, but still it is difficult to imagine Abraham's relief. "And the angel of the Lord," speaking on behalf of Jehovah, "called unto him out of heaven, and said, Abraham, Abraham: and he said, Here am I. And he said, Lay not thine hand upon the lad, neither do thou any thing unto him: for now I know that thou fearest God, seeing thou hast not withheld thy son, thine only son from me." Only then, after all their preparations, did Abraham notice "behind him a ram caught in a thicket by his horns," which he took and offered up "for a burnt offering in the stead of his son." Significantly, Abraham called the name of that place "Jehovah-jireh," meaning "the Lord will see or provide" (Genesis 22:9–14 and note 14a).[39]

At the conclusion of this ultimate test of faithfulness, the Lord, speaking through the angel, reconfirmed all of the blessings He had sealed upon Abraham and Sarah—"because thou hast done this thing, and hast not withheld thy son, thine only son: That in blessing I will bless thee, and in multiplying I will multiply thy seed as the stars of the heaven, and as the sand which is upon the sea shore; and thy seed shall possess the gate of his enemies; And in thy seed shall all the nations of the earth be blessed; because thou hast obeyed my voice" (Genesis 22:16–18).

Prophetic Testimonies of Abraham's Faithfulness

Jacob 4:5—Behold, [ancient Israel] believed in Christ and worshiped the Father in his name, and also we worship the Father in his name. And for this intent we keep the law of Moses, it pointing our souls to him; and for this cause it is sanctified unto us for righteousness, *even as it was accounted unto Abraham in the wilderness to be obedient unto the commands of God in offering up his son Isaac,* which is a similitude of God and his Only Begotten Son.

As noted above, Jacob, with many other prophets, testified of the importance of Abraham's example of faith and faithfulness. The Lord Himself underscored the importance of Abraham's example in our day, noting that he chose to put God's command above every other consideration, including not only that Isaac was his son, but the moral imperative not to take an innocent life. "Abraham was commanded to offer his son Isaac; nevertheless, it was written: Thou shalt not kill. Abraham, however, did not refuse, and it was accounted unto him for righteousness" (Doctrine and Covenants 132:36). But for me, more impressive than Abraham's desire and ability to always "let God prevail" in his life, was the *end* of all that obedience or faithfulness. The end or result was that, as the scriptures declare, he became the "friend [of God] forever" (2 Chronicles 20:7). "But thou, Israel," the Lord spoke through the prophet Isaiah, "art my servant, Jacob whom I have chosen, the seed of Abraham *my friend*" (Isaiah 41:8). Equally impressive was the faithfulness of his son Isaac and grandson Jacob, whose stories of faithfulness are summarized in appendix 2.

Why focus so extensively in a study about the temple and temple doctrine on the lives of Abraham, Isaac, and Jacob, and their wives?

What can we learn from their examples? If each of these patriarchs and their wives, as President Nelson taught, received the same temple ordinances that we receive,[40] and, in the process, had such glorious views and communion with the Lord, then is it not reasonable to hope that in the course of our temple experiences we might enjoy similar views and develop a similar deep and abiding relationship with our Father and Redeemer? In Doctrine and Covenants 132, the Lord again affirms the importance of the examples of these patriarchs, explaining perhaps in the process what it means ultimately to have the "blessings of Abraham, Isaac and Jacob" sealed upon us: "Abraham . . . abode in my law; as Isaac also and Jacob did none other things than that which they were commanded; and because they did none other things than that which they were commanded, they have entered into their exaltation, according to the *promises*, and sit upon thrones, and are not angels but are gods" (v. 37).

Endnotes

1. Nelson, "Let God Prevail."
2. For a comprehensive overview of the divine duties and principles given to ward and stake organization leaders (as well as all of us members) for the accomplishment of "God's Work of Salvation and Exaltation," see *General Handbook* 2, 3, 4.1, 6–13 and all of the sections under "God's Work of Salvation and Exaltation."
3. Bible Dictionary, "Elias" ("We have no specific information as to the details of [this last Elias's] mortal life or ministry"). Note that the Bible Dictionary was prepared under the direction of Elder McConkie, who wrote that "there was a man named Elias who came to Joseph Smith and Oliver Cowdery on April 3, 1836, in the Kirtland Temple to restore 'the gospel of Abraham' (Doctrine and Covenants 110:12)," but "whether he was Abraham himself or someone else from his dispensation, we do not know" (*Millennial Messiah: The Second Coming of the Son of Man* [Salt Lake City, Utah: Deseret Book, 1982], 102–104). See also McConkie, *Mormon Doctrine*, 219 ("We have no information, at this time, as to the mortal life or ministry of Elias. Apparently he lived in the days of Abraham, but whether he was Abraham, or Melchizedek, or some other prophet, we do not know").
4. Joseph Fielding Smith, "Joseph Smith's First Prayer," *Improvement Era*, June 1960, 402; see also Conference Report, April 1960, 71–73, https://archive.org/details/conferencereport1960a/page/n73/mode/2up (adding in a footnote, "It was Gabriel who appeared to Zacharias and promised him a son, and who appeared to Mary and announced the coming of the Son of God as recorded by Luke. It was also Gabriel as an Elias who is mentioned in the Doctrine and Covenants, section 27, verse 7. It was Gabriel, or Noah, who stands next to Michael or Adam in the priesthood"), as quoted in Monte S. Nyman, "The Covenant of Abraham," BYU Religious Studies Center, note 1, https://rsc.byu.edu/pearl-great-price-revelations-god/covenant-abraham#_edn1.
5. *Teachings of the Prophet Joseph Smith*, 157 (stating that Gabriel, the premortal Noah, "stands next in authority to Adam in the Priesthood").
6. Joseph Fielding Smith, "Joseph Smith's First Prayer."
7. Nyman, "The Covenant of Abraham," note 1. See also Doctrine and Covenants 77:9, 14 (Elias "was to come to gather together the tribes of Israel and restore all things"). For contrary apostolic views on this subject, see "Elias and Elijah at the Kirtland Temple," Fair: Faithful Answers, Informed Response, https://www.fairlatterdaysaints.org/answers/Elias_and_Elijah_at_the_Kirtland_Temple#cite_note-2.

   For further details on how the span of Abraham's life overlapped with Noah's and Shem's (and thus how they might have interacted), see "Appendix—Explanatory Notes on the Chronological Time Table Covering the Period of the Patriarchs" in W. Cleon Skousen, *The First 2,000 Years* (Salt Lake City, Utah: Bookcraft, 1953), 346–51. Skousen notes that Noah, nine generations from Adam, was 600 years old at the time of the flood (Genesis 7:11) and lived thereafter 350 years (Genesis 9:29), dying at age 950. According to Skousen, Abraham was about 47 when Noah died and Shem, who was 108 at the time of the flood and lived another 502 years, outlived Abraham by about five years—so these three great prophets would have been contemporaries during a portion of their lives and would have lived in the same general area of the world. For a description of the patriarchs and their acquaintance with one another, from Adam to Abraham, see Lecture 2 of *The Lectures on Faith*, paragraphs 37–53, in *The Lectures on Faith in Historical Perspective* (Larry E. Dahl and Charles D. Tate, Jr., eds. [Provo, Utah: Religious Studies Center, Brigham Young University, 1990], 46–50).

Bruce H. Porter posts among the research materials on his website a 1974 study or translation by Geza Vermes, entitled *Scripture and Tradition in Judaism*, of an eleventh century A.D. "rewritten Bible," the "Sefer ha-Yashar," which includes a "detailed story of Abraham's life, from his birth until his arrival in Haran," derived from ancient Jewish apocryphal or "Midrashic" sources. In summary, these apocryphal sources describe how Abram lived with and was raised by Noah and Shem in his youth, which would explain why, later in his life, he so keenly "sought for the blessings of the fathers" (Abraham 1:2). Abram's father, Terah, "the son of Nahor, the commander of Nimrod's army," was highly esteemed and "greatly exalted" by Nimrod (Noah's great-grandson through Ham), the king, and his princes. The night Abram was born, many of the king's sages and magicians came to Terah's house to celebrate the birth. As they left, these sages and magicians "saw a great star come from the east and run through the heavens, and it swallowed forty stars from the four sides of the heavens." They saw it as a sign that Abram "shall grow and flourish and multiply, and shall inherit for himself and his sons the whole earth forever." After counseling together the next morning, the sages and magicians determined that, to preserve their own lives, they needed to reveal the sign to the king (otherwise, if the sign came to pass and the king found out they had known and not told him, he would kill them), which they did. The king sent for Terah and demanded that he "give the child to me so that they may kill him before his evil increases upon us, and I will give you his price and fill your house with silver and gold." Terah agreed. But because "the Lord was with Terah in this affair that Nimrod might not kill Abram," Terah instead hid "Abram, his son, secretly, and his mother and his wet-nurse, and brought them to a cave," where he supplied them with provisions, and, instead, gave the king the son of one of his concubines, who "was born the same day as Abram" and "received his price" and the concubine's son "was killed in the place of Abraham."

Later, when Abram was about ten, and "the king, and all his princes and servants, all the magicians and sages of the king," imagining "that Abram was slain," "had forgotten the affair of Abram," Abram, "his mother, and his nurse, departed from the cave" and "went to Noah, and to Shem, his son," where they stayed. Thus, Abram learned "the discipline of the Lord and His ways; and no man recognized him. He spent thirty-nine years in the house of Noah." "The Lord was with" Abram and "gave to him an attentive heart, and understanding, and he knew that all the works of that generation were vain, and that all the gods which they served were vain and useless." (See https://www.bhporter.net/_files/ugd/c71091_1390933179144023b6c4f1257cb3ea74.pdf).

8. Joel A. Flake, "Gospel of Abraham," *Encyclopedia of Mormonism*, https://eom.byu.edu/index.php/Gospel_of_Abraham.
9. Russell M. Nelson, "Covenants," *Ensign*, May 2011. See also Nelson, *Teachings of Russell M. Nelson*, 7–8, 245, 246–47; Nelson, "The Everlasting Covenant."
10. For an overview of the coming forth and translation of the book of Abraham, see Kerry Muhlestein, *Let's Talk About the Book of Abraham* (Salt Lake City, Utah: Deseret Book, 2022). See also "Translation and Historicity of the Book of Abraham," Gospel Topics Essays, https://www.churchofjesuschrist.org/study/manual/gospel-topics-essays/translation-and-historicity-of-the-book-of-abraham?lang=eng under "Books and Lessons"— "Church History" in the Gospel Library app.
11. See, for example, Nelson, "Becoming Exemplary Latter-day Saints."
12. In his seminal conference address, "Let God Prevail," President Nelson noted that "in Hebrew, Abram is a noble name meaning 'exalted father.' But when God changed that name to Abraham, the name took on even greater significance, meaning 'father of a multitude.' Indeed, Abraham was to be the 'father of many nations.' (See Genesis 17:5; Nehemiah 9:7.)" (Nelson, "Let God Prevail," note 2).
13. Abraham was the tenth great-grandson of Noah (Shem, Arphaxad, Salah, Eber, Peleg, Reu, Serug, Nahor, Terah and Abraham). Abraham's home was Ur "in the land of the Chaldeans" (Genesis 11:28; Abraham 1:1), which scholars place variously in southern Iraq (today Tell el-Muqayyar), about 860 miles from Jerusalem, the head of the Persian Gulf (see Smith`s Bible Names Dictionary, 1866, in "Reference Overviews/Places of the Bible/Ur," https://biblecentral.info/places/ur/), or possibly in various sites, much closer to Jerusalem, in Syria or northern Mesopotamia (Stephen O. Smoot, "'In the Land of the Chaldeans'—The Search for Abraham's Homeland Revisited," *BYU Studies*, https://byustudies.byu.edu/article/in-the-land-of-the-chaldeans-the-search-for-abrahams-homeland-revisited/ [accessed February 8, 2022]).
14. Bible Dictionary, "Abraham."
15. Bible Dictionary, "Sarah or Sarai." "Sarai 'means princess in Hebrew but *queen* if based on Akkadian *sharratu*'" (Hardison, 138 note 26 [citation omitted]).
16. We learn from the Joseph Smith Translation that Melchizedek was the king of Salem, which is believed to have been in the area that later became Jerusalem (see JST, Genesis 14:25–40). Some believe that he was Shem, Noah's birthright son (and therefore would have "reigned" under him), who held the keys to the priesthood, was "the great high priest of his day" (see Doctrine and Covenants 138:41), and "walked with God" (Moses 8:27). Melchizedek, in Hebrew (מַלְכִּי־צֶדֶק) is a title (malkī-sedeq), meaning "king of righteousness." Alma E. Gygi, in "Is it possible that Shem and Melchizedek are the same person?" *Ensign*, November 1973, cites the following as evidence that Melchizedek was Shem: (i) the "inheritance given to Shem included the land of Salem. Melchizedek appears in scripture as the king of Salem, who reigns over this area"; (ii) "Shem, according to later revelation, reigned in righteousness and the priesthood came through him. Melchizedek appears on the scene with a title that means 'king of righteousness'"; (iii) Shem was the great high priest of his day, [whom]

Abraham honored . . . by seeking a blessing at his hands and paying him tithes"; (iv) "Abraham stands next to Shem in the patriarchal order of the priesthood and would surely have received the priesthood from Shem; but Doctrine and Covenants 84:5–17 says Abraham received the priesthood from Melchizedek"; (v) "Jewish tradition identifies Shem as Melchizedek" ["When Abraham returned from the war, Shem, or, as he is sometimes called, Melchizedek, the king of righteousness, priest of the Most High God. ..." (Ginsberg, *Legends of the Jews*, 233); "Jewish tradition pronounces Melchizedek to be a survivor of the Deluge, the patriarch Shem." (Smith's Bible Dictionary, 393); "And Adonizedek king of Jerusalem, the same was Shem. ..." (Book of Jasher 16:11)]; (vi) "President Joseph F. Smith's remarkable vision names Shem among the great patriarchs, but no mention is made of Melchizedek" (Doctrine and Covenants 138:41); (vii) Joseph Smith speaks of "Shem, who was Melchizedek" in *Times and Seasons* (vol. 5, 746). Some read Doctrine and Covenants 84:14, Gygi notes, which states that "Abraham received the priesthood from Melchizedek, who received it through the lineage of his fathers, even till Noah," as indicating that there are perhaps several generations between Melchizedek and Noah. However, this language could as easily be interpreted to mean that "priesthood authority commenced with Adam and came through the fathers, even till Noah, and then to Shem." Assuming Melchizedek was Shem, he would have been 465 years old when Abram was 75. See also Ron Phillips, *Unexplained Mysteries of Heaven and Earth*, 2013, 33, https://books.google.com/books?id=Htpk1wea0soC&pg =PA33&lpg=PA33&dq=Book+of+Jasher+%22Abraham+lived+with+Noah%22 &source=bl&ots=-VANZi9–Te&sig=ACfU3U2Yc5F6Np_8JYWHEP69AVN mDlq5cA&hl=en&sa=X&ved=2ahUKEwibgLORqb38AhXwmmoFHcfPDbg Q6AF6BAguEAM#v=onepage&q=Book%20of%20Jasher%20%22Abraham-%20lived%20with%20Noah%22&f=false. See discussion about Abraham's possible tutoring under the hands of Noah and Shem in note 7 above.
17. See generally *The Patriarchal Priesthood and Order: Notes, Quotes, and References*, compiled by Bruce H. Porter, self-published, 2018.
18. President Nelson cites Melchizedek as an example of the "privileges" that can be ours, as described in JST, Genesis 14: "Now Melchizedek," the inspired rendering of Genesis 14 recounts, "was a man of faith, who," through that faith, "wrought righteousness" and, even "when a child," "feared God, and stopped the mouths of lions, and quenched the violence of fire," suggesting that age is no limitation to accomplishing great things in God's holy cause. Moreover, the record reflects, it has ever been thus since the beginning. "For God having sworn unto Enoch and unto his seed with an oath by himself; that every one being ordained after this order and calling," which we have learned repeatedly from counsel from the Brethren and General Organization Officers of the Church (as summarized in chapter 18) includes women who are endowed and called and set apart by those holding or acting under priesthood keys, "should have power, by faith, to break mountains, to divide the seas, to dry up waters, to turn them out of their course; To put at defiance the armies of nations, to divide the earth, to break every band, to stand in the presence of God; to do all things according to his will, according to his command, subdue

19. principalities and powers; and this by the will of the Son of God which was from before the foundation of the world" (JST, Genesis 14:26–28, 30–31) (Nelson, "Ministering with the Power and Authority of God," 69 and note 3).
19. Kerry Muhlestein made the point in Scripture Central's Come, Follow Me lesson on "Genesis 12–17; Abraham 1–2" that Jehovah's identification of Himself by name and Abraham by name signals the beginnings of the covenantal relationship that is described throughout the history of Abraham. See https://www.youtube.com/watch?v=ssiOVNImLZY (accessed February 8, 2022). As we noted in chapter 5, the Lord followed a similar pattern in calling Moses, as He does with each of us (see chapter 11 and footnote 3).
20. Skousen observes that "priesthood of thy father" "probably had reference to the patriarchal priesthood, which follows a particular lineage from father to son as noted in Doctrine and Covenants 107:40–41: "The order of this priesthood was confirmed to be handed down from father to son, and rightly belongs to the literal descendants of the chosen seed, to whom the promises were made. This order was instituted in the days of Adam, and came down by lineage in the following manner," namely, from Adam to Seth, Enos, Cainan, Mahalaleel, Jared, Enoch and Methuselah, all of whom were blessed by Adam in the Valley of Adam-ondi-Ahman (vv. 42–53). Methuselah's son, Lamech, was ordained by Seth and Lamech's son, Noah, was ordained at age ten by Methuselah (vv. 51–52).
21. Skousen, 273. As explained in note 13 above, Abraham was also of this same royal lineage.
22. Abraham 2:23–24.
23. Haran, "almost universally identified with Harran, a city whose ruins lie within present-day Turkey" (Wikipedia, "Haran (biblical place)," https://en.wikipedia.org/wiki/Haran_(biblical_place), is about a 770-mile drive from the site traditionally identified as Ur. See note 13 above. Haran was named after Abraham's brother, who had passed away during the famine. Abraham's father, Terah, seems to have undergone something of a "reactivation" to the gospel, because he also went with Abraham. However, the conversion, if there was one, seems to have been short-lived, because several years later when Abraham was commanded by the Lord to leave for Canaan, which later would become the "promised land" of the Bible, Terah remained behind and eventually "turned again to his idolatry" (see Genesis 11:31).
24. "And I took Sarai, whom I took to wife when I was in Ur, in Chaldea, and Lot, my brother's son, and all our substance that we had gathered, *and the souls that we had won in Haran*, and came forth in the way to the land of Canaan, and dwelt in tents as we came on our way" (Abraham 2:15).
25. Skousen points out that "the principal populations of Europe, North, Central and South America, the islands of the Pacific and certain portions of Eurasia can all trace some branch of their lineage back to Abraham" (*First 2,000 Years*, 277).
26. As Skousen notes, Abraham was blessed both temporally—he "was very rich in cattle, in silver and gold" (Genesis 13:2)—and spiritually (Ibid.)
27. Abraham is honored by the two largest world religions, Christianity and Islam, together numbering more than 4 billion in 2015 according to the Pew Research Center. (See Conrad Hackett and David McClendon, "Christians

remain world's largest religious group," https://www.pewresearch.org/fact-tank/2017/04/05/christians-remain-worlds-largest-religious-group-but-they-are-declining-in-europe/#:~:text=Christians%20remained%20the%20largest%20religious,Pew%20Research%20Center%20demographic%20analysis.) Of course, he is also honored by more than 14 million Jews.

28. Thus, the statement in Genesis 12:4 that Abraham was seventy-five years old when he left Haran must be a scribal error.

29. Nelson, "Children of the Covenant." For a detailed study of the "transcendent significance" of the covenants God made with Abraham, and that he makes with each of us, which in part was a response to "President Nelson's invitation to make a list of the blessings promised to the children of Israel," see Kerry Muhlestein, *Finding Promised Blessings on the Covenant Path* (American Fork, Utah: Covenant Communications, Inc., 2023).

30. Nelson, "Children of the Covenant" (footnotes omitted). The Lord reminds us repeatedly in the Doctrine and Covenants of the renewal of the Abrahamic covenant. For example, President Nelson cites Doctrine and Covenants 132:30–31: "Abraham received promises concerning his seed, and of the fruit of his loins—from whose loins ye are, . . . my servant Joseph. . . . This promise is yours also, because ye are of Abraham." Another reference is found in Doctrine and Covenants 86:8–11: "Therefore, thus saith the Lord unto you, with whom the priesthood hath continued *through the lineage of your fathers*—For ye are lawful heirs, according to the flesh, and have been hid from the world with Christ in God—Therefore your life and the priesthood have remained, and must needs remain through you and your lineage until the restoration of all things spoken by the mouths of all the holy prophets since the world began. Therefore, blessed are ye if ye continue in my goodness, a light unto the Gentiles, and through this priesthood, a savior unto my people Israel."

31. "The Family: A Proclamation to the World" ("All human beings—male and female—are created in the image of God. Each is a beloved spirit son or daughter of heavenly parents, and, as such, each has a divine nature and destiny").

32. See Abraham 4:12, 18, 21 ("And the Gods saw that [after commanding the organization of the plants, sun, moon and stars and animals, respectively] they were obeyed"). See also Doctrine and Covenants 93:29–30; Skousen, *First 2,000 Years*, 288, quoting Brigham Young that intelligences are "in all matter throughout the vast extent of all the eternities; [they] are in the rock, the sand, the dust, in water, air, the gases, and in short, in every description and organization of matter . . . particle operating with particle" in *Brigham Young's Discourses*, 566.

33. "To the King of Sodom," Abraham said, "I have lift up mine hand unto the Lord, the most high God, the possessor of heaven and earth, that I will not take from a thread even to a shoelatchet" or "any thing that is thine, lest thou shouldest say, I have made Abram rich" (Genesis 14:22–23).

34. "Sarah . . . received the same ordinances that we as members of the Lord's restored Church today have made: those covenants that we receive at baptism and in the temple" (Nelson, "Come Follow Me").

35. In her discussion of the meaning and power of divine names received in the endowment, Amy Hardison notes: "The names we take on in our religious covenants are usually some form of the name of Christ. The difference between *Abram* and *Abraham* and *Sarai* and *Sarah* is in both cases the letter *h*. *H* is the dominant letter in the divine name Yhwh. This may indicate that Abraham and Sara, whose names are already pretty impressive (Exalted Father and Queen), are taking on another dimension of the name and nature of God" (Hardison, 138 [footnote omitted]).
36. Indeed, the Lord Himself cited this trial as a type and an example for all the faithful, who "must needs be chastened and tried, even as Abraham, who was commanded to offer up his only son" (Doctrine and Covenants 101:4).
37. "Genesis 18–23: Abraham—A Model of Faith and Righteousness," *Old Testament Student Manual—Genesis–2 Samuel*, 78, quoting Spencer W. Kimball, Conference Report, October 1952, 48. Elder Melvin J. Ballard described Abraham's possible feelings thus: "Can you feel what was in the heart of Abraham on that occasion? You love your son just as Abraham did, perhaps not quite so much, because of the peculiar circumstances, but what do you think was in his heart when he started away from Mother Sarah, and they bade her goodbye? What do you think was in his heart when he saw Isaac bidding farewell to his mother to take that three days' journey to the appointed place where the sacrifice was to be made? I imagine it was about all Father Abraham could do to keep from showing his great grief and sorrow at that parting, but he and his son trudged along three days toward the appointed place, Isaac carrying the fagots that were to consume the sacrifice" ("Genesis 18–23," *Old Testament Student Manual—Genesis–2 Samuel*, quoting Melvin J. Ballard, "The Sacramental Covenant," *New Era*, January 1976, 9–10).
38. "Genesis 18–23," *Old Testament Student Manual Genesis–2 Samuel*.
39. "Adam Clarke, citing other scholars, said that the proper translation should be 'on this mount the Lord shall be seen.' Clarke then concluded: 'From this it appears that the sacrifice offered by Abraham was understood to be a representative one, and a tradition was kept up that Jehovah should be seen in a sacrificial way on this mount. And this renders . . . more than probable . . . that Abraham offered Isaac on that very mountain on which, in the fulness of time, Jesus suffered.' (Bible Commentary, 1:141.) Jesus was sentenced to death within the walls of the Antonia fortress, which was only about a hundred yards from the traditional site of Abraham's sacrifice. He was put to death at Golgotha, part of the same ridge system as Moriah. Scholars not only have noted the significance of the site for the sacrifice of Jesus Himself but also have pointed out that it related to the site of Solomon's temple where the sacrifices under the Mosaic dispensation took place. 'The place of sacrifice points with peculiar clearness [to] Mount Moriah, upon which under the legal economy all the typical sacrifices were offered to Jehovah; . . . that by this one true sacrifice the shadows of the typical sacrifices might be rendered both real and true'" (Keil and Delitzsch, *Commentary*, 1:1:253, as quoted in "Genesis 18–23," *Old Testament Student Manual*).
40. Nelson, "Come, Follow Me."

CHAPTER 17

The Spiritual Treasures from the Mission and Keys of Elijah

"Under the direction of the Father and Son, . . . Elijah . . . restored the authority to join families together forever in eternal relationships that transcend death."[1]

—Russell M. Nelson

In this chapter, we review the significance of the mission and keys held by Elijah through the lens of the scriptural record of his life. Again, our focus is on how his life and ministry illuminate the powers of godliness and other spiritual treasures that are available to all of us by receiving, and honoring the covenants made and regularly participating in, the endowment and sealing ordinances. These spiritual treasures are available to us because of the priesthood keys the Lord entrusted to Elijah (and other prophets) and directed him to restore in this, the dispensation of the fulness of times (Ephesians 1:10; Doctrine and Covenants 112:30; 124:41; 128:18, 20).

Elijah's Mission and the Sealing Power

Malachi 4:5–6—Behold, I will send you Elijah the prophet before the coming of the great and dreadful day of the Lord: And he shall turn the heart of the fathers to the children, and the heart of the children to their fathers, lest I come and smite the earth with a curse (see also Doctrine and Covenants 128:17).

As David A. Bednar taught in April 2020 general conference, "Elijah was the last prophet to hold the sealing power before Christ."[2] Descriptions of the nature and importance of his mission are found in all four standard works, including the prophet Malachi's prophecy in the last verses of the Old Testament cited above. The Savior shared Malachi's prophecy with the Nephites, knowing that it would come forth to us as part of the Book of Mormon. "And it came to pass that he [the Savior] commanded them that they should write the words which the Father had given unto Malachi, which he should tell unto them" (3 Nephi 24:1). After reciting Malachi's prophecies in Malachi 3 and 4, including verses 5 and 6 of Malachi 4,[3] the Savior expounded them. Mormon did not record his explanation, but he did include the Savior's explanation as to one important reason He commanded the Nephites to record Malachi's prophecy: "These scriptures," he said, "which ye had not with you, the Father commanded that I should give unto you; for it was wisdom in him that they should be given unto future generations" (3 Nephi 26:2). Thus, in ratifying these prophecies, the Savior was telling *us* of their importance.

On September 21, 1823, three and a half years after the First Vision and after Joseph prayed for a "forgiveness of all [his] sins and follies," Moroni appeared to the Prophet Joseph Smith, calling him by name and telling him that God had a work for him to do—translating the Book of Mormon with the aid of the Urim and Thummim. Then, after telling Joseph Smith these things, Moroni quoted the fourth chapter of Malachi, "though with a little variation from the way it reads in our Bibles. . . He quoted the fifth verse thus: Behold, I will *reveal unto you the Priesthood*, by the hand of Elijah the prophet, before the coming of the great and dreadful day of the Lord. He also quoted the next verse differently: And he shall *plant in the hearts of the children the promises made to the fathers*, and the hearts of the children shall turn to their fathers. If it were not so, the whole earth would be utterly wasted at his coming" (Joseph Smith—History 1:36–39).[4]

President Joseph Fielding Smith taught that Malachi's reference to "promises made to the fathers," which would be "planted" in the hearts of their children, refers to "certain promises made to those who died without a knowledge of the gospel, and without the opportunity of receiving the sealing ordinances of the Priesthood in matters pertaining to their exaltation. According to these promises, [their] children in the latter days are to perform all such ordinances in behalf of the dead."[5] In other words, some premortal spirits agreed to come to the earth knowing that the gospel would not be available but were comforted by the assurance that other premortal spirits, their children or descendants, had *promised* that, as they had opportunity to receive the gospel themselves, either by being born in the covenant or baptized as new converts, they would do the family history work and temple ordinances for their progenitors, without whom they could not have been born. President Nelson added that Malachi's reference to "fathers" and Moroni's rephrasing of Malachi's prophecy to include the "promises to the fathers" "surely include Abraham, Isaac, and Jacob,"[6] or the promises God made to Abraham and his seed, as outlined in the previous chapter.

Who Was Elijah and What Ministry Did the Lord Give Him?

1 Kings 17:1—And Elijah the Tishbite, who was of the inhabitants of Gilead, said unto Ahab, As the Lord God of Israel liveth, before whom I stand, there shall not be dew nor rain these years, *but according to my word.*

Elijah first makes his appearance in ancient Israel during a time of apostasy. The ten tribes of Israel had separated some years previous from the tribes of Judah and in the process introduced a perverted form of worship of Jehovah in the Northern Kingdom involving golden calves. He is introduced suddenly, around 864 BC[7] in 1 Kings 17, challenging King Ahab, who "did more to provoke the Lord God of Israel to anger than all the kings of Israel that were before him" (1 Kings 16:33). Ahab, for political expediency, had begun promoting the worship of the pagan god Baal alongside the Northern Kingdom's corrupted worship of Jehovah. By authority of the sealing power of the Melchizedek Priesthood, Elijah confronted wicked Ahab, sealing the heavens so that there would be neither "dew nor rain" until the

Lord decreed.[8] To escape the ensuing wrath of the king, "the word of the Lord came unto [Elijah], saying, Get thee hence, and turn thee eastward, and hide thyself by the brook Cherith, that is before Jordan. And it shall be, that thou shalt drink of the brook; and I have commanded the ravens to feed thee there. So he went and did according unto the word of the Lord" (1 Kings 17:2–5).

A simpler "example of faithful obedience would be hard to find," Byron R. Merrill comments in his biography of the prophet Elijah. "The introductory verses about Elijah" show him to be a type of Christ, Brother Merrill and others have observed,[9] "first in his declaring his commission from God in speaking the Lord's words and second in his departing into the desert," as his story unfolds, following the example of the great lawgiver, Moses, and foreshadowing Christ's forty-day fast.[10] Elijah was fed by the ravens, as the Lord had promised, but after some months, as the famine progressed and the brook dried up, the Lord directed him to a widow in Sidon, who was not of the house of Israel (1 Kings 17:6–10).[11] Again, Elijah's obedient response is impressive—the record states, he simply "arose and went" as the Lord asked. The unnamed widow's faith and obedience, as the Savior noted,[12] were equally exemplary. Arriving at "the gate of the city," Elijah called to the widow, "Fetch me, I pray thee, a little water in a vessel, that I may drink. And as she was going to fetch it, he called to her, and said, Bring me, I pray thee, a morsel of bread in thine hand. And she said, As the Lord thy God liveth, I have not a cake, but an handful of meal in a barrel, and a little oil in a cruse: and, behold, I am gathering two sticks, that I may go in and dress it for me and my son, that we may eat it, and die" (1 Kings 17:9–12).

Like the widow whom the Savior observed giving two mites— "all that she had" (Mark 12:41–44)—the Lord through His prophet asked the widow of Zarephath to give all that she had, for it is doubtful that her handful of meal would have been sufficient for the starving prophet and for her and her son.[13] But to her great credit and blessing, in response to the prophet's promise from the "God of Israel," that "the barrel of meal shall not waste, neither shall the cruse of oil fail, until the day that the Lord sendeth rain upon the earth," she "went and did" just that (1 Kings 17:13–15). Her blessings, as always happens with the Lord, far exceeded her sacrifice—she and her only son did "eat many days." Later, when her son fell sick and died, the widow called upon the "man of God"—"art thou come unto me to call my sin to remembrance, and to slay my son?" (1 Kings 17:17–18). In her plea, Brother Merrill suggests, the widow did not blame either God or the prophet for her son's death but looked inward at some personal "sin" or regret, a reminder to us when tribulation and loss come to resist the temptation to blame God. Through the power of the Melchizedek Priesthood he held,[14] Elijah raised the boy from the dead. "Just as the miracle of the meal and the oil foreshadowed the miracles of the loaves and the fishes in Jesus' ministry," and reminds us of the Lord, at Moses's pleading, feeding the children of Israel manna in the wilderness,[15] "the circumstances surrounding the raising of the widow's son present Elijah as a type of the Savior, . . . [who raised] another widow's only son, the son of the widow of Nain (see Luke 7:11–16)."[16]

In the third year after sealing the heavens, the Lord commands Elijah to return to King Ahab and charge him to gather Israel to witness Jehovah's challenge to the false prophets supported by the wicked king and queen—450 of the prophets of Baal and 400 of "the prophets of the groves." When Ahab, his 850 "prophets," and "all the children of Israel" gathered to Mount Carmel, Elijah challenged them, "How long halt ye between two opinions? if the Lord be God, follow him: but if Baal, then follow him" (1 Kings 18:19–21). At El Muhrakah, the traditional site of the contest, at the southern end of the Mount Carmel range, overlooking the Mediterranean Sea to the west and the valleys and mountains of the Kingdom of Israel to the east, there was an old, broken altar to Jehovah (perhaps destroyed by the very priests Elijah challenged), apparently an altar to Baal, indicating that Baal's followers claimed supremacy over an area that had previously been given by Jehovah to Israel,[17] and a spring from which jars of water could be filled. Elijah's efforts to fortify the faith of his fellow Israelites by boldly challenging the false gods and ideas of his day and time reminds us of our opportunity to boldly defend the doctrine of Christ and fortify our families and neighbors against the false ideologies of our day.

We know the dramatic result that followed. After dressing the bullock and placing it on their altar, those false prophets of Baal "called on the name of Baal from morning even until noon, saying, O Baal, hear us. But there was no voice, nor any that answered. And they leaped upon the altar" and, in response to Elijah's mocking, "cut themselves after their manner with knives and lancets, till the blood gushed out upon them" (1 Kings 18:25, 28). Notwithstanding the extremity and supposed sincerity of their pleas,[18] "there was neither voice, nor any to answer, nor any that regarded." Then, about the time of evening sacrifice, "Elijah said unto all the people, Come near unto me. And all the people came near unto him." We likewise daily call upon our families to come near as we study *Come, Follow Me* and join in family prayer. "And he repaired the altar of the Lord that was broken down" (1 Kings 18:29–30). Sometimes we also have some repairing to do before we can effectively teach and testify to our loved ones.

"And Elijah took twelve stones, according to the number of the tribes of the sons of Jacob" (1 Kings 18:31), symbolizing Elijah's efforts to restore "the twelve tribes into one people again, a reuniting and sanctification of a people broken into two kingdoms both by idolatry and by political schism." In a magnificent object lesson to the demonstration of Jehovah's existence and power that follows, Elijah digs a large trench, orders it filled with twelve barrels or jars of water, each representing again the twelve tribes of Israel, and then turns his eyes and raises his arms to heaven and prays: "Lord God of Abraham, Isaac, and of Israel, let it be known this day that thou art God in Israel, and that I am thy servant, and that I have done all these things at thy word. Hear me, O Lord, hear me, that this people may know that thou art the Lord God, and that thou hast turned their heart back again. Then the fire of the Lord fell, and consumed the burnt sacrifice, and the wood, and the stones, and the dust, and licked up the water that was in the trench. And when all the people saw it, they fell on their faces: and they said, The Lord, he is the God; the Lord, he is the God" (1 Kings 18:36–39).

Elijah's sole purpose in this great teaching moment, as is ours in all of our teaching moments, was not to draw attention to himself or even primarily to ridicule or prove another religion or ideology false. It was to turn the *hearts* of the people back to their Father and their God. As the Savior lamented after the destruction among the Nephites at the time of his crucifixion, "O all ye that are spared because ye were more righteous than they, will ye not now return unto me, and repent of your sins, and *be converted, that I may heal you?*" (3 Nephi 9:13).

As Brother Merrill explains, while a literal, historical event, the challenge of the false priests and false religion at Mount Carmel is a dramatization of the doctrine of Christ—a call to faith, to "believe" in Jehovah, the "one true God," and to repentance, symbolized by the reconstruction or mending of the altar; of baptism, symbolized by the immersion of the sacrifice in water; and lastly of the cleansing power of the Holy Spirit, represented by the consummation of everything— sacrifice, wood, stones, water and even the dust—by fire. Likewise, "the offering at Carmel . . . foreshadowed the future offering of the Holy One of Israel as the sacrificial substitute for the sins of all mankind, including those in attendance at Carmel that day."[19]

After overseeing the execution of the false priests of Baal, as required by the law of Moses,[20] Elijah dismisses King Ahab and the people with the phrase, "for there is a sound of the abundance of rain" (v. 41). At that point undoubtedly the sound was only Elijah's consummate faith in that which the Lord was directing Him to do, which was then to climb to the top of the mountain and pray for rain, or more precisely, to exercise the keys of the sealing power he held to unlock the previously sealed heavens. "And Elijah went up to the top of Carmel; and he cast himself down upon the earth, and put his face between his knees, And said to his servant, Go up now, look toward the sea. And he went up, and looked, and said, There is nothing. And he said, Go again seven times" (1 King 18: 42–44). Notice that even though Elijah was praying, exercising the power of the holy Melchizedek Priesthood as directed by the Lord through the power of the Holy Ghost, he was not exempt from the principle that the grace, or power of the Lord, comes only after "all we can do" (2 Nephi 25:23). Pouring out his whole soul in prostrate, humble prayer, Elijah continues to plead as the servant returns seven times (note the teaching significance of that sacred number representing completion or perfection) before the object of Elijah's faith and hope becomes reality—"a great rain."

The Lord then directs Elijah to go from the north of Israel to its southern-most city, Beersheba, and then into the wilderness of the Negev desert "a day's journey." Elijah is so discouraged by Israel's unfaithfulness that "he requested [of the Lord] for himself that he might die; and said, It is enough; now, O Lord, take away my life; for I am not better than my fathers" (1 Kings 19:4). Nevertheless, after being nourished twice by an angel with "a cake baken on the coals and a cruse of water" (1 Kings 19:6), he remains in the desert forty days without food or water, reminiscent of both Moses[21] and Jesus.[22] Significantly, Horeb is the same mountain, Sinai, where Moses communed with God "face to face."[23] There he (and we) are taught, among many other things, that marvelous lesson about how to hear the voice of the Lord. When asked by the Lord as he camped in a cave on the mountain, "What doest thou here?" Elijah pours out his despair about how Israel had "forsaken thy covenant, thrown down thine altars, and slain thy prophets" "and I, even I only, am left; and they seek my life, to take it away." In response, the Lord asks Elijah to go to the cave's entrance and "stand upon the mount before the Lord." Then, in a spectacular demonstration of His power, the Lord "passed by, and a great and strong wind rent the mountains, and brake in pieces the rocks before the Lord; but the Lord was not in the wind: and after the wind [the Lord caused] an earthquake; but the Lord was not in the earthquake. And after the earthquake," He caused a fire to rage on the mountainside, "but the Lord was not in the fire." After these awesome and miraculous displays of His power over nature, the Lord spoke directly to Elijah's spirit, as He does to us, in "a *still small voice*" (1 Kings 19:9–12).

Like Moses before him[24] and all of us at times, Elijah felt discouraged and overwhelmed by the immensity of his mission to bring backsliding Israel back to their loving Parents and heavenly home. He felt, as we often feel, oppressed by and alone in his task. But the Lord reassures him, as He does us, that He would and does send not only His "Spirit to be in [our] hearts" but His "angels round about [us], to bear [us] up" (Doctrine and Covenants 84:88). Moreover, notwithstanding the multitude of evidence to the contrary, the Lord reassures Elijah that he is not alone, that He (Jehovah) had yet "left me seven thousand in Israel, all the knees which have not bowed unto Baal, and every mouth which hath not kissed him" (1 Kings 19:18). Often in our own efforts to live the standards of the gospel, we, and perhaps more concerning our spiritually maturing children, feel alone against the onslaught of social media-driven messages that seem to suggest "everyone is doing it" or "believing" it—"it," of course referring to everything that is contrary to the truths of the gospel. But even our seemingly worst moments and days, months, and even years, as the Lord explained to the Prophet Joseph Smith, teach us important lessons and give us "experience" (Doctrine and Covenants 122:7). In his extremity during his forty-day trial in the wilderness, as Brother Merrill envisions in his reading of this account, Elijah comes to *know* God, as each of us must in our own lives and ministries, as the God of heaven, the Mighty Jehovah, speaks peace to his soul through the power of the Holy Spirit.[25] In our own efforts to leave the world with its stresses and challenges and come to the Lord's Holy Mountain, it may seem at times we literally leave temporal and emotional gale-force winds, earthquakes, and fires. How grateful we should be, then, to have such places where, if spiritually prepared, we can *always* feel the still small voice of the Lord speaking peace, love, and comfort to our souls.

The remainder of the record of Elijah's earthly ministry in 1 Kings 19–22 and 2 Kings 1–2 shows that he had not been alone and that his work was not yet finished. Equally instructive as the events described above are the accounts of his call and training of his successor, Elisha (1 Kings 19:19–21; 2 Kings 2); his call of new kings appointed by the Lord (1 Kings 19:15–16); his and Israel's witness of the fulfillment of the Elijah's divinely inspired prophecies against the wicked King Ahab, Queen Jezebel, and their son, Ahaziah (1 Kings 21; 22:34–38, 51–53; 2 Kings 1:1–8, 13–17); Elijah's calling down fire from heaven, no doubt as directed by the Lord, to consume the soldiers sent by Ahab's son to apprehend him (2 Kings 1:9–13); and, perhaps most spectacularly in his singular ministry, his miraculous translation into heaven in a chariot of fire, in effect a "transfer" by the Lord to a new area of labor. "And it came to pass, as [Elijah and Elisha] went on, and talked, that, behold, there appeared a chariot of fire, and horses of fire, and parted them both asunder; and Elijah went up by a whirlwind into heaven. And Elisha saw it, and he cried, My father, my father, the chariot of Israel, and the horsemen thereof. And he saw him no more" (2 Kings 2:11–12).

Elijah's Ministry to the Savior and His Apostles in the Meridian of Time

In order to later confer upon Peter, James, and John on the Mount of Transfiguration the keys of the sealing power he held, Elijah needed to have a physical body.[26] As a translated being, Elijah was able to do this. About six months before the end of His ministry, Jesus "asked his disciples, saying, Whom do men say that I the Son of man am?" Peter answered with impressive surety, "Thou art the Christ, the Son of the living God." In response to Peter's expression of testimony, the Savior promised to confer upon him, together with James and John, "the keys of the kingdom of heaven" that "whatsoever thou shalt bind on earth shall be bound in heaven: and whatsoever thou shalt loose on earth shall be loosed in heaven" (Matthew 16:18–19). Matthew describes the occasion, one of the most important in the Savior's ministry:

> **Matthew 17:1–3**—Jesus taketh Peter, James, and John his brother, and bringeth them up into an high mountain apart, And was transfigured before them: and his face did shine as the sun, and his raiment was white as the light. And, behold, there appeared unto them Moses and Elias [Elijah] talking with him. . . . Behold, a bright cloud overshadowed them: and behold a voice out of the cloud, which said, This is my beloved Son, in whom I am well pleased; hear ye him.

The Prophet Joseph Smith explained that on this occasion, "the Savior, Moses, and Elias [Elijah], gave the keys to Peter, James, and John, on the mount, when they were transfigured before him."[27] *General Handbook* 3.4.1 defines "priesthood keys" as the "authority to direct the use of the priesthood on behalf of God's children." On the Mount of Transfiguration, "Moses conferred the keys of the gathering of Israel on Peter, James, and John, who, as the First Presidency, would soon be sending out missionaries to gather the righteous into the gospel. Elijah conferred the sealing power of the priesthood, which made it possible for ordinances performed on earth to be bound or loosed in heaven." Joseph Smith summarized the importance of Elijah's mission as follows: "The spirit, power, and calling of Elijah is, that ye have power to hold the key of the revelation, ordinances, oracles, powers and endowments of the fullness of the Melchizedek Priesthood and of the kingdom of God on the earth; and to receive, obtain, and perform all the ordinances belonging to the kingdom of God."[28] However, the sealing power that Peter, James, and John received could only be exercised at that time on behalf of the living. After the resurrection of Christ, President Joseph Fielding Smith explained, such keys could also be used on behalf of the dead.[29] President Smith added, "Christ told these three men, *who I believe received their endowments on the mount*, that they were not to mention this vision and what had taken place until after he was resurrected."[30]

Elijah's Ministry to the Prophet Joseph Smith and What It Means to Us

The week after the dedication of the Kirtland Temple, on the afternoon of Easter Sunday, April 3, 1836, and during the Jewish celebration of Passover, after administering the sacrament and lowering the curtains around the uppermost pulpit on the west side of the ground-floor assembly hall, Joseph Smith and Oliver Cowdery knelt in silent prayer. After their prayers, the Savior appeared in front of them. His "countenance shown above the brightness of the sun" (Doctrine and Covenants 110:3). Immediately after the Savior's visit, Moses appeared, restoring the keys of the gathering of Israel; then Elias came, restoring, as noted in the preceding chapter, the "dispensation of the gospel of Abraham" (Doctrine and Covenants 110:12).

> **Doctrine and Covenants 110:14–16**—After this vision had closed, another great and glorious vision burst upon us; for Elijah the prophet, who was taken to heaven without tasting death, stood before us, and said: Behold, the time has fully come, which was spoken of by the mouth of Malachi—testifying that he [Elijah] should be sent, before the great and dreadful day of the Lord come—To turn the hearts of the fathers to the children, and the children to the fathers, lest the whole earth be smitten with a curse—Therefore, the keys of this dispensation are committed into your hands; and by this

ye may know that the great and dreadful day of the Lord is near, even at the doors.

President Joseph Fielding Smith explained the importance of the keys conferred by Elijah: "These keys of the binding, or sealing power, which were given to Peter, James and John in their dispensation, are keys which make valid *all* the ordinances of the gospel. . . . During the days of his ministry Elijah held this authority, and the Lord gave him power over *all things* on earth and that through his ministry whatever was done should be ratified, or sealed, in the heavens and recognized of full force by the Eternal Father. This power effects [sic] and vitalizes every ordinance performed by duly commissioned officers holding divine power on the earth." As we will discuss in greater detail in the next chapter, "ordinances are performed in the temples" by virtue of the authority restored by Elijah "for both the living and the dead." This power "unites for eternity husbands and wives" and "makes eternal the family in the kingdom of God."[31]

President Boyd K. Packer described the keys conferred by Elijah on Joseph Smith and Oliver Cowdery as "the consummate authority on this earth for man to act in the name of God."[32] President Henry B. Eyring similarly described the sealing power Elijah held as "the greatest power God gives to His children."[33] President Nelson eloquently brought these grand truths down to earth, even to our figurative hearth stones, when during the midst of the COVID-19 pandemic he taught: "Elijah restored the keys of the priesthood that allow our families to be sealed together forever. *That is why it felt so good to administer the sacrament in your home.* . . . What will you do to retain that sacred feeling in your family?"[34] God be praised for prophets like Elijah—and President Nelson, who helps us understand the depth and breadth of the supernal spiritual treasures the Lord has bestowed upon us in these latter days, including being able to draw upon the spirit of Elijah and the very powers of heaven to minister to our loved ones at home.

Endnotes

1. Nelson, "Hear Him," quoting from "The Restoration of the Fulness of the Gospel of Jesus Christ: A Bicentennial Proclamation to the World," The First Presidency and Council of the Twelve Apostles of The Church of Jesus Christ of Latter-day Saints, chrome-extension://efaidnbmnnnibpcajpcglclefindmkaj/ https://newsroom.churchofjesuschrist.org/multimedia/file/restoration-proclamation-2020-april.pdf.
2. Bednar, "Let This House Be Built unto My Name," 85, citing Guide to the Scriptures, "Elijah."
3. See 3 Nephi 24–25.
4. Moroni's version of Malachi 4:5–6 is also included as Doctrine and Covenants 2, the headnote to which explains that these verses were given by "the angel Moroni to Joseph Smith the Prophet, while in the house of the Prophet's father at Manchester, New York, on the evening of September 21, 1823." See Doctrine and Covenants 2:1–3; see also references to Malachi's prophecies in Doctrine and Covenants 133:64 and Doctrine and Covenants 138:46. See generally Kenneth L. Alford, "'I Will Send You Elijah the Prophet,'" in *You Shall Have My Word: Exploring the Text of the Doctrine and Covenants*, Scott C. Esplin, Richard O. Cowan, and Rachel Cope, eds. (Provo, Utah: Brigham Young University Religious Studies Center, 2012), 34, https://rsc.byu.edu/you-shall-have-my-word/i-will-send-you-elijah-prophet.
5. Joseph Fielding Smith, "The Promises Made to the Fathers," *Improvement Era*, July 1922, 829. President Joseph Fielding Smith further taught, "The fathers are our dead ancestors who died without the privilege of receiving the gospel, but who received the promise that the time would come when that privilege would be granted them. The children are those now living who are preparing genealogical data and who are performing the vicarious ordinances in the temples. The turning of the hearts of the children to the fathers is placing or planting in the hearts of the children that feeling and desire which will inspire them to search out the records of the dead. Moreover, the planting of the desire and inspiration in their hearts is necessary. This they must have in order that they might go into the house of the Lord and perform the necessary labor for their fathers, who died without a knowledge of the gospel, or without the privilege of receiving the fulness of the gospel (*Doctrines of Salvation*, 2:127–28," as quoted in "Chapter 2: The Mission of Elijah," *Introduction to Family History Student Manual*, https://www.churchofjesuschrist.org/study/manual/introduction-to-family-history-student-manual/chapter-2?lang=eng).
6. Nelson, "The Everlasting Covenant," citing Doctrine and Covenants 27:9–10.
7. Austin Cline, "Biography of Elijah, Old Testament Prophet," https://www.learnreligions.com/elijah-profile-and-biography-248833.
8. Compare Nephi's similar exercise of the sealing power in Helaman 11. See Joseph Fielding Smith, "Elijah the Prophet and His Mission," a discourse originally delivered at the Salt Lake Assembly Hall and originally printed in *Utah Genealogical and Historical Magazine* 12, no. 1, January 1921, reprinted in the

Instructor, December 1951 and January 1952 (accessed in Kindle Reader, 61 of 444).
9. See, for example, Andrew C. Skinner, *Prophets, Priests, and Kings* (Salt Lake City, Utah: Deseret Book, 2005), 83–89.
10. Byron R. Merrill, *Elijah: Yesterday, Today, and Tomorrow* (Salt Lake City, Utah: Bookcraft, 1997), 13.
11. Ironically, Sidon was in prosperous Phoenicia, where Ahab's wicked queen, Jezebel (which means literally "Baal is prince"), was born and raised. Jezebel was the daughter of Ethbaal, a priest of the goddess Astarte, who usurped the throne of his brother, the King of Tyre, one of the principal cities of Phoenicia. Jezebel's arranged marriage with Ahab, the son of the King of Israel, represented a giant step in Israel's further apostasy, as Ahab "not only married Jezebel but also married her god." Ahab built a temple to Baal in the capital city Samaria. Jezebel, at taxpayer expense (i.e., establishing these false gods as a state-supported religion), brought to Israel 400 priests of Baal and 400 of Asherah. Under her influence, altars to Jehovah (Yahweh) were destroyed and defiled and many of Israel's prophets were killed. See generally entries under "Jezebel" at https://en.wikipedia.org/wiki/Jezebel and *Encyclopedia Britannica*, https://www.britannica.com/biography/Jezebel-queen-of-Israel.
12. See Luke 4:26.
13. Merrill, 18–19.
14. See Merrill, 38.
15. See Exodus 16.
16. Merrill, 23.
17. Ibid., 29, 38.
18. Merrill notes that "Baal was the god of nature who, with his consort Asherah—also known as Astarte or Ashtaroth (sometimes translated as 'the grove(s) in the Old Testament')—presided over the pantheon of gods worshiped in much of the territory surrounding the kingdom of Israel." "The issue presented to the [Israelites by Elijah] essentially questioned whether Elijah had offended Baal or whether the Canaanite god existed at all. One of the ancient writings known as the Ras Shamra texts boasts of Baal's supposed power over the elements: 'Moreover Baal will send abundance of his rain,/ Abundance of moisture with snow;/ He will utter his voice in the clouds,/ (He will send) his flashing to the earth with lightning.' If Baal was truly this powerful god of weather, why had there been no rain for so long? Elijah's contest thus challenged Baal to prove his divinity and show himself by sending fire to burn a sacrifice offered to him. The use of fire as the sign was a specifically chosen witness of divinity, for the god who could bring fire from heaven to the altar was the one who controlled lightning, and whoever could produce lightning could also produce rain to end the drought" (Merrill, 5, 37–38. See also "Baal," *Encyclopedia Britannica*, https://www.britannica.com/topic/Baal-ancient-deity).
19. Merrill, 44–45.
20. Ibid., 45.
21. Exodus 2:15; 34:28; Deuteronomy 9:9, 11, 18, 25; 10:10.
22. Matthew 4:2.

23. Exodus 33:11.
24. Merrill, 53, citing Numbers 11:15. See chapter 6, "Wandering in the Wilderness," above.
25. See Alma 58:11 (The Lord "did speak peace to our souls, and did grant unto us great faith, and did cause us that we should hope for our deliverance in him"); Doctrine and Covenants 6:23 ("Did I not speak peace to your mind concerning the matter? What greater witness can you have than from God?"); see also Alma 38:8; Doctrine and Covenants 121:7.
26. "Chapter 2: The Mission of Elijah," *Introduction to Family History Student Manual*, https://www.churchofjesuschrist.org/study/manual/introduction-to-family-history-student-manual/chapter-2?lang=eng.
27. "Chapter 6: Matthew 16–18," *New Testament Student Manual* (Salt Lake City, Utah: Seminaries and Institutes of Religion Curriculum The Church of Jesus Christ of Latter-day Saints, 2018), 105, https://www.churchofjesuschrist.org/study/manual/new-testament-student-manual/introduction-to-matthew/chapter-6?lang=eng, quoting Joseph Smith, *Teachings*.
28. Ibid., quoting Joseph Smith, *Teachings*, 311. As the Lord notes in Doctrine and Covenants 63:21, we will not have the full account of what happened on the Mount of Transfiguration until the Millennium: "When the earth shall be transfigured, even according to the pattern which was shown unto mine apostles upon the mount; of which account the fulness ye have not yet received." See also Spencer W. Kimball, "Our Great Potential," *Ensign*, May 1977, 49.
29. Resurrection is also an ordinance, the keys of which are held by Jesus Christ. President Kimball taught that after they have been resurrected, faithful priesthood holders "will be ordained, by those who hold [or act under] the keys of the resurrection, to go forth and resurrect the Saints, just as we receive the ordinance of baptism then receive the keys of authority [or authorization by keyholders] to baptize others for the remission of their sins. This is one of the ordinances we can not receive here [on the earth], and there are many more" (Kimball, "Our Great Potential," 49, citing President Brigham Young, *Journal of Discourses*, 15:137. See also Dallin H. Oaks, "The Keys and Authority of the Priesthood," *Ensign*, May 2014, 50, who cites President Kimball's foregoing general conference address.)
30. "Chapter 6: Matthew 16–18," *New Testament Student Manual*, quoting Joseph Fielding Smith, *Doctrines of Salvation*, 2:164–65 (emphasis added).
31. Smith, *Doctrines of Salvation*, 2:119, 117 (emphasis in original). See also D. Todd Christofferson, "The Sealing Power," *Liahona*, November 2023 ("We tend to think of the sealing authority as applying only to certain temple ordinances, but that authority is necessary to make any ordinance valid and binding beyond death").
32. Packer, The Holy Temple, 84.
33. "Chapter 2: The Mission of Elijah," *Introduction to Family History Student Manual*, quoting Henry B. Eyring, "Hearts Bound Together," *Ensign*, May 2005, 78.
34. Nelson, "What We Are Learning and Will Never Forget."

CHAPTER 18

The Spiritual Treasure of Eternal Families

"The blessings of the Abrahamic covenant are conferred in holy temples. These blessings allow us, upon being resurrected, to 'inherit thrones, kingdoms, powers, principalities, and dominions, to our "exaltation and glory in all things" [Doctrine and Covenants 132:19].'"[1]

—President Russell M. Nelson

The Crowning Ordinance of the Gospel of Jesus Christ

Everything that has preceded this point in this study, and in a sense everything that precedes this "crowning ordinance"[2] of the temple, is prelude to the new and everlasting covenant of marriage. The Lord explained simply and powerfully that "in order to obtain the highest ['heaven or degree' in the 'celestial glory'],[3] a man must enter into this *order of the priesthood* [meaning the *new and everlasting covenant of marriage*]; And if he does not, he cannot obtain it. He may enter into the other [lesser degrees of heaven], but that is the end of his kingdom; he cannot have an increase" (Doctrine and Covenants 131:2–4). In this chapter we focus on the meaning and significance of this crowning ordinance, what is often referred to as "celestial marriage."[4]

In one of the more poignant pleas he has made to those who have not yet sought, understood, gained a testimony of, or received this most supernal of all spiritual treasures from God, President Nelson in April 2019, speaking about "what is required for a family to be exalted forever," explained that "God weeps" and "I also weep" for "friends and relatives," "wonderful men and women, devoted to their family and civic responsibilities," who choose "not to make covenants with God. They have not received the ordinances that will exalt them with their families and bind them together forever." "They need to understand that while there is a place for them hereafter—with wonderful men and women who also chose not to make covenants with God—that is *not* the place where *families will be reunited and be given the privilege to live and progress forever*. That is not the kingdom where they will *experience the fulness of joy—of never-ending progression and happiness*. Those *consummate blessings* [spiritual treasures] can come **only** by living in an exalted celestial realm with God, our Eternal Father; His Son, Jesus Christ; and our wonderful, worthy, and qualified family members."[5]

The recently updated Church history, *Saints*, describes the reaction of the early Saints to the revelation on celestial marriage, which was recorded in 1843. For example, "Joseph taught [Benjamin and Melissa Johnson] that a woman and man could be sealed together for eternity in the new and everlasting covenant of marriage. Only by entering into this covenant, *which was an order of the priesthood*, he taught, could they obtain exaltation." William Clayton, Joseph Smith's secretary who was present and recorded the conversation, felt awe in learning about this truth from God. "I feel desirous to be united in an everlasting covenant to my wife and pray that it may be soon," he wrote in his diary.[6]

The apostles began administering the endowment in December 1845 in the newly completed attic of the Nauvoo Temple under the direction of Brigham Young, the president of the Quorum of the Twelve. Shortly thereafter, in January 1846, "the apostles began sealing couples together for time and eternity." So great was their enthusiasm that "more than a thousand couples received the new and everlasting covenant of marriage," many of them early converts to the Church "who had followed the church from place to place, consecrating their lives to Zion." "The apostles also sealed children to parents and men and women to spouses who had passed away. Joseph Knight Sr., who had rejoiced with Joseph on the morning he brought the gold plates home, was sealed vicariously to his wife, Polly, the first Saint buried in Jackson County, Missouri."[7] Notwithstanding the controversy that accompanied the revelation and practice of *plural* marriage,[8] the Saints who sought and acquired testimonies of the eternal nature of *celestial* marriage, which was contained in the same revelation (Doctrine and Covenants 132), rejoiced in the privilege they had to receive this supernal ordinance.

As the headnote to Genesis 2 states, "Adam and Eve [were] married by the Lord."[9] "And they were both naked, the man *and his wife*" (Genesis 2:25; see also Genesis 3:6 [Eve gave fruit of the tree of knowledge of good and evil to her *husband*] and 3:8 ["Adam and his *wife* hid themselves"]. Of course, such a union, administered before the Fall by God Himself, could not have been anything other than an eternal union, as intimated in the scriptures. "Thus all things were confirmed unto Adam by an holy ordinance" (Moses 5:59). The Prophet Joseph Smith taught, "marriage was an institution of heaven, instituted in the Garden of Eden, [and] it is necessary it should be solemnized by the authority of the everlasting priesthood," doctrine which President Nelson as affirmed.[10]

Brigham Young taught similarly, "We can tell some things with regard to [eternal marriage]; it lays the foundation for worlds, for angels, and for the Gods; for intelligent beings to be crowned with glory, immortality, and eternal lives. In fact, it is the thread which runs from the beginning to the end of the holy Gospel of Salvation—of the Gospel of the Son of God; it is from eternity to eternity."[11] In this vein, referring to the Apostle John's statements in Revelation (that Christ "hath made us kings and priests unto God and his father"), Elder McConkie wrote that "if righteous men have power through the gospel and its crowning ordinance of celestial marriage to become kings and priests to rule in exaltation forever, it follows that the women by their side (without whom they cannot attain exaltation) will be queens and priestesses. (Rev. 1:6; 5:10.) Exaltation grows out of the eternal union of a man and his wife. Of those whose marriage endures in eternity, the Lord says, 'Then shall they be gods' (Doctrine and Covenants 132:20); that is, each of them, the man and the woman, will be a god. As such they will rule over their dominions forever."[12]

How Do Faithful Women Receive and Exercise Priesthood Authority and Power?

When Joseph Smith organized the Relief Society, he taught several important principles as prelude to the restoration of temple ordinances: "(1) that he organized the Relief Society according to the same pattern as he did the priesthood quorums [eg. with a president and two counselors], (2) that he taught Relief Society members the same 'doctrine of the priesthood' he had taught the priesthood quorums, (3) that he delegated to the Relief Society certain 'keys,' or authority, and (4) that the inclusion of women within . . . the Church organization reflected the . . . perfect union of man and woman . . . essential to the restoration of the fullness of the priesthood."[13] As noted earlier, the restoration of the fulness of the priesthood included not only the restoration of the Aaronic and Melchizedek Priesthoods by John the Baptist in 1829 and Peter,[14] James, and John soon thereafter, but the restoration of priesthood keys in the Kirtland Temple by Moses, Elias, and Elijah in 1836. Moreover, the organization of the Relief Society under the prophetic direction and keys held by the Prophet Joseph Smith in 1842 facilitated and enabled the later restoration of temple endowment and sealing ordinances. As the Prophet explained, "The Church was never perfectly organized until the women were thus organized."[15]

Leaders of the Church have increasingly emphasized in recent years that the ongoing restoration of the Church involves continued revelation or explanation by the Lord through His servants to help us better understand and appreciate doctrines of the priesthood, including the role of men and women in exercising priesthood power and authority both in the home and in the Church. As Sister Joy Jones, General Primary President, acknowledged, "As a woman I didn't realize, earlier in my life, that I had access, through my covenants, to the power of the priesthood."[16] President Nelson highlighted the importance of such increased understanding in his 2019 "Spiritual Treasures" address to the sisters: "How I yearn for you to understand that the restoration of the priesthood is just as relevant to you as a woman as it is to any man." Through their temple endowment, President Nelson explains, women "are authorized to perform and officiate in priesthood ordinances every time [they] attend the temple. Your temple endowment prepares you to do so."[17] It is perhaps commonly understood that women who are set apart as ordinance workers in the temple "perform" or "officiate" in priesthood ordinances, which they do, for example, on behalf of sister patrons in the initiatory ordinances. But in this seminal conference address, President Nelson expands our understanding by clarifying that when men and women serve as proxies in the temple, whether in the washing, anointing, clothing, endowment, or sealing ordinances on behalf of the dead, they are "performing" or "officiating in" a priesthood ordinance, authorization for which is received as part of the endowment.

President Ballard likewise taught that women and men "are both endowed with the same power, which by definition is priesthood power." He said, "Our Father in Heaven is generous with His power. All men and women have access to this power for help in their lives. All who have made sacred covenants with the Lord and who honor those covenants are eligible to receive personal revelation, to be blessed by the ministering of angels, to commune with God, to receive the fulness of the gospel, and, ultimately, to become heirs alongside Jesus Christ of all our Father has."[18]

Section 2 of the *General Handbook* defines the priesthood generally as "the power and authority of God." "In mortality," including the Church and the home, "the priesthood is the power and authority that God gives to man [meaning mankind generally] to act in all things necessary for the salvation of God's children. The blessings of the priesthood are available to all who receive the gospel." As President Oaks teaches, "The priesthood is the power of God used to bless all of His children, male and female. Some of our abbreviated expressions, like 'the women and the priesthood,' convey an erroneous idea. Men are not 'the priesthood.'" He goes on to emphasize, as did President Ballard, that "the blessings of the priesthood," including all gospel ordinances performed by proper priesthood authority, "are available to men and women alike. The authority of the priesthood functions in the family and in the Church, according to the principles the Lord has established."[19]

As reviewed in chapter 5, men and young men receive or have the priesthood *conferred* upon them and are *ordained* to specific offices of the priesthood by or under the direction of priesthood leaders who hold priesthood keys, which are "the authority God has given to priesthood leaders to direct, control, and govern the use of His priesthood on earth" "within a jurisdiction."[20] Women and young women, including Primary, Young Women, and Relief Society presidencies, class officers, teachers, and other leaders "receive delegated [priesthood] authority to function in their callings" when they are set apart, as do sister temple ordinance workers. President Nelson explained, "When you are set apart to serve in a calling under the direction of one who holds priesthood keys—such as your bishop or stake president—you are given priesthood authority to function in that calling."[21] President Dallin H. Oaks commented in general conference about the priesthood authority exercised by women and young women:

> We are not accustomed to speaking of women having the authority of the priesthood in their Church callings, but what other authority can it be? When a woman—young or old—is set apart to preach the gospel as a full-time missionary, she is given priesthood authority to perform a priesthood function. The same is true when a woman is set apart to function as an officer or teacher in a Church organization under the direction of one who holds the keys of the priesthood. Whoever functions in an office or calling received from one who holds priesthood keys exercises priesthood authority in performing her or his assigned duties.[22]

The endowment, including the initiatory ordinances, can be viewed in a very real way as the means by which women—and men—receive the ultimate *blessings* and *power* of the priesthood.[23] Receipt of these ordinances and striving to keep the covenants made therein constitute the endowment of priesthood or godly power that the Lord said He had in store through the restoration of temples and temple ordinances. This priesthood power, God's power, is not received by conferral of, and ordination to offices in, the priesthood *per se*. Rather, ordination to priesthood offices, including the offices of bishop and/or high priest that are held by those who authorize members to hold temple recommends and recommend temple ordinances workers, serve to make the blessings and the power of the priesthood available to men and women. Thus, as the Lord explained in the Doctrine and Covenants, in the *ordinances* of the priesthood, especially the holy endowment administered by men and women in the temple, "the power of godliness is manifested" (Doctrine and Covenants 84:20).

Exercising "Priesthood Authority" and Priesthood Power versus "Holding" the Priesthood

Having authority to act in our callings as men and women or young men and young women, of course, is important. But more important is learning how to obtain *power* to bless others in our service—at home and in the Church. As we learn so well from the scriptures, this "power and authority" mentioned so often in the Book of Mormon[24] and applicable to both men and women[25] is none other than *priesthood* power or *God's* power, which He taught can only be governed by priesthood principles. Doctrine and Covenants 121 is perhaps the quintessential expression of how we obtain power in the priesthood, "only by *persuasion*, by *long-suffering*, by *gentleness* and *meekness*, and by *love unfeigned*; By *kindness*, and *pure knowledge*, which shall greatly enlarge the soul without hypocrisy, and without guile—Reproving betimes with sharpness, when moved upon by the Holy Ghost;[26] and then showing forth afterwards an *increase of love* toward him whom thou hast reproved, lest he esteem thee to be his enemy; That he may know that thy *faithfulness* is stronger than the cords of death." The Lord further counsels us to "be full of *charity* towards all men, and to the household of faith" and to "let *virtue* garnish thy thoughts unceasingly." On the other hand, our priesthood power is diminished and ultimately nullified "when we undertake to cover our sins, or to gratify our pride, our vain ambition, or to exercise control or dominion or compulsion upon the souls of the children of men, in any degree of unrighteousness." As we—again, men and women—exercise our priesthood authority righteously, we are promised supernal blessings or spiritual treasures: "thy confidence [shall] wax strong in the presence of God; and the doctrine of the priesthood shall distil upon thy soul as the dews from heaven. The Holy Ghost shall be thy constant companion, and thy scepter an unchanging scepter of righteousness and truth; and thy dominion shall be an everlasting dominion, and without compulsory means it shall flow unto thee forever and ever" (Doctrine and Covenants 121:36–38, 41–46). In short, persuasion, long-suffering, gentleness, meekness, love unfeigned, kindness, pure knowledge, discernment, judgment, wisdom, faithfulness, increased love, and charity are principles of priesthood power that apply in all of our roles, as parents and grandparents, siblings and extended family, and in our callings.

The Sealing Power

To begin to understand the promises of the new and everlasting covenant of marriage, one must understand the nature of the authority by which it is performed. President Gordon B. Hinckley explained that "no king, no president of a nation, no official of any entity in the world of which we are a part has any authority over matters beyond the grave. Everyone is helpless before the reach of death, but the humblest, good, righteous high priest who has received the sealing authority may bind in the heavens that which is bound on the earth."[27] Boyd K. Packer, then president of the Quorum of the Twelve, taught that to "understand both the history and the doctrine of temple work, we must understand what the sealing power is." As discussed in the preceding chapter, the Lord told Peter He would give him "the keys of the kingdom of heaven," to "bind" on earth and in heaven (Matthew 16:18–19), which He did together with, among others, Moses and Elijah on the Mount of Transfiguration. These keys have been passed down to "the President of the Church—to the prophet, seer, and revelator [today]. That sacred sealing power is with the Church now. Nothing is regarded with more sacred contemplation," President Packer said, "by those who know the significance of this authority. Nothing is more closely held. There are relatively few men who have been delegated this sealing power upon the earth at any given time—in each temple are brethren who have been given the sealing power. No one can get it except from the prophet, seer, and revelator and President of The Church of Jesus Christ of Latter-day Saints."[28]

Andrew Skinner offers this beautiful insight about the profound nature of the sealing power, the true depth and extent of which we are not able to fully comprehend in this life:

> The fulness of the authority of the priesthood includes the sealing power. The sealing power is the highest authority and the greatest power on earth. Although Satan is waging an all-out war against righteousness, especially righteous families on this earth, God's power—the power of the priesthood—is infinitely greater. The sealing power will conquer every enemy, sin, death, hell, and the devil.
>
> Some aspects inherent in the sealing power of the priesthood are more perceptible and obvious than others. One dramatic and visible aspect is control over the elements: the sealing and unsealing of the heavens and the invocation and revocation of famine (see 1 Kings 17:1; 18:41–45; Helaman 10:7; 11:5). Thus, the sealing power gives its possessor power over all things on earth and the right and ability to have his actions recognized and ratified in heaven by the Father. It is stunning to realize that the sealing together of husbands, wives, and children is done by the same power that seals shut the heavens and changes the elements of the earth.
>
> Once sealed, husbands, wives, and children are changed—they belong to each other. In a way we cannot explain scientifically or even understand completely, the sealing power welds together a husband, wife, and children for eternity. The sealing power is a real power in the universe. It affects the physical elements; it changes them, whether it be in the heavens, the weather, the waters and seas, or the binding together of families.[29]

The New and Everlasting Covenant of Marriage—The Promises of Abraham and the Power of Elijah

The Prophet Joseph Smith said he was frequently asked, "'Can we not be saved without going through with all those ordinances, etc.?' I would answer, No, not the fullness of salvation. Jesus said, 'There are many mansions in my Father's house, and I will go and prepare a place for you.' [See John 14:2.] House here named should have been translated kingdom; and any person who is exalted to the highest mansion has to abide a celestial law, and the whole law too."[30] In other words, to receive the "fulness of salvation," all that the Father desired through His perfect plan of happiness to bestow upon His children, one must prepare for, receive, and then live worthy of the covenants made in this crowning ordinance of the temple. Joseph Fielding Smith taught: "There is no ordinance connected with the Gospel of Jesus Christ of greater importance, of more solemn and sacred nature, and more necessary to [our] eternal joy . . . than [eternal] marriage. The fullness and blessings of the Priesthood and the Gospel grow out of Celestial marriage. This is the crowning ordinance of the Gospel and crowning ordinance of the temple."[31] Elder Cree-L Kofford of the Seventy observed that "sometimes the word 'sealed' is visualized as attaching or bonding a man and a woman together. While that is one of the results of being sealed, it is much too restrictive to be accurate. It has always seemed to me that the word 'sealed' refers much more to the act of conferring the blessings of God upon the husband and wife *individually* and *jointly* (and *upon their children*) than it does to just 'uniting' a man and a woman."[32] These blessings, as noted in the previous chapter, include the greatest blessings that God can bestow upon any of His children, the blessings of Abraham, Isaac, and Jacob.

The best source of information about the covenants and promises made and received in the new and everlasting covenant of marriage is the revealed language of the ordinance itself. Couples who are preparing to be sealed would be wise, either before, if possible, or soon after their sealing to participate as patrons in proxy sealings to be able to hear and ponder the inspired and inspiring covenants and promises contained in the sealing ordinances for both the sealing of husbands and wives and children to parents. Much can also be learned, however, by studying the actual doctrinal statements contained in the scriptures that describe this ordinance. In the following verses from Doctrine and Covenants 132, for example, I have numbered with brackets the blessings, or spiritual treasures, that the Lord promises in connection with the new and everlasting covenant of marriage, as well as highlighted in bold certain other conditions that He prescribes:

Doctrine and Covenants 132:18–21—Verily I say unto you, if a man **marry a wife by my word, which is my law**, and **by the new and everlasting covenant**, and it is **sealed unto them by the Holy Spirit of promise**, by him who is anointed, unto **whom I have appointed this power and the keys of this priesthood** [reminding us that a sealer must not only be duly ordained, as was Abraham, to an office in the Melchizedek Priesthood, but must also receive the sealing power by the laying on of hands by someone expressly authorized by the prophet to do so, who holds the keys of such power];

[1] Ye shall come forth in the first resurrection; . . . and shall inherit
[2] thrones,
[3] kingdoms,
[4] principalities, and
[5] powers,
[6] dominions,
[7] all heights and depths . . .
and *if ye abide in my covenant,* . . . **it shall be done unto them in all things whatsoever my servant hath put upon them, in time, and through all eternity**; and
[8] [their sealed marriage] shall be of full force when they are out of the world; and
[9] they shall pass by the angels, and the gods, which are set there, to their
[10] exaltation and
[11] glory in all things, as hath been sealed upon their heads, which glory shall be a fulness and a
[12] continuation of the seeds forever and ever (v. 19).
[13] Then shall they be gods, because they have no end; therefore shall they be from everlasting to everlasting, because they continue; then
[14] shall they be above all, because all things are subject unto them. Then shall they be gods, because
[15] they have all power, and
[16] the angels are subject unto them.

> Verily, verily, I say unto you, except ye abide my law ye cannot attain to this glory.

These verses set forth the elements of a celestial or "temple" marriage and how it is administered: first, it is a marriage administered only by a sealer called and authorized by the prophet ("him whom I have appointed unto this power") in a dedicated temple of The Church of Jesus Christ of Latter-day Saints; second, in this marriage the man and woman each make covenants with each other and with God "for time and for all eternity" (as the Church's Temples page succinctly states, "a husband and wife who are sealed in the temple make sacred covenants *with the Lord* and with each other"[33]); third, to be effective, such covenants must be made "by [Christ]," or as He said, "by my word, which is my law," meaning in the manner prescribed by God through His living prophet, who oversees all temple department personnel and procedures that govern every aspect of temple ordinances and operations; fourth, in order to receive the blessing promised in this ordinance, the parties must "abide" in, or faithfully keep, their covenants; and, fifth, their doing so must be ratified or "sealed by the Holy Spirit of promise."

Moreover, these verses also show by whom these glorious promises are received. In Doctrine and Covenants 132:13–21 it is made clear twenty-four times that the blessings of the new and everlasting covenant of marriage are received *only* as a couple. This idea is communicated by use of the pronouns "they" (e.g., "they shall pass by the angels, and the gods, which are set there" and "by whom they [can] pass"), "them" (e.g., "all things are subject unto them"), and "their" (e.g., "their exaltation"). In a devotional given at Brigham Young University—Idaho, Elder Paul B. Pieper echoed this doctrinal truth, that the fulness of the blessings of the priesthood are only received by a man and a woman *together* through the crowning ordinance offered in the House of the Lord:

> Our loving Father wants each of His children to receive everything—a fulness, His fulness. This does not mean giving us the deed to a nice little galaxy in a beautiful tropical universe. Rather, it implies His desire to share a fulness of His

knowledge, His attributes, His power, His glory, and His joy. In another revelation, we learn that in order to receive this fulness "a man must enter into this order of the priesthood [meaning the new and everlasting covenant of marriage]" [Doctrine and Covenants 131:1–2].

Eternal marriage and all that it is designed to help us learn and experience are the key to obtaining all of the blessings that the Father wants to give His children. Only a family—a man and a woman who live worthy to enter the house of the Lord and are sealed to each other—can be eligible. *The full blessings of the priesthood are received together, as husband and wife, or not at all.*

It is interesting that in the oath and covenant of the priesthood, the Lord uses the verbs *obtain* and *receive*. He does not use the verb *ordain*. It is in the temple that men and women—together—obtain and receive the blessings and power of both the Aaronic and Melchizedek Priesthoods. Having received these blessings in the house of the Lord, it is principally in their home life where they develop godly characteristics and attributes—sacrificing for and serving each other, loving each other with full fidelity, and being united in their love for each other and God.[34]

What effect does divorce have on a temple sealing? The important principle is that gospel blessings are conditioned on worthiness of the individual promised those blessings. According to the *General Handbook*, "If a couple was sealed and later divorced, the blessings of that sealing remain in effect for individuals who are worthy unless the sealing is canceled. A member who remains faithful to temple covenants will receive every blessing promised in the temple, even if the person's spouse has broken the covenants or withdrawn from the marriage" (38.4.1.8). The same principle applies to children whose parents are divorced.[35]

Another important doctrinal source of revealed truth about the new and everlasting covenant of marriage that we should all become familiar with is "The Family: A Proclamation to the World." As we "treasure up in [our] minds continually the words of life" (Doctrine and Covenants 84:85) contained in this vital doctrinal statement, the scriptures, the teachings of modern apostles and prophets, and the multiple meanings and import of the everlastingly important words of temple ordinances will be like the life-giving water the Savior promised to give the woman at the well (and each of us), as noted in the introduction of this book, even "a well of water springing up into everlasting life" (John 4:14). Ponder just a few possible examples. (1) The scriptural phrase "*if* a man marry a wife by my word, which is *my law*" reminds us that the decision to be sealed according to God's law is a choice. As Elder Robert D. Hales taught, we can attain eternal life "*if* we are obedient and *faithful* to the laws, ordinances, and covenants [of the gospel,] which we accept with our free agency, *of our own free will and choice*."[36] (2) The essence of the marriage covenant is captured in the scriptural injunction for "a man [to] leave his father and his mother, and . . . *cleave unto his wife*" (Genesis 2:24) or, in modern revelation, to "love [his] wife," or a wife her husband, "with all thy heart, and shalt *cleave unto her* [or him] and none else" (Doctrine and Covenants 42:22).[37] (3) The divinely appointed roles of husbands and fathers and wives and mothers from the Family Proclamation, including such statements as: "Husband and wife have a solemn responsibility to love and care for each other and for their children." "By divine design, fathers are to *preside over their families in love and righteousness*"; "Mothers are primarily responsible for the nurture of their children. In these sacred responsibilities, fathers and mothers are obligated to help one another as equal partners."[38] (4) "Through the temple sealing, a woman and a man enter the *holy order of matrimony in the new and everlasting covenant.*"[39]

What Are the Rites of the Gospel and How Do They Differ from Ordinances and Laws?

When a sister asked me this question once in a proxy sealing session, I had to confess that though I had asked myself the same question, I did not know the answer. I did know, however, that our Heavenly Father understands every language perfectly, particularly the meaning of words, and uses them deliberately and precisely.[40] *Divine law* is defined variously as the "body of commandments which express the will of God with regard to the conduct of His intelligent creatures"[41] and "the commandments or rules of God upon which all blessings and punishments are based both in heaven and on earth."[42] Elder Bruce R. McConkie taught that "all things are governed by law; nothing is exempt . . . in the divine economy the same in varying result always flows from the same cause. These principles are immutable, eternal, everlasting; they apply to all things both temporal and spiritual."[43] The term *ordinance*, as used in the Church, means "a sacred, formal act or ceremony performed by the authority of the priesthood." Ordinances which "are essential to our exaltation include baptism, confirmation, ordination to the Melchizedek Priesthood (for men), the temple endowment," which as noted previously include the washing, anointing, and clothing ordinances, "and the marriage sealing."[44] These ordinances define the covenant path. *General Handbook* 18.2 lists the following "other ordinances . . . [that] make it possible for God's children to receive His power, healing, comfort, and guidance": (1) naming and blessing children; (2) the sacrament; (3) conferral of the Aaronic Priesthood and ordination to an office (for young men and men); (4) setting apart members to serve in callings; (5) consecrating oil; (6) administering to the sick; (7) blessings of comfort and counsel, including father's blessings; (8) dedicating homes; (9) dedicating graves; and (10) patriarchal blessings by ordained patriarchs. Instructions about how each of these ordinances should be performed are found in the handbooks of the Church.

How do *rites* differ from ordinances? Entries in the Church's Gospel Library often use these terms synonymously. For example, in the Guide to the Scriptures, the term "ordinances" is defined as "sacred rites and ceremonies."[45] The *Oxford English Dictionary* defines the word "rite" variously as "a prescribed act or observance in a religious or other solemn ceremony" and "the custom or practice of a religious group, spec. the prescribed *form of service* or *order of worship*."[46] Its synonym, "ritual," is similarly defined as "of or relating to the performance of rites," "the prescribed form or order of religious or ceremonial rites."[47] Thus, the ordinances of the gospel of Jesus Christ, the actions or ceremonies for which are carefully prescribed by the leaders of the Church,[48] could be (and often are) included within the term "rites." But the term "rites," I would suggest, includes forms of service or worship that are broader than the ordinances listed above from the *General Handbook*.

For example, recently I observed how the stake president in a ward we were attending in São Paulo, Brazil, followed procedures to release an outgoing and sustain an incoming bishopric, exactly as I had seen done in meetings in the United States. This experience reminded me that these procedures, founded upon the principles of common consent found in Doctrine and Covenants 26:2,[49] and what President Packer referred to as the "unwritten order of things,"[50] are important "forms of service or worship," even rituals, that encourage leaders of our congregations to focus worshippers' attention on the Savior, not themselves, during every aspect of our sacred worship services.

One blogger explained the difference between "ordinances" and "rites" or "rituals" this way: "An *ordinance* is a religious commandment that is considered to be of great importance and significance. It is usually accompanied by a specific action or ceremony that has a symbolic meaning." "Some examples of ordinances in Christianity include baptism, confirmation, and the sacrament of the Lord's Supper." Rites or rituals "in religious contexts," on the other hand, "are often used to create a sense of community and to connect believers with their faith. Some examples of religious rituals include prayer, meditation, and the lighting of candles." Another example found in "many religions," this commentator recites, would be "a prayer before meals." He concludes, "It is important to note that not all religious practices are ordinances."[51]

In my home growing up (and when we were raising our children), blessings on the food at every meal, kneeling personal and family prayers, family home evening, and regular family scripture study were ritual practices that, indeed, helped us feel connected to God and to each other. Over the years these rituals have brought my family, as well as my siblings' families, immeasurable blessings. In the segment of the Church's Bible videos showing the Savior and His apostles entering the room prepared for their last supper together, each apostle, and then the Savior Himself, is shown participating in a beautiful Jewish ritual or rite as they touched the mezuzah by the doorpost and then touched their lips, as commanded in Deuteronomy 6:4–9.[52] President Oaks often referred to such rites as "holy habits."[53] We are taught about these rites, of course, in the scriptures and by prophets[54] and apostles. Similarly today, regular individual and family *Come, Follow Me* study has become an important gospel rite with demonstrable blessings. Faithfulness to each gospel rite or ritual, as well as gospel ordinances, laws, or principles—such as the first laws or principles of the gospel, faith and repentance—entitle us to specific blessings. As the Lord declared, "When we obtain any blessing from God, it is by obedience to that law [or rite or ordinance] upon which [such blessing] is predicated" (Doctrine and Covenants 130:21). In a beautiful way, the concepts of "laws, rites, and ordinances" encompass the broad spectrum of God's will for His children, from His most universal laws (such as justice and mercy), to the rites He encourages us through His living prophets to make part of our daily lives and, finally and most importantly, to the essential ordinances of exaltation.

What Does It Mean to Have Our Ordinances Sealed by the Holy Spirit of Promise?

The Holy Spirit of Promise, as Bruce R. McConkie and others have taught, is the Holy Ghost. "This name-title is used in connection with the sealing and ratifying power of the Holy Ghost, that is, the power given him to ratify and approve the righteous acts of men so that those acts will be binding on earth and in heaven." "To seal is to ratify, to justify, or to approve. Thus an act which is sealed by the Holy Spirit of Promise is one which is ratified by the Holy Ghost; it is one which is approved by the Lord; and the person who has taken the obligation upon himself is justified by the Spirit in the thing he has done." Elder McConkie goes on to explain that the Holy Ghost's "ratifying seal of approval is put upon an act" or ordinance when the individual is "worthy," "righteous," and "just and true" (citing Doctrine and Covenants 76:53).[55]

How do we know whether our ordinances—baptism, ordinations, endowment, and even sealing—have been sealed by the Holy Spirit of Promise? I believe that if we are worthy of the companionship of the Holy Ghost, particularly as we learn to recognize His influence in our lives, we can also be assured at those times that our ordinances have been sealed by the Holy Ghost. Seen in this light, President Nelson's urging for us to repent daily takes on added importance. If, on the other hand, we drift further and further from the covenant path, we can, before we know it, become as the Nephites shortly before the Lord's birth, who "saw that . . . the Spirit of the Lord did no more preserve them; yea, it had withdrawn from them because the Spirit of the Lord doth not dwell in unholy temples" (Helaman 4:24; see also Mosiah 2:37; Alma 7:21; Alma 34:36). Elder McConkie uses the example of someone being baptized: "An unworthy candidate for baptism might deceive the elders and get the ordinance performed, but no one can lie to the Holy Ghost and get by undetected. Accordingly, the baptism of an unworthy and *unrepentant* person would not be sealed by the Spirit; it would not be ratified by the Holy Ghost." But if later such individual were to become "worthy *through repentance and obedience*, the seal would then be put in force. Similarly, if a worthy person is baptized, with the ratifying approval of the Holy Ghost attending the performance, yet the seal may be broken by subsequent sin." "These principles apply to every other ordinance and performance in the Church."[56] Just as King Benjamin taught us how to "retain a remission" of our sins "from day to day" (Mosiah 4:26), we can walk daily in the comfort and assurance that our temple marriages and the sealings of our children to us, whether born in the covenant or sealed to us in the temple, are sealed by the Holy Spirit of Promise by simply striving daily to keep our covenants, including sincerely renewing them weekly in the all-important ordinance of the sacrament.

Endnotes

1. Nelson, "The Everlasting Covenant."
2. This phrase, "crowning ordinance," is used repeatedly in Church resources to describe the new and everlasting covenant of marriage. For example, "Being sealed as a family is the crowning ordinance of the temple and the greatest of God's blessings for His children" (Families and Temples, https://www.churchofjesuschrist.org/study/manual/families-and-temples/what-is-the-temple-sealing?lang=eng, located in Gospel Library under "Handbooks and Callings"—"Mission Callings"—"Teaching Pamphlets").
3. See Dallin H. Oaks, "Kingdoms of Glory" ("In the 'celestial' glory there are *three levels, of which the highest is exaltation* in the celestial kingdom. . . . The Church of Jesus Christ of Latter-day Saints focuses on [the eternal laws, ordinances, and covenants that must be observed to develop the godly attributes necessary to realize this divine potential] because the purpose of this restored Church is to prepare God's children for salvation in the celestial glory and, more particularly, for *exaltation in its highest degree.*")
4. "Marriages performed in the temples for time and eternity, by virtue of the sealing keys restored by Elijah, are called celestial marriages. The participating parties become husband and wife in this mortal life, and if after their marriage they keep all the terms and conditions of this order of the priesthood, they continue on as husband and wife in the celestial kingdom of God" ("Marriage for Eternity," *Eternal Marriage Student Manual*, quoting McConkie, *Mormon Doctrine*, 117).
5. Nelson, "Come, Follow Me." See also Nelson, *Heart of the Matter*, 71–72 (section on celestial marriage). It is noteworthy to me that President Nelson has repeated this admonition, including quoting its doctrinal underpinning from Doctrine and Covenants 132:19, in multiple conference messages (see, eg., Nelson, "The Temple and Your Spiritual Foundation," 95 and note 17; Nelson, "Think Celestial!"; see also Nelson, *Heart of the Matter*, 68, 182).
6. *Saints*, vol. 1, 487.
7. *Saints*, vol. 1, 580.
8. See generally, "Plural Marriage in Kirtland and Nauvoo," Gospel Topics Essays.
9. See Chapter 38, "Eternal Marriage," *Gospel Principles*, https://www.churchofjesuschrist.org/study/manual/gospel-principles/chapter-38-eternal-marriage?lang=eng#p2 ("Adam and Eve were married by God before there was any death in the world. They had an eternal marriage").
10. Skinner, *Temple Worship*, 102 (quoting from Smith, *Doctrines of Salvation* 2:70); Nelson, "Come, Follow Me" ("Adam and Eve . . . received the *same* ordinances that we as members of the Lord's restored Church today have made . . . in the temple")(emphasis in original).
11. *Teachings of Presidents of the Church: Brigham Young*, https://www.churchofjesuschrist.org/study/manual/teachings-brigham-young/chapter-23?lang=eng.
12. "Marriage for Eternity," *Eternal Marriage Student Manual*, 168, quoting McConkie, *Mormon Doctrine*, 613.

13. Leslie Bluhm, "The Priesthood Power and Authority of Women," remarks at Richardson Stake Conference, September 11, 2021 (copy on file with author), quoting Jill Mulvay Derr, Janath Russell Cannon, Maureen Ursenbach Beecher, *Women of Covenant—The Story of Relief Society* (Salt Lake City, Utah: Deseret Book), 42. See also Nelson, *Heart of the Matter*, 178 (After "Elijah committed the keys of the sealing authority to Joseph Smith in the Kirtland temple" in 1836, the Prophet "continued to receive revelations that furthered the restoration of the endowment and sealing ordinances" "until his martyrdom," including the restoration of the "fulness of the priesthood.")
14. For a discussion of Peter's possible special "role with temples," see Hafens, *Contrite Spirit: How the Temple Helps Us Apply Christ's Atonement*, 53–54.
15. Bluhm, citing Joseph Smith, quoted in Sarah M. Kimball, "Auto-biography," *Women's Exponent*, September 1, 1883, 51; see also *Teachings of Presidents of the Church: Joseph Smith* (Salt Lake City, Utah: The Church of Jesus Christ of Latter-day Saints, 2007), 451, https://www.churchofjesuschrist.org/study/manual/teachings-joseph-smith/chapter-22?lang=eng, and *Daughters in My Kingdom: The History and Work of Relief Society* (Salt Lake City, Utah: The Church of Jesus Christ of Latter-day Saints, 2017), 7.
16. Joy D. Jones, "An Especially Noble Calling," *Ensign*, May 2020.
17. Nelson, "Spiritual Treasures."
18. M. Russell Ballard, "Men and Women and Priesthood Power," *Ensign*, September 2014.
19. Dallin H. Oaks, "Priesthood Authority in the Family and the Church," *Ensign*, November 2005.
20. *General Handbook* 2.1.1. Section 2.4.1, entitled "Receiving Authority" states: "For information about ordaining brethren to priesthood offices, see 20.7. For information about the process of calling, sustaining, and setting apart members to serve in Church callings," in other words, how men and women alike receive "priesthood authority" to act in specific callings, "see chapter 19." For a discussion of Joseph Smith's teaching on this subject, see generally Gospel Topics Essays, "Joseph Smith's Teachings about Priesthood, Temple, and Women," https://www.churchofjesuschrist.org/study/manual/gospel-topics-essays/joseph-smiths-teachings-about-priesthood-temple-and-women?lang=eng.
21. Nelson, "Spiritual Treasures," 78. *General Handbook* 3.4.3.1 adds to our understanding that "when men and women are set apart under the direction of those who hold priesthood keys, they are given authority from God to act in that calling." See also Nelson, *Heart of the Matter*, 86 (The work which sisters do in the Church "is done by divine authority," quoting Joseph Fielding Smith, "Relief Society—An Aid to the Priesthood," *Relief Society Magazine*, January 1959, 5); 88–90 [section entitled "Women Have Access to Divine Power"]; 93 (quoting President M. Russell Ballard: "Those who have priesthood keys . . . literally make it possible for all who serve faithfully under their direction to exercise priesthood authority and have access to priesthood power" [in "Men and Women in the Work of the Lord," *New Era*, April 2014]).
22. Oaks, "Priesthood Authority in the Family and the Church." See also, Oaks, "The Keys and Authority of the Priesthood."

23. Anthony Sweat begins his discussion of temple covenants by helping us understand that while "the Order of the Son of God" referred to in Doctrine and Covenants 107:3 and other scriptures is appropriately understood "in some contexts" as referring to "men being ordained to certain priesthood offices," the concept of an "order of the priesthood" is not limited to this, as evidenced, for example, by the Lord's description in Doctrine and Covenants 131:2 of receiving, or "enter[ing] into," the new and everlasting covenant of marriage as entering into "an order of the priesthood." While verse 2 of section 131 says that "in order to obtain the highest" "heaven" or the celestial kingdom, "a man must enter into this order of the priesthood [meaning the new and everlasting covenant of marriage]," the Lord could just as well have said that to be exalted in the celestial kingdom a woman must enter into this order of the priesthood. "Seeing the holy order through the lens of the temple," Brother Sweat observes, meaning the "ancient order" men and women became part of beginning with Adam and Eve by receiving and keeping all of the covenants of the gospel, "broadens our vision of priesthood to apply to all members, including women. When we view entering into the holy order of the Son of God through receiving temple ordinances and keeping temple covenants, it becomes a way for all to enjoy the gifts, power, authority, and blessings of the holy priesthood, as modern prophets have pled for us to better understand. We can see how priesthood isn't only an ecclesiastical office for men; it's a covenant order for us all" (*The Holy Covenant*, 5–9 and note 15. See also Jean B. Bingham, "Women and Covenant Power," *Liahona*, January 2021).
24. See, for example, Words of Mormon 1:17; Mosiah 13:6; 18:26; Alma 17:3; Helaman 5:18; 6:5; 11:18; 3 Nephi 7:17. See also "Exercising Priesthood Power" in Nelson, *Heart of the Matter*, 97–100.
25. In his first address as Prophet and President of The Church of Jesus Christ of Latter-day Saints, made in a general priesthood session, President Nelson taught boldly about how women, through "their endowment and other temple ordinances," as well as through their Church callings issued ultimately by holders of priesthood keys, receive the power and authority of God to do good and bring about much righteousness. Moreover, he referred to covenant-keeping women and men who "know how to call upon the powers of heaven to protect and strengthen their" families and "live up to their privileges as bearers of the priesthood." Having said this, however, he went on to "voice a concern"—"too many of our brothers and sisters do not fully understand the concept of priesthood power and authority" (Nelson, "Ministering with the Power and Authority of God," 68).
26. "The phrase 'reproving betimes with sharpness when moved upon by the Holy Ghost' [verse 43] means to correct someone quickly, promptly, and with clarity when inspired to do so by the Holy Ghost" ("Lesson 47: Doctrine and Covenants 121:11–46," *Doctrine and Covenants Teacher Manual*, https://www.churchofjesuschrist.org/study/manual/doctrine-and-covenants-teacher-manual-2017/lesson-47-doctrine-and-covenants-121-11-46?lang=eng).
27. Gordon B. Hinckley, *Teachings of Gordon B. Hinckley* (Salt Lake City, Utah: The Church of Jesus Christ of Latter-day Saints, 1997), 639.

28. Boyd K. Packer, "The Holy Temple," *Ensign*, October 2010.
29. Skinner, *Temple Worship*, 71–73, citing *Doctrines of Salvation* 2:117.
30. *Teachings of Presidents of the Church: Joseph Smith*, 418.
31. "Chapter 51: Doctrine and Covenants 131; 132:1–33," *Doctrine and Covenants Student Manual*, quoting Joseph Fielding Smith, *Teachings of Presidents of the Church: Joseph Fielding Smith* (Salt Lake City, Utah: The Church of Jesus Christ of Latter-day Saints, 2013), 194, https://www.churchofjesuschrist.org/study/manual/doctrine-and-covenants-student-manual-2017/chapter-51-doctrine-and-covenants-131-132-1-33?lang=eng.

    Speaking about the "solemn and sacred" nature of the crowning sealing ordinance of the temple, President Boyd K. Packer reminded brides and grooms that in the temple "we are not in the world. The things of the world do not apply here and should have no influence upon what we do here. We have come out of the world into the temple of the Lord. This becomes the most important day of your lives" (*Preparing to Enter the Holy Temple*, 15). Brides and grooms who are spiritually mature and carefully prepare for this highest ordinance of the gospel of Jesus Christ will more likely avoid the trap of confusing the "things" or ways of the world with the ways of God as they approach this ordinance. As we know from other ordinances, such as baptism and the sacrament and our worship services generally, the ways of the world tend to more outward pomp and ostentation than the simplicity and meekness of Christ's ways. Much less important in this ordinance than the current stylishness or elegance of the bride's dress or the lavishness of the wedding reception, for example, are the sacred *words* of this ordinance—God's words. He is careful and precise in His expressions and knows how to communicate meaning in all languages. As noted earlier in the introduction, God's words, particularly the words of His ordinances, "are not of men nor of man, but *of me*" (Doctrine and Covenants 18:34).
32. Cree-L Kofford, "Marriage in the Lord's Way, Part One," *Ensign*, June 1998 (emphasis in original).
33. "About Temple Sealings," https://www.churchofjesuschrist.org/temples/what-happens-in-a-temple-sealing?lang=eng.
34. Paul B. Pieper, "The Realities of Mortality," Brigham Young University-Idaho Devotional, February 19, 2013, https://www2.byui.edu/Presentations/Transcripts/Devotionals/2013_02_19_Pieper.htm#_edn3, quoted in, Paul B. Pieper, "Revealed Realities of Mortality," *Ensign*, January 2016, 21. See also "Lesson 31: Doctrine and Covenants 84," *Doctrine and Covenants Teacher Manual*, https://www.churchofjesuschrist.org/study/manual/doctrine-and-covenants-teacher-manual-2017/chapter-31-doctrine-and-covenants-84?lang=eng.
35. "If my parents were sealed in the temple and then got divorced, which one am I sealed to?" *New Era*, August 2015, https://www.churchofjesuschrist.org/study/new-era/2015/08/to-the-point/if-my-parents-were-sealed-in-the-temple-and-then-got-divorced-which-one-am-i-sealed-to?lang=eng.
36. Robert D. Hales, "Making Righteous Choices at the Crossroads of Life," *Ensign*, November 1988, 9.

37. See Ezra Taft Benson, "To the Fathers in Israel," *Ensign*, November 1987 ("What does it mean to 'cleave unto [your wife]'? It means to stay close to her, to be loyal and faithful to her, to communicate with her, and to express your love for her"); Matthew O. Richardson, "Three Principles of Marriage," *Ensign*, April 2005 ("The term cleave, as used in Genesis, is derived from the Hebrew *dawbak*, meaning 'cling, adhere, stick, catch by pursuit' or 'follow close.' When the Savior speaks of cleaving to one's wife in Matthew 19:5, the source word of cleave is from the Greek *poskallah*, meaning 'glue or join.' By scriptural definition, then, we find that God expects us to 'cling' to our spouse or to 'stick' with him or her"). Brown, 69 (Cleave "has two [diametrically opposed] meanings . . . 'to part, divide, or separate,' and . . . 'to stick, adhere, or cling.' . . . What began as one (*adam* or 'humanity') became two (male and female), and those two are now directed to once again become one through the balanced unity of eternal marriage. As they are united both spiritually and physically as husband and wife, their unique qualities and roles perfect and complete each other")(emphasis in original).
38. Quentin L. Cook, "Great Love for Our Father's Children," *Ensign*, May 2019, 76 ("Women and men have unique roles as outlined in 'The Family: A Proclamation to the World,' but their stewardships are equal in value and importance. They have equal power to receive revelation for their family. When they work together in love and righteousness, their decisions are heaven blessed. Those who seek to know the will of the Lord as individuals and for their families must strive for righteousness, meekness, kindness, and love").
39. Ulisses Soares, "In Partnership with the Lord," *Liahona*, November 2022 ("By way of this order of the priesthood, they are given eternal blessings and divine power to direct their family affairs as they live according to the covenants they have made.") See also Cook, "Great Love for Our Father's Children" ("When a man and woman are sealed in the temple, they enter the holy order of matrimony in the new and everlasting covenant, an order of the priesthood").
40. For example, see Alonzo Gaskill's explication of the different meanings of the words "pertaining" and "appertaining" as used in gospel rituals in *Temple Reflections: Insights into the House of the Lord*, chapter 10 ("while there may be no difference between these words in common English language usage," in legal usage "'appertain' usually means to 'to belong to rightfully' <the privileges appertaining to this degree>, whereas pertain usually means 'to relate to; concern' <the appeal pertains to defendant's Fifth Amendment rights>'").
41. "Law," n., I.ii. "Divine Law," https://www.oed.com/dictionary/law_n1?tab=meaning_and_use#39479557.
42. Guide to the Scriptures, "Law," https://www.churchofjesuschrist.org/study/scriptures/gs/law?lang=eng.
43. A. Theodore Tuttle, "Principles with a Promise," BYU Speeches, January 31, 1978, https://speeches.byu.edu/talks/theodore-a-tuttle/principles-promise/ (quoting McConkie, *Mormon Doctrine*, 395). Another term the Brethren often use to convey the same idea as divine law is "principle." "A principle is an enduring truth, a law, a rule you can adopt to guide you in making decisions," President Boyd K. Packer taught. Unlike "procedures,

programs, . . . administrative policies, even some patterns of organization, [which] are subject to change . . . the principles, the doctrines [of the gospel] never change" ("Principles," *Eternal Marriage Student Manual, Preparing for an Eternal Marriage, Religion 234; Building an Eternal Marriage, Religion 235*, The Church of Jesus Christ of Latter-day Saints, [Salt Lake City, Utah: Church Educational System, 2003]). As the Lord declared, "There is a law, irrevocably decreed in heaven before the foundations of this world, upon which all blessings are predicated—And when we obtain any blessing from God, it is by obedience to that law upon which it is predicated" (Doctrine and Covenants 130:20–21). See also Dallin H. Oaks, "Love and Law," *Ensign*, November 2009, 26.
44. Topics and Questions, "Ordinances," https://www.churchofjesuschrist.org/study/manual/gospel-topics/ordinances?lang=eng. See also General Handbook 18.1 "Ordinances of Salvation and Exaltation."
45. See, e.g., Boyd K. Packer, "Preparing to Enter the Holy Temple," *Ensign*, November 2010, 30 ("All who are worthy and qualify in every way may enter the temple, there to be introduced to the sacred rites and ordinances"); *Preach My Gospel*, Lesson 3 ("An ordinance is a sacred ceremony or rite that shows that we have entered into a covenant with God").
46. "Rite," n. https://www.oed.com/search/dictionary/?scope=Entries&q=rite
47. "Ritual," adj. & n. https://www.oed.com/search/dictionary/?scope=Entries&q=ritual.
48. In my efforts to grow in my understanding and appreciation for the detailed instructions provided by the leaders of the Church for the administration of temple ordinances, I found it instructive to review the directions for administering the sacrament found in *General Handbook* 18.9. Section 18.9.4 contains a list of twelve instructions, including such matters as "the bishop makes sure the sacrament prayers are spoken clearly, accurately, and with dignity. If someone makes an error in the wording and corrects himself, no further correction is needed. If the person does not correct his error, the bishop kindly asks him to repeat the prayer. The bishop uses discretion when asking for the prayer to be repeated. He ensures that doing so does not cause undue embarrassment or detract from the ordinance. Another person at the sacrament table can help as needed."

   The instructions are quite detailed, including the directive that "members partake with their right hand when possible" and "*those who blessed* the sacrament place a cloth over the trays" (emphasis added). At the same time, there are also guidelines, which have more to do with how leaders can help those who administer this ordinance focus on the needs of worshippers, not merely how to go about preparing, blessing, and passing the sacrament. For example, leaders help young men and men remember the "sacred nature of the sacrament" and its essential purpose for members "to remember the Savior's sacrifice of His flesh and blood and to renew their sacred covenants," including such counsel as "priesthood leaders should prepare carefully so it is orderly and reverent" and encourage "those who administer the sacrament . . . to ponder the Savior's Atonement as they prepare, bless, and pass the sacrament."

Leaders also teach priesthood holders to remember "that they are representing the Lord"; they teach those who administer the sacrament the principle of non-distraction—to "not wear clothing or jewelry that might detract from the worship and covenant making that are the purpose of the sacrament"; they ensure that "the passing of the sacrament [is] natural and not overly formal. For example, certain actions (such as holding the left hand behind the back) or appearances (such as dressing alike) should not be required." Such counsel is analogous to what temple ordinance workers are taught as they seek to administer temple ordinances with "exactness" (see Alma 57:21)—to always remember the overarching principles about the "patron experience."

49. See "Common Consent," Church History Topics, https://www.churchofjesuschrist.org/study/history/topics/common-consent?lang=eng#title1.
50. Boyd K. Packer, "The Unwritten Order of Things," Brigham Young University Devotional, October 15, 1996, in *Principles of Leadership Teacher Manual, Religion 180R*, https://www.churchofjesuschrist.org/bc/content/shared/content/english/pdf/language-materials/36180_eng.pdf?lang=eng. See generally *General Handbook* 29.2, "Sacrament Meeting."
51. Shawn Manaher, "Ordinance vs Ritual: When And How Can You Use Each One?" https://thecontentauthority.com/blog/ordinance-vs-ritual.
52. See https://www.churchofjesuschrist.org/media/video/2011-10-0013-the-last-supper?lang=eng&alang=eng&collectionId=00b01a73c6fe4b218464982d5be32a8e; "Mezuzah," *Wikipedia: The Free Encyclopedia*, https://en.wikipedia.org/wiki/Mezuzah. Bible translators used the word "rite" to refer to the specific acts and ceremonies the Lord commanded ancient Israel to follow in celebrating passover each year: "In the fourteenth day of this month, at even, ye shall keep [the passover] in his appointed season: according to all the *rites* of it, and according to all the *ceremonies* thereof, shall ye keep it" (Numbers 8:3) (emphasis added). The headnotes to different Old Testament chapters also use the word "rites" to describe important elements of the Law of Moses. See, for example, the headnotes to Exodus 29 ("various sacrificial rites shall be performed"); Leviticus 14 ("Laws, rites, and sacrifices revealed for cleansing lepers"); Leviticus 15 ("Laws, rites, and sacrifices for cleansing those who have an issue and other types of uncleanness").
53. See, e.g., Dallin H. Oaks, "Mexican Saints Told to Form Holy Habits, Righteous Routines," https://www.churchofjesuschrist.org/prophets-and-apostles/unto-all-the-world/mexican-saints-told-to-form-holy-habits-righteous-routines?lang=eng.
54. President Joseph F. Smith and his counselors in the First Presidency instituted home evenings as a Church-wide practice by letter to local Church leaders dated April 27, 1915: "We advise and urge the inauguration of a 'Home Evening' throughout the church, at which time fathers and mothers may gather their boys and girls about them in the home and teach them the word of the Lord" (R. Scott Lloyd, "2015 Marks Two Milestones for Family Home Evening," *Church News*, February 3, 2015, https://www.churchofjesuschrist.org/church/news/2015-marks-two-milestones-for-family-home-evening?lang=eng#:~:text=Smith%2C%20sixth%20President%20

of%20the%20Church%2C%20introduced%20family%20home%20-evening,gospel%20in%20the%20home%20frequently. See also https://www.churchofjesuschrist.org/topics/family-home-evening?lang=eng).
55. "Holy Spirit of Promise," *Eternal Marriage Student Manual*, quoting McConkie, *Mormon Doctrine*, 361–62 (certain citations omitted).
56. Ibid.

CHAPTER 19

The Temple's Ultimate Promise and Spiritual Treasure

Beholding the Faces of the Father and the Son

"Without the ordinances . . . and the authority of the priesthood, the power of godliness is not manifest unto men in the flesh; For without this no man can see the face of God, even the Father, and live."

—Doctrine and Covenants 84:20

The Temple Prepares Us to See the Face of God and Enter into His Presence

President Nelson has said, "God, our Heavenly Father, wants you to choose to come home to Him."[1] Quoting President Boyd K. Packer, President Nelson taught that the way to "come home" is through "ordinances and covenants," which "become our credentials for admission into [God's] presence. To worthily receive them is the quest of a lifetime; to keep them thereafter is the challenge of mortality."[2] In short, "the covenant path is the only path that leads to exaltation and eternal life."[3]

In order to "exercise faith [in God] unto life and salvation," which is the end to which the covenant path leads, the Prophet Joseph Smith taught that a person must know that "the course of life which they pursue is according to the will of God."[4] Giving us this assurance or "comfort" and helping us regain it when we deviate even slightly from the path is one of the primary missions of the Holy Ghost. But there is another spiritual treasure, or Comforter, promised to temple patrons for which we should all strive. Jesus told His disciples at the Last Supper, "I will pray the Father, and he shall give you *another Comforter*, that he may abide with you forever; . . . I will not leave you comfortless: *I* will come to you. . . . He that hath my commandments, and keepeth them, he it is that loveth me: and he that loveth me shall be loved of my Father, and I will love him, and will *manifest myself to him*" (John 14:16, 18, 21). In other words, entering into God's presence need not await our transfer to the spirit world or the Resurrection and Final Judgment. In what He described as "another," or as it is commonly referred to, the "second" Comforter, the Lord taught that "if a man love me, he will keep my words: and my Father will love him, and *we will come unto him, and make our abode with him*" (John 14:23). This appearance "of the Father and the Son," the Lord revealed, "is a *personal* appearance; and the idea that the Father and the Son dwell in a man's heart is an old sectarian notion, and is false" (Doctrine and Covenants 130:3).

Joseph Smith taught, "After a person hath faith in Christ, repents of his sins, and is baptized for the remission of his sins, and receives the Holy Ghost (by the laying on of hands) which is the first Comforter, then let him continue to humble himself before God, hungering and thirsting after Righteousness, and living by every word of God, and the Lord will soon say unto him, Son thou shalt be exalted. . . . When the Lord has [thoroughly] proved him, and finds that the man is determined to serve him at all hazard, then the man will find his calling and Election made sure, then it will be his privilege to receive the *other Comforter* which the Lord hath promised the Saints, as is recorded in [John 14:12–27]. . . . What is this other Comforter? It is no more nor less than the Lord Jesus Christ himself. . . . When any man obtains this last Comforter he will have the personage of Jesus Christ to attend him or appear unto him from time to time, and even he will manifest the Father unto him, and they will take up their abode with him."[5]

That faithful Saints may "see" God is declared throughout the scriptures and is amply attested to by the examples of prophets highlighted throughout this study—Adam, Enoch, Noah, Abraham,

Moses, and Joseph Smith, who saw the Savior on multiple occasions.[6] In the temple we both symbolically enter God's presence and are promised we can feel His presence.[7]

Doctrine and Covenants 88:68—Therefore, sanctify yourselves that your minds become single to God, and the days will come that you shall see him; for he will unveil his face unto you, and it shall be in his own time, and in his own way, and according to his own will.

Doctrine and Covenants 93:1—Verily, thus saith the Lord: It shall come to pass that every soul who forsaketh his sins and cometh unto me, and calleth on my name, and obeyeth my voice, and keepeth my commandments, shall see my face and know that I am.

"God hath not revealed anything to Joseph," the Prophet declared, "but what He will make known unto the Twelve, and even the least Saint may know all things as fast as he is able to bear them, for the day must come when no man need say to his neighbor, Know ye the Lord; for all shall know Him . . . from the least to the greatest [see Jeremiah 31:34]."[8] In fact, from the earliest revelations received by the Prophet, and in particular the earliest revelations about the initiatory temple ordinances of washing and anointing, "the ultimate goal was to sanctify the [Saints] and prepare [them] to meet God. Seeing God was what Joseph wanted all the Saints to experience in mortality," as he and many others had.[9]

Elder Larry R. Lawrence of the Seventy shared his feelings about the process of preparing ourselves for this consummate privilege: "Years ago I read these words of President Spencer W. Kimball, which had a lasting impact on me. He said: 'I have learned that where there is a prayerful heart, a hungering after righteousness, a forsaking of sins, and obedience to the commandments of God, the Lord pours out more and more light until there is finally power to pierce the heavenly veil. . . . A person of such righteousness has the priceless promise that one day he shall see the Lord's face and know that he is.'"[10]

In his message during the 2021 First Presidency Christmas devotional, Elder Dale G. Renlund graciously shared the sweet story of how the temple's promise was fulfilled in his father's life, as recounted in a *Church News* summary of his remarks:

> Elder Renlund said as he grew older, he saw his parents love and serve others, keep covenants, minister to others, go to the temple and accept Church callings. And each year, on Christmas Eve, his father testified with Simeon of the Savior, Jesus Christ. Over the years, his father extended his invitation to "know it, too" to in-laws and grandchildren.
>
> Elder Renlund's father was 92 years old when Elder Renlund spoke for the first time in October 2009 general conference. He said his sisters made sure his father could watch the conference and his talk. Afterward, he went over to their home.
>
> "I asked, 'Dad, did you watch conference?' He responded, 'Ja.' I asked, 'Did you hear me speak?' He responded, 'Ja.' With some exasperation, I blurted out, 'Well, Dad, what did you think?' He replied, 'Oh, it was alright. I was almost proud.'"
>
> Elder Renlund then realized that while he was fishing for a compliment, his father was preoccupied. He told his son he had something he needed to tell him.
>
> "Last night I had a dream," Elder Renlund's father said to him. "I dreamed I died, and I saw the Savior. He took me in His arms and told me my sins were forgiven. And it felt so good."
>
> "That was all he said out loud," said Elder Renlund. "But the look on his face spoke volumes; he knew Jesus Christ. He knew that the babe in Bethlehem, who had 'increased in wisdom and stature, and in favour with God and man,' was his salvation, that the Son of God had grown up, and atoned for his sins. And my father knew it long before this dream."
>
> Elder Renlund said the dream was a tender mercy—a gift—from a loving Heavenly Father to a man who died two months later.[11]

John A. Widtsoe, a member of the Quorum of the Twelve, addressed the question, "What does [the promise] mean" that "to the temples God will come and that in them man shall see God?" Elder Widtsoe said, "Does it mean that once in a while God may come into the temples, and that once in a while the pure in heart may see God there; or does it mean the larger thing, that the pure in heart who go into the temple, may, there, by the Spirit of God, always have a wonderfully rich communion with God? I think that is what it means to me and to you and to most of us. We have gone into these holy houses, with our minds freed from the ordinary earthly cares, and have literally felt the presence of God. In this way, the temples are always places where God manifests himself to man and increases his intelligence."[12]

What Does It Mean to Have Our "Calling and Election Made Sure" or to Receive the "More Sure Word of Prophecy"?

In his epistle, Peter shares that he, James, and John received "a more sure word of prophecy" and had their calling and election made sure on the Mount of Transfiguration, where they "were eyewitnesses of [Christ's] majesty" and heard the voice "from God the Father" to His Son saying, "This is my beloved Son, in whom I am well pleased" (2 Peter 1:16–17, 19).[13] The Prophet Joseph Smith explained that the term "more sure word of prophecy" and making our calling and election sure "means a man's knowing that he is sealed up unto eternal life, by revelation and the spirit of prophecy, through the power of the Holy Priesthood (Doctrine and Covenants 131:5)."[14] Peter encouraged the Saints of his day that they would "do well" to seek the same assurance, giving diligence to "make your calling and election sure" (2 Peter 1:16–19). Likewise the Prophet encouraged members of the Church in our day "to go on and continue to call upon God until you make your calling and election sure for yourselves, by obtaining this more sure word of prophecy, and wait patiently for the promise until you obtain it."[15]

How do we do this? Peter answered, through Christ's "divine power." Because He was enabled by the power of the Father to accomplish the Atonement, Christ and His Father have given each of Their covenant children *"exceeding great and precious promises"*

(2 Peter 1:3–4). Bruce R. McConkie explains that this phrase refers to "promises of eternal life, which is 'the greatest of all the gifts of God' [Doctrine and Covenants 14:7]." As we rely in faith on these precious promises and draw upon Christ's power, Peter adds, each of us is assured that we "might be partakers of the divine nature" (1 Peter 1:4). This means that in time and through the power of the Atonement we can "become as God is, enjoying to the full every characteristic, perfection, and attribute which he possesses and which dwell in him independently."[16] The temple enables and accelerates this process as no other activity can. "Giving all diligence," as Peter encourages, we add to our "faith virtue; and to [our] virtue knowledge; And to [our] knowledge temperance; and to [our] temperance patience; and to [our] patience godliness; And to [our] godliness brotherly kindness; and to [our] brotherly kindness charity." For as these things become part of our natures, and "abound" in us, "they make [us] that [we] shall neither be barren nor unfruitful in the knowledge of our Lord Jesus Christ" (2 Peter 1:5–8). "Knowledge" refers here to our character or natures—"this is life eternal, that they might *know* thee the only true God, and Jesus Christ, whom thou hast sent" (John 17:3).

What Is the "Fulness of the Priesthood" and How Do We Receive It?

Less than two years after the Prophet Joseph Smith arrived from his ordeal in Liberty Jail, while the Saints were still settling into their new homes in Nauvoo after their expulsion from Missouri, the Lord commanded them to "build a house unto my name" "that I may reveal mine ordinances therein unto my people" (Doctrine and Covenants 124:27, 40). Until then, the Lord had allowed the Saints to perform baptisms for the dead in the Mississippi River, but now He commanded them to stop the ordinance until they had dedicated a baptismal font in the temple. "This ordinance," He declared, "belongeth to my house." Moreover, He promised to reveal additional temple ordinances and inspiring new truths for, He said, "I deign to reveal unto my church things which have been kept hid from before the foundation of the world, things that pertain to the dispensation of the fulness of times." He also said, "And I will show unto my servant Joseph all things pertaining to this house, and the priesthood thereof."[17] As He did to ancient Israel, the Lord commanded the Saints to bring "all your gold, and your silver, and your precious stones . . . all your precious things of the earth; and build a house to my name, for the Most High to dwell therein. For there is not a place found on earth that he may come to and restore again that which was lost unto you, or which he hath taken away, even *the fulness of the priesthood*" (Doctrine and Covenants 124:26–28).[18]

What is the "fulness of the priesthood"? Simply stated, the fulness of the priesthood is received when a man and woman are sealed together in the temple and keep the covenants received in that ordinance. As they "abide" in or keep their covenants (Doctrine and Covenants 132:19), their temple marriage will be certified or ratified by the Holy Spirit of Promise.[19] President Joseph Fielding Smith wrote that "'if a man gets a fulness of the Priesthood of God, he has to get it in the same way that Jesus Christ obtained it, and that was by keeping all the commandments and obeying all the ordinances of the house of the Lord.' I hope we understand that. If we want to receive the fullness of the Priesthood of God, then we must receive the fullness of the ordinances of the house of the Lord and keep His commandments." Anciently, President Smith added, "the Lord could give these things on the mountain tops—no doubt that is where Moses got it, that is no doubt where Elijah got it. . . . But now you will have to go into the house of the Lord, and you cannot get the *fulness of the priesthood unless you go there*."[20]

In his vision of the kingdoms of glory, Joseph Smith described those who receive of the "fulness" of the Father and the Son:

- "And we beheld the glory of the Son, on the right hand of the Father, and *received of his fulness*" (Doctrine and Covenants 76:20);
- "They are they who are priests and kings, who have *received of his fulness*, and of his glory" (Doctrine and Covenants 76:56);
- "And again, we saw the terrestrial world, and behold and lo, these are they who are of the terrestrial, whose glory differs from that of the church of the Firstborn who have received *the fulness of the Father*, even as that of the moon differs from the

sun in the firmament" (Doctrine and Covenants 76:71);
- "They who dwell in [Christ's] presence are the church of the Firstborn; and they see as they are seen, and know as they are known, having *received of his fulness* and of his grace" (Doctrine and Covenants 76:94).[21]

In the Resurrection, those who receive a celestial body will be "quickened by a portion of the celestial glory" and "shall then receive of the same, even a fulness" (Doctrine and Covenants 88:29). "Fulness" in these contexts refers to a fulness of the glory, power, abilities, and blessings that the Father and Son enjoy. As noted in the discussion of the new and everlasting covenant of marriage, these are the blessings of Abraham, Isaac, and Jacob, the blessings pronounced upon those who are sealed in the House of the Lord, who receive the "fulness of the priesthood." This is the consummate blessing included in the endowment and sealing ordinances to which the Lord referred in the revelation on priesthood in Doctrine and Covenants 84, even the "power of godliness" or power to become like our Heavenly Parents and enter into Their rest, "which rest is the *fulness* of [Their] glory" (Doctrine and Covenants 84:24).

President Joseph Fielding Smith may also have had in mind another temple ordinance, also referred to as the "fulness of the priesthood" or the "second anointing." Due to the sacred nature of this ordinance, the Church has chosen to say very little publicly about it and generally discourages discussion of it in public teaching venues such as seminary and institute.[22] As noted in the non-Church website, FairLatterDaySaints, which is dedicated to responding accurately to arguments against the Church and its doctrines, "the second anointing is an ordinance performed in the temple. It is not regarded as an essential ordinance which one must receive in this life for exaltation; but will be necessary in the next life. In the early Utah period, this ordinance was performed more openly than it is today."[23] In her recounting of the history of the unfolding of temple doctrine by the Prophet Joseph Smith, Jennifer Ann Mackley notes that the Prophet taught that receiving the "new and everlasting covenant of marriage" was a prerequisite to receiving the fulness of the priesthood ordinance. However, she notes, the Prophet also made it clear "that simply participating in an ordinance was not the only requirement; each person would need to prove to the Lord that he or she is willing 'to serve him at all hazards.'"[24]

According to Mackley, "Joseph and Emma were the first to receive their second anointings, on September 28, 1843. Six other couples also received their second anointings later that year, including Brigham Young and his wife Mary Ann." "Before Joseph Smith's death two years later, sixty-six men and women had been anointed as priests and priestesses to God, receiving the 'fulness of the priesthood,' and been promised eternal life."[25] Significantly, each of these crowning ordinances, the new and everlasting covenant and the fulness of the priesthood, were only received by husband and wife together, consistent with the Lord's statement that "in order to obtain the highest" degree of the celestial kingdom, "a man [and his wife] must enter into this order of the priesthood [meaning the new and everlasting covenant of marriage]" (Doctrine and Covenants 131:2).[26]

What about those who do not receive their second anointing in mortality? The Lord assures us, "Blessed are they who are faithful and endure, whether in life or in death, for they shall inherit eternal life" (Doctrine and Covenants 50:5). Andrew Skinner echoes this assurance: "Whether such a guarantee [of eternal life] comes before death or after mortality has concluded, it makes no difference. The result is the same—exaltation. That is why it is so important for all of us to endure faithfully, patiently, and cheerfully to the end of our mortal lives."[27]

Endnotes

1. Nelson, "The Temple and Your Spiritual Foundation."
2. Nelson, "Personal Preparation for Temple Blessings," quoting Boyd K. Packer, "Covenants," *Ensign*, May 1987, 24.
3. Nelson, "The Power of Spiritual Momentum."
4. Lecture Sixth, *Lectures on Faith*, https://lecturesonfaith.com/. See also "Lectures on Theology ('Lectures on Faith')," Church History Topics, https://www.churchofjesuschrist.org/study/history/topics/lectures-on-faith?lang=eng.
5. "Chapter 50: Doctrine and Covenants 129–30," *Doctrine and Covenants Student Manual*, quoting *Manuscript History of the Church*, vol. C-1 addenda, pages 8–9, josephsmithpapers.org (emphasis in original).
6. As reported in the *Church News*, in his remarks at the 2020 Mission President's Seminar, "President Nelson said Joseph's divine tutoring began in 1820 in answer to his questions about his standing before God and his confusion over which church to join. In response, Heavenly Father and His Son Jesus Christ appeared in glory and magnificence to Joseph. . . . On at least eight other occasions—in addition to the First Vision—Joseph saw the Father or the Son, said President Nelson. . . . Four of these visions included both the Father and the Son, while the Savior appeared another four times by Himself" (Sara Jane Weaver, "President Nelson at Mission Leadership Seminar: How to receive divine tutoring like the Prophet Joseph Smith," *Church News*, June 21, 2020, https://www.thechurchnews.com/leaders-and-ministry/2020–06–27/president-nelson-mission-leadership-seminar-joseph-smith-187832).
7. See Pinegar, 232–33.
8. *Teachings of Presidents of the Church: Joseph Smith*, from a discourse given by Joseph Smith on June 27, 1839, in Commerce, Illinois; reported by Willard Richards, *History of the Church*, 3:380.
9. Mackley, 42–43. For a list and description of many who, during the Kirtland period, were eyewitnesses of the Father, the Son, and/or Their holy angels, in addition to the Prophet Joseph Smith and his closest associates (even "hundreds of others"), see Anderson, *The Savior in Kirtland*, 127–43 (quoting George Q. Cannon, in *Journal of Discourses*, 25:158). Brother Anderson noted that many such appearances were "connected with temple or other significant events," as the Lord had promised (Ibid., 129).
10. Larry R. Lawrence, "What Lack I Yet?" *Ensign*, November 2015.
11. Mary Richards, "Elder Dale G. Renlund testifies of Christ and says 'You can know it, too'," *Church News*, December 5, 2021, https://www.thechurchnews.com/leaders-and-ministry/2021–12–05/elder-renlund-first-presidency-christmas-devotional-you-can-know-it-too-235464.
12. Madsen, *The Temple: Where Heaven Meets Earth*, 93, quoting John A. Widtsoe, "Temple Worship," *Utah Genealogical and Historical Magazine*, April 1921, 62.
13. For a description of their consummate experience on the Mount of Transfiguration, during which, President Joseph Fielding Smith asserted, Peter, James, and John were endowed, see "Elijah's Ministry to the Savior and

His Apostles in the Meridian of Time" in chapter 17 and text accompanying note 30. Joseph Smith encouraged members of the Church to also seek this blessing: "Oh! I beseech you to go forward, go forward and make your calling and election sure" (Pinegar, 229, quoting Joseph Smith, *Teachings of the Prophet Joseph Smith*, 366).

14. *History of the Church*, 5:389, as quoted in "Chapter 51: 1 Peter and 2 Peter," *New Testament Student Manual*.
15. Ibid. The Lord affirmed that Joseph Smith's calling and election was made sure in Doctrine and Covenants 132:49 ("Verily I seal upon you [Joseph Smith] your exaltation, and prepare a throne for you in the kingdom of my Father, with Abraham your father"). See also Mosiah 26:20 ("Thou [Alma] art my servant; and *I covenant with thee that thou shalt have eternal life*; and thou shalt serve me and go forth in my name, and shalt gather together my sheep.")
16. "Chapter 51: 1 Peter and 2 Peter," *New Testament Student Manual*, quoting McConkie, *Doctrinal New Testament Commentary*, 3:352. The Joseph Smith Translation of 2 Peter 1:19 states: "We have therefore a more sure knowledge of the word of prophecy, to which word of prophecy ye do well that ye take heed" (2 Peter 1:19, footnote a).
17. *Saints*, vol. 1, 426–27, citing Doctrine and Covenants 124:29–38, 41–42.
18. While there are many scriptural references to the "fulness of the gospel" or "fulness of my everlasting gospel" (see, e.g., Doctrine and Covenants 14:10; 20:9; 27:5; 35:12, 17; 39:11, 18; 42:12; 45:28; 66:2; 76:14; 90:11; 109:65; 133:57; 135:3) and other uses of the term "fulness" (for example, "fulness of times" (see, e.g., Doctrine and Covenants 27:13; 76:106; 112:30; 121:31; 124:41; 128:18, 20; 133:57; 138:48, 53), "fulness of joy" (see, e.g., Doctrine and Covenants 93:33, 34; 138:17, 48), "fulness of my scriptures" (see, e.g., Doctrine and Covenants 42:15; 104:58), "fulness of the earth" (see, e.g., Doctrine and Covenants 59:16), "fulness of the Holy Ghost" (see, e.g., Doctrine and Covenants 109:15), Doctrine and Covenants 124:38 is the only scriptural reference to "fulness of the priesthood."
19. See Richard G. Ellsworth and Melvin J. Luthy, "Priesthood," in *Latter-day Saint Essentials: Readings from the Encyclopedia of Mormonism*, John W. Welch and R. Devan Jensen, eds. IProvo, Utah: BYU Studies and the Religious Studies Center, 2002), https://rsc.byu.edu/latter-day-saint-essentials/priesthood#:~:text=Fulness%20of%20the%20priesthood%2C%20which,132%3A18%E2%80%9319. President Joseph Fielding Smith added, "Do not think because anybody has a higher office in this Church than you have, that you are barred from blessings [speaking in the context of receiving a "fulness of the priesthood"], because you can go into the temple of the Lord and get all the blessings there are that have been revealed, if you are faithful, have them sealed upon you as an elder of this Church, and then you have all that any man can get. There have to be offices in the Church, and we are not all called to the same calling, but you can get the fulness of the priesthood in the temple of the Lord by obeying [the revelations]. I want to make this emphatic." He also emphasized that this blessing can only be received by a husband and wife together: "No man shall receive the fulness of eternity, of

exaltation alone; no woman shall receive that blessing alone; but man and wife, when they receive the sealing power in the temple of the Lord, shall pass on to exaltation, and shall continue and become like the Lord" (*Elijah the Prophet and His Mission*, Kindle Reader), 421 of 444.

20. "Section 124, A Solemn Proclamation: The Priesthood Order is Established," *Doctrine and Covenants Student Manual*, https://www.churchofjesuschrist.org/manual/doctrine-and-covenants-student-manual/section-124-a-solemn-proclamation-the-priesthood-order-is-established?lang=eng.

21. Additional scriptural references to witnessing the "fulness" of the Lord's glory, which can occur only when one is transfigured spiritually, receiving the "fulness of the Father" and the "fulness of the Son," which appears to be a blessing accompanying the resurrection and entry into the celestial kingdom or "rest" and "fulness" of the glory of God, can be found in Doctrine and Covenants 93, the dedicatory prayer on the Kirtland Temple found in Doctrine and Covenants 109, and the revelation on eternal marriage in Doctrine and Covenants 132.

22. "Chapter 19: Eternal Life," *Doctrines of the Gospel Teacher Manual*, https://www.churchofjesuschrist.org/study/manual/doctrines-of-the-gospel/chapter-19?lang=eng ("Exercise caution while discussing the doctrine of having our calling and election made sure. Avoid speculation. Use only the sources given here and in the student manual. Do not attempt in any way to discuss or answer questions about the second anointing.")

23. Fair: Faithful Answers, Informed Response, "Question: What is the 'second anointing'," https://www.fairlatterdaysaints.org/answers/Question:_What_is_the_%22second_anointing%22%3F.

24. Mackley, 84 and note 300, quoting *Joseph Smith, Discourse*, ca. June 1839, Willard Richards Pocket Companion, 19; the Joseph Smith Papers, http://josephsmithpapers.org/paperSummary/report-or-instructions-circa-june-1839-as-reported-by-willard-richards.

25. Ibid., 85–86.

26. See Mackley, 86. Andrew Skinner notes that through the sealing power of the priesthood the Lord's servants, when duly authorized, may "perform an ordinance granting [men and women (couples)] eternal life once they pass beyond mortality, to place a seal on them so that no matter what happens in the world, no matter what desolation sweeps the earth, yet they shall be saved in the day of the Lord Jesus. (Doctrine and Covenants 88:84–85; 109:38, 46; 124:124; 131:5; 132:19, 46, 49)" (*Skinner, Temple Worship*, 74 [quoting McConkie, *Mormon Doctrine*, 683]). See also Ronald K. Esplin, "Joseph, Brigham and the Twelve: A Succession of Continuity," *Brigham Young University Studies* 21 no. 3, 301–342, file:///C:/Users/Owner/Downloads/21.3esplinjoseph-4272ddbf-638d-4ba2-a06b-180a8d152e98.pdf.

27. Skinner, *Temple Worship*, 75.

Epilogue

"Let us never lose sight of what the Lord is doing for us now. He is making His temples more accessible. . . . He is accelerating the pace at which we are building temples."[1]

—Russell M. Nelson

This Remarkable Era of Temple Building

In his Sunday morning conference address in April 2011, President Thomas S. Monson marveled at the increased pace of temple building in our day: "During the first 150 years following the organization of the Church, from 1830 to 1980, 21 temples were built, including the temples in Kirtland, Ohio, and Nauvoo, Illinois. Contrast that with the 30 years since 1980, during which 115 temples were built and dedicated."[2] Nine years later Elder Bednar, then Chairman of the Temple and Family History Executive Council, put this dramatic increase in the number of announced and operating temples in the context of President Nelson's life and apostolic ministry: "When President Nelson was sustained as President of the Church, 159 temples were operating, an increase of 133 temples in the 34 years during which he served as a member of the Quorum of the Twelve. . . . Ninety-six percent of the existing temples have been dedicated during President Nelson's lifetime; 84 percent have been dedicated since he was ordained an Apostle."[3]

As of October 2023 general conference, the *Church News* announced, "In less than six years as its prophet, President Russell M. Nelson has announced 153 new temples for The Church of Jesus Christ of Latter-day Saints" (more temples than any other prophet in this dispensation, 75 more than President Hinckley, who announced 78 new temples during his prophetic tenure).[4]

What might the Lord be trying to teach us through this remarkable record of temple building? President Nelson answers simply that "making covenants and receiving essential ordinances in the temple, *as well as seeking to draw closer to Him there*, will bless your life in ways no other kind of worship can. For this reason, we are doing all within our power to make the blessings of the temple more accessible to our members around the world."[5] It used to be, one temple leader told me, that it was sufficient to be "active" in the Church, praying, studying your scriptures, and attending church regularly. No more. It is increasingly important that we be in the temple as often as our circumstances permit in order to survive the temptations and trials of the last days.[6]

Why the Need for More Frequent Temple Worship?

The Lord repeatedly promised His saints from the earliest days of the restoration to endow them with "power from on high" (Doctrine and Covenants 38:32, 38). This "power of godliness " (Doctrine and Covenants 84:20, 21), available only through the ordinances of the gospel, is quite simply the power or motivation to do and be a little better each day. As we participate in the gathering of Israel, which means gathering individuals to the Church and members of the Church ultimately to the temple, we become the people who will be able, ready, and worthy to receive the Savior when He comes again, "a people who have already chosen Jesus Christ over this fallen world."[7] Notwithstanding our day is a "perilous time" indeed,[8] it is also a time when "we will see the *greatest* manifestations of the Savior's power that the world has *ever* seen. Between now and the time He returns 'with power and great glory,' He will bestow countless blessings, privileges and miracles upon the faithful."[9] This is why President Nelson has, and all the prophets who follow him will, urge us to increase our faith, thus enabling Jesus Christ to "increase [our] ability to move the mountains" of "loneliness, doubt, illness, weakness with a particular temptation" and other challenges to our personal spiritual progression[10] and, as we do, to "expect miracles."[11] "Increased time in the temple," the Lord's prophets have repeatedly testified, will bring such miraculous results "in ways nothing else can."[12]

The blessings or spiritual treasures the Lord has promised us from receiving temple ordinances and "establish[ing] a pattern of regular temple attendance" include learning "how to draw upon [Christ's] priesthood power with which [we] have been endowed in His temple."[13] How often have we been counseled to be in the temple? According to the *General Handbook*, as "often as [our individual] circumstances allow."[14]

The Spiritual Treasures of the Temple

We end this study where we began, with President Nelson's expressed hope that all members of the Lord's restored Church "understand the spiritual treasures that are theirs in the temple."[15] These treasures, so well and often described by many commentators about temple ordinances and doctrines,[16] have perhaps never been so well summarized than by the Lord Himself in His revealed dedicatory prayer on the Kirtland Temple found in Doctrine and Covenants 109, which has become a pattern for all temple dedicatory prayers. From the explicit and implicit promises or spiritual treasures, which are quoted from various verses of section 109 below,[17] we see and feel the love of Heavenly Parents and a Savior who want to help and bless us in so many extraordinary ways:

- When we come to the temple, a "house to [Jehovah's] name," we are privileged to abide for a time in a place where "the Son of Man" "manifest[s] himself to his people" (v. 5) and where His renewing and strengthening "power" and "glory . . . rest down upon [us, His] people, and upon [His] house," "sanctify[ing]" it by His presence, making it a "place of [His] holiness," "clean" from the "pollutions" of the world, where His "holy presence continually" abides (vv. 12–13, 20) and where we feel, as we did premortally, at home, at peace, and joyously in His presence, even if only for a moment in the busyness, the worries, and stresses of our important sojourn in mortality, away from our eternal home (v. 16);
- We can feel that He calls us, and we indeed are, His "friends" (v. 6);
- As a result of our regular "worship in [God's holy] house," we are taught through the power of the Holy Ghost, line upon

line, in the temple and through our scripture study, "out of the best books," which includes today all of the means the Church utilizes to communicate the words and ministries of ancient and modern prophets, "words of wisdom," being blessed thereby with "learning" and knowledge "by [our] study and also by [our] faith" how to apply such learning to increase our faith in Jesus Christ, enabling us to receive godly power to move the mountains and receive the miracles the Lord has promised (vv. 7 and 14);

- Regular temple worship "organizes" or prioritizes our lives, reminding us of our eternal origin, natures, and divine destinies, the purposes and needful priorities of our mortal probation, giving us power, in turn, to "organize" and prioritize our families and homes, "establishing" them in temple patterns, as we covenant to do in the new and everlasting covenant of marriage, as houses "of prayer," "of fasting," "of faith," "of learning [especially learning of the divine]," "of glory," "of order," and "of God," (v. 8), making them indeed what President Nelson described as "center[s] of gospel learning";[18]
- We are blessed that our "incomings," "outgoings," even "all [our] salutations may be in the name of the Lord," suggesting the possibility of His divine guidance and blessing over our daily social interactions and relationships in and outside the home (vv. 9, 17– 19);
- We will be "assist[ed]" "with [God's] grace" (v. 10);
- We can come to feel that the Lord finds us "worthy in [His] sight" and that "the promises" He has made to us "in the revelations given unto us," especially the ultimate promises received in the temple, will be "fulfilled" (v. 11);
- Over the years of our regular service in the temple, we will "grow up in [Christ]," as Paul promised, into the "stature of the fulness of Christ" (Ephesians 4:13), "receive a fulness of the Holy Ghost," being "prepared to obtain every needful thing," including, most importantly, eternal life (v. 15);
- We receive assurances that when we "transgress, *any* of [us]," which the Father's perfect plan contemplated that we all would do, as we learn from our own experience the difference

between choosing God and Satan, we are blessed with power to "speedily repent and return unto [God and to His temple], and find favor in [His] sight, and be restored to the blessings which [He] hast ordained to be poured out upon those who shall reverence [Him] in [His] house" (vv. 21, 34);
- From each visit to the temple, we have the opportunity to "go forth" "armed with [God's] power," with His "name" (or authority or blessing) "upon" us, His "glory . . . round about" us and His "angels hav[ing] charge over us" (v. 22);
- We are promised that as we keep our temple covenants, we will "honorably hold a name and standing in [God's house], to all generations and for eternity" (v. 24);
- We will be given God's "power" to do His work (v. 33);
- Our temple "anointing[s]" will "be sealed upon [us] with power from on high," meaning that through our faithfulness the promises in the anointing ordinance will be fulfilled (v. 35);
- We will be strengthened to live the law of consecration, "to say" and desire, "with thy grace assisting" us, "Thy will be done, O Lord, and not [mine]" and so choose in our daily lives (v. 44);
- As we endure faithfully in keeping our covenants, we are promised "that when the trump shall sound for the dead, we shall be caught up in the cloud to meet [God], that we may ever be with the Lord; That our garments may be pure, that we may be clothed upon with robes of righteousness, with palms in our hands, and crowns of glory upon our heads, and reap eternal joy for all our sufferings" (vv. 75–76).[19]

May God grant that in our efforts to sustain and follow our living prophets we will recommit ourselves to seek, study, recognize, be grateful for, and share the magnificent spiritual treasures the Lord so anxiously desires to bestow upon us in and through the ordinances of His holy house.

Endnotes

1. Nelson, "Focus on the Temple," 121.
2. Thomas S. Monson, "The Holy Temple—a Beacon to the World," *Ensign*, May 2011, 90.
3. Bednar, "'Let This House Be Built unto My Name," 87.
4. Tad Walch, "'Temples closer to the people,'" *Church News*, November 10, 2023, https://www.deseret.com/2023/11/10/23941131/president-nelson-more-lds-mormon-temples.
5. Russell M. Nelson, "The Answer Is Always Jesus Christ," *Liahona*, May 2023, 127–28. See also David A. Bednar, "Come to Zion," *Church News* video, https://www.thechurchnews.com/leaders/2023/4/13/23682283/video-elder-bednar-temple-building-called-to-zion?utm_campaign=Church%20News%20-%20English&utm_medium=email&_hsmi=254856064&_hsenc=p2ANqtz-8dMN0DEbv64xveWr1NeJCmDAionZ8F1WjJ3oJFeBXSs_4FpqxzkNWvW_atUDS5JcC3AkSb2g7kKDX9XDaKpe0DlF1KVw&utm_content=254856064&utm_source=hs_email ("I can think of few invitations President Nelson has offered more frequently than be in the temple as often as your circumstances allow").
6. Personal conversation in September 2022 with Emron Pratt, then serving as president of the Monticello Utah Temple. Used by permission.
7. Nelson, "Overcome the World and Find Rest," 98. A few of President Nelson's references to the Second Coming include his statement in the priesthood session of April 2018 general conference: "Think of your duty as God's mighty army to help prepare the world for the Second Coming of the Lord. This is our charge. This is our privilege" (Nelson, "'Ministering with the Power and Authority of God," 75); from the women's session of the October 2018 general conference, "Together we can do all that our Heavenly Father needs us to do to prepare the world for the Second Coming of His Beloved Son" (Nelson, "Sisters' Participation in the Gathering of Israel," 70); from the women's session of the October 2019 general conference: "We Latter-day Saints are not of the world; we are of covenant Israel. We are called to prepare a people for the Second Coming of the Lord" (Nelson, "Spiritual Treasures," 78); from his closing remarks in the October 2019 general conference: "Of course, the crowning jewel of the Restoration is the holy temple. Its sacred ordinances and covenants are pivotal to preparing a people who are ready to welcome the Savior at His Second Coming" ("Closing Remarks," 120); from his closing remarks in the April 2020 general conference: "May we go forward together to fulfill our divine mandate—that of preparing ourselves and the world for the Second Coming of the Lord" (Nelson, "A New Normal," 119); from the October 2020 general conference: "For centuries, prophets have foretold [the] gathering [of Israel], and it is happening right now! As an essential prelude to the Second Coming of the Lord, it is the most important work in the world!" (Nelson, "Let God Prevail," 92). See also Nelson, "The Future of the Church," 9.

8. Henry B. Eyring, "Steady in the Storms," *Liahona*, May 2022, 27 ("Each of us, wherever we are, knows that we live in increasingly perilous times").
9. Nelson, "Overcome the World and Find Rest," 95 (emphasis in original).
10. Nelson, "Christ Is Risen; Faith in Him Will Move Mountains," 102–03. Nelson, *Heart of the Matter*, 125. President Nelson adds: "The mountains in our lives do not always move how or when we would like. But our faith will always propel us forward. Faith always increases our access to godly power" (Ibid., 127).
11. Nelson, "The Power of Spiritual Momentum," 99.
12. Nelson, "Focus on the Temple," 121.
13. Nelson, "Sisters' Participation in the Gathering of Israel," 70. Availing ourselves of the blessing of the online appointment system, made available to us during the COVID-19 pandemic by the Brethren, can help us make our regular temple worship and service more intentional. See "Adjustment to Temple Scheduling," News Release, June 3, 2022, https://newsroom.churchofjesuschrist.org/article/adjustment-temple-scheduling ("Allowing members to reserve temple appointments has provided many advantages, including reduced wait times for patrons and ensuring members can participate in the ordinances (ceremonies) as they choose").
14. See *General Handbook* references listed in note 22 of chapter 9.
15. Nelson, "Spiritual Treasures," 76.
16. See, for example, David J. Ridges, *Temples—Sacred Symbolism, Eternal Blessings* (Springville, Utah: CFI, 2019), which includes in pages 19–20 a paraphrased list of the "blessings of temple attendance" from Doctrine and Covenants 109. In *Finding Promised Blessings on the Covenant Path*, Kerry Muhlestein recites dozens (if not hundreds) of scriptures that describe the many and varied blessings that come from entering into and keeping the "new and everlasting covenant" or Abrahamic covenant, which "are the same thing." These blessings could and should also be viewed as "spiritual treasures" that come from entering into and keeping temple covenants, which are part of the crowning covenants of the gospel and the Abrahamic covenant.
17. In this dedicatory prayer, which the Prophet Joseph Smith "received by revelation," the Lord "described many of the extraordinary blessings that are bestowed upon those who worthily enter the temples of the Lord" (Benjamín De Hoyos, "The Work of the Temple and Family History—One and the Same Work" *Liahona*, May 2023, 52). For another wonderful overview of the promises and "enlightening treatment" the Lord gives us about the temple in Section 109, see Hugh W. Nibley, "A House of Glory," in *Temples of the Ancient World: Ritual and Symbolism*, 29, https://www.ldsscriptureteachings.org/staging/4108/wp-content/uploads/2019/10/Temples-of-the-Ancient-World-Ritual-and-Symbolism-Parry-full-text.pdf.
18. Nelson, "What We Are Learning and Will Never Forget," 79. President Nelson repeated in his 2023 review of "what 100 years of living have taught" him that not only he, speaking from his own experience, but the Lord, *Jesus Christ* "is the One who wants you to understand with great clarity exactly what you are making covenants to do. *He* is the One who wants you to comprehend

your privileges, promises, and responsibilities. *He* wants you to have spiritual insights and awakenings you've never had before" (*Heart of the Matter*, 180–81) (emphasis in original).

19. Other express promises or spiritual treasures are promised in Doctrine and Covenants 109 to temple worshipers as we "love, share, and invite" others to receive the blessings of the gospel God desires for all of His children. We are promised power (i) to "bear exceedingly great and glorious tidings, in truth, unto" our neighbors and in the circles of our influence, even unto "the ends of the earth," "[our] testimony of the covenant," "that [our friends and family] may know [because of our testimonies and examples] that this is [God's] work, and that [God] hast put forth [His] hand, to fulfil that which [He] hast spoken by the mouths of the prophets, concerning the last days," that our friends' and family members' "hearts may be softened when [we, as God's] servants" "go out from [God's] house," that we of the Church and they who heed our testimony may be "prepared" "for all those judgments [God is] about to send, in [His] wrath, upon the inhabitants of the earth," that we and they "may not faint in the day of trouble" and that God's "peace and salvation" may be with such converts, enabling them to "know that we, [God's] servants, have heard [His] voice, and that [He] has sent us," that they may "come forth to Zion, or to her stakes, the places of [God's] appointment, with songs of everlasting joy" and that "the gathering of [God's] people may roll on in great power and majesty, that [His] work may be cut short in righteousness" (vv. 23, 38–39, 56–59; see also v. 73); (ii) "that no weapon formed against [us] shall prosper" in the long run; "that he who diggeth a pit for [us, in the Lord's time] shall fall into the same himself" (v. 25); and (iii) "that no combination of wickedness shall have power to rise up and prevail over [us] upon whom [God's] name [has been] put in" the temple by virtue of the ordinances we receive there, that God's "anger [will] be kindled against" all enemies of righteousness and purveyors of evil cultural and other influences, and He "will fight for" us, our children and our grandchildren, who are immersed in such worldly influences, as He did "in the day of battle, that [we] may be delivered from the hands" of all such wicked influences, that those who spread falsehoods about or misrepresent the Church, its beliefs and its leaders, or good and truth generally, will be "confounded," "astonished," brought "to shame and confusion," and their "works . . . brought to nought" and "swept away by the hail" and by God's judgments, if they do not repent when taught the truth (vv. 26–31, 42).

APPENDIX 1

Sacrifices and Offerings of the Mosaic Law[1]

Name of the Ordinance and Type of Offering	Emblematic Objects Used for the Ordinance	Purpose of the Ordinance	When Administered
BURNT OFFERING (Lev. 1; Lev. 6:9–13) This is another name for the ordinance of sacrifice practiced by the patriarchs from Adam down to Israel. (See "The Priesthood Ordinance of Sacrifice," p. 49.) See "The Priesthood Ordinance of Sacrifice," p. 49 [page references are to the page of the December 1973 issue of the *Ensign* in which this chart was first published. See https://www.churchofjesuchrist.org/study/ensign/1973/12/the-priesthood-ordinance-of-sacrifice?lang=eng].)	Male animal without blemish (Ex. 12:5; Lev. 1:3; Lev. 22:18–25; Num. 28:3–4; Deut. 15:21; Deut. 17:1). Originally the animal was to be a firstborn (Gen. 4:4; Ex. 13:12; Lev. 27:26; Num. 3:41; Num. 18:17; Deut. 12:6; Deut. 15:19–21). The animal used varied according to the position and personal possessions of the individual, as well as the occasion of the sacrifice: bull, ram, he-goat, turtledoves, or young pigeons (Lev. 1:5, 10, 14; Lev. 5:7; Gen. 15:9).	"… This thing is a similitude of the sacrifice of the Only Begotten of the Father. …" (Moses 5:7; see also Lev. 1:4, 9; Lev. 14:20; Heb. 9:14; 1 Pet. 1:19; 2 Ne. 11:4; 2 Ne. 25:24–27; Jacob 4:5; Jarom 1:11; Mosiah 3:15.)	PUBLIC OFFERINGS Regularly appointed times: Daily—morning and evening (Ex. 29:38–42; Num. 28:3–4). Sabbath—double portion given (Num. 28:9–10). New Moon—monthly (Num. 28:11–15). Seasonally appointed times: Feast of Passover and Unleavened Bread Feast of the Harvest, Feast of the Tabernacles New Year, and the Day of Atonement (See "Feasts or Holidays in Ancient Israel," p. 49). PRIVATE OFFERINGS Given for family events—birth, marriage, reunions, etc., and at times of personal need. Most often, private or individual offerings were given during the times of appointed feasts.

Name of the Ordinance and Type of Offering	Emblematic Objects Used for the Ordinance	Purpose of the Ordinance	When Administered
PEACE OFFERING (Lev. 3; Lev. 7:11–38)	Male or female animal without blemish (Lev. 3:1, 12) and cattle, sheep, or goats, but no fowl or other substitutes (Lev. 22:27). The animal was to be meat for a sacrificial meal. The fat and inward portions were burned upon the altar (Lev. 3:3–5), a specified part was given to the priests (see Heave and Wave Offerings below), and the remainder was used for meat in the special dinner (Lev. 7:16).	The threefold purpose of peace offerings is suggested in the following titles or descriptions given. THANK OFFERING is given to thank God for all blessings (Lev. 7:12–13, 15; Lev. 22:29). VOW OFFERING (Lev. 7:16; Lev. 22:18, 21, 23; Num. 15:3, 8; Num. 29:39; Deut. 12:6) signifies the taking or renewing of a vow or covenant. FREE-WILL OFFERING (Lev. 7:16; Lev. 22:18, 21, 23; Num. 15:3; Num. 29:39; Deut. 12:6, 17; Deut. 16:10; Deut. 23:23) suggests voluntary receiving of covenants with attendant responsibilities and consequences. An individual could seemingly give the offering for any of the above declared purposes separately or together.	These were only private offerings or personal sacrifice for family or individuals. (See Private Offerings under Burnt Offering above.)

Sacrifices and Offerings of the Mosaic Law

Name of the Ordinance and Type of Offering	Emblematic Objects Used for the Ordinance	Purpose of the Ordinance	When Administered
SIN OFFERING (Lev. 4; Lev. 5:1–13; Lev. 6:25–30)	Male or female animal or fowl without blemish. The offering according to the position and circumstances of the offerer: the priest offered a bull (Lev. 4:3; Num. 8:8), the ruler among the people a he-goat (Lev. 4:22–23), the people in general a she-goat (Lev. 4:27–28), the poor two turtledoves or two young pigeons (Lev. 5:7), and those of extreme poverty an offering of fowl or meal (Lev. 5:11; Num. 15:20–21). The offering is not consumed by fire, but is used by the Levitical priesthood as a sacrificial meal. The meat and hide are for their sustenance and use. (Lev. 5:25–30; Lev. 7:7–8; Lev. 14:13.)	Sin offerings were given for sins committed in ignorance (Lev. 4:2, 22, 27), sins not generally known about by the people (Num. 15:24), sins in violation of oaths and covenants (Lev. 5:1, 4–5), and ceremonial sins of defilement or uncleanness under the law of carnal commandments (Lev. 5:2–3; Lev. 12:1–8; Lev. 15:28–30). The purpose of sin offerings, after true repentance on the part of the parties involved, was to prepare them to receive forgiveness as a part of the renewal of their covenants. (Lev. 4:26, 35; Lev. 5:10; Lev. 10:17; Num. 15:24–29.) This same blessing is possible by partaking of the sacrament today. (JST, Matt. 26:24.)	A special sin-offering affecting all the people was offered on the Day of Atonement. (Ex. 30:10; Lev. 16:3, 6, 11, 15–19; see "Feasts or Holidays in Ancient Israel," p. 49.) All other sin offerings were private and personal offerings, most often given at the times of the appointed feasts.

Name of the Ordinance and Type of Offering	Emblematic Objects Used for the Ordinance	Purpose of the Ordinance	When Administered
TRESPASS OFFERING (Lev. 5:15–19; Lev. 6:1–7; Lev. 7:1–10)	Ram without blemish (Lev. 5:15, 18; Lev. 6:6; Lev. 19:21). A leper was to offer a lamb (Lev. 14:12), and a Nazarite was also to give a lamb (Num. 6:12).	Trespass offerings were given for offenses committed against others: i.e., false testimony (Lev. 6:2–3), forceful and unlawful possession of property (Lev. 6:4), disrespect for sacred things (Lev. 5:16–17), acts of passion (Lev. 19:20–22). The purpose of the trespass offering was to bring forgiveness. (Lev. 6:7.) This was possible after repentance (Lev. 26:40–45) and after fulfilling the law of restitution that required, where possible, that the guilty individual restore completely the wrong and an additional 20 percent (Lev. 5:16; Lev. 6:5–17; Lev. 27:13, 15, 19, 27, 31; Num. 5:6–10).	All trespass offerings were private and personal offerings, most commonly given at the times of the appointed feasts.

Name of the Ordinance and Type of Offering	Emblematic Objects Used for the Ordinance	Purpose of the Ordinance	When Administered
MEAL OR MEAT OFFERING GIFTS (Ex. 29:40–41; Lev. 2; Lev. 6:14–23; Lev. 7:9–10; Num. 15:4–24; Num. 28; Num. 29)	An unleavened bread. Few ingredients were permitted with the basic flour—salt (Lev. 2:13), oil (Lev. 2:5), even incense (Lev. 2:15), but no leavening or honey (Lev. 2:11). However, it could be baked or fried in various ways.	This offering completed the sacrificial meal of the burnt and peace offerings. It was then given to the priests for their service and sustenance. (Lev. 7:8–10)	This offering was always given with the burnt offerings and peace offerings and could even substitute for a sin offering in the stress of poverty (Num. 15:28; Num. 29).

Name of the Ordinance and Type of Offering	Emblematic Objects Used for the Ordinance	Purpose of the Ordinance	When Administered
HEAVE OFFERING (Ex. 29:26–27; Lev. 7:14, 32–34; Num. 18:19)	The heave offering is the right shoulder and the wave offering the breast of the peace offering animal given in payment by the offerer for the services of the priest. Whatever the Levites received for their priesthood service—heave or wave offering, meat offering, or tithe (Num. 18)—they were required to offer to the Lord in sacrifice a portion as a memorial offering (Lev. 2:2, 9, 16; Lev. 5:12; Lev. 6:15; Num. 5:26; Lev. 18:26–29). "Heave" and "wave" refer to gestures of lifting the offerings up and extending them toward the priest who received them on behalf of the Lord.	This is the priest's portion (Lev. 7:35–36; Deut. 18:1–8). This memorial offering was a type of peace or thank offering to the Lord, as well as a remembrance of God and service to him. The Levites also received the hides of all the animals sacrificed for their labors and services. (Lev. 7:8.)	These were given at the times of burnt offerings and peace offerings. These were given at the time the offerings were given.

Endnotes
1. Edward J. Brandt, "The Priesthood Ordinance of Sacrifice," *Ensign*, December 1973, 50–5 used by permission.

APPENDIX 2

Promises Made and Ordinances Given to Abraham Were Renewed with Isaac and Jacob

Abrahamic Covenant Renewed with Isaac

One of the most important lessons learned from the lives of Abraham, Isaac, and Jacob is the importance of marrying the right person by the right authority, that is by the power of the holy priesthood. Thus, when "Abraham was old," he "said unto his eldest servant of his house, that ruled over all that he had, Put, I pray thee, thy hand under my thigh."[1] In other words, the servant was to make an oath and solemn covenant that in fulfilling Abraham's sacred charge to find a wife for Isaac, he would "not take a wife . . . of the daughters of the Canaanites," but go to Haran and among Abraham's relatives find the girl whom Isaac should marry. In so charging him, Abraham then promised him by the authority of the priesthood he held that the Lord would "send his angel before thee" and lead him to the woman whom the Lord would choose for Isaac (Genesis 24:1–9).

Abraham, of course, married Sarai, a faithful princess of the royal lineage of Shem, thus entitling her to receive all of the blessings of the priesthood. Now, he needed to ensure that Isaac, his son of the covenant, to whom Abraham had given "all that he had" (Genesis 25:5), including, most importantly, a testimony of the true and living God, also married a woman who believed in Jehovah and lived His gospel and would thus be entitled to "marry in the temple," so to speak. This meant, for his day and time, that he must find for Isaac a faithful descendant of Shem. The story of that marriage holds many lessons for our day and time, in particular, how the Lord will be in the details as we approach this greatest decision in life—who and where we should marry. It is also a very romantic story!

Upon accepting his sacred charge, "the servant took ten camels of the camels of his master, and departed; for all the goods of his master were in his hand: and he arose, and went to Mesopotamia, unto the city of Nahor." Arriving at the city well at the time of the evening watering, he prayed, "O Lord God of my master Abraham, I pray thee, send me good speed this day, and shew kindness unto my master Abraham." In short, he asked God to guide him to know who among all the women who would be arriving shortly at the well was to be Isaac's wife. In great faith, he petitioned Jehovah, "Let it come to pass, that the damsel to whom I shall say, Let down thy pitcher, I pray thee, that I may drink; and she shall say, Drink, and I will give thy camels drink also: let the same be she that thou hast appointed for thy servant Isaac." "And it came to pass, *before he had done speaking*, that, behold, Rebekah came out, who was born to Bethuel, son of Milcah, the wife of Nahor, Abraham's brother, with her pitcher upon her shoulder." Rebekah must have been very striking, for the record states that she "was very fair to look upon." But more importantly, it turns out that she is Abraham's great-niece, the granddaughter of Abraham's brother, Nahor. When he saw her go to fill her pitcher, he "ran to meet her" and asked her if he could "drink a little water" from her pitcher. In fulfillment of Abraham's blessing and the servant's faith, Rebekah responded, "Drink, my lord" and quickly "let down her pitcher [and] gave him drink. And when she had done giving him drink, she said, I will draw water for thy camels also, until they have done drinking. And she hasted, and emptied her pitcher into the trough, and ran again unto the well to draw water, and drew for all his camels.

"And the man wondering at her held his peace, to wit whether the Lord had made his journey prosperous or not" (Genesis 24:10–28). The servant's faithfulness is surely a tribute to Abraham's influence and missionary zeal to share the truths of the gospel with all his household, indeed all his "neighbors." The Lord answered him even before he finished praying.

The servant gave Rebekah precious jewelry—"a golden earring of half a shekel weight, and two bracelets for her hands of ten shekels weight of gold"—and asked who she was and whether there was room in her father's house for him and his company to lodge. When he learned that she was indeed Abraham's relative (and, perhaps more importantly, that her actions reflected that she was a faithful follower of Jehovah), he "bowed down his head, and worshipped the Lord," saying, "blessed be the Lord God of my master Abraham, who hath not left destitute my master of his mercy and his truth: I being in the way, the Lord led me to the house of my master's brethren."

Rebekah's brother, Laban, and her father, Bethuel, then invited the servant and those accompanying him to dine with them. But before the servant met any of his own needs, he attended first and foremost to his mission. Describing Abraham's faith in the Lord, the servant recounted Abraham's promise that the Lord, "before whom [he] walk]ed]," would "send his angel" and "prosper" the servant's way and help him accomplish his divine mission to identify a worthy wife and companion for his son (Genesis 24:40). Bethuel and Laban recognize the hand of the Lord in what has happened and consent to the marriage, for which blessing the servant again worships the Lord, "bowing himself to the earth" (v. 52). When they naturally suggested that Rebekah be given "a few days, at least ten" to adjust to the news and take leave of her family, the servant, once again, showed his unwavering loyalty: "Hinder me not, seeing the Lord hath prospered my way; send me away that I may go to my master" (v. 56). They left the decision to Rebekah, who showed her faith by responding simply, "I will go" (v. 58). Isaac would be forty when he married Rebekah (Genesis 25:20).

Rebekah again showed her faith about nineteen barren years later when she "enquired of the Lord" (Genesis 5:22), who revealed that she was pregnant with twins and that "the elder shall serve the younger" (v. 23). Notably, President Nelson teaches that "Isaac and Rebekah's son Jacob was born in the covenant," meaning, of course, that Isaac and Rebekah had been sealed in the new and everlasting covenant of marriage.[2] When Esau and Jacob were born, Isaac was sixty (v. 26). His sons were fifteen when Abraham died.

As his sons grew, Isaac preferred Esau, "because [Isaac] did eat of [Esau's] venison." Esau became a "cunning hunter, a man of the field," while Jacob became a sheep herder, a "plain man, dwelling in tents." "But Rebekah loved Jacob" (Genesis 25:27–28), whom the

Lord had revealed would be served by his older brother. Undoubtedly her influence, as well as his grandfather Abraham's example, who had "sought" diligently the right to be ordained to the priesthood, kindled in Jacob early in his life a desire for the birthright blessing, or right to receive the priesthood, which traditionally belonged to the oldest son, a gift, in fact, that Esau "despised." When Esau came famished "from the field" or the hunt, he asked Jacob to give him some of the "red pottage" or lentil stew he was making. Jacob responded, no doubt guided by the Spirit, that he would in exchange for Esau's birthright. Apparently with no thought other than his empty stomach, Esau agreed to the sale, rationalizing, "Behold, I am at the point to die: and what profit shall this birthright do to me?" To ensure that Esau understood the seriousness of Jacob's offer, Jacob demanded that Esau "swear to me this day; and he sware unto him: and he sold his birthright unto Jacob. Then Jacob gave Esau bread and pottage of lentiles;[3] and he did eat and drink, and rose up, and went his way: thus Esau despised his birthright" (Genesis 25:29–34).

Like his father, the Lord greatly blessed Isaac (see Genesis 25:11), including in the fruit of the field "an hundred fold" (Genesis 26:12). When another great famine arose and Isaac contemplated fleeing to Egypt, as Abraham had, the Lord appeared to him, warned him not to go to Egypt but to "sojourn in this land." He then renewed with Isaac the Abrahamic covenant—"I will be with thee, and will bless thee; for unto thee, and unto thy seed, I will give all these countries, and I will perform the oath which I sware unto Abraham thy father; And *I will make thy seed to multiply as the stars of heaven*, and will give unto thy seed all these countries; and *in thy seed shall all the nations of the earth be blessed*; Because that Abraham obeyed my voice, and kept my charge, my commandments, my statutes, and my laws" (Genesis 26:2–5).

In time, however, Isaac's success caused envy among his Philistine hosts in the city of Gerar. The king asked Isaac to leave, "for thou art much mightier than we" (Genesis 26:16). Isaac moved from the city to the surrounding valley of Gerar, re-dug the well his father had originally dug (and the Philistines had filled with earth), and was again ejected by the Philistines. He moved a third time and then a fourth and final time to Beer-sheba, where Abraham had also dwelt and where the Lord appeared to him again: "And the Lord appeared unto him the same night, and said, I am the God of Abraham thy father: fear not, for I am with thee, and will bless thee, and multiply thy seed for my servant Abraham's sake." Isaac built an altar there, "and called upon the name of the Lord and pitched his tent there: and there Isaac's servants digged a well" (Genesis 26:24–25). Almost immediately after receiving this blessing, Abimelech, the King of Gerar, returned and sued for formal peace, which Isaac accepted, making a feast for his former self-declared enemy. "And it came to pass the same day, that Isaac's servants came, and told him concerning the well which they had digged, and said unto him, We have found water" (Genesis 26:27–32). Thus, faithful Isaac was blessed both temporally and spiritually. Esau at this time was forty and Isaac one hundred years old. Age had deprived him of sight, a key element in the story of how Jacob finally obtains the birthright, or right to the priesthood.

As Prophesied to Rebekah, Jacob's Worthiness Qualifies Him for the Blessings of Abraham

When Rebekah overheard Isaac asking Esau to bring him venison so that he could "bless [Esau] before the Lord" before he died, she told Jacob: "Now therefore, my son, obey my voice according to that which I command thee. Go now to the flock, and fetch me from thence two good kids of the goats; and I will make them savoury meat for thy father, such as he loveth: And thou shalt bring it to thy father, that he may eat, and that he may bless thee before his death." Jacob wondered how this would work, since, he told her, Esau "is a hairy man, and I am a smooth man," something Isaac would easily detect, resulting in a cursing for Jacob rather than a blessing. But Rebekah was determined: "Upon me be thy curse, my son: only obey my voice, and go fetch me them." Jacob obeyed. Rebekah made the savory meat, clothed Jacob in Esau's clothes ("which were with her in the house" [v. 15], meaning in her care) and puts "the skins of the kids of the goats upon his hands, and upon the smooth of his neck."

Jacob entered with the meat and greeted his father, "My father." Isaac answered, "Here am I; who art thou my son? And Jacob said unto his father, I am Esau thy firstborn" (vv. 18–19). The subterfuge appears to be working. However, when Jacob offers his father the meat, Isaac said, "Come near, I pray thee, that I may feel thee, my son, whether thou be my very son Esau or not. And Jacob went near unto Isaac his father; and he felt him, and said, The voice is Jacob's voice, but the hands are the hands of Esau. And he discerned him not, because his hands were hairy, as his brother Esau's hands: so he blessed him." Isaac ate the meal Rebekah prepared, kissed Jacob, and "smelled the smell of his raiment, and blessed him, and said, See, the smell of my son is as the smell of a field which the Lord hath blessed: Therefore God give thee of the dew of heaven, and the fatness of the earth, and plenty of corn and wine: Let people serve thee, and nations bow down to thee: be lord over thy brethren, and let thy mother's sons bow down to thee: cursed be every one that curseth thee, and blessed be he that blesseth thee" (Genesis 27:5–29).

Notwithstanding Jacob's reservations about "tricking" his father into receiving the birthright blessing, Rebekah was undeterred as she *knew* by the power of the Spirit, as Isaac at this point apparently does not, that this particular blessing the Lord had reserved for Jacob, not Esau. "As soon as Isaac had made an end of blessing Jacob," Esau returned. "And he also had made savoury meat, and brought it unto his father, and said unto his father, Let my father arise, and eat of his son's venison, that thy soul may bless me. And Isaac his father said unto him, Who art thou? And he said, I am thy son, thy firstborn Esau. And Isaac trembled very exceedingly, and said, Who? where is he that hath taken venison, and brought it me, and I have eaten of all before thou camest, and have blessed him? yea, and *he shall be blessed*" (Genesis 27:26–33). A blessing given under false pretenses, of course, conveys nothing. However, Isaac realized, when Esau returned, the hand of the Lord is in his wife's actions and ratifies the blessing pronounced on Jacob.[4]

Rebekah's anxiety that Jacob secure the birthright blessing was also motivated by the earlier choices Esau had made to marry two Hittite women, Judith and Bashemath, outside the gospel covenant, bringing "grief of mind" to his parents (Genesis 26:34–35).[5] In order to receive the fulness of the blessings of the gospel, it was not enough for Jacob to receive the Melchizedek Priesthood. He must also be sealed in the new and everlasting covenant of marriage. Rebekah reminded Isaac that Esau's decision to marry outside the covenant would most likely deprive them of the promise of a righteous posterity that would be sealed to them. This promise, of course, was, and always is, dependent upon the faithfulness of such posterity. Esau's decision to marry outside the covenant dramatically reduced the odds that his children and grandchildren would enter into covenants with and remain true to Jehovah, the author and source of all covenant blessings. Rebekah reminded Isaac that, notwithstanding all their efforts to raise their sons in the admonition and nurture of the Lord, if Jacob followed his older brother's example, her life would lose all meaning. "And Rebekah said to Isaac, I am weary of my life because of the daughters of Heth: if Jacob take a wife of the daughters of Heth, such as these which are of the daughters of the land, what good shall my life do me?" (Genesis 27:46).

Bruce R. McConkie applauds Rebekah's courage in counselling with her husband about Jacob's eligibility to receive the crowning blessings of the temple:

> Rebekah had great anxiety as to whom Jacob would marry. She was fearful that he, too, might depart from the teachings of his parents and marry someone who was not eligible to receive the blessings of eternal marriage. . . . That is to say, Rebekah thought her whole life would be wasted if Jacob married out of the Church. She knew he could not enter the gate leading to exaltation unless he was married in the new and everlasting covenant of marriage, and so she brought the matter to Isaac's attention. This, I think, is a great object lesson. The mother was greatly concerned about the marriage of her son, and she prevailed upon the father to do something about it. She was acting as a guide and a light to Isaac, as my wife often does to me.[6]

The important point in all of this is that worthiness, not birth position, qualifies one for blessings from God. In ways that the record does not fully reflect (but his later life certainly did), Jacob qualified, as the Lord knew he would, for the sacred responsibilities, as well as blessings, bestowed upon him. His worthiness was amply demonstrated in significant subsequent sacred experiences in which he, like his fathers, saw and communed with the premortal Christ.

Jacob Receives the Endowment and a New Name Preparatory to His Eternal Marriage

Before sending Jacob to Abraham's relatives to find a wife, Isaac "blessed him, and charged him," saying, "Thou shalt not take a wife of the daughters of Canaan. Arise, go to Padan-aram, to the house of Bethuel thy mother's father; and take thee a wife from thence of the daughters of Laban thy mother's brother. And God Almighty bless thee, and make thee fruitful, and multiply thee, that thou mayest be a multitude of people; And *give thee the blessing of Abraham, to thee, and to thy seed with thee*; that thou mayest inherit the land wherein thou art a stranger, which God gave unto Abraham" (Genesis 28:1–4).

As he travelled to Haran in obedience to his parents, Jacob had a remarkable spiritual experience, preparatory to one of the most important decisions of his life—marrying in the covenant. According to inspired commentary on Genesis 28, Jacob received the endowment *before* he met and married Rachel, his chosen companion, setting an example for all of covenant Israel.

> **Genesis 28:10–17**—And Jacob went out from Beer-sheba, and went toward Haran. And he lighted upon a *certain place*, and tarried there all night, because the sun was set; and he took of the stones of that *place*, and put them for his pillows, and lay down in that *place* to sleep [v. 11]. And he dreamed, and behold a ladder set up on the earth, and the top of it reached to heaven: and behold the angels of God ascending and descending on it. And, behold, the Lord stood above it, and said, I am the Lord God of Abraham thy father, and the God of Isaac: the land whereon thou liest, to thee will I give it, and to thy seed; And *thy seed shall be as the dust of the earth*, and thou shalt spread abroad to the west, and to the east, and to the north, and to the south: and in thee and *in thy seed shall all the families of the earth be blessed*. And, behold, *I am with thee, and will keep thee in all places whither thou goest*, and will

bring thee again into this land; for *I will not leave thee.* . . . And Jacob awaked out of his sleep, and he said, Surely the Lord is in this *place*; and I knew it not. . . . This is none other but the *house of God, and this is the gate of heaven* [v. 17].

Commentators focus on the three uses of the word "place" in Hebrew in verse 11 to suggest that it was "not any ordinary place. Jacob happens upon *the* place . . . a sacred site."[7] In fact, after awaking he referred to it as "the house of God" and "the gate of heaven" (v. 17). In vision he saw the Lord, who spoke with him.[8] As Michael Wilcox noted, "the word *ladder* is better translated 'stairway.' Here is one of the finest descriptions of a temple in scripture. A temple is a stairway set up on earth whose top reaches to heaven. It is the meeting place of heaven and earth, a place where the dead and the living communicate with one another and where the Spirit teaches beautiful lessons. It is a place where those who have preceded us in the spirit world descend to us while we ascend to them."[9]

Notably, the Lord enters into a covenant with Jacob, even the Abrahamic covenant, that through him and his seed "all the families of the earth [would] be blessed," even with the blessings of the gospel, including, most importantly, the blessing of exaltation. The Lord's promises to "be with" and "keep thee in all places whither thou goest," and "not leave thee" are the same promises he extends to us in the temple. "Above the stairway and through the gate, the Lord stood, waiting to receive Jacob into his kingdom, but first the stairway had to be climbed and the gate passed. . . . The temple is a stairway. We must climb it in order to reach our Father in Heaven. Everything in the Church funnels us toward the stairway and encourages us to climb. The climb will require effort, but even the effort is rewarding. The temple is also a gate. We must pass through it or forever remain outside the kingdom of God."[10]

"Just as God renewed the Abrahamic covenant with Jacob, those portions of the Abrahamic covenant 'which pertain to personal exaltation and eternal increase are renewed with each member of the House of Israel who enters the order of celestial marriage.'"[11] Given all of the associations to the endowment, it is likely that "Jacob received his endowment at Bethel" as part of the sacred experience recorded in

Genesis 28.¹² Following his sacred experience, Jacob arose "early in the morning" and took one of the stones he had slept on "and set it up for a pillar, and poured oil upon the top of it. And he called the name of that place Bethel," meaning gate of heaven. "And Jacob vowed a vow, saying, If God will be with me, and will keep me in this way that I go, and will give me bread to eat, and raiment to put on, So that I come again to my father's house in peace; then shall the Lord be my God: And this stone, which I have set for a pillar, shall be God's house: and of all that thou shalt give me *I will surely give the tenth* unto thee" (Genesis 28:18–22). Significantly, Jacob honors God's renewal of the Abrahamic covenant by covenanting to live the law of tithing, a key separator of those worthy to receive the ordinances of the temple.

Jacob Follows the Counsel and Example of His Parents, Marrying in the Covenant

Jacob's courtship with Rachel is one of the greatest love stories in scripture. When Jacob arrived at a well in a field in "the land of the people of the east," he inquired of those watering their sheep where they were from. When they responded "Haran," he asked if they knew "Laban the son of Nahor," to which they responded affirmatively and noted that at that very moment "Rachel his daughter cometh with . . . her father's sheep: for she kept them. And it came to pass, when Jacob saw Rachel the daughter of Laban his mother's brother [he] went near, and rolled the stone from the well's mouth, and watered the flock of Laban his mother's brother. And Jacob kissed Rachel, and lifted up his voice, and wept."

After Jacob introduced himself, Rachel "ran and told her father." He, in turn "ran to meet" Jacob "and embraced him, and kissed him, and brought him to his house." What a grand reunion! While their guest for the next month, it appears that Jacob had been helping with the "chores," because Laban said, "Because thou art my brother [close relative], shouldest thou therefore serve me for nought?" In other words, Laban was saying that it wouldn't be right for him to accept Jacob's free labor indefinitely. So he asked, "Tell me, what shall thy wages be?" By then, if not at first sight, Jacob had fallen head over heels for Rachel (or as ancient scribes describe it, "Jacob loved Rachel"), who was described as being "beautiful and well favoured" (compared to her older sister, Leah, who was described as "tender eyed").[13] He offered to serve Laban "seven years for Rachel thy younger daughter," which Laban accepted. The next verse 20 reads almost like a fairy tale. "And Jacob served seven years for Rachel; and they seemed unto him but a few days, for the love he had to her" (Genesis 29:1–2, 4–6, 9–20).

But, of course, there is the inevitable plot twist. The headnote to Genesis 29 states that "Laban gives to Jacob, first Leah, then Rachel in marriage." After the wedding and accompanying feast, Laban brought Leah (who probably is veiled as was customary at the time) to Jacob "in the evening" (obviously, when it is dark). Jacob "went in unto her," not realizing until morning that he had consummated his marriage with the wrong girl! After remonstrating that he had been cheated, Laban justified his deception, saying, "It must not be so done in this country, to give the younger before the first born" (v. 26). He then consented to give Rachel to Jacob in marriage *if* he served him another seven years. "And Jacob did so" (v. 28), the record states, no doubt gladly. Cleon Skousen estimates that Jacob at the time "was at least 64 years of age."[14] In addition to laboring for seven years, Jacob had worked almost a lifetime (by our reckoning) to marry the love of his life.

Jacob Again Communes with God upon His Return to "the Land of His Fathers"

Over the ensuring years, thirteen children came to Jacob and his four wives (he married the handmaidens of each of Leah and Rachel, Bilhah and Zilpah)—twelve sons, who become heads of the twelve tribes of Israel,[15] and a daughter, Dinah. The challenge of providing for such a large family was compounded greatly by the greedy and deceitful character of his father-in-law, which began with his betrayal in Jacob's marriage and continued throughout the possibly four or so decades[16] Jacob served his father-in-law. Jacob notes that throughout this time Laban "deceived me, and changed my wages ten times" (Genesis 31:7). But as promised, God was with Jacob, protecting and prospering him.[17] In fact, after Jacob was warned by God to flee from

Laban, who then pursued Jacob with an army of men, God warned Laban in a dream not to harm Jacob and, no doubt through God's influence, they were reconciled (see Genesis 31:24–55).

But Laban was not the only one who presented a mortal danger to Jacob and his family. Jacob was "greatly afraid and distressed" (Genesis 32:7) that Esau, his older twin brother, would make good on his vow to slay Jacob after Isaac died (Genesis 27:41–42). In this critical moment of Jacob's life, when he was almost one hundred years old[18] and had arrived home near a brook that emptied into the Jordan River,[19] Jacob was met by "the angels of God" or "God's host" (Genesis 32:1, 2), which in Hebrew means "God's camp" or army. "In this instance, the word reveals that Jacob must have seen a vast number of angels,"[20] reminiscent of when Elisha prayed for the Lord to open his servant's eyes and he saw the mountain full of horses and chariots of fire (2 Kings 6:17). Jacob sent servants in separate parties with dozens of animals as gifts to placate Esau, divided his family in groups so if one was attacked "then the other which is left may escape" (v. 8), and sent them across the brook. Now alone, Jacob poured out his heart all night to God. Expressing thanks—"I am not worthy of the least of all the mercies, *and of all the truth*, which thou hast shewed unto thy servant"—he prayed for deliverance "from the hand of Esau: for I fear him, lest he will come and smite me, and the mother with the children" (Genesis 32:10–11).

> **Genesis 32:9–11, 24–30**—And Jacob was left alone; and there wrestled a man with him until the breaking of the day. And when [the man] saw that he prevailed not against [Jacob], he touched the hollow of his thigh; and the hollow of Jacob's thigh was out of joint, as he wrestled with [the man]. And he said, Let me go, for the day breaketh. And he said, I will not let thee go, except thou bless me. And he said unto him, What is thy name? And [Jacob] said, Jacob. And [the man] said, Thy name shall be called no more Jacob, but Israel: for as a prince hast thou power with God and with men, and hast prevailed. And Jacob asked him, and said, Tell me, I pray thee, thy name. And [the man] said, Wherefore is it that thou dost ask after my name? And [the man] blessed [Jacob] there. [v. 29] And Jacob called the name

of the place Peniel: for I have seen God face to face, and my life is preserved [v. 30].

This capstone experience in Jacob's life serves as a living example of what it means to have the blessings of Abraham, Isaac, and Jacob sealed upon us in the new and everlasting covenant of marriage. As one commentator summarized, "While the wrestling between Jacob and this angel is represented as a physical struggle, this may be metaphorical for the exhaustive spiritual wrestlings that precede the greatest blessings from God."[21] Another commentator on this event quotes President Brigham Young, who said that "all of us are situated 'upon the same ground' [as Jacob], in that we must 'struggle, *wrestle*, and strive, until the Lord bursts the veil and suffers us to behold His glory, or a portion of it.'"[22] Jacob's struggle at the veil, so to speak, follows a familiar pattern to all regular temple-goers—Jacob is asked for his given name; he is given a new name; he then asks the angel, who represents God, "Tell me, I pray thee, thy name" (Genesis 32:29).

"Following this conversation, the record states that the angel blessed Jacob. It does not elaborate on the nature of this blessing. However, the next thing that Jacob says is, 'I have seen God face to face, and my life is preserved.' Indeed, this is an iceberg event. The most important part of the exchange is under the surface. Since Jacob received his endowment . . . earlier, it would seem that this experience is something more. It may well be that 'the event occurring between verses 29 and 30, though only implied, was no less than the ultimate theophany of Jacob's life—his being ushered into the presence of God to have every promise of past years sealed and confirmed upon him.'"[23] Thus, in the life of Jacob, as in the lives of his father Isaac and his grandfather Abraham, we have clear examples of what it looks like to receive the ultimate spiritual treasures of the temple.

Endnotes

1. For a discussion of possible meanings of this symbolic gesture, see Hardison, 147 and note 58.
2. Nelson, "The Everlasting Covenant."
3. "In Jewish tradition, it is said that the lentil stew Jacob cooked was meant for his father Isaac, who was mourning the death of his father Abraham (Jacob and Esau's grandfather). Lentils are a traditional mourner's meal for the Jews" (Tori Avey, "What the Ancient Israelites Ate—Jacob's Lentil Stew," April 19, 2022, https://toriavey.com/jacobs-lentil-stew-2/#:~:text=In%20Jewish%20tradition%2C%20it%20is,mourner's%20meal%20for%20the%20Jews).
4. As explained in the Primary lesson on this event, "The Lord knew that Jacob would be worthy of the birthright blessing from the beginning and had revealed this to Rebekah before the twins were born. (See Genesis 25:23.) Explain that when Isaac became aware that he had blessed Jacob instead of Esau, he could have revoked the blessing, but he did not. Isaac recognized that the blessing was right when he stated, 'And he shall be blessed' (Genesis 27:33)" ("Lesson 13: Jacob and Esau," *Primary 6: Old Testament* [Salt Lake City, Utah: The Church of Jesus Christ of Latter-day Saints 1996], 52–55, https://www.churchofjesuschrist.org/manual/primary-6-old-testament/lesson-13?lang=eng).

   Bruce Porter provides another perspective on Rebekah's actions based on her rights and responsibility as a matriarch—equal in importance to her husband's rights and responsibilities as the patriarch—in the new and everlasting covenant of marriage or the patriarchal priesthood. The "ancient patriarchal order consists of a husband and wife with equal power but divided responsibilities. The husband's duty was to administer the ordinances of salvation and exaltation to his family and posterity, setting apart a new patriarch for the extended family before his death. One of the wife's responsibilities in this order of the priesthood would be to present, or 'bear' physically, as well as spiritually her children to the patriarch for his acceptance, naming, and blessing." Notably the Lord spoke to Rebekah, not Isaac, about which of her sons would receive the birthright or priesthood (Genesis 25:23). Thus, when she understands that Isaac has asked Esau to bring "savoury meat" that Isaac may eat and bless his son before he dies, she knows that he is preparing for "a sacramental or ritual meal" with which she is familiar and for which she then prepares Jacob, whom the Lord has entrusted her to prepare, throughout his life, for that which the Lord revealed he should receive. Interestingly, the ritual involves Isaac asking Jacob, "'Who are thou, my son?' or 'what is your name?'" Jacob responds by giving the first or given name of the firstborn, Esau, "as a key word to legitimize the blessing" and perhaps other "signs of recognition" (which right Jacob purchased from Esau previously). When Isaac invites Jacob to "'come near' (vs. 21) so that he may 'feel' or touch Jacob" to assure himself that he is prepared for the ritual for which Rebekah has prepared him, he appears to be testing the birthright son. "Come near now, and kiss me, my son," Isaac asks (Genesis. 27:26). "While in this mutual and ritual embrace

Isaac surrenders to the signs he was looking for" and proceeds to utter the inspired birthright blessing, a blessing which in the next chapter "is expanded and explained as the familiar Abrahamic covenant" in connection with the impending marriage of Jacob "so that the rights/rites of this blessing might continue in the family lines."

Porter continues: "The involvement of Rebekah in the blessing of Jacob was one of decision and responsibility, not deception, and should not be ignored in an interpretive exegesis of male and female relationships in Genesis. Likewise we should not gloss over the involvement of the wives and mothers of patriarchs, prophets, and kings as recorded in ancient scripture. Only the mother can verify the father and lineage of the child. She alone may testify who her firstborn is, and to whom the birthright belongs. Thus by revelation, Rebekah knew which child should receive the birthright. She then prepared and presented that son for the endowed blessing from his father when the time had arrived. With this patriarchal authority and right that Rebekah held, Isaac could not rebel against his wife, the presented son, or the inspired blessing given under his hand. The ['matrilineal patriarchy'] pattern espoused here is a motif inherent in the patriarchal order of Genesis and can be seen elsewhere in Old Testament examples," including, he cites, the case of Egypt and her son, Pharaoh (Abraham 1:25–26); Moses and Pharaoh's daughter, who "had the right to present 'her son' (Exodus 2:10)" "as the heir to the throne" (see Hebrews 11:24); Sarai and Hagar; Judah and Tamar; and Moses and Zipporah ("Deception vs. Decision, Matriarchal Authority and Patriarchal Responsibility," https://www.bhporter.net/deception-vs-decision).

5. Bruce R. McConkie explained Rebekah's preoccupation this way: "When Jacob and Esau had grown to maturity, the greatest concern of their parents was the matter of whom they should marry. The record says that Esau 'took to wife Judith . . . and Bashemath . . . ; which were a grief of mind unto Isaac and to Rebekah.' (Genesis 26:34, 35.) What this means is that Esau married out of the Church. Esau did not enter the Lord's system of celestial marriage, and his marriage brought great sorrow to his parents" ("Lesson 7: Genesis 24–36," *Old Testament Instructor's Guide,* Religion 301–2, https://www.churchofjesuschrist.org/study/manual/old-testament-instructors-guide/genesis-24-36?lang=eng, quoting from Conference Report, Sydney Australia Area Conference 1976, 34–35).

6. Ibid. Significantly, President Nelson refers to this example of Rebekah's influence on Isaac and Jacob in support of the following statement about faithful women in the Church: "It would be impossible to measure the influence that such women have, not only on families but also on the Lord's Church, as wives, mothers, and grandmothers; as sisters and aunts; as teachers and leaders; and especially as exemplars and devout defenders of the faith" (Nelson, "A Plea to My Sisters," 96 and note 3).

7. Hardison, 169.

8. Ibid. note 20, quoting scholars who observes that Jacob's statement, "Surely the Lord is in this place," suggests that "Yaweh's immediate presence" was on the earth with Jacob "rather than in heaven at the top of the stairway." Alternatively,

it could mean that "Jacob had ascended the ladder and entered into the presence of the Lord." In either event, it is clear that Jacob is having the type of experience for which the endowment prepares us. As described on the Church's website, at the conclusion of the endowment, patrons "symbolically return to the Lord's presence as they enter the celestial room." See chapter 15 above.
9. Wilcox, *House of Glory*, 103–04.
10. Ibid.
11. Hardison, 170–71, quoting McConkie, *Mormon Doctrine*, 13.
12. Andrew C. Skinner, "Jacob in the Presence of God," *Sperry Symposium Classics: The Old Testament*, ed. Paul Y. Hoskisson (Provo and Salt Lake City, Utah: Religious Studies Center, Brigham Young University and Deseret Book), 117–32, https://rsc.byu.edu/sperry-symposium-classics-old-testament/jacob-presence-god.
13. "Some translations (such as NJPS, RSV, NEB, and REB), perhaps influenced by Jacob's preference for Rachel, render [tender eyed] as "dull-eyed" or "weak eyes," but the more appropriate translation is "soft eyes" (as in NRSV and NAB)—what we might call "cow eyes," Jewish Women's Archive, https://jwa.org/encyclopedia/article/leah-bible#:~:text=Leah%20and%20her%20sister%20Rachel,(Gen%2029%3A17).
14. Skousen, *Third Thousand Years*, 43, 54–56 and note 96.
15. In birth order, Reuben, Simeon, Levi, Judah, Dan, Naphtali, Gad, Asher, Issachar, Zebulon, Joseph, and Benjamin.
16. See Skousen, *Third Thousand Years*, 54.
17. See, for example, Genesis 31:7–13 (the Lord reveals to Jacob how he had multiplied his flocks and that He was "the God of Bethel" who had promised Jacob that He would be with him and keep him "in all places whither" he should go).
18. Skousen, *Third Thousand Years*, 54 note 96.
19. Genesis 32:22. The brook is located about halfway between the Sea of Galilee and the Dead Sea (Skousen, 58–59).
20. Hardison, 171.
21. Ibid. 172–73 (citations omitted).
22. Skinner, "Jacob in the Presence of God," quoting Brigham Young, in *Journal of Discourses*, 3:192 (London: Latter-day Saints' Book Depot, 1856) (emphasis in original). President Nelson refers to this important event in Jacob's life as an illustration of Jacob's willingness to "let God prevail" in his life, as we should let God prevail in our lives: "For a moment, let us recall a crucial turning point in the life of Jacob, the grandson of Abraham. At the place Jacob named *Peniel* (which means 'the face of God'), Jacob wrestled with a serious challenge. His agency was tested. Through this wrestle, Jacob proved what was most important to him. He demonstrated that he was willing to let God prevail in his life. In response, God changed Jacob's name to Israel, meaning 'let God prevail.' God then promised Israel that all the blessings that had been pronounced upon Abraham's head would also be his" (Nelson, "Let God Prevail," 92 [emphasis in original, footnotes omitted]).
23. Hardison, 171, quoting Skinner, "Jacob in the Presence of God," 146.

WORKS CITED

Resources Available on ChurchofJesusChrist.org and other Church Resources

Silvia H. Allred, "Holy Temples, Sacred Covenants," *Ensign*, November 2008, 112.

Neil L. Anderson, "We Talk of Christ," *Liahona*, November 2020, 88.

_____, "My Mind Caught Hold upon This Thought of Jesus Christ," *Liahona*, May 2023.

Richard D. Anthony, "I Was a Bishop before I Really Learned to Pray," *Ensign*, January 1976.

Brian K. Ashton "The Doctrine of Christ," *Ensign*, November 2016.

Marvin J. Ashton, "Know He Is There," *Ensign*, February 1994.

M. Russell Ballard, "God's Love for His Children," *Ensign*, May 1988, 57.

_____, "Men and Women and Priesthood Power," *Ensign*, September 2014.

_____, "Men and Women in the Work of the Lord," *New Era*, April 2014.

David A. Bednar, "And Nothing Shall Offend Them," *Ensign*, November 2006.

_____, "Ask in Faith," *Ensign*, May 2008, 94.

_____, "Honorably Hold a Name and Standing," *Ensign*, May 2009, 97.

_____, "In the Strength of the Lord," *Ensign*, October 2004.

_____, "Let This House Be Built Unto My Name," *Ensign*, May 2020, 84.

_____, "Meek and Lowly of Heart," *Ensign*, May 2018, 30.

———, "Missionary, Family History, and Temple Work," *Ensign*, November 2014.

———, "Pray Always," *Ensign*, November 2008, 41.

———, "Prepared to Obtain Every Needful Thing," *Ensign*, May 2019, 101.

———, "The Hearts of the Children Shall Turn," *Ensign*, November 2011, 24.

Ezra Taft Benson, "Because I Live, Ye Shall Live Also," *Ensign*, April 1993, 4.

———, "Life is Eternal," *Ensign*, June 1971, 32.

———, "To the Fathers in Israel," *Ensign*, November 1987.

———, "What Manner of Men Ought We to Be?" *Ensign*, November 1983.

Jean B. Bingham, "Women and Covenant Power," *Liahona*, January 2021.

Book of Mormon Student Manual, "Chapter 26: Alma 13–16," Salt Lake City, Utah: Seminaries and Institutes of Religion Curriculum Services, The Church of Jesus Christ of Latter-day Saints, 2009.

Book of Mormon Teacher Manual, "Chapter 26: Alma 13–16," Salt Lake City, Utah: Seminaries and Institutes of Religion Curriculum Services, The Church of Jesus Christ of Latter-day Saints, 2009.

Edward J. Brandt, "The Priesthood Ordinance of Sacrifice," *Ensign*, December 1973, 50–51.

Douglas A. Callister, "Our Heavenly Home," *Ensign*, June 2009.

Matthew L. Carpenter, "Wilt Thou Be Made Whole?" *Ensign*, November 2018.

D. Todd Christofferson, "Abide in My Love," *Ensign*, November 2016.

———, "The Power of Covenants," *Ensign*, May 2009, 19.

———, "The Sealing Power," *Liahona*, November 2023.

———, "When Thou Art Converted," *Ensign*, May 2004, 11.

Umberto Controzorzi, "The Word of Wisdom Changed My Life," *Liahona*, October 1983.

Gene R. Cook, "Receiving Divine Assistance through the Grace of the Lord," *Ensign*, May 1993.

Quentin L. Cook, "Great Love for Our Father's Children," *Ensign*, May 2019, 76.

———, "Safely Gathered Home," *Liahona*, May 2023.

Elaine Dalton, "Stay on the Path," *Ensign*, May 2007, 11.

Benjamín De Hoyos, "The Work of the Temple and Family History—One and the Same Work," *Liahona*, May 2023, 52.

Daughters in My Kingdom: The History and Work of Relief Society. Salt Lake City, Utah: The Church of Jesus Christ of Latter-day Saints, 2017.

Doctrine and Covenants and Church History: Gospel Doctrine Teacher's Manual "Lesson 14: The Law of Consecration." Salt Lake City, Utah: The Church of Jesus Christ of Latter-day Saints, 1999.

Doctrine and Covenants Teacher Manual—Religion 324 and 325, "Lesson 31: Doctrine and Covenants 84"; "Lesson 34: Doctrine and Covenants 88:70–141"; "Lesson 39: Doctrine and Covenants 101"; "Lesson 47: Doctrine and Covenants 121:11–46." Salt Lake City, Utah: Seminaries and Institutes of Religion Curriculum Services The Church of Jesus Christ of Latter-day Saints, 2017.

Doctrine and Covenants Student Manual—Religion 324–325, "The Law of Consecration and Stewardship—L-7 The History of Consecration"; "Section 124, A Solemn Proclamation: The Priesthood Order is Established"; "Chapter 50: Doctrine and Covenants 129–30"; "Chapter 51: Doctrine and Covenants 131; 132:1–33." Salt Lake City, Utah: Seminaries and Institutes of Religion Curriculum Services, The Church of Jesus Christ of Latter-day Saints, 2018.

Endowed from on High—Temple Preparation Seminar, Teacher's Manual. Salt Lake City: The Church of Jesus Christ of Latter-day Saints, 2003.

Eternal Marriage Student Manual; Preparing for an Eternal Marriage—Religion 234; Building an Eternal Marriage, Religion 235, "Holy Spirit of Promise"; "Marriage for Eternity." Salt Lake City, Utah: Church Educational System of The Church of Jesus Christ of Latter-day Saints, 2003.

Henry B. Eyring, "Faith and the Oath and Covenant of the Priesthood," *Ensign*, May 2008.

———, "Hearts Bound Together," *Ensign*, May 2005, 77.

———, "Steady in the Storms," *Liahona*, May 2022, 27.

Families and Temples, https://www.churchofjesuschrist.org/study/manual/families-and-temples/what-is-the-temple-sealing?lang=eng, located in Gospel Library under "Handbooks and Callings"—"Mission Callings"—"Teaching Pamphlets."

James E. Faust, "Eternity Lies before Us," *Ensign*, May 1997.

———, "A Royal Priesthood," *Ensign*, May 2006, 51.

———, "The Restoration of All Things," *Ensign*, May 2006.

Joel A. Flake, "Gospel of Abraham," *Encyclopedia of Mormonism*, https://eom.byu.edu/index.php/Gospel_of_Abraham.

For the Strength of Youth: A Guide for Making Choices. Salt Lake City, Utah: The Church of Jesus Christ of Latter-day Saints, 2022, https://www.churchofjesuschrist.org/study/manual/for-the-strength-of-youth/02-choices?lang=eng.

General Handbook: Serving in The Church of Jesus Christ of Latter-day Saints. Salt Lake City: The Church of Jesus Christ of Latter-day Saints, 2022.

Gerrit W. Gong, "Happy and Forever," *Liahona*, November 2022.

———, "Room in the Inn," *Liahona*, May 2021.

Gospel Principles, "Chapter 39: The Law of Chastity." Salt Lake City, Utah: The Church of Jesus Christ of Latter-day Saints, 2011.

David B. Haight, "Personal Temple Worship," *Ensign*, May 1993, 23.

Robert D. Hales, "Making Righteous Choices at the Crossroads of Life," *Ensign*, November 1988, 9.

Gordon B. Hinckley, *Teachings of Gordon B. Hinckley*. Salt Lake City, Utah: The Church of Jesus Christ of Latter-day Saints, 1997.

Howard W. Hunter, "Christ, Our Passover," *Ensign*, May 1985, 17.

———, "Chapter 9: The Law of Tithing." *Teachings of Presidents of the Church: Howard W. Hunter*, The Church of Jesus Christ of Latter-day Saints, Salt Lake City, Utah, 2015, 134–35.

"If my parents were sealed in the temple and then got divorced, which one am I sealed to?" *New Era*, August 2015, https://www.churchofjesuschrist.org/

study/new-era/2015/08/to-the-point/if-my-parents-were-sealed-in-the-temple-and-then-got-divorced-which-one-am-i-sealed-to?lang=eng.

Introduction to Family History Student Manual—Religion 261, "Chapter 2: The Mission of Elijah"; "The Spirit World and the Redemption of the Dead," 9.2.2. Salt Lake City, Utah: Seminaries and Institutes of Religion Curriculum The Church of Jesus Christ of Latter-day Saints, 2012.

Jesus Christ and the Everlasting Gospel Teacher Manual, "Lesson 5— Jesus Christ Was Jehovah of the Old Testament." Salt Lake City, Utah: Seminaries and Institutes of Religion Curriculum Services, The Church of Jesus Christ of Latter-day Saints, 2016.

Marianne Dahl Johnson, "The Windows of Heaven," *Ensign*, September 2005.

Joy D. Jones, "An Especially Noble Calling," *Ensign*, May 2020.

_____, "Value Beyond Measure," *Ensign*, 2017.

L. Lionel Kendrick, "Enhancing Our Temple Experience," *Ensign*, May 2001, 78.

Spencer W. Kimball, "Our Great Potential," *Ensign*, May 1977, 49.

_____, "Privileges and Responsibilities of Sisters," *Ensign*, November 1978.

_____, "The Blessings and Responsibilities of Womanhood," *Ensign*, March 1976.

Cree-L Kofford, "Marriage in the Lord's Way, Part One," *Ensign*, June 1998.

Larry R. Lawrence, "What Lack I Yet?" *Ensign*, November 2015.

Bruce R. McConkie, "Christ and the Creation," *Ensign*, June 1982.

_____, "Obedience, Sacrifice and Consecration," *Ensign*, May 1975.

Robert L. Millett, "The Man Adam," *Ensign*, January 1994.

Thomas S. Monson, "Obedience Brings Blessings," *Ensign*, May 2013.

_____, "The Holy Temple—a Beacon to the World," *Ensign*, May 2011.

Dale C. Mouritsen, "The Spirit World, Our Next Home," *Ensign*, January 1977.

Marcus B. Nash, "The New and Everlasting Covenant," *Ensign*, December 2015.

Russell M. Nelson, "A New Normal," *Ensign*, November 2020, 118.

———, "A Plea to My Sisters," *Ensign*, November 2015, 95.

———, "Becoming Exemplary Latter-Day Saints," *Ensign*, November 2018, 113.

———, "Children of the Covenant," *Ensign*, May 1995.

———, "Choices for Eternity," Worldwide Devotional for Young Adults with President Nelson—May 2022," https://www.churchofjesuschrist.org/study/broadcasts/worldwide-devotional-for-young-adults/2022/05/12nelson?lang=eng.

———, "Christ Is Risen; Faith in Him Will Move Mountains," *Liahona*, May 2021.

———, "Closing Remarks," *Ensign*, May 219.

———, "Closing Remarks," *Ensign*, November 2019.

———, "Constancy Amid Change," *Ensign*, November 1993.

———, "Come Follow Me," *Ensign*, May 2019, 88.

———, "Covenants," *Ensign*, May 2011.

———, "Divine Love," *Ensign*, February 2003, 24.

———, "Drawing the Power of Jesus Christ into Our Lives," *Ensign*, May 2017, 39.

———, "Embrace the Future with Faith," *Ensign*, November 2020, 73.

———, "Focus on the Temple," *Liahona*, November 2022, 121.

———, "Go Forward in Faith," *Ensign*, May 2020.

———, "Hear Him," *Ensign*, May 2020, 88.

———, *Heart of the Matter: What 100 Years of Living Have Taught Me.* Salt Lake City: Deseret Book, 2023.

———, "Hope of Israel," Worldwide Youth Devotional, June 3, 2018, HopeofIsrael.lds.org.

———, "Jesus Christ Is Our Savior," *Liahona*, April 2023.

———, "Lessons from Eve," *Ensign*, November 1987, 86.

———, "Lessons from the Lord's Prayers," *Ensign*, May 2009, 46.

———, "Let God Prevail," *Ensign*, November 2020.

———, "Make Time for the Lord," *Liahona*, November 2021.

———, "Ministering with the Power and Authority of God," *Ensign*, May 2018.

———, "Moving Forward," *Ensign*, November 2020.

———, "Now Is the Time," *Liahona*, May 2022.

———, "Opening the Heavens for Help," *Ensign*, May 2020.

———, "Overcome the World and Find Rest," *Liahona*, November 2022, 95.

———, "Personal Preparation for Temple Blessings," *Ensign*, May 2001, 32.

———, "Prophets, Leadership, and Divine Law," Worldwide devotional for Young Adults, Jan. 8, 2017, https://www.churchofjesuschrist.org/church/events/january-2017–worldwide-devotional-for-young-adults?lang=eng.

———, "Peacemakers Needed," *Liahona*, May 2023.

———, "Prepare for Blessings of the Temple," *Ensign*, March 2002.

———, "Sisters' Participation in the Gathering of Israel," *Ensign*, November 2018.

———, "Spiritual Treasures," *Ensign*, November 2019, 76.

———, "Sweet Power of Prayer," *Ensign*, May 2003, 7.

———, "The Answer Is Always Jesus Christ," *Ensign*, May 2023, 127.

———, "The Atonement," *Ensign*, November 1996, 33.

———, "The Correct Name of the Church," *Ensign*, November 2018.

———, "The Creation," *Ensign*, May 2000.

———, "The Everlasting Covenant," *Liahona*, October 2022, 4.

———, "The Exodus Repeated," *Ensign*, April 2002.

———, "The Future of the Church: Preparing the World for the Savior's Second Coming," *Liahona*, April 2020, 9.

———, "The Gathering of Scattered Israel," *Ensign*, November 2006.

———, "The Power of Spiritual Momentum," *Liahona*, May 2022.

———, *Teachings of Russell M. Nelson*. Salt Lake City, Utah: Deseret Book, 2018.

———, "The Temple and Your Spiritual Foundation," *Liahona*, November 2021, 93.

———, "Think Celestial!" *Liahona*, November 2023.

———, "We Can Do Better and Be Better," *Ensign*, May 2019, 67.

———, "What We Are Learning and Will Never Forget," *Ensign*, May 2021, 78.

New Testament Student Manual, "Chapter 6: Matthew 16–18"; "Chapter 51: 1 Peter and 2 Peter," Salt Lake City, Utah: Seminaries and Institutes of Religion Curriculum The Church of Jesus Christ of Latter-day Saints, 2018,

Dallin H. Oaks, "Divorce," *Ensign*, May 2007.

———, "Kingdoms of Glory," *Liahona*, November 2023.

———, "Priesthood Authority in the Family and the Church," *Ensign*, November 2005.

———, "Taking upon Us the Name of Jesus Christ," *Ensign*, May 1985, 80.

———, "The Blessing of Commandments," BYU Speeches, https://speeches.byu.edu/talks/dallin-h-oaks/blessing-commandments/.

———, "The Great Plan," *Ensign*, May 2020.

———, "The Great Plan of Happiness," *Ensign*, November 1993, 72.

———, "The Keys and Authority of the Priesthood," *Ensign*, May 2014.

———, "Trust in the Lord," *Ensign*, November 2019, 26.

———, "Truth and the Plan," *Ensign*, November 2018.

Old Testament Instructor's Guide, Religion 301–2, "Lesson 7: Genesis 24–36"; "Exodus 25–30; 31:1–11; 35–40." Salt Lake City, Utah: Church Educational System, The Church of Jesus Christ of Latter-day Saints, 1982.

Old Testament Student Manual Genesis-2 Samuel—Religion 301, "Genesis 18–23: Abraham—A Model of Faith and Righteousness"; "Exodus 1–10"; "Exodus 11–19: The Passover and the Exodus"; "Exodus 21–24; 31–35: The Mosaic Law: A Preparatory Gospel"; "Exodus 21–24; 31–35: The Mosaic Law: A Preparatory Gospel," "Exodus 25–30; 35–40: The House of the Lord in the Wilderness," "Numbers 1–12 and Enrichment Section E: The Problem of Large Numbers in the Old Testament," "Numbers 13–36: Wilderness Wanderings, Part 2"; "Leviticus 1–10: A Law of Performances and Ordinances, Part 1: Sacrifices and Offerings," "Leviticus 1–16" "Leviticus 11–18: A Law of Performances and Ordinances, Part 2: The Clean and the Unclean." Salt Lake City, Utah: Church Educational System, The Church of Jesus Christ of Latter-day Saints, 2003.

Old Testament Student Manual-Kings-Malachi—Religion 302, "Solomon: Man of Wisdom, Man of Foolishness: 1 Kings 1–11"; "The Last Days and the Millennium: Isaiah 55–66"; "Prophecies of the Restoration: Ezekiel 25–48." Salt Lake City, Utah: Church Educational System, The Church of Jesus Christ of Latter-day Saints, 2003.

Old Testament Student Study Guide, "Exodus 3: The Burning Bush." Salt Lake City, Utah: Church Educational System, The Church of Jesus Christ of Latter-day Saints, 2002.

Old Testament Teacher Resource Manual, "Leviticus 1–16." Salt Lake City, Utah: Church Educational System, The Church of Jesus Christ of Latter-day Saints, 2003, 90.

Our Heritage: A Brief History of The Church of Jesus Christ of Latter-day Saints, Chapter 9, "The Expanding Church." Salt Lake City, Utah: The Church of Jesus Christ of Latter-day Saints, 1996, 109.

Boyd K. Packer, "Atonement, Agency and Accountability," *Ensign,* May 1988, 69.

_____, "Covenants," *Ensign,* May 1987, 24.

_____, "Inspiring Music—Worthy Thoughts," *Ensign,* November 1973, 28.

_____, "Our Moral Environment," *Ensign,* May 1992, 66.

_____, "These Things I Know," *Ensign,* May 2013, 5.

_____, "Preparing to Enter the Holy Temple," *Ensign,* November 2010, 28.

Dennis R. Peterson, "To Love the Things God Loves," *Ensign,* March 1981.

Paul B. Pieper, "Revealed Realities of Mortality," *Ensign*, January 2016.

Preach My Gospel: A Guide to Sharing the Gospel of Jesus Christ. Salt Lake City, Utah: The Church of Jesus Christ of Latter-day Saints, 2023.

Preparing to Enter the Holy Temple, adapted from Boyd K. Packer, *The Holy Temple*. Salt Lake City, Utah: The Church of Jesus Christ of Latter-day Saints, 2002.

Primary 6: Old Testament, "Lesson 13: Jacob and Esau." Salt Lake City, Utah: The Church of Jesus Christ of Latter-day Saints, 1996, 52–55.

Dale G. Renlund, "Accessing God's Power through Covenants," *Liahona*, May 2023.

———, "A Framework for Personal Revelation," *Liahona*, November 2022.

———, "Choose You This Day," *Ensign*, November 2018.

Matthew O. Richardson, "Three Principles of Marriage," *Ensign*, April 2005.

Marion G. Romney, "Church Welfare Services' Basic Principles," *Ensign*, May 1976, 120–23.

———, "Living the Principles of the Law of Consecration," *Ensign*, February 1979.

———, "The Oath and Covenant Which Belongeth to the Priesthood," *Ensign*, November 1980.

Saints: The Story of the Church of Jesus Christ in the Latter Days, vol. 1, *The Standard of Truth, 1815–1846* & vol. 2, *No Unhallowed Hand—1846–1893*. Salt Lake City, Utah: The Church of Jesus Christ of Latter-day Saints, 2018 and 2020, respectively.

Jonathan S. Schmitt, "That They Might Know Thee," *Liahona*, November 2022.

Evan A. Schmutz, "Trusting the Doctrine of Christ," *Ensign*, May 2021, 48.

Joseph Fielding Smith, "Joseph Smith's First Prayer," *Improvement Era*, June 1960, 402.

Ulisses Soares, "In Partnership with the Lord," *Liahona*, November 2022, 42.

Dr. Sidney B. Sperry, "Ancient Temples and Their Functions," *Ensign*, January 1972.

Vern P. Stanfill, "The Imperfect Harvest," *Liahona*, May 2023.

Works Cited

James E. Talmage, *The House of the Lord: A Study of Holy Sanctuaries Ancient and Modern*. Salt Lake City, Utah: The Church of Jesus Christ of Latter-day Saints, 1912.

N. Eldon Tanner, "The Administration of the Church," *Ensign*, November 1979.

Teachings of the Living Prophets Student Manual—Religion 333, "Chapter 4: The Quorum of the First Presidency." Salt Lake City, Utah: Seminaries and Institutes of Religion Curriculum, The Church of Jesus Christ of Latter-day Saints, 2010.

Teachings of Presidents of the Church: Joseph Smith. Salt Lake City, Utah: The Church of Jesus Christ of Latter-day Saints, 2007.

Teachings of Presidents of the Church: Joseph Fielding Smith,. Salt Lake City, Utah: The Church of Jesus Christ of Latter-day Saints, 2013.

The Eternal Family Teacher Manual—Religion 200, "Lesson 12—Temple Ordinances and Covenants." Salt Lake City, Utah: The Church of Jesus Christ of Latter-day Saints, 2016.

"The Living Christ: The Testimony of the Apostles," https://www.churchofjesuschrist.org/study/scriptures/the-living-christ-the-testimony-of-the-apostles/the-living-christ-the-testimony-of-the-apostles?lang=eng#p2.

"The Family: A Proclamation to the World," The First Presidency and Council of the Twelve Apostles of The Church of Jesus Christ of Latter-day Saints, https://www.churchofjesuschrist.org/study/scriptures/the-family-a-proclamation-to-the-world/the-family-a-proclamation-to-the-world?lang=eng.

The Gospel and the Productive Life Student Manual—Religion 150, "Chapter 7: Recognizing and Developing Talents and Abilities." Salt Lake City, Utah: Church Educational System, The Church of Jesus Christ of Latter-day Saints, 2004.

The Pearl of Great Price Student Manual, "Moses 1:1–11: God Revealed Himself to Moses." Salt Lake City, Utah: Seminaries and Institutes of Religion Curriculum Services, The Church of Jesus Christ of Latter-day Saints, 2017.

"Translation and Historicity of the Book of Abraham," Gospel Topics Essays, https://www.churchofjesuschrist.org/study/manual/gospel-topics-essays/translation-and-historicity-of-the-book-of-abraham?lang=eng under "Books and Lessons"—"Church History" in the Gospel Library app.

True to the Faith, "Repentance." Salt Lake City, Utah: The Church of Jesus Christ of Latter-day Saints, 2004, 132.

Dieter F. Uchtdorf, "Jesus Christ Is the Strength of Youth," *Liahona,* November 2022.

Orson F. Whitney, "Gospel Classics: The Divinity of Jesus Christ," *Ensign,* December 2003.

Bradley R. Wilcox, "Worthiness Is Not Flawlessness," *Liahona,* November 2022.

Other Resources

Kenneth L. Alford, "'I Will Send You Elijah the Prophet,'" in *You Shall Have My Word: Exploring the Text of the Doctrine and Covenants*, Scott C. Esplin, Richard O. Cowan, and Rachel Cope, eds. Provo, Utah: Brigham Young University Religious Studies Center, 2012, 34.

Karl Ricks Anderson, *The Savior in Kirtland*. Salt Lake City, Utah: Deseret Book, 2012.

Nelson Baker, *The Process of Atonement*, 2016 (self-published).

Richard E. Bennett, *Temple Rising: A Heritage of Sacrifice*. Salt Lake City, Utah: Deseret Book, 2019.

Christopher Kimball Bigelow, *Temples of the Church of Jesus Christ of Latter-Day Saints*. San Diego, California: Thunder Bay Press, 2108.

Jeffrey M. Bradshaw, "An Old Testament KnoWhy—Gospel Doctrine Lesson 13: Bondage, Passover, and Exodus (Exodus 1–3; 5–6; 11–14)," The Interpreter Foundation, April 4, 2018, https://interpreterfoundation.org/knowhy-otl13b-what-can-we-learn-about-the-historical-exodus-from-outside-the-scriptures/.

Matthew B. Brown, *The Gate of Heaven: Insights on the Doctrine and Symbols of the Temple*. American Fork, Utah: Covenant Communications, Inc., 1999.

Melinda Wheelwright Brown, *Eve and Adam: Discovering the Beautiful Balance*. Salt Lake City, Utah: Deseret Book, 2020.

Beverly Campbell, *Eve and the Choice Made in Eden*. Salt Lake City, Utah: Bookcraft, 2003.

D. Cecil Clark, "New and Everlasting Covenant," *Encyclopedia of Mormonism*, https://eom.byu.edu/index.php/New_and_Everlasting_Covenant.

Spencer J. Condie, *Russell M. Nelson: Father, Surgeon, Apostle*. Salt Lake City, Utah: Deseret Book, 2003.

Richard O. Cowan, *Temples Dot the Earth*, Cove Fort, 1997.

Sheri Dew, *Insights from a Prophet's Life: Russell M. Nelson*. Salt Lake City, Utah: Deseret Book, 2019.

Richard G. Ellsworth and Melvin J. Luthy, "Priesthood," in *Latter-day Saint Essentials: Readings from the Encyclopedia of Mormonism*. John W. Welch and R. Devan Jensen, eds. Provo, Utah: BYU Studies and the Religious Studies Center, 2002, https://rsc.byu.edu/latter-day-saint-essentials/priesthood#:~:text=Fulness%20of%20the%20priesthood%2C%20which,132%3A18%E2%80%9319.

Ronald K. Esplin, "Joseph, Brigham and the Twelve: A Succession of Continuity," *Brigham Young University Studies*, 21 no. 3, 301–342, file:///C:/Users/Owner/Downloads/21.3esplinjoseph-4272ddbf-638d-4ba2-a06b-180a8d152e98.pdf.

Alonzo L. Gaskill, *Sacred Symbols: Finding Meaning in Rites, Rituals, & Ordinances*. Springville, Utah: Bonneville Books, 2011.

———, *Temple Reflections: Insights into the House of the Lord*. Springville, Utah: CFI, 2016.

Kim Gibbs, *Understanding the Sacred Symbolism of Temple Clothing*. American Fork, Utah: Covenant Communications, Inc., 2019.

Fiona and Terryl Givens, *All Things New: Rethinking Sin, Salvation, and Everything in Between*. Meridian, Idaho: Faith Matters Publishing, 2020.

Mark H. Green, III, *The Scriptural Temple*. Bountiful, Utah: Horizon Publishers & Distributors, Inc., 2000.

Alma E. Gygi, "Is it possible that Shem and Melchizedek are the same person?" *Ensign*, November 1973.

Bruce C. and Marie K. Hafen, *Contrite Spirit: How the Temple Helps Us Apply Christ's Atonement*. Salt Lake City: Deseret Book, 2016.

Gerald E. Hansen Jr., *Sacred Walls: Learning from Temple Symbols*. American Fork, Utah: Covenant Communications, Inc., 2009.

Amy Hardison, *Understanding the Symbols, Covenants and Ordinances of the Temple*. American Fork, Utah: Covenant Communications, Inc., 2016.

Steven C. Harper, "Historical Context and Background of D&C 131," Scripture Central, http://doctrineandcovenantscentral.org/historical-context/dc-131/.

Heart Turned to the Fathers, ed. James B. Allen, Jessie L. Embry, Kathleen B. Mehr. Provo, Utah: BYU Studies, 1995.

Joseph Heinerman, *Temple Manifestations*. Salt Lake City, Utah: Joseph Lyon and Associates, Inc., 1974.

Works Cited

Jeffrey R. Holland, *Christ and the New Covenant*. Salt Lake City, Utah: Deseret Book, 1997.

Daniel K. Judd, "The Fortunate Fall of Adam and Eve," in *No Weapon Shall Prosper: New Light on Sensitive Issues*, Robert L. Millett, ed., BYU Religious Studies Center, 2011, https://rsc.byu.edu/no-weapon-shall-prosper/fortunate-fall-adam-eve.

David J. Larsen, "Ascending into the Hill of the Lord: What the Psalms Can Tell Us About the Rituals of the First Temple," *Interpreter: A Journal of Latter-Day Saint Faith and Scholarship*, https://journal.interpreterfoundation.org/ascending-into-the-hill-of-the-lord-what-the-psalms-can-tell-us-about-the-rituals-of-the-first-temple/.

Steve Law, "Ancient Pilgrim's Road Up the Temple Mount Uncovered," *Patterns of Evidence*, August 16, 2019, https://www.patternsofevidence.com/2019/08/16/ancient-pilgrims-road-up-the-temple-mount-uncovered/; https://www.generationword.com/jerusalem101/47-southern-temple-wall.html.

N. B. Lundwall, *Temples of the Most High*. Salt Lake City, Utah: Press of Zion's Printing & Publishing Company, 1944.

Jennifer Ann Mackley, *Wilford Woodruff's Witness: The Development of Temple Doctrine*. Seattle, Washington: High Desert Publishing, 2018.

Truman G. Madsen, *The Temple: Where Heaven Meets Earth*. Salt Lake City, Utah: Deseret Book, 2008.

Truman G. Madsen, ed., *The Temple in Antiquity: Ancient Records and Modern Perspectives*. Provo, Utah: Religious Studies Center, 1984.

Bruce R. McConkie, *Doctrinal New Testament Commentary*, 3 vols. Salt Lake City, Utah: Bookcraft, 1965–74.

———, "Eve and the Fall," in *Woman*. Salt Lake City, Utah: Deseret Book, 1979, 57–68.

———, *Mormon Doctrine*. Salt Lake City, Utah: Bookcraft, 1966.

———, *The Mortal Messiah: From Bethlehem to Calvary*, 4 vols. Salt Lake City: Deseret Book, 1979–81.

———, *The Promised Messiah: The First Coming of Christ*. Salt Lake City: Deseret Book, 1978.

———, *Millennial Messiah: The Second Coming of the Son of Man*. Salt Lake City, Utah: Deseret Book, 1982.

Byron R. Merrill, *Elijah: Yesterday, Today, and Tomorrow*. Salt Lake City, Utah: Bookcraft, 1997.

Dwight E. Monson, *Understanding the LDS Temple*. M&M Global, LLC, 2014.

Kerry Muhlestein, *Let's Talk About the Book of Abraham*. Salt Lake City, Utah: Deseret Book, 2022.

———, *Finding Promised Blessings on the Covenant Path*. American Fork, Utah: Covenant Communications, Inc., 2023.

Lee Nelson, *Beyond the Veil*, vol. 1. Orem, Utah: Cedar Fort, Inc., 1988.

Russell M. Nelson, *Teachings of Russell M. Nelson*. Salt Lake City, Utah: Deseret Book, 2018.

Hugh W. Nibley, *Temple and Cosmos: Beyond This Ignorant Present*, ed. Don E. Norton, *The Collected Works of Hugh Nibley*, vol. 12. Salt Lake City, Utah: Deseret Book, 1992.

Monte S. Nyman, "The Covenant of Abraham," BYU Religious Studies Center, note 1, https://rsc.byu.edu/pearl-great-price-revelations-god/covenant-abraham#_edn1.

Boyd K. Packer, *The Holy Temple*. Salt Lake City, Utah: Bookcraft, Inc., 1980.

———, "The Holy Temple," *Ensign*, October 2010.

———, "A House of Glory," in *Temples of the Ancient World: Ritual and Symbolism*, ed. Donald W. Parry, Salt Lake City: Deseret Book and FARMS, 1994, 29, https://www.ldsscriptureteachings.org/staging/4108/wp-content/uploads/2019/10/Temples-of-the-Ancient-World-Ritual-and-Symbolism-Parry-full-text.pdf.

Donald W. Parry, *175 Temple Symbols and Their Meanings*. Salt Lake City, Utah: Deseret Book, 2020.

———, ed., *Temple of the Ancient World: Ritual and Symbolism*. Salt Lake City, Utah: Deseret Book, 1994.

Donald W. Parry and Jay A. Parry, *Understanding the Signs of the Times*. Salt Lake City, Utah: Deseret Book, 1999.

Daniel C. Peterson, "De Profundis," *Interpreter: A Journal of Latter-Day Saint Faith and Scholarship*, https://journal.interpreterfoundation.org/de-profundis/.

———, "The Temple as a Place of Ascent to God," https://www.fairlatterdaysaints.org/conference/august-2009/the-temple-as-a-place-of-ascent-to-god.

Mark E. Peterson, *Moses: Man of Miracles*. Salt Lake City, Utah: Deseret Book, 1977.

Ed J. Pinegar, *The Temple: Gaining Knowledge and Power in the House of the Lord*. American Fork, Utah: Covenant Communications, Inc., 2014.

Bruce D. Porter, *Endowed with Power: The Purpose of Creation Accounts*, 2018 (self-published).

Mary Richards, "Elder Dale G. Renlund testifies of Christ and says 'You can know it, too,'" *Church News*, December 5, 2021, https://www.thechurchnews.com/leaders-and-ministry/2021-12-05/elder-renlund-first-presidency-christmas-devotional-you-can-know-it-too-235464.

Chaim Richman, *A House of Prayer for All Nations: The Holy Temple of Jerusalem*. Carta, Jerusalem: The Temple Institute, 1997.

David J. Ridges, *Temples—Sacred Symbolism, Eternal Blessings*. Springville, Utah: CFI, 2019.

Mark A. Shields, *Your Endowment*. Springville, Utah: CFI, 2018.

Andrew C. Skinner, "Jacob in the Presence of God," *Sperry Symposium Classics: The Old Testament*, ed. Paul Y. Hoskisson. Provo and Salt Lake City, Utah: Religious Studies Center, Brigham Young University and Deseret Book, 117–32, https://rsc.byu.edu/sperry-symposium-classics-old-testament/jacob-presence-god.

———, *Prophets, Priests, and Kings*. Salt Lake City, Utah: Deseret Book, 2005.

———, *Temple Worship: 20 Truths That Will Bless Your Life*. Salt Lake City, Utah: Deseret Book, 2007.

Eric N. Skousen, *Earth in the Beginning*. Orem, Utah: Verity Publishing, 1996.

W. Cleon Skousen, *The First 2,000 Years*. Salt Lake City: Bookcraft, 1953.

———, *The Third Thousand Years*. Salt Lake City: Bookcraft, 1964.

Joseph Smith, *Teachings of the Prophet Joseph Smith*. Joseph Fielding Smith, ed., The Deseret News Press, 1946.

Joseph Fielding Smith, *Doctrines of Salvation*, 3 vols., compiled by Bruce R. McConkie. Salt Lake City: Bookcraft, 1954–56.

———, *Elijah the Prophet and His Mission*, a discourse delivered at the Salt Lake Assembly Hall and originally printed in *Utah Genealogical and Historical Magazine* 12, no. 1, January 1921, reprinted in the *Instructor*, December 1951 and January 1952.

Stephen O. Smoot, "'In the Land of the Chaldeans'—The Search for Abraham's Homeland Revisited," *BYU Studies*, https://byustudies.byu.edu/article/in-the-land-of-the-chaldeans-the-search-for-abrahams-homeland-revisited/ (accessed February 8, 2022).

Anthony Sweat, *The Holy Covenants: Living Our Sacred Temple Promises*. Salt Lake City: Deseret Book, 2022.

———, *The Holy Invitation: Understanding Your Sacred Temple Endowment*. Salt Lake City: Deseret Book, 2017.

James E. Talmage, *Jesus the Christ: A Study of the Messiah and His Mission according to Holy Scriptures both Ancient and Modern*. Salt Lake City, Utah: Deseret Book, 2006.

The Lectures on Faith in Historical Perspective, Larry E. Dahl and Charles D. Tate, Jr., eds. Provo, Utah: Religious Studies Center, Brigham Young University, 1990.

The Words of Joseph Smith: The Contemporary Accounts of the Nauvoo Discourses of the Prophet Joseph, "5 October 1840 (Monday Morning)," Andrew F. Ehat and Lyndon W. Cook, eds., https://rsc.byu.edu/words-joseph-smith/5–october-1840–monday-morning.

M. Catherine Thomas, "The Brother of Jared at the Veil," in *Temples of the Ancient World: Ritual and Symbolism*, ed. Donald W. Parry. Salt Lake City, Utah: Deseret Book and FARMS, 1994, 388, www.ldsscriptureteachings.org/staging/4108/wp-content/uploads/2019/10/Temples-of-the-Ancient-World-Ritual-and-Symbolism-Parry-full-text.pdf.

Brent L. Top, *What's on the Other Side? What the Gospel Teaches Us about the Spirit World*. Salt Lake City, Utah: Deseret Book, 2012.

———, "What's on the Other Side? A Conversation with Brent L. Top on the Spirit World," *Religious Educator*, vol. 14, no. 2, 2013, 48, https://scholarsarchive.byu.edu/cgi/viewcontent.cgi?article=1623&context=re.

Clark D. Webb, "Mysteries of God," *Encyclopedia of Mormonism*, https://eom.byu.edu/index.php/Mysteries_of_God.

Brent L. & Wendy C. Top, *Glimpses Beyond Death's Door*. American Fork, Utah: Covenant Communications, 2012.

Rodney Turner, *This Eternal Earth: A Scriptural and Prophetic Biography*. Orem, Utah: Granite Publishing and Distribution, Second Edition 2000.

Wendy Ulrich, *The Temple Experience: Passage to Healing and Holiness*. Springville, Utah: CFI An Imprint of Cedar Fort, Inc., 2017.

M. Richard and Kathleen H. Walker, *House of Learning: Getting More from Your Temple Experience*. Salt Lake City, Utah: Deseret Book, 2010.

Sara Jane Weaver, "President Nelson at Mission Leadership Seminar: How to receive divine tutoring like the Prophet Joseph Smith," *Church News*, June 21, 2020, https://www.thechurchnews.com/leaders-and-ministry/2020-06-27/president-nelson-mission-leadership-seminar-joseph-smith-187832.

John W. Welch, *Illuminating the Sermon at the Temple & the Sermon on the Mount: An Approach to 3 Nephi 11–18 and Matthew 5–7*. Provo, Utah: Foundation for Ancient Research and Mormon Studies, 1999.

S. Michael Wilcox, *House of Glory: Finding Personal Meaning in the Temple*. Salt Lake City, Utah: Deseret Book, 1995.

Lynne Wilton Wilson, "The Holy Spirit Creating, Anointing, and Empowering throughout the Old Testament," in *The Gospel of Jesus Christ in the Old Testament*, eds. D. Kelly Ogden, Jared W. Ludlow, and Kerry Muhlestein. Provo, Utah: BYU Religious Studies Center, 2009, https://rsc.byu.edu/gospel-jesus-christ-old-testament/holy-spirit.

About the Author

Stephen L. Fluckiger received his BA from Princeton University and JD from Brigham Young University. He practiced law for thirty-two years with the international law firm Jones Day, becoming a partner in 1988. He and his wife, Dorothy, served as mission leaders in the Portugal Lisbon Mission, senior missionaries in the Brazil area office, and president and matron of the Dallas Texas Temple. Previous to these assignments, Brother Fluckiger served as a bishop, stake president, and Area Seventy. He currently serves as a sealer in the San Antonio Texas Temple.

Brother and Sister Fluckiger live in Georgetown, Texas, and are the parents of five children with seventeen grandchildren.

DRAWING UPON THE SPIRITUAL TREASURES OF THE TEMPLE is a captivating exploration of our faith inspired by the visionary teachings of President Russell M. Nelson. As the prophet who has announced more temples than any other in this dispensation, President Nelson invites us to move beyond routine to better understand the spiritual treasures received through temple ordinances.

IN THIS INSIGHTFUL STUDY, Stephen Fluckiger shares the incredible blessings he unearthed after accepting President Nelson's call, including the power to recognize and feel God's divine love, the life-changing influence of consistent temple worship, and the profound understanding of covenant-making central to God's perfect plan. Delve into the ministries and priesthood keys restored by Moses, Elias, and Elijah, and gain greater power to part the veil and receive divine guidance through prayer.

FROM THE SUPERNAL BLESSINGS sealed upon us through the new and everlasting covenant of marriage to the ultimate power to become one with God, this book unveils the richness of temple ordinances. More than an exploration, it serves as a guide, revealing not just the promised treasures but how to harness their power. President Nelson promises that as we do so, our families will be more "united, sealed in the temple of the Lord, and full of love for our Heavenly Father and for Jesus Christ."

GAIN AN EXCLUSIVE LIBRARY OF videos, audiobooks, podcasts, and more with the CEDAR FORT APP!
Scan QR code to download the App and get 3 months free!

ALSO AVAILABLE AS AN EBOOK

CFI
AN IMPRINT OF
CEDAR FORT, INC.

CEDAR FORT
Publishing & Media

ISBN 978-1-4621-4701-4   USA $28.99

WWW.CEDARFORT.COM